REV. IVAN STANG
IS THE AUTHOR OF
THE BOOK OF THE SUBGENIUS
(WITH MANY OTHERS)
HIGH WEIRDNESS BY MAIL

SHORT STORIES IN THE SUBGENIUS MYTHOS

THREE-FISTED

EDITED BY REVEREND IVAN STANG

TALES OF

A FIRESIDE BOOK   PUBLISHED BY SIMON & SCHUSTER INC.   NEW YORK   LONDON   TORONTO   SYDNEY   TOKYO

"BOB"

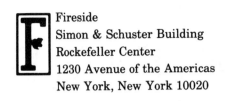

Fireside
Simon & Schuster Building
Rockefeller Center
1230 Avenue of the Americas
New York, New York 10020

This book's stories and characters are fictional creations of the SubGenius Foundation. Certain real locations, institutions, and public figures are mentioned to bring a sense of realism to the fictional stories. This work is entirely the product of the authors' imagination.

FIRESIDE and colophon are registered trademarks of Simon & Schuster Inc.

Designed by Bonni Leon

"Bob" mandalas artwork by Byron Werner.
Manufactured in the United States of America

10 9 8 7 6 5 4 3 2 1

Library of Congress Cataloging in Publication Data
Three-fisted tales of "Bob" / edited by Ivan Stang.
   p. cm.
   "A Fireside book."
   1. Science fiction, American. I. Stang, Ivan. II. Title:
3-fisted tales of "Bob."
PS648.S3T5 1990
813'.0876208—dc20
ISBN 0-671-67190-1   89-26042
                       CIP

We are grateful to the following authors and publishers for permission to use the material indicated:

"Behind-ForeEverAfterword: SECTS AND DEATH" from *ROOSEVELT AFTER IN-AUGURATION and Other Atrocities* by William S. Burroughs. Copyright © 1979 by William S. Burroughs. Originally published by City Lights Books. Reprinted by permission.

"Stompin' at the Savoy" by Lewis Shiner. Copyright © 1985 by Flight Unlimited. First published in *Shayol* #7. Reprinted by permission.

FOR MY KIDS, XANDY AND TEVIS.
MAY I GROW UP TO BE JUST LIKE THEM.

CONTENTS

·DOBBS·

—Artwork by Kenneth
Huey

Plastic Model Kit of
J. R. "BOB" DOBBS
1:8 Scale

Long, long ago, during the Years of Trouble, when all the Northern Fathers still slept under the glaciers, there lived the being we now know as J. R. "Bob" Dobbs.

This man, Dobbs, was chosen by JHVH-1 for the Primary *Communionications* from our alien benefactors, the Xists. As "Bob" moved through the stars, he changed the face of them. His ten billion Quasi-modalities now vibrate in each of us, and have transformed him into the ETERNAL INCARNATION OF SLACK.

From Dobbs came the UnReasoned Utterances which will remain forever unerasable. His brave experimentation with Excremeditation and Fornicationalism, using all Humankind as his test flock, resulted in the rule of the SubGenius for the next twelve thousand years.

During his Span, disaster followed Dobbs, resulting in the outright obliteration of his physical vessel. Only by careful, Church-supervised studies can we now have our first look at the Dobbshell. Here is the approved Religiofficial Bioreconstructoid, perfect in every detail: *Our Salesman.*

His skull is shaped a bit differently than is ours today. It is somewhat flattened in the rear and bulges over the brow. His brain was well devolved. Some theocraticians think that Dobbs did not speak at all, or that if he did, he did not have what we would call a language.

He wears the Suit. His hands and feet are like ours. He was left-handed. The Briefcase he holds sent the signals that launched the Rockets of Cleansing, the blessed vehicles of our birth.

He stands here in the wreckage of Earth, his native planet.

—**Paul Mavrides**

BEFOREWORD

raditionally, there are only two reasons for any book to have an introduction, or foreword, or preforeword or whatever the hell the editor decides to call that thing in the front of a book.

Reason #1: To Boost Sales

Someone discovered long ago that an artfully dropped name can establish instant credibility in certain situations. In the publishing industry, this translates into the practice of inviting some celebrity or well-known expert to introduce a work. All too often, that is the sole "kicker" which sells it. Unfortunately, there is no guarantee that the quality of the introduction will be commensurate with the selling power of the introducer's name.

Reason #2: Sentimental Obligations

The editor bestows the honor of writing the introduction upon an old buddy—some harmless but washed-up has-been to whom he owes a favor—just to give the doddering hack a break, "for old times' sake." While this approach sometimes makes for a more enlightening and sincere introduction, sales may suffer from the lack of status attached to the decrepit old bum's name.

As difficult as it may be to believe, a book's ultimate success depends *entirely* upon which of these traditional paths is chosen by the editor. Since I fit neither category of introducers, this book may conceivably be one of those "wild cards" that shatter all accepted norms of publishing . . . if not even civilization as we know it, considering the nature of our mission!

Some readers may also be surprised to learn that the foreword is usually the last part of a book to be written, and that the foreword actually contains the afterthoughts. A common afterthought is that readers might wonder why in the world the book was ever written . . . which may be particularly true in this case, so an especially lengthy attempt at an explanation, or at least an excuse, is required.

The public generally associates my name with J. R. "Bob" Dobbs and the Church of the SubGenius, and well it should. I have known "Bob" since our college days, when I saved him from drowning in a mud puddle after he had been knocked unconscious during a panty raid. (His skull was fractured by a bra with ice frozen into its cups—a bra hurled by none other than his wife-to-be, the attractive and gracious "Connie" Marsh. Yes, all three of us met simultaneously on that fateful night in 1946.)

After several years of casual friendship and countless poker games, my win/loss ratio with "Bob" was hopelessly lopsided and my family fortune exhausted. I prevailed upon his boundless good nature to let me earn back some of my money. Pitying me, Dobbs proffered an opportunity by which I could both repay him my debts and recover my own losses many times over. Promising a get-rich-quick scheme unparalleled in history, he enlisted my aid in founding the Church of the Sub-Genius and its public relations arm, The SubGenius Foundation, Inc. Utilizing my experience and numerous contacts in the advertising business, I chose the then-destitute Rev. Ivan Stang to fill the open Sacred Scribe position at Foundation headquarters in Dallas. Ivan's task was to compile and organize the encrypted instructions provided by Dobbs: arcane trance memos and codices that ultimately became the early SubGenius pamphlets. "Bob" had long since undergone his Divine Emaculation, and had consequently amassed a personal fortune in the eleven-figure range. He then pretended to retire from public life. (It was even rumored in the Pentagon that he had actually fled our solar system!)

Nevertheless, in 1979, in caves hidden in the vastness of the Himalayas, the Most High Tibetan Lamas surgically altered my brain under the direct tutelage of Dobbs—performing that perilous operation, *the Opening of the Third Nostril*. This enabled me to receive, unimpeded, dogmatic revelations directly from interstellar Silent Radio signals. It simultaneously prepared me for that painful somatic mutation to literal, physical OverManhood which so drastically warped my appearance that I now must conceal my visage from the squeamish, bigoted eyes of normal humans. Despite arduous spiritual preparations, I underwent the very tortures of Hell when first I channeled the brain-scorching direct transmissions required for *The Book of the SubGenius* (Fireside/Simon & Schuster trade paperback, $10.95).

But who, some few may ask, *is* this man J. R. "Bob" Dobbs? As difficult as it is for me to imagine that there are still so many mired in ignorance, it yet remains a most challenging question to answer— possibly the most challenging of our time. After all, how does one describe the indescribable, and define the indefinable? I shall attempt nonetheless to paint a portrait of "Bob"—one equating not so much to a photograph, but at best to a child's broken-crayon stick-figure scrawl.

J. R. "Bob" Dobbs: on the surface, an average, good-looking all-American "Joe," though of debated parentage; perpetual smoker of a sacred briar Pipe filled with mysterious and, some claim, hallucinatory admixtures; master omni-salesman of legendary abilities (very probably the historical "Traveling Salesman" of mythology), to whom has been widely attributed total command of *the Luck Plane* by virtue of, not skill, but *sheer and unadulterated* intuitive ignorance; recognized as Patron Saint of Salesmen the world over; contacted and Emaculated in his youth by the alien space-god JHVH-1 to receive instructions for initiating select individuals into the secrets of Original Slack, its attainment, abuse and true purpose; founder of a burgeoning cult religion with literally countless schisms and heretical spin-offs; purportedly assassinated in 1984 by the renegade Church Hierarchite D. Woodman Atwell (aka *Puzzling Evidence* and *Überbrow*), but also allegedly resurrected in 1987 at Dokstok, a pagan convocation of fanatical upper-echelon Church executives; prophesied savior of the dogma-following and dues-paying Chosen on **X-Day**, July 5, 1998, when his "customers" **the Xists** arrive from "Planet X"; Honorary Pilot of the pleasure-saucer Escape Vessels of the Sex Goddesses; and captain of the Church softball team.

"Bob's" teachings promote awareness of the Original Slack with which all bipeds, MereHumans and SubGenii alike, are endowed at birth, allowing us to exercise and financially exploit our *Abnormality Potentials*. He fights to ensure that this innate Slack is not squandered or, worse yet, stolen outright by that Conspiracy of Normals which presently controls this planet. Only if the Universal Slack levels are high enough, and the smoke from "Bob's" Pipe sufficiently thick, will the Xists materialize and save all paid-up, Yeti-descended Ordained SubGenius Ministers☻—while trashing in their interplanetary "beer run" not only the faithless human Conspiracy dupes (or "Pinks," "Menialitites," "Mediocretins," etc.), but their entire hellhole planet as well.

These are but a few reasons you owe it to yourself to purchase *The Book of the SubGenius*—if you haven't already—and to buy additional copies with which to save your loved ones . . . but NOT, necessarily, excuses for waiting to purchase this third book. (*High Weirdness by Mail*, an exposé of rival false cults, is the second.☻☻)

☻ Ordainment, membership documents and subscription to the Church journal, *The Stark Fist of Removal*, are $20 from SubGenius, Box 140306, Dallas, Texas 75214 ($30 overseas); $1 for catalog of audio- and videotapes, pamphlets, posters, clothing and other Churchly items.
☻☻ *High Weirdness by Mail*, the cyclopedic directory of kookified mutation and artistic frenzy, is, partially, our way of repaying those early collaborators who gobbled up the bait, for it promotes hundreds of their own secular rantzines, scientific discoveries, performance projects, UFO contacts, forbidden musical recordings and shunned comic books, all created independently of the Dobbsword—indeed, created as if in psychic rebellion against the insidious spiritual grip within which Dobbs had, in many cases, threatened to engulf their minds. Dobbs was proud of them for that, and rewarded them. Both *High Weirdness* and *The Book of the SubGenius* are $12 each postpaid from The SubGenius Foundation, Box 140306, Dallas, Texas 75214. They may also be ordered by better bookstores everywhere through the publisher, Simon & Schuster.

The Book of the SubGenius presented the Teachings of Dobbs in a formal, almost Biblical "textbook" style. It succeeded in luring into the fold those brilliant collaborators who have made the Church relentlessly grow and grow, like the Blob of pop mythology or the Sceptre of Priapus in classical legendry—simultaneously inoculating our endeavors against the entropic stagnation which afflicts all rival religions.

The intentions, then, of this anthology of fables, parables and dramatic historical retellings is to help students transcend the hidebound, stodgy formality of earlier revealed dogma, to grasp by example Dobbs' more subtle characteristics, and simply to enjoy his true-life adventures as he seeks to accomplish his Nameless Mission: a mission whose origin and purpose remain a total mystery, certainly unfathomable through mere rote memorization of PreScripture. Indeed, it's possible that those who *haven't* researched previous SubGenius litany may, ironically, glean more pure Slack from this collection than will the "Bobbies" who've memorized Dobbs' every recorded utterance. For they will be inculcating themselves with Dobbs Knowledge *from context*—which, preliminary studies suggest, is the most expeditious way to extract that "Grail of the Philosophers"! "Bob's" is a living church, a dynamic social organism better understood through even *vicarious* experience than through the simplistic doctrines and embarrassing rituals which hobble lesser faiths.

What exactly is a "Three-Fisted Tale of "Bob" "? Any answer lies only in what the Tales are *not*.

They aren't just gripping yarns of action and suspense, nor whimsical fantasy, nor pathetic cuteness-and-light New Age prattlings. Nor are they limited to the strictures of science fiction or lurid murder-mystery traditions. One cannot label them simply "romance"; and it is impossible to pigeonhole any solely as spy thrillers, humor, or sword-and-sorcery. They are, instead, a revolutionary amalgamation of all of the above, and far more!

Defying all basic literary genres, they lie more in the realm of Apocrypha—dictated not by Dobbs, as was *The Book of the SubGenius,* but instead by his Apostles, his Fishers of Wallets. A few Tales may even seem heretical in content . . . but, more often, they represent inspired prophetic visions, biographical reenactments, and outright *but no less valid* fabrications. Whether solidly researched, untarnishable histories, or strictly metaphorical parables, they fill out the previously sketchy picture of "Bob" Dobbs the man.

To protect his family, Dobbs himself insists that we never identify which are true histories and which (if any) are fables; he trustingly leaves that determination up to you, our dearly beloved Reader. Thus, if any given Tale seems particularly distasteful to you personally, it is your right to rank it among the subversive lies; those that you enjoy, on the other hand, may be taken as irrefutable and factual chronicles worthy of being etched into the Rock of Ages.

Being true SubGeniuses all, each author sees "Bob" differently, depending upon his or her own ethical development. One writer may be accurately recounting the Master's deeds, while the next is a schismatic reprobate intent upon destruction of the Church from within. "Bob" still insists that you be the judge.

Our contributors hail from all walks of life: occultists, astrologers, rich jet-setters, doctors, minimum-wage slaves, yardmen, poverty-stricken geek visionaries, upper-level corporate managers, Berkeley egghead intelligentsia, right-wing fascists, frothing Commie radicals, filmmakers, technical writers, Christian missionaries, suicidal wretches both successful and failed, cartoonists, avant-garde painters, rock musicians ... even gorgeous, slinky housewives in sheer, silken evening gowns. (*One* manages to combine *all* of the above callings!) Some have had absolutely no prior professional writing experience, yet were obviously inspired by what can only be termed "Higher Powers." Two or three have actually built successful careers as accomplished, paid storytellers!

As for the editor of this anthology, the Rev. Ivan Stang is a celebrated and erudite man of distinction known the world over—an accomplished author, radio personality, film auteur ... and regular family man. Known for his ranting "Southern preacher"–style sermon delivery, Rev. Stang has organized soul-saving Church Devivals across this country (and several foreign nations) to great critical and even supernatural acclaim.

He has arranged these Tales not chronologically, but rather by stringent (but seductively simple) Drummondian subliminal Silent Radio mind-control techniques. The first few stories provide a perspective for new readers unfamiliar with the orthodox dogma: introductory Tales, if you will. At the same time, they serve to remind self-proclaimed "Sub-Genius experts" of those sound basic doctrines whence sprang the Church's pythonic, back-to-the-Pamphlet, dogma-scrubbing redeformation movement.

Once the explanatory narratives have been digested, the newly illuminated reader may hurtle uncontrollably *but safely* into the more profound, esoteric and, mayhaps, *frightening* tales—those designed to disconnect established thought patterns and sabotage habitual mental logic. Gliding effortlessly into a euphoric haze of real or imaginary happenings, the reader will imbibe freely of the fermented fruits of those who are not-quite-geniuses, becoming "drunk as a lord" with enlightenment.

Finally, when the maximum limit of enlightenment absorption is reached, the reader (if he or she can still be referred to as such) may stealthily dare to approach the last stories—hideous necropoli of soul-lessly rotting, maleficent, stench-filled pre-/post-histories wherein mysterious apparitions gleefully carve their unspeakable names upon the foolish mortal reader's heart and soul. Tales of this depth simply defy all earthly description.

This arrangement allows the reader to become gradually familiar not only with the ancillary characters who populate the later stories, *but even with their writing styles*—for did not these so-called "characters" *write* half the stories??

This is the first One True Anthology to represent the entire gamut of the Before-, After-, and In-Between Resurrection annals—the first (of, hopefully, many volumes) to dare cover ALL conceptual bases, charging cheerfully and unfalteringly into the colossal sales fray that is the marketplace, battling head to head with any and all competitive comers, even the shallowest of best-sellers. And it shall surely come up smiling, delivering Dobbs' Ultimate Punch Line in its pristine virgin state—unsullied and uninterpreted.

By promising nothing, "Bob" both gives us the world and grants us the final laugh . . . that laugh which will surely last all the way to the bank, no matter how this book's sales figures may be impugned by any pencil-necked geek of a market-myopic chain-bookstore accountant.

We sincerely hope that these Tales somehow allow the elusive awareness of Slack to delicately insinuate itself into our readers' consciousnesses, preferably without damaging their abilities to do their day jobs. After all, we value their money almost as highly as their souls.

It is therefore my most profound privilege to declare to you, dear Reader: **READ ON IF YOU DARE!**

This is my testament!

> **—Dr. Philo Drummond**
> **OverMan 1st Degree,**
> **First Authorized FisTem-**
> **ple Lodge, Church of the**
> **SubGenius/Drummondian**

IN REMEMBRANCE OF TIM MCGINNIS

(1953–1988)

On July 11, 1988, our editor of six years, Tim McGinnis, died of lymphatic cancer at the age of thirty-four. To call it a blow and a shock would be a severe understatement. Most people outside his family and close friends had no idea how sick he was; he wasn't one to complain.

He was a good buddy; we shared a few hair-raising adventures above and beyond our business relationship. Some of these were merely phone conversations, but Tim could make a long-distance discussion into an adventure. He was a truly *funny* guy, in a quirky way entirely his own, which luckily for us was big enough to also encompass the SubGenius style. Even if he'd had nothing to do with publishing our books, he'd have been "SubGenius Hierarchy" through and through.

It took months for the fact of his death to sink in, for me to realize what had been lost to so many—including hundreds of people he never met, but who were part of dozens of SubGenius projects and spin-offs, from books to stage productions to radio and films. And I'm not so sure it ever really *can* sink in fully; I doubt I'm doing justice to his memory here. How could I? I probably owe him my career, without which even my marriage and therefore my life might well have been jeopardized. And all friends of the SubGenius Church certainly owe him for its visibility and commercial success.

More than a hundred publishers had rejected the proposals for *The Book of the SubGenius* before Tim suddenly, in our darkest days, appeared as if by magic and ramrodded it into print against all odds. He never saw the pamphlet/proposal I'd originally sent to his then employer, McGraw-Hill; it'd been trashcanned by some secretary. Instead, during a picnic, my friend Leslie Gaspar showed him a beat-up copy she'd found lying in the backseat of my sister-in-law's car. Alone among those hundred-plus editors, he saw the potential and made us an offer the very next day. (In publishing, an offer leads to an agent, which leads to other offers, which leads to a track record. It isn't what you know, but who; we were very lucky to know Tim McGinnis.) As Tim said, "Dobbs works in *extremely* mysterious ways."

Once news got around, via our agent, Jane Jordan Browne, that Tim was working with us, editors who'd previously shunned SubGenius started bidding on it themselves. Rather ironic, but illustrative of Tim's originality and willingness to go out on limbs.

I knew by then that Tim, alone among the rival editors, understood "Bob" and what we were really trying to do. Whereas the others had all manner of Mickey Mouse ideas about how we should water down the Dobbsword to make it more palatable to idiots (retitling it *The Book of Bob* was the most frequent telltale suggestion), Tim intended to bring it to press with its purity intact. Today I cringe to think how insipidly cutesy the book would have become in any other hands. It might have sold better, but all SubGenii would have felt dirty and tainted forever. "Bob" himself must have brought Tim to us. He never censored a word. He guided, he collaborated, he advised, and he somehow managed to make his superiors *think* they understood it. He practically risked his job sticking up for us when the PR department thought he was nuts. He stuck to his guns throughout what became a public-relations night-mare. There were McGraw-Hill employees who repeatedly denied (even to book chains with money in hand) that our troublemaking tome had ever been printed by their Great Father Company. SubGenius was, in fact, something of a publishing legend simply because Tim had conned such a straitlaced outfit as McGraw-Hill into distributing it in the first place.

When he changed jobs over to *Rolling Stone*'s book publishing branch, he continued to look out for us, and after becoming an editor at Simon & Schuster's Fireside Books he miraculously convinced the powers that be that SubGenius could do well with better PR. (It did; *The Book of the SubGenius* is still in stores, and getting plenty of attention despite its uncanny propensity for frightening timid media moguls.) So great was his concern for artistic integrity that when all twenty thousand new copies were accidentally printed with an appendix page missing, he managed to have the entire run reprinted correctly!

Tim then sold Fireside on *High Weirdness by Mail,* although nothing like it had existed before. It did much better than expected. At that point, any other editor would've said, "Do another *High Weirdness!*" Instead, Tim encouraged us to compile *Three-Fisted Tales of "Bob."*

He got us the contract, phoned occasionally to advise us, and then suddenly died in his sleep when the chemotherapy and megavitamin therapies failed. We had talked two weeks before his death; that was the first time I'd had any inkling that the illness he'd fought through the years was mortally serious. But his main comment was, "I'm get-ting better, though . . . don't worry."

Speaking for myself alone, were it not for Tim I'd probably, at best, be slaving away in some Conspiracy job instead of enjoying the luxury of working on my true calling at home, with the sounds of my children playing in the next room. At worst, I'd be dead of hopelessness.

*   *   *

He left a real legacy. We aren't the only ones Tim McGinnis helped, or saved, not by a long shot. He had that rare talent for spotting unknown but worthwhile artists, and then selling corporate entities on their oddball projects even when they bore no earthly resemblance to current best-sellers. He stuck his neck out for dozens of struggling authors whose work met resistance elsewhere, but who went on to find critical and/or commercial success—thanks in large part to Tim's vision, tenacity, and skill at smooth-talking sales executives. That combination of artistic savvy, pure soul and mastery of corporate double-talk occurs all too infrequently in modern publishing.

He gave many of us our crucial first publications—putting his own foot in the door so that *we* could sneak in. Tim was one of those very few behind-the-scenes giants who do so much of the dirty work for none of the glory. And he did it at the expense of his own work; he was an excellent, funny, biting, gutsy, humane writer, but he tended to put off finishing *his* novels in order to ensure that his friends' works made it to the marketplace.

If any SubG sits at the right hand of "Bob," it's Tim McGinnis. Lest you think that a joke in poor taste, believe me when I say Tim would've appreciated it. He really was a "SubGenius," in the least jokey sense of the word. He worked hard to see that the truth might be present between the lines, which is usually the best place to stash the truth. I never heard him say a mean or jealous word about anyone, though, unlike many of us. He was capable of being as cynical as any of us, but could just as quickly drop that facade and become a real person, a nice young man with a wife and parents and dreams. And more guts than I can quite understand.

I'm sure Tim wouldn't mind my saying that he practiced what most religious people only preach. He didn't waste any of his limited and very valuable time paying lip service to anything; he *lived* and *did*. He didn't worship "Bob"—he *laughed with* "Bob," and gave thousands of others the chance to do so as well. He truly did unto others, etc., not for brownie points from any particular god, but simply because it made good sense to him.

And he hung in there to the bitter end, giving those last few deserving but unknown writers their big chance while he still could.

One of my most profound, if selfish, regrets is that he never got to finish his own "Bob" Tale for this book. When I was informed of his death, before the realness and sadness of it had quite sunk in, one of my first reactions was, "Damn!—now he'll never get to read these stories!" I must reluctantly admit that I also had the mercenary thought, "But—now who's going to support us in the commercial publishing world?"

But I realized he'd already taken care of that. His hard work, stubborn encouragement and advice gained us just enough of a track record to survive and then prosper. It's terribly ironic that he's not here to enjoy it with us. Or is he?

The Church of the SubGenius has had many "saints," but Tim McGinnis is the first real one.

—**Rev. Ivan Stang**

Sacred Scribe #273, Stangian Orthodox Covenant People's MegaFisTemple Lodge of Dobbs Yeti, Resurrected

The Iowa Review has established a literary humor award to honor Tim's memory and spirit. All inquiries or contributions to the award should be sent to David Hamilton, c/o *Iowa Review,* 308 EPB, University of Iowa, Iowa City, Iowa 52242.

Behind-ForeEverAfterword:
SECTS AND DEATH

I postulate that the function of art and all creative thought is to make us aware of what we know and don't know that we know. You can't tell anybody anything he doesn't know already. Like those folks living on the sea coast in the Middle Ages, watching those ships come in mast first year after year—then Galileo wises them up and they are ready to burn him as an egghead deviant. But they cool it out over the years and finally have to admit: "It's round, boys, it's round. We knew it all along." Cezanne showed the viewer objects seen from a certain angle in a certain light and they attacked his canvases with umbrellas at the first exhibition. Well, that doesn't happen any more and any child would recognize the objects in a Cezanne canvas. Joyce made readers aware of their own stream of consciousness and was accused of promulgating a cult of unintelligibility.

If the function of art is to make us aware of what we know and don't know we know, the function of the Christian Church and all its metastases has been and still is to keep us in ignorance of what we know. People living on the sea coast knew the earth was round. They believed it was flat because the Church said so. And hard-core Synanon members still believe the media put that rattlesnake in Paul Morantz' mail box to discredit Synanon. Is there any limit to brainwashing? Apparently not. Such cults as Synanon, Scientology, the Peoples Temple derive from the same infected source as Christianity. In fact they recapitulate the story of Christianity word for word, like the inevitable course of some unsightly disease: criminal ignorance, brutish stupidity, self-righteous bigotry, paranoid fear of outsiders. For the cultist, psychiatrists, the media, Government agencies have become Satan incarnate. Like the fundamental Christians, they have to be *right*.

Now Christianity sounded good at first to the naive convert. Love, peace and charity—what's wrong with that? I'll tell you what's wrong— a series of unprecedented horrors perpetrated by so-called Christians: the Inquisition, the Conquistadores, the American Indian wars, slavery, Hiroshima and the present-day Bible Belt. That poisonous old-time religion they brew up down there constitutes a menace to all passengers on spacecraft Earth. Why did this happen, and why does it happen with the sects that stem from Christianity? What was so wrong with Christianity in the beginning? In the beginning was the Word, and the Word was God.

There's an interesting book entitled *The Origin of Consciousness in the Breakdown of the Bicameral Mind.* The author, Julian Jaynes, postulates that the awe in which the ancient priest-king was held derived from his ability to produce his voice in the brains of his loyal subjects. This is the voice of God, which funnels through the non-dominant brain hemisphere. Jaynes cites clinical evidence; stimulation of the non-dominant hemisphere causes experimental subjects to hear voices. An attempted suicide who was rescued from drowning stated that a voice in his head told him to kill himself, and that for some reason he *had to obey that voice.* If you want to start a cult, the first step is to get your voice into the non-dominant brain hemisphere of your soon-to-be devoted followers. The Scientology course involves listening to hours of L. Ron Hubbard's voice on tape. The voice of Dederich, founder of Synanon, was said to drift from the air conditioning system, and Reverend Jim Jones had tapes of his voice continually broadcast over loudspeakers at Jonestown.

The second step: make enemies. If there is one thing a cult leader needs, it is enemies—real or imagined—from which to deliver his flock. Having postulated fiendish enemies, the leader then sets up commando squads to deal with this self-created emergency: the Sea Org of Scientology, the Imperial Marines of Synanon, the armed guards of the Peoples Temple. Aggressive acts by these protectors then produce counter-actions from outside. After all, what can you expect when you break into Government offices, put rattlesnakes in people's mail boxes, and murder a Congressman? These counterattacks, which the cultists bring on themselves, lead to escalating paranoia and more and more extreme measures.

Given the ability to project your voice into others' minds, here is a how-to blueprint:

ACT, the Anti-Cancer Temple, was founded by Tobias Antony Crump, a self-styled minister of the Radiant Church of Regenerate Christ. He leased an abandoned resort hotel in upstate New York where he offered for a reasonable fee to cure people of the smoking habit in seven days. The cure was effected by suggestions implanted in what he called "the other mind." The suggestions were administered through headphones which his parishioners were required to wear day and night throughout the seven days of the cure. At the end of this time all the reborn parishioners decided to stay on at the Temple and work for ACT. In return for the privilege of becoming ACTers they were required to turn over ten percent of their assets to ACT.

Crump prospered and expanded his facilities. More and more pressure was put on cured parishioners to stay on after completing the no-smoking course. They were told that the cure was not yet complete. If they returned to their old haunts they would inevitably relapse and die of cancer in a few years. Besides they had a sacred duty to help others. Cancer, he taught, was a Venusian plot to take over the planet. Aliens were landing in cancerous tissues as invisible parasites who were invading minds and bodies in all walks of life. Reverend Crump published a weekly tabloid in which he launched preposterous charges against all the enemies of ACT, a list that now included the tobacco companies, the drug companies, the FDA, the World Health Organization, the Cancer Research Society, the FBI, the CIA, the media, Interpol, the IRS, the Communist Party. A typical cartoon showed Uncle Sam hit in the face by a mass of cancerous putrescence like a custard pie: "From Russia With Love."

When a bomb partially destroyed an outbuilding of the Temple, Crump declared a state of absolute emergency. His followers must now turn over half their worldly goods and all their time to ACT. He declared all-out war on his Satanic adversaries. When an investigative reporter, sent to get the story on ACT, disappeared under mysterious circumstances, the founder proclaimed that the subsequent investigation "clearly and unequivocally proves a ten-year conspiracy on the part of Government agencies acting in concert with the media to suppress a Church."

Reverend Crump was involved in countless lawsuits bringing action against any critics of ACT. The resulting expenses were more than compensated by the constant influx of money with which he bought real estate. He now owned huge tracts of land in Florida, New Hampshire, East Texas and Montana where he set up Temples for his followers, who now numbered in the hundreds of thousands. He taught that they must all merge into one organism through what he called biologic fusion. Only in this way could they counter the Venusian virus which was taking over the rest of the world. To foster biologic fusion there were bizarre mass sex orgies and nudity feasts to break down residual resistance and let in the radiant light of Christ. He instituted Black Broadcasts, in which his followers gathered at synchronized times to concentrate in silent malevolence on the enemies of the week, whose names, addresses and pictures appeared on a screen. His followers were now required to turn over all their possessions to ACT, and were told that they must be ready to offer their life-blood if necessary. Desertion was made a crime punishable by death. There was continual practice in the martial arts, and the bestial howls and grunts and snarls could be heard for miles around. Any neighbor who complained was put on the enemy list. Crump boasted that he had only to lift his hand to dispatch his followers as one man on kamikaze missions of assassination and sabotage. He was rumored to have in readiness nuclear devices and enough nerve gas to blanket the East Coast. "He could knock the Government of this country down like a house of cards," a highly placed official stated flatly.

*   *   *

Richard Nixon exploded the Presidential image at Watergate. I think he will go down in history as a folk hero. The Reverend Jones has, by his example, called into question the leadership principle which is the very basis of authority. What else are churches, armies, nations built upon but leaders and the belief that these leaders know what they are doing and that the citizen owes them unquestioning obedience?

Anyone who believes he owns all the answers is a lunatic. And lunatics are dangerous to themselves and others. Spacecraft Earth is too small and too overcrowded to accommodate lunatic sects. The answer is very simple: instead of being tax-free, churches should be taxed double. They should be taxed right out of existence.

—William S. Burroughs

Rev. John Shirley

199619971998

She was a small soft thing walking in the shadow of great hard things, under the sullen gray sky of a November morning. She was in North Central California, and she was quite alone. She was Little Connie Depthcharge, taking a walk into the year 1996. That's how she thought of it. Every second, she reasoned, took her further into the year. And the year was unfolding around her, bleak and relentless, pervading this edifice of decay. The year 1996 was a place, Connie thought. This time is a place. Not all times are places, not so you'd notice, but this one was.

Connie was nine years old. Until this year she had perceived the world as a sort of efflorescence blossoming symmetrically out from her; she had imagined herself at the center of it. Now she saw that the world had no center, or none visible. Perhaps there was some great sucking whirlpool of events somewhere, like the black hole in that old Disney movie she'd panned in the videocassette section of her column for *Weekly Reader* (the column was called "The Cinematic Bitch." Now that the children's newspaper had gone yellow tabloid, with blaring headlines like "My Mom Has Sex with the Vacuum Cleaner and I'm, Like, So Embarrassed," it had room for Little Connie's penetrating if spiteful analyses.)

Connie was thinking about these things as she walked along the weed-thatchy railroad tracks. She was walking through the old industrial park. It was closed today. Much of it had been closed continuously since the Dream Plagues. The smokestacks were streaked with rust, marbled with cracks; the acid rains had pitted the gray and black walls of the monolithic buildings squatting on both sides of her. She liked to walk here because the place had a dreary, pleasantly obtuse *cinéma-vérité* quality that she found reassuring. It had no *affect*. It could be trusted, she thought, to remain itself. She was weary of the unpredictable, since the Dream Plagues; since the War of the Weirdos; since the jarring sight of the people spinning by overhead, high on antigravity drugs. . . . Here, at least, there were no surprises.

A lizard surprised her by scuttling from a hole. It seemed too cold for lizards to be about. The lizard was a leathery sizzle, here and gone. Then another, darting from another hole. And another. And then the warm-blooded things, rats and mice, oozing from holes in the ridges of cinders to either side of the rusty tracks, shimmying from the cracks in the dusty foundations of the old factories, small living things moving like a fear hormone through this industrial vein, scrambling randomly about, ignoring her, and she read the signs for what they were. She could feel it herself, then: felt it in the soles of her feet. In *that* spot, the place in her foot that Mother said contained a gland of some kind. (Poor crazy Mama; poor dead Mama; she'd insisted on a coffin shaped and painted like a Masters of the Universe lunchbox. It was, like, so embarrassing. But it was *her* funeral.)

Staggering to remain upright, Little Connie felt the vibrations ripple up from some epicenter below the railroad tracks; saw the dust rise in matched ripples to either side as it traveled outward; saw the symmetry become confusion as the vibrations collided with quake vibrations coming from the opposite direction. She thought of blenders and taffy machines and Mama's candy-striped vibrator.

She was too fascinated, just then, to be afraid. This was her first earthquake, and she thought of it as a storm in the earth, weather underfoot, and, swaying, she sought to find its groove, the way her mother had taught her. "Every storm has a groove," Mama had said.

But then the buildings began to move. They weren't falling, they weren't caving in. They were moving toward one another. The newer ones were moving faster, she noticed. They were moving with an impossible ease, sailing the ground like ships across water, either making the earthquake or made to move by the earthquake, thunderous but absurdly graceful. Like improbably swift icebergs, coming together . . . and she was going to be caught between them.

But still the terror refused to come. She wondered at its absence. Perhaps she was numb; perhaps resigned to death. She was alone in the world. Why not?

Closer. The buildings sailed across the open ground, plowing up the gravel, coming corner first like a prow making a wake in the dirt, raising fantails of dust, shrieking with the grind of metal and concrete like a ghost in chains. Closer, looming over her; she could smell friction, see sparks rising like spray from the prow of these industrial ships . . .

Maybe this was all hallucination, she told herself. But the Dream Plagues were over, and she knew what *that* felt like. Hallucinations had a distinctive quality. No, this was no dream, she knew, as a chunk of rock, smashed by one onrushing building against another, flew apart and a fragment hit her cheek. It stung nastily, and blood ran along her jawline. No, this was real. Objectively real.

The buildings loomed over her . . . and then the corners of the buildings had pushed past her on either side, grinding the railroad steel into tangled ribbons that whipped through the air. . . . She dodged a cobra of torn steel and, staggering in the shockwaves cracking the ground, she stepped into the interstice between the two onrushing prows, where outthrust bulkheads, passing one another, made a sort of alleyway a few feet wide. . . .

The buildings stopped moving; cacophony gave way to eerie silence. She waited, breathless, as the dust settled. The buildings on either side had moved together, leaving only a few gaps here and there, like the gaps between wrongly fitted jigsaw-puzzle pieces. She was safe in one of these, for the moment.

The buildings had moved very deliberately, she thought. Not like things nudged by some geologic randomness. Who is moving them? Why?

She knew it wasn't over. She could feel it.

That's when the smokestacks tilted over and began to snake toward one another. She watched as, overhead, a set of smokestacks from two separate buildings met mouth to mouth and, somehow, locked together.

The tortured metal squealed. The windows of the buildings shattered. Connie ducked flying shards of oily glass as sections of machinery thrust themselves through windows and moved click-click, snick-snick, creak-creak, together, locking into unity like the smokestacks: sections of pipe and wire and gauges and robotic arms and struts and more wire and tubing and gears and cogs and the rollers from conveyor belts and metal hooks and stamping units and stainless-steel presses and a thousand intricate variations of metal and plastic and rubber innard she couldn't identify; self-animated, they began to rewire and reconstruct themselves, grinding and caterwauling and moaning and sparking in the process, making a mazelike roof of odd machine parts a few feet over Connie's head. . . .

"Right this way, Little Connie! Big sale on small favors!" It was a man's voice, melodious and warm and perhaps a touch unctuous. But a voice to inspire confidence. She crawled toward the sound, under the writhing nest of living metal. Half expecting to be caught up by the wires and pipes, forced into the woof of their rigid weave, crushed and incorporated in living death.

No. She emerged from beneath the ceiling of the living unliving, and found herself on her knees before a doorway at the end of the alley. It was a cobwebby old back door of one of the factories, and standing in the open door was a sign shaped like a man. One of those cardboard cutout life-size photos you see promoting things in a supermarket. But then it moved and she saw it wasn't a sign, it was quite three-dimensional and human. Some quality of absolute emblematic expression—as if this man were *only* semiotics—had made him seem artificial at first. Looking at his face, the fixed expression of faintly self-deprecating glee, the drugged eyes and idiotic grin, the unwavering diagonal of the ordinary brown pipe clenched in teeth so white and even they looked all of a piece . . . the perfect quizzical brows and immaculate swept-back short black hair . . .

Looking up into that face she once more had the sense of emblem, of semiotic absolutes. . . .

And then he spoke. His mouth moved; the pipe bobbed—some noxious herb in it tracing a wavery line of blue smoke in the air—his head tilted . . . but the expression remained the same. "Connie," he said, "we have to move quickly. The Prototime is upon us. Am I right? You coming? Or do you prefer to die horribly, by remaining here?"

She blinked. He hadn't asked the question sarcastically, or facetiously. It was as if he sincerely thought she might actually *want* to die horribly. As if it were a viable option, like, Would you prefer to take the train or a jet? "Lead the way," she said.

They went through the door and behind her the buildings closed up the gaps, sidling and edging till they fit perfectly together. The right jigsaw-puzzle pieces after all.

The factory was reconstructing itself around them. It was merging with another factory; thesis, antithesis, synthesis, and the synthesis was heavy-metal pandemonium. The feverish self-redesigning was clearly guided, conscious—but what consciousness was the guiding force was a palpable mystery Connie could taste in her mouth and smell in her nostrils, along with the stink of random lightning bolts and the ancient scent of uneasy petroleum and tortured metal and ozone.

She walked in the lee of the briskly striding stranger, a tall man in a timeless suit, her eyes stung by the smoke from his pipe. They plunged through a mechanical Armageddon, as machines threw themselves through the air at one another—but instead of crashing the machine sections merged perfectly; machines that could not possibly have been designed to interface somehow *tilted and gyrated* to interface. She thought again of puzzle parts. All this time the puzzle parts have lain about us on the table and we didn't know they fit together. To make . . . what?

Sparks flew, smoke belched, wires whipped, pipes clanged, things flashed past, moved in a blur in search of unity, a dance of death all around them, and somehow, miraculously, they walked through the gauntlet untouched. The man never seemed to look around, never seemed to watch where he was going at all. He just blundered through and somehow, so far, was unhurt. Once, a year before, looking through the window of a factory, she'd seen a mouse run along a conveyor belt. The conveyor belt carried bits of soft metal to stamping presses that stamped the metal into Dabney the Poodle doorbell ringers, a faddish novelty item. The mouse ran under the stampers—and past them, narrowly avoiding getting crushed five times before it leapt free. Just the luck of the very stupid, she'd thought.

Was that what was happening now?

Not for everyone. She glimpsed people—maybe workmen, maybe caretakers—caught in the machinery, skewered and crushed like cockroaches caught in a garbage disposal . . . she couldn't bear to look, to think about it. She tried to think of something to talk to the man about, to get her mind off what she'd seen.

"How'd you know my name?" she asked, shouting it over the uneven racket of the place.

"It was written on your pstench!" he shouted. "I whiffread it! Your mom had it coded into your DNA so I could find you!"

A lunatic, she thought. But he had saved her life. "What's *your* name?"

He stopped and turned to her. An enormous razor-edged pendulum of metal swept by in the spot he would have been in had he kept going. It would have pulped him, she thought, if I hadn't asked him his name just then. He thrust out a hand to her, like an encyclopedia salesman who'd come to the door once. (Mom had broken the guy's fingers.) She shook his hand. Feverishly warm. Possibilities squirmed under the skin. "The name is Dobbs! J. R. "Bob" Dobbs!" You could hear the quotation marks around *"Bob."* He turned and swept onward, plunging recklessly through the storm of flying metal. She followed, trying not to look around, tasting the fear now.

Up ahead, a conveyor belt was taking cryptically shaped segments of crystal up an incline, toward the ceiling, and through a hole in the roof.

They stepped off the conveyor belt, onto the roof. Beside them, the fist-sized irregular chunks of crystal fell off the belt and rolled with effortless serendipity to fit perfectly into irregular holes pocking the roof. To the left the expanse of tar paper was unbroken. "Bob" strode off to the edge of the roof; Connie followed. When she got there she saw with a flush of embarrassment that he'd unzipped his pants and was peeing off the edge of the building. With his free hand he gestured sweepingly at the great world. "Behold, the Prototime!"

She gazed out over the city. The buildings on the Strip, beyond the edge of the industrial park, were moving and changing too. They were all franchises and chains of some sort: 7-Eleven, Soy-Boy, PetroPup, In-n-Out, PigeonPie, Pioneer Chicken, Colonel Sanders, McDonald's, Carl's Jr., Horse Habit, ArtiFish 'n' Chips, and the discount department store chains, K mart and Target and Bozo's Re-Cycled Goods and the other places like Kragoff's Soviet Auto Parts. . . .

They were all moving together, like a film of an explosion run backwards, leaping together, or stumping on their signs like they were crutches and falling together in some cryptic organization that, once achieved, seemed natural and normal . . . because they all fit. K mart fit with Pioneer Chicken and PetroPup fit with Carl's Jr., they locked together like machine parts, signs snicking into place in door slots, oddly angled roof peaks fitting neatly into drive-in windows, all the jumble of architectural ineptitude she'd always wondered about suddenly made sense when they were locked together, and an *über*building came about, the gestalt fruit of this fevered mating . . . an enormous quasi-crystalline structure that reached out multicolored limbs of fiberglass and plastic and impossibly flexible roofing tiles to interface neatly with the reconstructed shapes of the industrial park, all of it becoming One Thing, some minatory self-contained environment. . . .

The clangor and roar of it resonated the surface of the planet like a cymbal.

Afraid, feeling so tiny in the sight of this mighty reconstruction (and seeing that "Bob" had put his majestic privates back in his pants and zipped them up), Little Connie took "Bob's" hand and moved close beside him. " "Bob" . . . is it happening everywhere?"

"No. But it *will* happen everywhere, unless we stop it, Little Connie. This is the Prototime, the precursor to X-Day, Connie, the Con's prep for July 5th, 1998. They're setting a trap for us, so we will be lost to those charismatic strangers from Planet X when they arrive on Earth . . . a trap set by the Conspiracy and triggered by the Malign Sendings of the Yacatisma! What you're seeing is the Conspiracy preparing the way for the Yacatisma (not to be confused with Yacatizma) who seek to prevent me from interceding with the Xists. The Conspiracy hid this one from us, Connie . . . they hid it from us using the power of the Smog Monster, who blanketed the Earth with toxic complacency. The poisons spread through the air slowly, subtly, and we accepted them. The 'intelligent' among humanity found a thousand intelligent ways to rationalize them—so no one fought them . . . and they affected our minds. Made even those of us who See into the Higher Wire a little blind, just enough so they created a psychic smoke screen, enabling the Conspiracy to plant their submolecular nanotechnological machinery in the paint and insulation and plastics and lubricants of these structures— hence, this went unpredicted, Little Connie. Fuck! The Smog Monster fooled us all . . . for the Smog Monster is a sending of . . . *G'BROAG-FRAN!!!, the Rebel God from Deep Space!*" With the uttering of this arcane name, his voice took on an amplified reverb quality that should have been possible only with recording-studio equipment. "I was driving to Kragoff's Soviet Auto Parts to see if they had something that would work as a water pump for a '57 Studebaker, when I felt the submolecular Conspirals of self-organizing quantum-mechavibrational systems in the Material Reality Underpinnings—and knew we'd been snookered. *The Smog Monster is creating an enormous mechanized concentration camp for the processing and subjugation of SubGeniuses and non-Normals of all kinds!* We should have guessed, seeing the franchises and chain stores scab up around the periphery of the cities, like ringworm, like an encamped army around us, tightening the noose, subjecting us to bombardments of mind-numbing consumer-conditioning symbols. I should have guessed they were simply preparing the ground for this. . . ." He paused to stuff a wad of multicolored herb into his pipe—somehow the pipe never quite went out as he did this. . . . Puffing, talking out of the side of his mouth, chattering rapid-fire but offhandedly the whole time: "Lucky for you I came to investigate. *Lucky for you* is a blessing, dear child, that makes the mealymouthed prayers of the 'Holy Father' in the Vatican smell like a dog fart, my Little Connie. . . ."

"All of this"—Connie looked out at the gigantic artifact building itself around them—"is going to trap us? It's some kind of prison?"

"Exactly. A Conspiracy concentration camp . . . a camp without guards for it has *a life of its own* . . . it is its own guards. . . ."

"You talk just like my Mom," Connie observed. "Did you know my Mom? Betty Furnace? She used to talk about the Yacatisma and used to say 'not to be confused with Yacatizma' just the same way *you* did. . . ."

"Bob" turned to her and laid a hand on her head, ruffling her hair gently. "Yes," he said tenderly, allowing ashes from his pipe to drop into her eyes, "Yes, I knew your mother. Betty was—"

He was interrupted by an explosion.

There was a narrow section of ground—narrowing more as the concentration camp construct creaked and shuddered nearer—four stories beneath their roof edge. It had erupted, a fissure opening in it to gout violet and sulfur-yellow smoke that geysered upward, a furious spew that towered over them like a Djinn . . . and a sort of Djinn it was. . . .

Little Connie and "Bob" staggered backwards ("Bob" had a quality about him of having *planned* to stagger or stumble though he couldn't possibly have planned it . . .), Connie clinging to "Bob," choking in the stink of the thing, the rotten-eggs-mixed-with-semitruck-smoke gas-chamber stench of it, as its rolling mass shaped into . . .

"It is the one called AH'OOGAH!" "Bob" shouted. "The Smog Monster!"

"YOU MUST NOT INTERFERE WITH THE GESTATION!" came a voice from within the foul whirlwind. It was a voice belched from exhaust pipes and smokestacks . . . a voice without a muffler. "TRY YOUR FAMOUS LUCK OUT ON DEATH ITSELF!"

And AH'OOGAH swung toward them like a tornado wielded as a hammer—

—as "Bob" grabbed Connie's hand and stumbled with her off the edge of the roof.

She was falling. The Earth rushed up at her . . .

And then the Earth was *above* her. The ground was a sort of ceiling she was falling *up* to. "Bob" was beside her, still holding her hand, his head thrown back, the pipe clenched in his teeth gushing a locomotive cloud of blue (and green-sparkled) smoke that surrounded them, made her choke with its cloying incense . . . but somehow as she inhaled it, a certain ethereal clarity created a magnification lens for her perceptions, and she saw that "Bob," through the medium of this envelope of smoke, was clearing a path of some sort for them. All this she perceived in the half-second it took them to fall upward to the ground. . . .

And then they struck the ground, which was, despite appearing unyielding as concrete, a mist, an atomic illusion like all matter, mostly space, and the space came together around them so they passed harmlessly through, and emerged—

—in the midst of a city. Downward into an upside-down city. The city was hung from above like one of those trick rooms where the chairs are glued to the ceiling. The buildings were upside down. They fell past them, down toward the sky. And then her stomach flip-flopped, followed by her perceptions, as suddenly sky and ground changed places and they were ascending, levitating upward from the ground.

They ceased ascending, alighting on the roof of a bus laying over on a corner, where it blocked traffic and the crosswalk. The driver, unaware of them, smoked an angel dust joint and massaged his crotch.

Feeling detached and objective and weirdly bodiless—and yet *not at all dreamlike*—Connie looked around, and knew that the city had been vivisected for her.

The skin of its consensus reality had been peeled away; she saw now the pulsing inner organs of it, the skein of its hidden organic relationships, and she recognized it all.

"Where's the Smog Monster?" Connie asked.

"Hundreds of miles from here," "Bob" said. "We took a shortcut through the Luck Plane. By the time the Rebel Gods find us it'll be too late. With luck."

"Luck cuts both ways, "Bob," " Little Connie said.

"Little Connie, you were always too old for your age," "Bob" replied, through his ceaseless grin. "I was absent when you grew up and yet I was there. Where two and three gather in my name, there am I also: Can you not feel my hands in your pockets? (I love my own scriptures.) . . . Notice anything about this place?"

Connie was staring at a crowd of people milling on the sidewalks of the great city, people on their way somewhere, oblivious of the Ipsissimus of Sales and his charge atop the bus, and she saw now that a series of coruscating lines were connecting some of the people in the crowd; they were like translucent puppet strings of energy, defining relationships the people in the crowd were entirely unaware of. They belonged to herds within the herd; to cultural phyla whose attributes governed what they supposed to be their freewheeling impulses. And looking closer at those people she saw past their superficial semblances, saw them as they could not see one another: as they really were. There were tall men who were dwarfs and short men who were ten-foot giants from Hell; there were beautiful women who were revealed as twisted harridans, and hunchbacked, shrunken old women who were actually the stately winners of beauty contests; there were bankers who were actually giant worms with lamprey mouths, and there were smiling, friendly cops who were really werewolves in Nazi-SS uniforms; there was a priest who was a mincing drag queen and there was a mincing drag queen who was a genius of dizzying mathematical perceptions. She saw four men in tailored suits coming out of a Hilton, approaching their forty-foot eight-wheeled limousine. They were surrounded by bodyguards who wore black suits and sunglasses; looking beyond their veneers she saw that the men in the suits were hideous slug-bodied things of palpitating tendrils and oozing suckers, hungry aliens with the mouths of giant horseflies; their bodyguards were robots, she saw, things of sheer intent and nothing more. She shivered, and was grateful that "Bob's" psychic cloaking screen protected her from being seen.

Then "Bob" took her hand, and blew a plume of smoke above them, which somehow drew them with it into the air. Like a sex-changed and depraved Mary Poppins, Dobbs drew Little Connie higher and higher into the sky, till they reached the thirteenth-story level. There they drifted along, paralleling the impatient procession of traffic, gazing down at a whole new web of interrelationships. Connie saw, from this greater height, the oscillating blueprint of the Luck Plane superimposed on the street. She saw which cars were likely to collide (but weren't necessarily destined to) and which were likely to make it home unscathed; she saw which individuals would fall in with drug addicts and be sucked into the conditioning quicksand, and which would instead likely fall to a fundamentalist preacher or the deadly programming of network television; she saw which ones would accidentally become wealthy, and which would . . .

Wait. There was something more: She saw the skein of interrelationships as it stretched out to the event horizon . . . she saw something hideous and something glorious taking shape out there . . . she saw . . .

Saucers.

She blinked, and looked back at the present. Amongst the crowd she saw a few who were like self-propelling steel balls in a pinball game, making havoc of the rules, introducing a Brownian motion where the others strove for regimentary order. There was something about them that reminded her of her mother—could they be the ones Mother had described? The other race hidden amongst the humans . . . the privileged and divinely aberrant . . . the SubGenius?

"I see you perceive your tribe," "Bob" told her. "The tribe of the Untribal. Do you also see the webs of probability?"

"I do."

"Then keep your eyes on them and learn, Little Connie . . . because we're dive-bombing the Luck Plane!"

And with that "Bob" dove down, straight down, rocketing headfirst toward the bus they'd alighted on earlier. The bus had moved on, was entering the stream of traffic. And now they entered the bus through the roof—passing through it as if it were the skin of a soap bubble. "Bob" came to a screeching stop in the air over the driver, floating beside a sign that said, "PINKVILLE VOCATIONAL SCHOOL IS A STEP UP TO MORE WORK!"

"Bob" reached out and tapped the back of the man's head with his pipe . . . tapped it precisely. In a particular spot.

The man shuddered, and giggled, and jerked the wheel to the left—into the flow of oncoming traffic.

"Uh oh!" "Bob" said, grinning. "I made a mistake. Accident. Wrong car. We're going to cr—"

Crash, as the bus rammed the forty-foot limo they'd seen earlier, buckling it so it was shaped like a boomerang. The limo spun and struck a semitruck, which swerved and drove through the wall of a power station and crashed into a set of enormous transformers, causing a short circuit which caused a mighty power surge (Connie could see all this taking shape on the Luck Plane like a video animation) which roared through the wires to an airport a hundred miles away garbling the transmissions of the air traffic controllers causing the wrong signals to be sent to a Learjet crammed with undersecretaries of the Trilateral Commission who went into a screaming panic when the plane, its computer controls confused, veered wildly and went out of control, going into a tailspin, nosing down . . . crashing thunderously into the industrial park where Connie had met "Bob." The cargo of nanotechnological submolecular reprogramming proteins the undersecretaries had been carrying to Washington exploded along with the hundreds of gallons of fuel in the plane's tanks, spreading in a diffuse cloud over the living concentration camp construct, the nanoprogramming molecules colliding with submolecular guidance systems for the minatory mechanism, reprogramming it—quite by lucky accident—into a complete reversal of the process, so that the living concentration camp began to deconstruct itself . . . and in so doing released another cloud of deprogramming nanotech molecules that drifted over the land, reversing the process wherever they encountered it. . . .

"Whew!" "Bob" said. "That was lucky." He turned to Little Connie. "Young Miss, how would you like to visit your brothers and sisters in Malaysia?"

"Brothers and sisters? But I'm an only child!"

"Not at all. You're my daughter. You have hundreds of brothers and sisters, products of the Supreme Seed, thriving in Dobbstown, learning, awaiting X-Day . . . would you like to meet them?"

"You're my . . . Dad?"

"Yes!"

"Shit! What a disappointment . . . Mom told me you were a rock star."

The eternal grin almost wavered. Then he ruffled her hair tenderly. "You'll like your brothers and sisters," "Bob" said. "They're just as disrespectful as you are. Care for some 'Frop?"

And so, borne on a purposeful plume of green-sparkled blue, they rose from the twisted wreckage of the traffic accident, oblivious to the screams of the approaching sirens, and hurried on into the year 1996, on their way to a date with destiny, seeing the years 1997 and 1998 unfold ahead of them, like a place in the distance, where, clearly and far away, the Saucers were landing. . . .

Rev. Ivan Stang
THE THIRD FIST

A s Li Li-jing stood knee-deep in dinosaur manure, facing certain death in the jaws of a slavering Tyrannosaurus rex, he seriously regretted leaving China and joining the SubGeniuses. Had he foreseen this eventuality, he certainly would have declined Stang's invitation to the Church camp-out.

As the fetid typhoon of saurian's breath roiled over him, his mind raced at top speed, perhaps compensating for the lack of time remaining to it. At least he would die honorably. Being devoured in defense of all humanity, eighty million years before his own birth, by the most efficient killing machine nature had ever produced, until humankind anyway, wasn't really a bad way to cap off a life. Maybe someday the fossil of his skeleton might be found. That would certainly confound the historians. Perhaps, he mused in detached hysteria, the fossil of Peking man in the museum was his own skull!

Probably not, he realized. His half-digested bones would more likely dissolve, scattered among those of lesser animals in the droppings of this beast.

Was there anything he wanted to do before he died? Yes. He wanted to go to sleep. As the rows of gore-encrusted teeth drew nearer, he closed his eyes and thought back—ahead, technically—to his arrival at Dokstok in the early 1980s . . . the early years of the Church. . .

He really shouldn't have felt so insecure about meeting Ivan's friends. He was a proud and intelligent Han Chinese, and he'd managed to achieve something only one in five million of his countrymen had done: He had quit his job (as a sound recordist at Beijing Film Studios) and traveled to America.

In 1984, assigned to a Chinese-American documentary coproduction, he had become fast friends with the Texan film editor, Ivan Stang. Despite language barriers, each recognized a kindred spirit and they shared an almost telepathic rapport. Both were kindly but driven family men who had developed ornery, acutely sardonic senses of humor as buffers against their frustrations. Li had taken the culture-shocked Stang under his wing in Beijing, and in return Stang had offered to sponsor Li's American education. After three years of paperwork, Li had finally made it to the U.S. But . . . either both his English and jet lag were much worse than he'd imagined, or these people really *were* crazy.

In his Dallas home (a mansion by Li's standards, a hovel by its own-er's), Stang was an entirely different man than he'd been in China. Li had quickly realized that Stang actually made his living not by editing film, but by administrating his strange Church of the SubGenius. The "Church" had almost made sense to Li, the way Stang had explained it three years earlier in China; but Li now knew Stang had been holding something back.

Li still liked Stang, though; the bespectacled Caucasian behaved hon-orably, worked hard and had been sensitive to Li's loneliness and con-fusion in adjusting to the States. He'd struggled—vainly, of course—to help Li find work as a sound man.

But something was being left unsaid. Li was fairly certain Stang hadn't really wanted to take him to the big SubGenius party and wil-derness campout called Dokstok, that the invitation had been extended painfully, purely out of a sense of politeness. Stang kept stressing that this "SubGenius thing" wasn't "typically American," but would in the same breath almost shout that it embodied everything the Spirit of America stood for. Stang's mysterious ambiguity made Li all the more anxious to attend.

From Dallas, they'd driven a whole day to reach the island encamp-ment on a remote Arkansas lake. Li thought he'd prepared himself for the unearthly American propensity for obstreperous individuality; he was far wrong. The uneasy feeling began when Li first saw the Dokstok site.

An open-sided pavilion stood at the center of several rough cabins, with many vehicles parked randomly nearby. All else was clear lake and dense, breathtaking forest landscape. Li couldn't imagine more than a city park's worth of such rich land going uncultivated in China. Nor had he ever seen, not even on TV, such a crazy-quilt variety of round-eyes as peopled Dokstok.

Here a man was totally bald, but sported an enormous handlebar moustache, tweaked and curled fantastically. There a black man had shoulder-length hair in Rastafarian style and a beard uncut for years. And there was a woman without a shirt on, kissing a man with a full head of hair on his *neck* and *dozens of moustaches* on his otherwise shaven *scalp*. Altogether there must have been a hundred guests, few of them fitting Li's ideal of a normal American.

Stang leaped from his Japanese car and began excitedly talking with a large man wearing an extravagant goatee. Li understood only a few words of the high-speed stream they spewed at each other simulta-neously. He recognized several grossly indecent invectives, but, instead of coming to blows over the vulgar insults, the two men embraced. The big man was Doktor Sterno, one of the hosts of Dokstok. Li was then introduced to cohost Doktor Snavely, who looked twenty but who was, Li learned, well into his forties. This strangely childlike man was possessed of not only a crazed, manic friendliness, but also a "wandering eye" which seemed to look off towards distant horizons while his other was focused straight at Li.

Li had just begun to feel hypnotized by Snavely's weird eye when the fellow abruptly hopped into Li's arms, clinging to him like a lemur, causing him to stumble backwards in confusion. Just as suddenly, Snavely let go and jumped back to the ground, reverting to ordinary behavior as if this stunt had never occurred, offering Li food and drink from the nearby pavilion. He now seemed quite sincere and gentlemanly. Li hoped that Snavely's startling, overly familiar shenanigans had been meant as some sort of inscrutable friendship gesture; maybe Arkansas customs were as different from those of Dallas as were Beijing's from Shanghai's.

Li was rescued from his helpless befuddlement by the impersonal, merely physical task of helping Stang carry his gear—sleeping bags, a tent, and many recording decks—down to the pavilion area where crouched other little tents.

"Li," warned Stang under his breath, "these guys all act crazy. *I will too.* But, just remember, it's all okay. It's all just. . ." he looked off at the lake, sighing, ". . . it's all just SubGenius." He shook his head as if in resignation.

As they reached a clear spot and plunked down their burdens, at least a dozen aberrant people, apparently old friends, came to greet Stang and meet Li. Li was once again reminded that he hadn't thoroughly adjusted to these huge, heaving, loud, round-eyed, big-snouted Caucasians. Moreover, these particular Caucasians seemed somehow larger (or else much smaller), louder, more round-eyed, more big-snouted than most. And bigger-breasted. Everything about each person was extreme. Only one thing was obviously held in common: All bore, somewhere on their persons, a picture of "Bob." And they all seemed to be laughing, perpetually, some to the point of tears, but always at rapidly spoken words that meant nothing to Li. He was seized with an irrationally acute sense of his own incongruity. He was very Oriental, his English was rudimentary, his clothing shabby, and he had no money of his own to speak of.

Li was unanimously regarded as one of the funniest, hippest young fellows at Beijing Film Studios. But here, his skills were useless. Not that any of these "doktors"—as the SubGenius old-timers ranked themselves—were hostile; in fact, they were friendly to a degree that seemed to Li uncalled for and even undignified.

Li mulled over this as he surveyed the open-air pavilion. Several musicians had started setting up electric guitars, synthesizers and amplifiers on a crude stage made of planks. A huge sheet of plywood bearing "Bob's" image hung behind the stage. It must have been crafted by an extremely devoted artist, Li thought, for every one of the ten thousand dots of that grinning halftone face was perfectly hand-painted on the flimsy sheet of wood.

Striving to overcome his shyness, Li joined a group sitting on the ground in a big circle, laughing. He sat between Stang and a shirtless, bearded man in a straw hat who was by far the hairiest human being Li had ever seen outside of a circus. The hirsute man introduced himself as Rev. Buck Naked and happily engaged Li in conversation of a sort; Buck did most of the talking.

Much to Li's embarrassment, Buck immediately mentioned his own hairiness. "Bet you don't see many people like me in China, huh, Li?" he asked, proudly displaying his furred pelt. "It's because I'm part Yeti. You know what a Yeti is? Sure you do. You know, in Tibet— Himalayas—big hairy ape-man. We call 'em Abominable Snowman, too. And Bigfoot. I know you have them in China."

"Oh yes," laughed Li, hoping that laughter was the correct response. "We call them Wild Mans. But . . . I think maybe he is just big story. For children. Or just big monkey."

"Oh no, Li," said Buck quite seriously, now rocking rapidly back and forth on his heels like a hyperactive child. "My great-grandfather was a full-blood Yeti, I'm sure. You're probably part Yeti, too. . . ." He eyed Li up and down. "Yep. Long arms. Short legs. You're one of us, brother!" He chortled idiotically.

Li nervously lit one of his treasured Seven Heavens cigarettes. Then he noticed that several pipefuls of a foul-smelling, unidentifiable white vegetable were being passed from person to person. Li was startled to see that some, rather than smoking it, packed the leafy substance into their ears, even beneath their eyelids and down the backs of their pants and—he had to avert his eyes when he saw what one man was doing with it. Soon the talk became louder, more seemingly disjointed, finally reverting into a kind of ritualistic chanting peppered with strange hoots, ululations, vulgar farting noises, and bouts of hysterical laughter. Li laughed too at first, but it kept going on and on until, he realized, they sounded frighteningly like deranged savages in the Cambodian jungles. With a start, he wondered if this " 'Frop" might not actually be the opiumlike American drug marijuana. He didn't want to believe that; it smelled more like k'wang-ji, a harmless herb smoked by many old Mongolian and Tibetan gentlemen of the lower classes. His good friend Ivan couldn't possibly be a drug user! That would be heartbreaking. He steeled himself to ask.

"Ivan—is this bad drug?"

"Oh, hell no!" Stang assured Li in a hideous new croaking voice.

"That stuff's for sissies. This is 'Frop. Grows in Tibet." Then he coughed out the gigantic lungful he'd been holding in, tears welling in his eyes, which now seemed to *glow* ever so slightly with an inner light. Li thought it was a freak reflection, until he realized that all eyes in the group now displayed the same preternatural glow.

Li was most uncomfortable. This seemed dangerous. He politely excused himself and hurriedly made his way back towards the pavilion.

Dozens of people were eagerly crowding into one of the little cabins; others staggered out, clutching tightly inflated balloons and *sucking* on them. Curious, Li stood on tiptoe at the doorway to peer in. Over the crowd's shoulders, he spied a large metal canister boldly labeled "BOB-BIE SOULS." A tall Englishman with a gratingly loud, authoritative voice, Stang's friend G. Gordon Gordon, was filling balloons with gas from the canister and doling them out selectively to clutching hands. "Church Air, one soul per breath!" he growled repeatedly. People were so anxious for balloons that Gordon threateningly waved what Li hoped was one of the many replica toy handguns that littered Dokstok.

Outside, those with balloons were inhaling the gas from them and holding their breaths until they turned half blue; they would finally exhale, uttering cryptic statements in unnaturally deep voices. Others were rushing around tape-recording these odd, seemingly random statements. Conversations took on a dreamlike, surreal quality, disconnected from each other. Braying laughter echoed to the lake and back.

Li gawked in absolute bewilderment. This was a party? He looked down at a scrawny, swarthy, rather ratlike man sitting cross-legged on the ground, wearing an Egyptian-style goatee, with his kinky salt-and-pepper hair cut only on the sides so that its top rose like a pencil eraser. The man, Palmer Vreedeez, had just managed to inhale an entire balloon's worth of this Church Air, and the white streaks in his hair appeared to become visibly whiter, spreading further across his hairdo. Then, to Li's utter astonishment, the man literally levitated two or three feet off the ground, his eyes rolled back. He hovered briefly and then, as he slowly descended, exhaling, he looked at Li and solemnly intoned in a supernatural baritone, "Hi, Li. Your relatives in China are fine. Lao Wang honored your bribe. "Bob's" looking for you. He'll pick you up tonight. But it's all Stang and Drummond's fault, you know. Call . . . my . . . lawyer. . ." and then the man crashed over onto the ground, flat on his back, unconscious.

Li bent to the man's aid, his heart pounding. No one else seemed to even take notice! But suddenly the rodentlike man was again conscious, and forcing himself upright. A trembling wracked his bony, starved-looking form, and he dashed past Li holding out his balloon, shoving into line again as near the Air tank as possible. His emaciated claws clutched convulsively at the canister.

Both frightened and disgusted, Li turned away from the Church Air cabin and strode back to the pavilion. What a sad display, he thought. But at least they weren't throwing up. And . . . he halted in his tracks. How did that man know about Lao Wang and the bribe?? He started back to question Vreedeez when a man wearing a military jacket, sporting one continuous and very black eyebrow across the top of his otherwise handsome features, accosted him and held a cassette recorder up between their faces. He expectorated several sentences so fast that he sounded like a tape recorder in fast-forward mode. Then he made a sound with his mouth that mimicked exactly a high-speed rewinding, followed by a quiet chuckle. He then walked on, talking to himself or his recorder, ignoring Li completely.

That must be Puzzling Evidence, Stang's military friend, Li thought. Maybe he thinks I'm North Vietnamese. This was getting downright insulting. He quietly edged off towards the pavilion where a tall, skeletal man stood on the makeshift stage, shouting rhythmically into a microphone that wasn't plugged in, to an audience that wasn't there. He gestured frantically at the huge picture of "Bob" behind him. "You can't run from your own legs. How you gonna run from your own legs? 'Cause they're what you're using to run from 'em *with!* You can't run from your own legs, you can't hide from "Bob." 'Cause he's dumber than you. He packs more 'Frop up his exit wound than you do. His face has been mimeographed and stuck up in more places than yours has. You can't hide from J. R. "Bob" Dobbs! *Heunh!* Help me somebody! She ain't got no legs! Preacher, my legs are on fire! Pull the lever, down ya go." The man did a little dance to unheard music.

Nothing made sense. These people seemed harmless enough, but definitely crazy. Crazier even than any Japanese Li'd met, and that was saying a lot. Li's opinion of Stang had plummeted far.

It was getting dark and storm clouds were rolling in overhead. Making for the privacy of the lakeshore, Li noted a long line of men waiting before a filthy tent. One man emerged from it, zipping up his pants and grinning broadly, as another man ducked down to enter eagerly.

Li was appalled. There must be a woman in there—a prostitute! No wonder all Americans had AIDS!

G. Gordon Gordon, the loud Englishman from South America, accosted Li from behind, startling him. "Mr. Li! I'll bet it's been a while since you had yourself some good healthy prairie squid!"

"What? Sorry, I don't understand."

"Prairie squid." He leaned over towards Li, winking conspiratorially. "C'mon, I *know* you aren't one of these sissy guys who never heard of prairie squid."

"Squid? Squid is . . . is fish, with arms, right?"

"Yeah. But I'm talking about the *prairie squid*. That mighty land mollusk which is every country boy's delight. And girl's, too."

"Pray-ree squid," repeated Li. "What you do with it? Go in tent . . . play with animal?" He was profoundly puzzled.

"No, no, Li!" growled Gordon merrily. "You *fuck* it."

"What! No! You make, like, make love to *animal??*"

"You got it, sir. And never could a man ask for a more generous and tender helpmeet."

He laughed at Li's shocked expression.

"Go ahead, try that cephalopod out. I'm surprised you don't have those in China. But I'll bet some of your peasants in the Hubei countryside could tell you *a thing or two* about the *Yellow River* prairie squid."

Li looked towards the tent, aghast, as another man stepped in and the last came out, this one also lashing together his pants and grinning sheepishly.

Li made an immediate decision to return to China as soon as possible. He'd always thought that the Mao-inspired anti-American propaganda of his childhood was grossly exaggerated. But if this was America, it was *far* worse, morally, than his government had even begun to suspect!

He wasn't sure what to do. Perhaps hitchhike back to Dallas, where he'd left his passport, and then go to the Chinese embassy. He could never live in a place like this. These people . . . now he noticed how bad they all smelled: That unfortunate doglike odor common to white people seemed amplified here. Everything smelled, looked, sounded and tasted funny. He absolutely hated all the food these people ate, the raw vegetables, big, ugly chunks of meat, and unidentifiable synthesized junk foods.

And then the music started.

It was, beyond question, the most horrible and *physically painful* sound Li had ever heard. Normal American rock and roll was bad enough to his ears; he'd expected perhaps some weird jazz from these "doktors." But what now came crashing from the overamped speakers, pealing monstrously across the lake, was a wall of the most noxious and earsplitting noises he'd ever imagined. And yet the audience seemed to *enjoy* it! Indeed, many were tapping their feet in time to a rhythm Li couldn't hear, and a few were up and dancing. Then he noticed that *all were dancing or tapping to a different beat*. It wasn't just his ignorance; there *was* no beat. These drug-and-religion-addled people were simply imagining one!

Clamping his hands over his ears, Li grimaced and looked down at his feet where several bugs lay unsquashed yet dead on their backs. As he stared, a fat mosquito halted in flight and plunged to the floor to join the other dead insects.

This music was literally killing small animals by sheer sonic ugliness alone!

Filth. Vulgarity. Immorality. Sloth. Drugs of some heretofore unknown kind. What next? Violence? Enough was enough. He would bend like a reed in the wind—and *leave*. He strode rapidly away from the pavilion, unnoticed by the audience of Caucasian fools who sat entranced by the inhuman display.

The night bristled with lightning, and a downpour started. Li hurried towards a short causeway bridge that led back to the main highway. Drenching rain or not, he wasn't going to rot in an American jail with mentally ill people.

Lightning writhed overhead as Li toiled on through the pelting sheets of rain. Once off Dokstok Mountain and back on the mainland, he kept to the side of the road, hugging the tree line.

Soaked to the bone, shivering, Li finally spied ahead a lighted tavern, surrounded by pickups. He approached cautiously, suspecting that a soaked, penniless Chinese might bring out the worst in some of the more backward natives.

As he approached the ramshackle honky-tonk, he saw that his worries were entirely justified. A hand-lettered sign on the door read:

DO NOt INteR WeTHOut WHIT SKEN AN a gUNN

Li hurried away, clinging to the woods along the roadside. The rain grew colder and his teeth chattered in the cold. So this was America.

Headlights were approaching. Fearing for his health, he resolved to throw himself upon the mercy of the natives and pray for some shared sense of common humanity. As the car approached, he thrust out his thumb as he'd seen in American movies. He decided to say he was from Taiwan, not the Communist mainland.

He had worked up a whole story about escaping from the evil Communists when the large, powerful roadster—of an ancient make, at least twenty years old—pulled to a stop beside him. He yanked open the door and begged of the driver, whose face was swathed in dark, "Can you give me ride to nearer to city?"

"Ya got me," intoned a deep but amused voice, chuckling. "Me, I'm just as lost as can be! Maybe we can help each other!" As Li climbed into the front seat, thanking his benefactor, he began to distinguish the man's features.

The face was startling. It might have been molded of solid plastic! Li half expected to see a seam down the side. The head was almost too perfectly proportioned to be human. A remarkably high forehead, lantern jaw and strong smile denoted either a rare power of character, or severe mutation from inbreeding. His hair lay straight and smooth, as if molded from the same plastic as his skin but painted black and shellacked. A long, straight pipe jutted from his grinning mouth.

But most striking of all were his eyes—like pools of fine flake jade, swirling in depthless blue. These eyes possessed an almost hypnotic quality, a strange suggestion of being able to give orders at a glance, without speaking them.

Of course the personage was none other than J. R. "Bob" Dobbs.

Li stared, thunderstruck, as Dobbs pulled back onto the highway.

"Stang lie to me," uttered Li. "He say you dead man."

"Hmph," grunted Dobbs. "Is that so?" He looked thoughtful, drumming his fingers on the wheel. "Stang." Many cloying smoke clouds issued rapidly from the Pipe clenched in his teeth. "Name seems familiar," he allowed finally. He cocked an eyebrow at Li, as if expecting an explanation.

Li had trouble answering, as he'd realized that Dobbs was driving back towards Dokstok and, in fact, already crossing the causeway. Even with the car windows up, they could already hear the awful "music" pulsating from the island.

"Hmm," mused "Bob." "Listen to that horrible noise. I could swear it sounds just like a Dokstok. Now, wouldn't that be a coincidence!"

Li gaped at Dobbs in dumbfoundment. Could this be happening?

"Well, might as well stop in and see the boys," announced Dobbs happily as he pulled his enormous old car into the parking area.

"But, "Bob"! These people. . . There will be police! Big trouble! I don't know. . . I think maybe they crazy criminals!"

"Tell me something new," quipped Dobbs, quitting the car and striding purposefully towards the pavilion. In his business suit and tidy haircut, he looked as out of place as an FBI agent.

Stang, Sterno, and many others were clustered together, jabbering excitedly. The band, which had dwindled to three guitar players, thumped out slow, tired blues. Dozens of people had retired to tents or had fallen asleep right on the ground around the pavilion.

No one noticed Dobbs as he stepped gingerly over the prostrate bodies and stood on the outskirts of the chattering group. He tried repeatedly to interrupt the conversation—"Hey, boys—ahem. . . hey, uh . . ." But so absorbed were they in recounting past antiestablishment exploits, none noticed him.

Finally, Dobbs became bored. He wandered over to the stage and watched the musicians, none of whom looked up from their instruments. He stood next to a young man with a balloon taped over his face so that he could breathe and rebreathe his Church Air without interruption. The young man looked up at "Bob," did a surprised double take, then shrugged his shoulders and turned his attention back to the band, shaking his head as if amazed at the concrete realness of this "Church Air hallucination."

Dobbs walked back to Li, who had waited by the car.

"Those fucked-up hopheads can't see past their own 'Fropsticks," chuckled Dobbs without a trace of resentment. "Should've known." He clamped a broad hand on Li's shoulder. "Li Li-jing, you're probably the only one here innocent enough to believe in me," he said absentmindedly, gazing off into the distance. Then he turned and looked directly into Li's eyes. Li found he could not turn away . . . nor did he want to. Dobbs exuded a friendliness of almost seductive purity.

"Say, you're a Chinese fellow, or something, aren't you? You speak Chinese?"

"Well, yes, "Bob," " answered Li, puzzled. "Of course. Three dialects. But is many kind Chinese. . ."

"Great!" interrupted Dobbs. "How about kung fu? Can you do kung fu fighting? Like a ninja, or whatever, you know, HYAH! HAH!" Dobbs playfully executed a clumsy imitation of karate against imaginary foes.

"I am good boxer," admitted Li. He saw no use in false modesty with Dobbs, who seemed as sincere and direct as he was simpleminded.

"Ah, what luck!" He suddenly became quite serious. "Listen, I need your help, Li. But don't feel you have to join me in this noble quest. It could be very dangerous. We'll be facing madmen, mudmen and dinosaurs."

Li leaned in closer, suspecting he hadn't understood "Bob" correctly. Dinosaurs? Mudmen? Madmen he'd already faced.

"I'm on a quest to save the human race," continued the inappropriately grinning white man. "Other than that, it isn't really your concern. But I need a SubGenius boxer who can fight like a son-of-a-bitch, and I need someone to translate Chinese, because the Chinese "Bob" doesn't speak English. It hasn't been invented in his time. Do you have a minute?" he suddenly asked, rather belatedly. "I'd like to tell you about this once-in-a-lifetime chance."

Despite the feeling that he was being sold something, Li felt an irresistible urge to trust this odd man. This *holy* man, he realized. For there was no question now in Li's mind, despite Dobbs' manipulative air and lack of miraculous performances, that this man Dobbs was all that legend claimed him to be. Proof wasn't required; in the actual presence of "Bob," rationality was as nothing compared to the charisma veritably oozing from his dotlike pores. That Dobbs had chosen Li over his supposed Hierarchites—most of whom were now snoring drunkenly—had much to be said for it as well.

"Please. I want to help you, "Bob," " said Li awkwardly.

"All right, Li. Now this is all going to sound crazy, and I won't blame you if you don't believe me. But it could be the most crucial mission of my life. JHVH-1 Itself bespoke to me what I must do." Dobbs pronounced *JHVH-1* almost nonverbally, yet in a manner which grated on Li's nerves. "The very fate of the universe hinges on the success or failure of this mission, the outcome of which will dictate whether all mankind shall crumple under the jackboot of history, or scale the heights of its rightful destiny as decreed in our genetic inheritance!"

Dobbs regarded Li gravely for a second, then burst into laughter.

"Ha! Had you going for a minute there, didn't I?" Then his laughter was stifled as suddenly as it had begun. "But seriously now, JHVH-1 has told me in a mystic vision that the AntiBob is gaining power in our Past-That-Might've-Happened. The Beforelife, I like to call it. If he isn't stopped, he will—or did—taint and pervert all humanity, and all Sub-Geniuskind, even worse than they already are. Eventually this evil will culminate in his literally *fucking* the earth . . . and Li, I don't mean that figuratively. This won't be just acid rain and volcanoes and plagues and monsters and nuclear war. I mean he will actually take out a gigantic *AntiBob dick* and *fuck* this planet with it." To Li's shock, Dobbs held up his hands and made a grossly obscene, childish "fuck" gesture, pumping away at a "hole" formed by circled fingers on one hand with one straight finger of another hand. "He will do this, *or has possibly already done this,* by manipulating the past . . . indeed, his villainous actions may just be what has made our present, all this world around us, the way it is!"

For some reason, when "Bob" uttered such statements, they didn't sound at all ridiculous.

"And worse than that," continued "Bob," his eyes starting to water with tears, his grin changing almost imperceptibly into a grimace of agony, "even worse than that—*the AntiBob has kidnapped my wife and taken her somewhere back in time!*"

"Let me show you a picture of my beloved," sniffed "Bob." "Check this out. . . ." He unfolded his wallet and slid out a snapshot of a lovely woman in her thirties, wearing her hair in an old-fashioned "beehive" hairdo. " "Connie"!" snurfled "Bob" to the picture, his hands trembling. "I would do anything to get you back." Li then noticed another picture which remained in the wallet, a crude Polaroid that had been revealed when Dobbs removed the snapshot. It showed the same woman, grinning lasciviously, stark naked, her legs spread wide open. . . .

Li averted his eyes in shame, and Dobbs, noticing, coughed with embarrassment and shoved the snapshot back into his wallet.

"Anyway," he continued, granite-voiced now, "The only way I can rescue my beloved, and smite the AntiBob for the sake of humanity's Slack, is to journey back in time via . . ."

He paused portentously.

"... the Vortex. You see, the AntiBob's antiluck powers shield him from even my 4-D vision. To learn his identity, I must travel back in time and consult with all the other "Bobs"!"

As Dobbs spoke, lightning crackled dramatically in the sky behind him. Li shuffled uneasily.

Dobbs solemnly intoned, "As I'm sure you know, I am merely the Caucasian "Bob." Even though I'm half Mayan." He halted, inwardly emotional. "I must travel through the Dream Time to meet in days of yore with the Oriental "Bob," the African "Bob" and the American Indian "Bob" ... for they will help me reach the most ancient "Bob" of all, the First "Bob," the King of Atlantis called the Yeti "Bob." You follow me so far?"

Li blinked in a sort of semicomprehension that smacked of schizophrenia. "Yes, "Bob." I think so. But what about ... Aborigine "Bob"? Australia man?"

"Oh yeah, him too," exclaimed Dobbs, slapping himself on the forehead. "That's right! I always forget those guys! Anyway, I have to cross the backside of reality, and I will need help—translating and fighting."

Li stood, staring blankly. There seemed little to say. His exhaustion had hit him viscerally. He hadn't slept well since leaving China; in this dreamlike condition, rational decisions seemed irrelevant. But this was Dobbs, *the* Dobbs, asking him to risk his life for what would be either an authentic magical quest or a stupid drug-induced wild goose chase.

Why not?

"Okay. I go," said Li Li-jing.

"Well," said Dobbs, "nothing left to do now but summon the Vortex."

Dobbs put his fingers to his mouth and whistled. Then he stood expectantly, striking a noble pose. He held this overly self-conscious pose for a full minute.

But nothing happened.

"Hmm," he reconsidered. "Musta changed the frequency. Oh well. I'll try it the old-fashioned way."

He held his arms up to the sky, his Pipe jutting skywards. It occurred to Li that he had seen Dobbs neither refill nor light the Pipe, yet it had incessantly smoldered, relentlessly productive of abundant, cloying fumes.

Dobbs chanted, "From the Land Beyond Beyond, from the World Past Hope and Fear, I bid you, Vortex, now appear!" He winked at Li. "I got that from a movie!"

The brightest bolt of lightning in Li's experience rent the sky—but no thunder followed. A vast glow began at the distant horizon and swelled as if a great curtain of darkness and stars were being rolled up across the sky. Revealed behind this curtain of reality was a psychedelic, ever-metamorphosing fountain of spiraling shapes in colors too intense for names. The swirling light show swallowed more and more of the sky until it passed over and behind them. It reminded Li of computer animation from Japan that he'd seen at the Studios. When it had almost reached the far horizon behind them, also somehow obliterating most of the ground around them, Dobbs suddenly shouted, "Oh, golly-gosh-darn-it! Wait a minute! I forgot, we need something to ride on!"

He dashed off into the colored fog of the Vortex momentarily, but reappeared carrying a huge sheet of plywood with his face painted on one side. It was the backdrop that had been mounted above the stage in the pavilion. A few bent nails protruded from its edge.

He threw the plywood to the ground—Dobbsface down, Li noted—and led Li onto it with him.

Li instantly felt the board lurching forward like a Disneyland ride. The ground itself vanished, leaving only the quasi-material whorls of light around and below them. There were two layers to the vista of color-light waves, however—one moving beneath the plywood, carrying them, while another field of cloudlike light flowed more gradually overhead as they passed beneath it. Li and "Bob" were *riding* the plywood through a "sea" of light, Dobbs standing at the front and holding his arms outward exactly as if he were surfing. And now Li felt it—a heaving up-and-down motion combined with a sense of zooming forward at high speed against a strong wind. They *were* surfing on light waves!

"Hey, there's a curl starting up!" yowled Dobbs. "Let's hang ten into Indian territory!"

The sense of velocity increased. They were speeding headlong into some new whorl in the Vortex, a spinning tunnel of light that had forked away from the main, sweeping stream of energy. As they banked into it, they accelerated so fast that they spiraled end over end along the tube of the Vortex as if riding the screw of a great whirlpool into the bowels of Inner Reality. Up and down were nonexistent. All was Vortex.

Li could see nothing but the tunnels of light, the board beneath his feet, and "Bob."

"Fun, huh?" quizzed Dobbs, winking. Then, as they gained even more speed, he howled, "KOWABUNGAAAAAA!"

Dobbs was enjoying this immensely, somehow using his inborn sense of cosmic balance to guide the board in its headlong careening. His movements had a flowing smoothness, like great springs uncoiling in oil. Though his necktie flapped in the solar winds, his perfect hair was unruffled.

"But . . . how you do this?" queried Li, only now becoming less stunned than incredulous with admiration at Dobbs' surfing skills.

"Bob" returned a startled look, as if he'd never before considered that detail. "Huh! Good question! I dunno . . . path of least resistance, I suppose. Hmmm. . ." He looked thoughtful. "Hell, ya got me!"

"But. . ." stammered Li, "how you know where we going?"

"I'll be honest with ya, Li. I don't really know *where* the hell I'm going. But what the heck, I always seem to get there! Just kind of follow my nose, you know? It always seems to work out. . . ." Again, Dobbs gazed off into the distance, the center of the Vortex. "But, you know, this reminds me of those nights . . . with "Connie". . . ." He sniffed piteously, his grin now an ironic one. "Whoa—this is where we get off! Hang on!"

"Bob" suddenly gave the board a downward push with his feet, and the Vortex skinned itself back from around them, revealing a dismal, smoky landscape. They were now skidding wildly over grass and mud, the Vortex gone.

The board went into a spin as they decelerated, throwing both Li and Dobbs off. Li bumped to a stop on his behind, but "Bob" managed to maintain his footing. His fine, straight hair remained undisturbed.

The duo took in their surroundings. It was cold, daytime, and a light fog covered an endless vista of ruined, bombed-out, European-style buildings. Clouds of smoke wafting through smelled of gunpowder.

"Hmmm," pondered Dobbs. "This was supposed to be the American West of one hundred years ago, but I could swear this looks like wartime Germany. And if I remember my war days right, we're just outside Berlin."

Strange lights came into his azure eyes as he evidently arrived at some conclusion. "I would deduce from our surroundings, Li," he intoned distractedly, "that I either took a wrong turn at that last Mutron, or else the AntiBob himself is aware of my movements and has sabotaged our Vortex journey with his insidious tricks, trying to distract us with such trivialities as World War Two. He knows full well how I hate Nazis." "Bob" smirked grimly.

They were standing on a muddy road, with not a soul in sight. But a deep rumbling captured their attention.

Emerging from the fog was an army tank, sporting a swastika on its tattered flag!

"Panzer!" shouted "Bob." "Yep, this is Germany all right. Well, while we're here, might as well strike a blow for freedom, truth and Jews. Some of my best friends are Jewish," he added.

Li stood agog as Dobbs broke into a full-speed sprint, charging the massive tank head-on. The turret swiveled menacingly and the barrel came to bore on "Bob." Li was thunderstruck. Did this fool "Bob" think he could destroy a German tank by himself??

It looked like curtains for Dobbs and Li!

But, within a few dozen yards of the juggernaut, Dobbs lost his footing and tripped spectacularly over a long, bent piece of gas pipe exposed by some previous explosion. He fell flat on his face in the mud. But, in the process of tripping on the pipe, he'd caused it to swivel sideways towards the treads of the tank now bearing down on him. Just before the machine could crush Dobbs beneath it, the broken pipe slammed into the gears at its side upon which the treads rolled. Caught in the machinery, the pipe was drawn into the works of the relentless juggernaut. It must have then impaled some crucial mechanism, for the tank suddenly slammed to a halt.

Nazi soldiers threw open the hatch, about to spray Dobbs and Li with machine-gun fire, when a hideous scraping noise erupted from the bowels of the tank. The entire machine shuddered like a wet dog, groaning horribly, and suddenly exploded in a ball of hot gas. Machine and bloody Nazi parts sprayed into the air.

" "Bob!" You saved us! Are you all right?" demanded Li as he rushed to help extricate Dobbs from the mud that had shielded him from the explosion.

"I'm fine, Li. Thanks," muttered Dobbs as he stood up, scraping mud off his suit, his composure again perfect. "Those goddamn Nazis. Boy, I *hate* Nazis. In fact, I don't hate anybody BUT Nazis. And the AntiBob!"

They continued down the destroyed road, approaching a deserted, bombed-out German village.

"You know," mused "Bob," "Nazis are like Commies. No offense if you're a poor misguided Commie, Li." Li shook his head in the negative. Dobbs continued. "They cannot understand the eternal verities of Patriopsychotic Anarchomaterialism—you know, 'every yard a kingdom.' It is beyond their beaten-down emotional grasp. They perceive Slack only for other Nazis. Why, I remember the time I killed Hitler. Now that was a blast, I tell you."

Li, dazed, barely listened to Dobbs' insane reminiscing.

"Yep, that one time when I killed Hitler. I'd been prepping him all along, you know, waiting for the right moment. I'd infiltrated the Reich for the Allies . . . Churchill said it was our only hope. All I had to do was put on a devil mask and a blanket, like a Dracula cape . . . that dumb Kraut never suspected I wasn't really the New Man of the Age of Thule from Atlantis, or whatever! First I drove him crazy, showing up when he least expected, telling him just what he wanted to hear in bad German and Latin I got from notes I wrote on my hand. That dumbshit fell for it," Dobbs chuckled. "I'd give him these completely fucked-up suggestions, then he'd go and force these suicidal strategies on his generals . . . finally, I throttled the nasty son-of-a-bitch with my own bare hands, in his bunker. Took my sweet time doing it, too. Played cat and mouse with the un-American bastard. Just when he thought Death had come, I'd allow him just enough air to prolong his terror. Yep," he chuckled with undisguised cruelty, "I taught that fuckhead a lesson. Not that it did him much good in the end! Pardon my language. . . . In fact, I wouldn't be surprised if I wasn't *also* in downtown Berlin right now, strangling him even as we speak!"

"Bob" stooped to pick up trash as they toiled down the cratered road, conscientiously pocketing the shreds of paper. "People shouldn't litter," he muttered disapprovingly.

They discovered an old woman begging by the roadside—almost blind, judging by her pitiful movements. Her clothing was shabby and she looked to be starving. "Bob" gazed upon her pityingly.

He dug in his pocket for loose change. "Darn, I left my wallet in the car!" Then, to Li's dismay, he retrieved from his pocket two random pieces of trash he had collected, one a slip of paper, the other a ruined paperback book. He gave them to the pathetic hag, a look of grand benevolence on his face, and walked on. At first, neither the old woman nor Li could believe "Bob" had done such a callous, mocking thing.

But the old woman held the piece of paper close to her face, scanning it. Then she blinked in astonishment. For the ragged piece of paper was the business card of the top German eye specialist. And from between the pages of the tattered paperback fell a hundred-thousand-mark bill.

The old woman burst into tears. It was enough money to cure her blindness, and put her grandchildren through Harvard as well.

This seemed a strange thing for a man to do who had just dealt cold and terrible justice to a tankful of soldiers. But, thought Li, "Bob" Dobbs was indeed a strange man, at least when judged by the look-out-for-yourself code of civilization.

"Well, gosh," exclaimed Dobbs suddenly. "Enough of Nazi killing. We have to find the Indian "Bob" ASAP, or it's curtains for "Connie." And humanity," he added, rather parenthetically. "Let's scram back to the Vortex."

Dobbs again summoned the Vortex, and it rose from the horizon with a great wind—which, with uncanny synchronicity, just happened to blow the piece of Dobbshead-stenciled plywood from the road far behind them to a spot right under their feet.

"Lucky break," mused Dobbs as they boarded the plywood and were swept up once again into the whirlpool-like whorls of Vortex light.

This time the trip was much shorter. Riding the plywood back into the main Vortex tunnel, and then down another smaller one, they came sliding to a stop in the middle of a Western prairie on a bright sunny day. A light breeze ruffled the prairie grass like waves on an ocean as the Vortex rolled back. But the breeze also bore the unmistakable stench of death.

Just behind them was a flaming, overturned American stagecoach. Its two drivers, obviously dead of gunshot wounds, sprawled nearby, their gore pooling in the dust. Four horses lay dead on the ground, still bridled to the coach, their throats cut.

Two people in turn-of-the-century suits, evidently passengers, were tied to a nearby tree stump, likewise dead—but also scalped, their raw heads buzzing with flies in the hot sun. That, and the profusion of wounds on their bodies, bespoke that they had been waylaid and tortured into revealing how to open their box of money.

Gagging, Li whispered, "Indians?"

"No, Li, only white outlaws could have perpetuated this heinous act! They scalped these poor innocent monopoly bankers to make it look like the work of Indians. The Sioux around these parts don't do that kind of thing." He gazed disapprovingly at the bloody spectacle. "No, they usually cut the balls off their enemies. And they'd *never* kill the horses. White bandits, or corrupt cavalry soldiers, did this. We must warn the Indians!"

Before they could act, a hue and cry of distant battle wafted to them on the wind. They climbed a bluff and ascertained the source of the increasingly dreadful sounds of cries and gunshots: a valley nestled just below amid the rolling amber hills.

A regiment of well-armed U.S. cavalry had surrounded a small Sioux encampment. Most of the warriors must have been occupied elsewhere, for only helpless women, children, and oldsters were visible dashing back and forth among the teepees in a futile attempt to repel the mounted soldiers gaily firing rifles and Gatling guns into their midst.

"Why, those dirty bastards," shouted "Bob," enraged. "It was never like this in the movies!" To Li's horror, Dobbs dashed to one of the prone corpses and scavenged from it a white cowboy hat and gun belt. "I need a horse," he muttered as he hurriedly donned them.

As if at Dobbs' command, an entire herd of Indian ponies thundered up onto the bluff, apparently fleeing the horror below. Without time for thought, Dobbs leaped upon one of the horses as it passed. The animal immediately came to a halt, and, as if according to orders whispered by Dobbs into its ear, spun around and carried him, riding bareback and firing his new six-guns into the air, back down towards the battle. Li could hear Dobbs hollering "Yeeeee-HAW!" as he vanished over the bluff's peak.

Li, without a mount, and unfamiliar with horses on any account, could but watch helplessly as the mighty Dobbs rode straight into the heat of battle. The evil cavalry rednecks were routed in confusion upon seeing this white man in a white hat blasting six-guns in all directions, each shot somehow finding its target. Cavalrymen plunged from their horses all around Dobbs.

Finally, one rifleman downed the horse upon which Dobbs rode. Even before the luckless steed hit the ground, Dobbs was airborne in a flying leap, landing amidst the blue-clad bullies. His guns now emptied, Dobbs waded into the fray bare-handed, lashing out with what looked to Li like a peculiar form of martial arts. Without really even *seeing* his victims, Dobbs became a blurred tornado of whirling and jabbing fists. In scant seconds, the area around him was peppered with dead or injured cavalrymen. Hundreds of shots had been fired at him, but, miraculously, none had hit their mark. Most had, in fact, struck other soldiers.

Within the space of ten seconds, Dobbs had rubbed out some forty men. Li was staggered by the Pipe-Bearer's amazing luck powers. "Bob" had merely closed his eyes and struck blindly at his attackers—and with far more ease, seemingly, than an average man would exert in zipping up his pants. It showed how little "Bob" needed either strength or agility.

With the tides turned, the embattled Indians surged from their camp and overpowered the few remaining soldiers. Before Li reached the Sioux camp, the battle was won. Surviving soldiers were already being bound and hauled into the camp to be slowly castrated by joyous Sioux women.

Li felt dizzy as he entered the Indian camp, so long had it been since he'd slept. The unfamiliar stench of the Indian camp—composed entirely of skin and bone, sewn together with sinew—hardly affected him. He had seen, heard and smelled too much in the last two hours; he was truly "freaked out."

Indian women knelt over their slain loved ones, wailing piteously. Dobbs strode through the center of the camp, supporting a limping but particularly attractive young Sioux woman who'd been grazed by a bullet. None took notice of Li; being Chinese, he simply looked much like a small-nosed Indian despite his blue jeans and plaid shirt.

A group of Sioux warriors on horseback belatedly topped the nearby hills and sped into camp trailing a cloud of dust. A tall, noble-looking Indian at the head of the group dismounted and strode straight to Dobbs.

Dobbs whirled around, dropping the injured young woman rather abruptly, so that she landed on her behind, squalling.

"Crazy Horse! You nutty bastard! Good to see you!"

"Hau, Dobbs," intoned the tall, severe Native American warrior in awkwardly pronounced English. "Once again you come to aid of our people."

Even Li had read of the exploits of Crazy Horse, mystic warrior hero of the doomed Sioux. Had he not already endured hours of equal impossibilities, he'd have doubted his own sanity.

"Crazy Horse," said Dobbs as Li sidled up to them, "Let me introduce my faithful Chinese companion, Li Li-jing. Li, this is Crazy Horse. Oh,

I'm sorry . . . his real name is Tashunka-Witco." Dobbs grinned sheep-ishly. "My Injun is a bit rustier than his English, I'm afraid."

Li ignored Dobbs' racist remark about a "faithful Chinese compan-ion." It was, after all, true.

"We hear of your mighty deeds even in my land, Mr. Witco," said Li, bowing.

"You resemble the people of the old lands whence came our forefa-thers," replied Crazy Horse, his brow furrowed. "We are honored by your presence. I have conversed with others of your kind held in slavery by the *Washeechu,* the pale boogie men who keep them slaves, making them work on the evil railroads which distract the buffalo and make them sick."

"Hey, Crazy," interrupted Dobbs, somewhat rudely. He leaned close to the proud warrior, whispering confidentially. "Listen, man, we need to do some business with the Indian "Bob" and the two Pipes." He pronounced *Indian* as "inden."

He pulled his own Pipe from his mouth and tamped it with his finger suggestively. "Pipes, you know? Savvy, Kimosabe? If I can get the two Pipes together, maybe I can get to the Yeti "Bob"—you know, the Chi-Chi Man, hairy guy. Me have-um big business with him. Dig?"

A scornful expression darkened the proud face of Crazy Horse mo-mentarily, but he chuckled and said, "Yes, "Bob," I understand. You are in luck, as always. In His Wisdom, Wakan Tanka, the grandfather of all things, has seen that the Great Pipe of the Lakota is in my possession now. We may combine the two powers of your Pipe and ours, and you will be taken to the Indian "Bob" who lives in the Dream Time."

"Wow, that's cool!" exclaimed Dobbs excitedly, jumping up and down like a child.

Crazy Horse disappeared into a teepee and emerged carrying, most gingerly, a package wrapped in smelly buffalo hide. From it he care-fully withdrew a "Peace Pipe"—a soapstone bowl attached to a long wooden stem hung with eagle feathers.

To Li's surprise, Dobbs gasped and fell prostrate before the revealed Peace Pipe. "My God," he mumbled into the dirt, "More juju than I remembered last time! Well, let's not waste a minute. God only knows what the AntiBob is trying to get my wife to do . . . on him. . . ."

He leaped to his feet and brandished his own Pipe. Crazy Horse held his Indian Pipe in the air facing Dobbs'. They pointed both Pipes to-wards the Spirits of the Four Winds, then touched the two together, stem to bowl, forming a magic rectangle. The other Indians drew back in fearful suspense.

A great flash of white light enveloped the two Pipes. Through the glow, Li discerned Dobbs and Crazy Horse grunting and heaving them back and forth with an almost sexual movement. Li thought he saw a great bulge rippling on Dobbs' pants near his groin. Suddenly, as if from the clear blue sky overhead, there dropped to the ground between the two men a third Pipe—strangely carved, of unidentifiable metallic composition, illuminated with intricate scrollwork.

"Hoooo-eee!" shouted "Bob," lifting it reverently from the ground. "It's the goddamned real thing! The Third Pipe! A goddamn Xist artifact! From outer space! What else could I need?"

" "Bob," " glowered Crazy Horse, "You are truly a Sacred Fool, a *heyoka*. It is a true thing that this is a Pipe from beyond the stars, from the Thunder Beings themselves. But you cannot smoke of it without the protection of the *Yuwipi Washeechu,* the White Stone of Strangeness, kept by the Indian "Bob" in his Dream Time lair."

"Yeah . . . right. . . . MWOWM . . ." mumbled Dobbs, dejectedly. "The only one on Earth until 1998. They'll be a dime a dozen then . . . but I need one *now* and I doubt the Indian "Bob" is gonna let his go cheap."

"Being a chief, I can accompany you and bargain the price down . . . for a percentage," said Crazy Horse, "but before we enter Dream Time, I insist that you honor us by making jig-jig with our sacred virgin."

"Hey—no prob!" exclaimed Dobbs. Doffing his white cowboy hat and eagerly shucking the shirt from his back so that he stood bare-chested, he darted to the teepee indicated by his host. His tongue hung out grossly, like a dog's, and he panted uninhibitedly.

Li noted that "Bob's" frame, stripped, was an amazing piece of organic machinery. While his muscles were not those of an Atlas, far less grossly knotted than a bodybuilder's, they yet resembled haphazardly bundled piano wire lacquered under deep plastic. He looked not unlike the "Popeye" character from American cartoons. The asymmetry of that great form was such as to stun an onlooker. Indian maidens swooned right and left.

Crazy Horse turned to Li. "Son of my forefathers," he spoke, "I suggest we now leave our friend "Bob" to pleasure himself with this unsullied woman and lend his strange but mighty *washeechu itomni* seed to our tribe."

Li and Crazy Horse sat outside the teepee, sipping from bowls of dog soup. Neither spoke for a time, preferring to listen to the almost laugh-provoking grunts and hollers from inside the teepee. Li nearly nodded into sleep.

Eventually, Dobbs emerged.

"Ahhh . . . I feel like a new man," he gloated, expansively. And then, to Li's embarrassment, Dobbs unzipped his slacks and exposed his inhumanly large, moray eel–like organ, urinating profusely on the grass. He accompanied the splashing sounds with indecently loud groans of pleasure.

Agog, Li witnessed bright yellow and blue prairie flowers springing up magically along the line of "Bob's" holy pee spray. However, as bladderial pressure dissipated, the flowers were replaced by thorns and thistles.

"Ouch," grumbled "Bob," addressing Li while tucking his prodigiously large self back into his pants. "It kinda burns at the end, ya know?"

Turning to Crazy Horse, he said, "Hey, thanks, man, thanks a million. No, really! I mean it! But Li here, and me, we gotta move on and meet up with the Indian "Bob," what's his name, uh . . . Smoking Butt or whatever?"

"He is our greatest *weechasha wakan,* "Bob," and I remind you that his name is Smokes-While-Trading. Do not insult this great medicine man. I suggest you approach him most cautiously, for he is now plagued with boils on his backside, and is possessed of a foul temper, making him almost as crazy as you," warned Crazy Horse.

"Ah, hell, it runs in the family. Well, *HEUNH,*" hooted Dobbs, stepping onto the magically decorated buffalo hide which Crazy Horse had laid out before them. Li and Crazy Horse followed. "You almost forgot this," Crazy Horse reminded Dobbs, holding out the Third Pipe.

"Oh, gosh," exclaimed Dobbs, exasperated. "What am I gonna do with myself??"

Almost immediately, they were enveloped by the Vortex.

Scant seconds of light-surfing later, the three found themselves standing astride the same hide rug, but now inside a vast cavern. Flickering torchlight dimly illuminated an altarlike rock throne. The walls swarmed with ritual carvings and hieroglyphs.

An incredibly ancient-looking Indian—remotely resembling "Bob," if in grin only—sat cross-legged on the natural rock throne (naked but for a pillow under his afflicted backside), surrounded by beautiful naked maidens. Li's groin heaved urgently.

"Hau, hau," the holy man muttered. "Of course, I saw in the spirit your coming, "Bob" Dobbs."

"Well, HOW, Chief!" exclaimed Dobbs loudly, stepping off the hide and proffering his hand. "Smokes-and-Sells, if I'm not mistaken? Have I got a deal for you!"

Smokes-While-Trading cast a baleful eye on "Bob." "Truly, you are the essence of your kind," he grumbled. "But no problem. Though the patterns of your smoke and the presence of Crazy Horse prove you are chosen by the *Wakinyan,* the thunder beings from the twin stars, this nevertheless warns the wise man to be most careful in trading with you. What deal? You talking firewater?" The medicine man sighed resignedly, shifting on his throne with the extreme caution befitting a severe hemorrhoidal condition.

"No, no!" exclaimed "Bob." "Not booze! I mean MONEY! You know, the mean green! Cabbage and gravel!" Winking, he rubbed his two forefingers and thumb together in the pancultural sign-language gesture for *greed*. Li cringed.

But the wizened medicine man's eyes lit up.

"Oh! You mean money! Hau, hau . . . MONEY! Yes, this is surely the Unknowing Clown-Man of the prophecy. With money, we can buy firearms . . . lawyers . . . senators. . . ." He gazed with a mad, vengeful, rapacious grin into unseen futures. "Not even the Mormons can seduce us, if we possess this 'money' of which you speak."

"Yeah!" shouted "Bob." "Right, Chief! Let's talk turkey." Extracting from his pocket a sheaf of Confederate bank notes, "Bob" suggested greasily, "Me give you bucks, you give me White Stone, tell me place to find Wild Man. Then me talk to First "Bob"! Savvy?"

The medicine man snorted derisively. "Not only do you speak down to me like a condescending white Pink man, Caucasian "Bob," but you take me for a fool. These notes are worth nothing; the Southern white men will lose their war. You must offer a better thing. Give me . . . give me your ring."

The old man was eyeing, with barely concealed lust, a cheap plastic toy ring on Dobbs' left pinkie. It sported the image of Ronald McDonald.

"This?" asked Dobbs, cautiously.

"Yes. It bears the image of the One Truly White Man, the Man of Pinkness. By possessing and gradually defacing his stupid image, I would attain new power over him and all he represents. Secret rites performed over this trinket, known only to me, will win many lawsuits over the next one hundred years for what's left of our tribe. The hexes empowered by this Future Object will be almost as sweet a revenge on your people as was tobacco."

"Fine! Great!" exclaimed Dobbs, wrenching the cheesy ring from his finger. "Take it! All yours! Now gimme the White Stone and tell me how to find a Yeti somewhere hereabouts!"

Shifting his buttocks with great care, the old man fetched from his loincloth what looked, to Li, to be a simple white river rock, its edges worn smooth by erosion.

" "Bob," you ask for a passkey to the Indian "Bob" and the Other "Bobs." This may be that which you seek. To me, this is nothing but a stupid piece of rock, useless to our tribe. But our legends say that this rock was once owned by the First "Bob" himself."

"Hot damn," muttered "Bob," reaching eagerly for the rock. "This motherfucker is a goddamn Xist computer and time radio!" Suddenly he covered his mouth. "Oops . . . language!"

"But even with this Stone and the Pipe, your luck is gone."

Dobbs looked stricken, grimacing.

"Yes. Wild Chi-Chi Man is no longer friend to Indians on this land.

Too many white mans with guns shoot at poor Chi-Chi. Too many Indians betray the Wild People for payment of firewater. You must go to the Next-to-First "Bob" in the land whence came your companion." The man indicated Li.

"Chinese "Bob" has the Bigfoot connection, eh, Chief?" said Dobbs. A crafty edge then came into his voice. "Okay, no prob. But one thing before we go, Chief. I just gave you a lot of money's worth of magic plastic." (He winked at Li.) "The rock's great, whatever the hell I'm supposed to use it for, but, well, since you can't give me the Yeti . . . don't you think I'm entitled to . . . oh, I dunno, a magic word or something?"

"White men . . . always finding something more to snatch up." The Indian snorted disgustedly, but from his medicine bag he extracted for Dobbs an ancient glass vial. Its faded label read faintly: "Rev. Dr. McNutt's Holy Snake Oil Tonic. Cures All Ailments Or Money Back."

"Is great medicine," said the Native American holy man. "Makes old men young, weak men strong, limp men hard. Oil of snake. Given to me by a great holy man as a gift for my services. Take it for magic protection against all curses save one—sores on backside." Only Li noticed the old man winking to Crazy Horse, just as Dobbs had winked to Li over the worthless Ronald McDonald ring.

Dobbs took the vial gratefully and pocketed it, gushing with unfeigned sincerity. "Hey, thanks, Chief. I dunno how to repay you."

The old man took a long draw on his peace pipe. "Just vanquish the AntiBob, and in so doing strain the shit from the bowels of the soulless *washeechus* who wreck our land. That is enough. Be always *itomni*—crazy, happy, drunken . . . slackful. But I warn you, bad spirits lay in wait for you. They serve AntiBob and know you are here to hurt them and aid the wise spirits, who meddle not in the silly affairs of men."

"Uh . . . right," nodded Dobbs enthusiastically. "Me kick ass on bad demons. No prob! ME BAD MOTHUHFUCKAH!!!!"

"Truly, your mouth is as great as your mind is simple," grunted the Indian "Bob," looking skeptical. "For this reason, and also to show good manners, I strongly urge you to consult the two remaining major "Bobs" along the way." Chuckling at some private joke, he added, "Give my regards to the African "Bob" especially!"

"Yes! How! Me comprendee, Chief! African "Bob"! Abo "Bob"! Me get big medicine from blackfellows!"

"One thing last, Dobbs," sighed the shaman. "Tell me. What will happen to our people in their battles against your relatives, the white-faced monsters?"

"Oh, you get mostly wiped out," replied Dobbs, grinning with insensitive joviality. "But the ones that are left, hell, they get free tract houses and canned food."

"Figures," muttered Smokes-While-Trading, shaking his head. "But enough banter. You must reenter the Vortex. Despite your stupid ways, I bless you. May you never be afflicted with incurable backside sores."

Li, Crazy Horse and "Bob" boarded a large beech canoe furnished by Smokes-While-Trading.

"Next stop: Africa!" "Bob" shouted above the airless rush and noiseless roar of the Vortex, as they were engulfed by the metamorphosing lights of that whirlpooling cosmic time-subway.

The canoe "landed" on dry ground . . . but in a northern forest, not a tropical jungle. Li was further surprised when a crude arrow appeared abruptly from nowhere, lodged in Dobbs' cowboy hat.

Spears and arrows suddenly rained upon them, pincushioning the canoe as Li and Crazy Horse ducked down into the bowels of the vessel.

"Hellfire—wrong goddamn spearchuckers!" shouted "Bob" to his confused companions, remaining carelessly upright. "More AntiBob sabotage! Backpaddle! Stern ho! Let's haul butt outa here!"

Dobbs' senseless paddling was ludicrously ineffectual, of course; they were far from any lake or stream. Though he was a nonsensically easy target, none of the countless missiles touched him. Human figures were increasingly visible as they darted closer and closer between the trees: pale-faced individuals with beards and furry clothing.

"We been screwed again," shouted Dobbs. "This ain't Africa! The AntiBob must've plunked us down right in pre-Roman England or some such place, in the middle of these fuckin' Druids!"

While Dobbs had been shouting, Crazy Horse and Li Li-jing had crept from the too-vulnerable canoe into a nearby creek bed. Dobbs ran to join them, but so heedlessly did he expose himself that when he reached the ditch his backside was almost comically pincushioned with arrows.

Dobbs suddenly howled in pain—but not from the arrows, which he scarcely seemed to notice. "Wait a minute! I . . . I have to . . . take a *shit . . . right NOW!*" "Bob" grimaced piteously, tears streaming down his face, his hands tearing his belt buckle loose. He was facing away from the Druids—and, as he bent over to yank down his pants, the arrows spontaneously flew backwards out of his butt, pelting their unseen attackers like quills shot from a porcupine.

Still doubled over behind the creek ridge, Dobbs strained with a fearsome effort, his whitened knuckles clutching his knees. He groaned loudly. Dobbs looked as if he were about to explode. Li backed away instinctively, noting strange markings on Dobbs' buttocks.

"Must . . . break . . . wind. . ." grunted Dobbs, sweat breaking out upon his brow. "Too . . . much . . . pressure. . ."

To Li's surprise, Dobbs suddenly thrust his buttocks over the edge of the protecting ridge. It was then that Li clearly saw two huge, reptilian eyeballs tatooed on Dobbs' rump. To the attack Druids, the Dobbs posterior must have resembled some hideous beast rearing up from the creek.

"Must . . . pyroflatulate. . ." gasped Dobbs through his clenched teeth. "Our . . . only . . . chance. . ." Grimacing in agony, Dobbs fetched a plastic lighter from his pocket and held it just under his bare, exposed rectum, past which arrows still flew.

"It comes . . . NOW!" Dobbs shrieked, and with that he flicked the lighter. An impossible burst of fiery blue gas sprayed like a flamethrower from his nether regions for at least a full minute, sweeping the woods as the SlackMaster wriggled his sacred booty back and forth in pain. From the now-burning woods came earsplitting screams loud enough to drown out the dreadful farting noise of Dobbs' "seizure."

Suddenly, the Druids across the clearing let out an even louder series of panicky yelps and babbling, independent of those of the burn victims mutilated by Dobbs' pyroflatulation. Arrows from some *third* party were now zinging overhead, from the opposite side of the woods! Many reached their marks, Li estimated, judging from the cries of pain and death gurgles. Soon it was evident that the Druids had fled. (And they carried with them the seed of all future Celtic legends of dragons. Their leader, Beowulf, would later brag about this episode interminably, in bad rhyme.) Of their benefactor, there was no visible sign.

"Well," Dobbs slurred to Li and Crazy Horse, pulling up his pants. "I hate doing that in front of you guys, but at least we're safe from those damn Limey cavemen."

"But who are the others that aided us?" wondered Li.

In answer, an unearthly, witchy voice squeaked from the forest, "Your enemies flee not only from your magic, but also from mine."

From the woods strode a seven-foot-tall, two-headed black man armed with a gigantic bow. Of the two heads, one was dusky and handsome, the other pallid and wrinkled, with straggly white hair.

Li, Crazy Horse and even Dobbs froze in astonishment.

"Fear not; for we are friends," bleated the pale head in modern English, as the monster bowed to them. It was then that Li discerned that this ebony two-headed giant was but a one-headed giant with a tiny, deformed Caucasian dwarf riding him papoose-style and peering over his shoulder. The wizened face of the dwarf lolled, the drool dribbled from its toothless mouth, but it spoke again quite clearly.

"The giant who carries me is Usuthu, once son of an Ethiopian slave, now a great warrior and magician. I am Janiti, an unfortunate cripple and Wiccan priestess gifted by the Moon Goddess with the magic of Speaking All Tongues."

"Holy shit! What the fuck is this?" griped Dobbs, bravely maintaining a false grin in the face of knuckle-gnawing fear.

"Hold your tongue, and earn our aid," snapped the dwarf. "My friend Usuthu and I are not demons, but mortals like yourselves. Our presence together, in this time and place, is no evil magic—only a product of whims of Fate so utterly improbable as to make the most inane religious superstitions seem logical by comparison. Until recently, Usuthu was the companion of the great Viking explorer, Halberd. As they were returning home from a quest in the Unknown World—the land whence you come, as I judge from my visions—they stopped for provisions on this Isle of the Picts and were separated. It so happened that I, due to my hideous appearance and witching skills, had been cast from my tribe to die in the forest. As I neared death, I experienced a vision of your quest. Then Usuthu found me, and recognized in me the magical abilities for which my own people had sentenced me to death—even though I was but a harmless woman wishing only to heal the sick."

"That retard is a woman?" gasped Dobbs, insensitively.

Usuthu again muttered in the dwarf's ear.

"My goal is to accompany you on your Quest so that the First "Bob" is not disgusted that only males have approached him. Usuthu determined to join me, for he is curious but not inexperienced regarding matters of the Dream Time."

Dobbs stood slack-jawed. "Well, I'll be goddamned," he muttered. "This is like something out of a really bad movie."

"Usuthu wishes to know," continued the dwarf, "whether you truly intend to meet with the great god of his mother's tribe, the fearsome and tyrannical Bahaab Dahaabs, who he imagines has aided him magically in many times past. If so, he will gladly join you and, moreover, continue to carry my pitiful physical vessel so that my gifts of speech might aid you in your infinite clumsiness . . . and that he may pay personal homage to his god. I would suggest," the dwarf croaked with a hint of sarcasm, "that you accept our offer to join you, as our skills are granted by the gods only once in a thousand generations, and the likelihood of our meeting this way by chance alone are so astronomical as to further suggest either divine or demonic intervention."

"Well . . . gosh," said Dobbs, after a short pause. "I can't hardly refuse that, now can I! You're both too weird to be agents of the AntiBob. One thing bothers me, though. Are you sure you're a woman?"

Li cringed in shame. Truly, Dobbs was an uncouth man. But the dwarf seemed happy to answer.

Scrunching up higher on Usuthu's back, she exposed her chest and flopped a droopy, stretch-marked teat over the black giant's shoulder.

Dobbs emitted a wolf whistle and nudged Li rudely with his elbow, winking lasciviously.

"I am indeed a woman, though not of the same mundane design as those of your world, nor of most others," she cackled, ignoring Dobbs' crudeness.

"Say," Dobbs queried sleazily. "Are you married, by any chance?"

"I am married to the spirits of the mind, through whom all could communicate, could they but hear truly," answered the crippled hag.

"Oh . . . yeah," said Dobbs, obviously not understanding. "Well . . . then . . . look, I'm supposed to be saving my wife and the universe, and the next stop is Bahaab's pad, dig? So what're we waiting for?"

The hag whispered once more into the ears of the warrior Usuthu. He nodded and she said, "You are impetuous, Caucasian "Bob," but right. We must all hurry to vanquish the forces of evil, lest they gain more strength by making your wife perform sexual acts upon them."

Smoke blew copiously from "Bob's" Pipe and every orifice of his head, even the corners of his eyes.

"Then we go! *Now!* Everybody get in the canoe! I MEAN FUCKING RIGHT GODDAMN *NOW!!*"

Because the canoe was scarcely large enough to hold even Usuthu alone, Crazy Horse, Li and Dobbs snuggled tightly together into it, while Usuthu tightened the strap holding Janiti to him, and clung with a viselike grip to the top sides of the vessel.

"Here goes!" shouted Dobbs, and once again they sped through the majestic Vortex.

Their canoe exited the Vortex, sliding and careening on brackish water before slamming into a riverbank in what was certainly Darkest Africa. Dobbs immediately quit the boat and motioned for the others to follow him. Jungle drums echoed in the humid distance. Li slapped at gigantic mosquitoes which buzzed his face as he and the others followed Dobbs.

The Great Beatnik Salesman seemed to be drawn by instinct, for he evinced no doubt as to his destination. By the way he sniffed the air, his eyes furtively scanning the woods before them, Li guessed that he followed an invisible trail.

Dobbs' form seemed to flow through the leaves and branches and snakes. Not a leaf fluttered, not a hair was ruffled out of place. "Bob" moved as instinctively as a great jungle cat. His going was as silent as a breeze-swept puff of pipe smoke.

They broke from the rain forest into a clearing filled with grass huts. Towering over these primitive structures was a palace—an imposing edifice of countless domed towers and architecturally fantastical cones. Yet no living being was to be seen. From the volume of the chanting voices inside the palace, it appeared that all the tribe had gathered therein.

Approaching the Cyclopean palace, Li observed that every piece of the amazing structure was carved of wood . . . much of it as intricately rendered as any Buddhist temple. It occurred to him that structures like this might have existed all over Africa, but, due to their wooden construction, would have left neither fossil nor ruin, having instead been swallowed by the constantly encroaching jungle.

The palace was humid with the sweat of naked dancing girls and chanting singers. Immediately, armed guards challenged them with spears. But Usuthu, who spoke a rough form of their dialect, commanded them swiftly and authoritatively. The adventurers were allowed entry on the condition that they hold their tongues until "the great M'Bugulu" saw fit to receive them.

At least three hundred Africans kowtowed before a gigantic throne dominating the seemingly measureless room. To Li, despite his state of exhaustion, the ebony-sheened, topless women dancing erotically around the throne looked much better than the blemished, half-starved waitresses in his Beijing neighborhood restaurant. Did all "Bobs" surround themselves with naked women?

Usuthu and Janiti translated to the others what was transpiring.

A sick man was brought before the obese, decoratively scarred shaman, the great M'Bugulu, Bahaab Dahaabs. A distraught woman raved at him begging him to save her "unworthy husband." Dahaabs leaned over the limp body of the stricken man, shaking his outlandishly huge feathered headdress. As he intoned a litany in some strange tongue, waving his hand in mystical gestures and twiddling the bone which pierced his nose, Li spied him surreptitiously slipping a piece of string into his mouth with his other hand. This went apparently unnoticed by the rapt audience.

"Now," announced the chieftain grandiosely, "My Magic Cord of the Spirit shall draw from this man all evil demons inhabiting him."

The overweight witch doctor leaned over his patient, extending the string from his mouth until it touched the sick man's heaving chest. Dahaabs then lowered his mouth to the man's breast, simultaneously sucking the cord back into his mouth.

He sucked strenuously at the man's chest, then lifted his head and spat out mouthfuls of blood.

"The spirits are leaving!" he announced.

He resumed sucking. Again he raised his head. "There is a particle of bad magic in this fine man," he moaned melodramatically. "I will strive to remove it. But it will surely require nothing less than a miracle."

Then—clearly, to Li's eyes—Dahaabs transferred a previously palmed piece of quartz crystal into his mouth—which he again lowered to the man's chest. Then he raised his head and spat the crystal into his hand.

"The evil is banished," he exulted triumphantly, holding aloft the crystal. "And I further see that this man was made sick not by normal illness, but by an evil spell cast by . . . by whom?"

He gazed suspiciously around the palace, from one cowering face to another. Then he looked into the smoke rising from an incense burner.

"In this smoke I see . . . the truth," intoned Dahaabs. "I see . . . the face of my rival, M'Gelbelo. He is the murderer who hexed this man."

A murmur ran through the crowd. Obviously, M'Gelbelo had little time left to live.

Suddenly the drums stopped. Both the dancers and audience fell prostrate, bowing before . . . before Dobbs and his companions, Li realized.

"I know who you are. Do not waste my time," thundered the obesely fat Black "Bob" from his huge bamboo throne. "I know why you strange and very ugly foreigners come," the chieftain bellowed. "You are "Bob" Dobbs of the Future Land, and you wish to anally or monetarily dominate him who is opposite of all True "Bobs," before he anally manipulates us." The four-hundred-pound African shaman's eyes and nostrils flared fearsomely.

"But I must ask of you one question, before I might aid you." He narrowed his fat-creased eyes shrewdly. "What can you give me?"

Through their translators, Dobbs and Dahaabs haggled.

"I hold many souls in my great banks of the future," wheedled Dobbs. "The souls of Bobbies—my followers in the depraved World of Tomorrow." He wiped some sweat from his brow, his right hand clenching and unclenching as if to grip a remembered briefcase full of demographic charts. "I have been granted power by JHVH-1 Himself to transfer ownership of said unclean souls to your psychic account."

The Black "Bob" regarded him doubtfully.

"Caucasian "Bob," you are every bit as stealthy and clever as Nasrudin, the Arab "Bob." I avoid doing business with such tricksters— they are too tricky even for me."

"Hey, wait a minute, Sambo," said "Bob," blustering loudly to hide his fear. "Don't speak too soon. Look, you ain't fooling me." He lowered his voice. "I'm onto your tricks. You sucked fake blood out of that sick dude by biting your own cheek. You spat out that damn mystic cord from your mouth."

"And yet the man will be healed, will he not? I help my people," argued the Black "Bob," also whispering confidentially. "I admit to certain simple tricks. I see ants moving to their holes, and frogs croaking, and then I announce that I am about to make rain. And so comes the rain. Likewise, I suck the evil objects from the bodies of ill people, and they become well. Simply because I always maintain an expression of utmost gravity and holiness, they *believe* they will become well. My people *are* both healed and given hope. So, out of our common "Bobhood," please do not blow my cover . . . or I will kill you."

"Okay. Just play fair with me, and I won't expose your scam to your fine people here."

"Agreed," Dahaabs conceded. "I will show mercy and assist you. . . . But, "Bob" Dobbs, you yourself are no better than me. You have tried to cheat me with your ludicrous 'payment in souls.' You would take me for another of your unquestioning, foolish customers . . . yet for that I respect you. Surely, you are as great a Salesman as myself, and you, like me, use your powers for any who come to you for help in their ignorance. Though you take their money, you yet give them Slack.

"But I cannot join your quest, for my people need me, and, moreover, I am too fat to travel the Vortex. I can offer only my magic submarine, and another thing unavailable from any of the other "Bobs" you may encounter. Gaze upon my mighty handiwork," he concluded, pointing proudly to an ordinary American phone booth half hidden behind his throne.

"However, I would expect some small token of payment," he added.

"Heck, if only I hadn't forgotten my Magic Wallet," groaned Dobbs, patting his pockets. "Ah! Wait! Here's something. O Mighty M'Bugulu," he declared ceremoniously, extracting the snake-oil vial and laying it at the feet of Dahaabs. "This is the oil of the magic snake, given me by none other than the Indian "Bob" of the Unknown World."

"By the Undulating Tail of M'Kele M'Bembe!" exclaimed Dahaabs, incredulous. "Simply for the use of my Magic Telephone and Submarine, you are willing to part with this rarest of elixirs?"

"I do so happily, to show my boundless respect for your own Sales Magic, which surpasses even my own," said Dobbs grandly, bowing from the waist.

As the crowd of natives kowtowed to this stranger who had dared wheel and deal with their Living God, "Bob" rushed to the phone booth. He dialed a short sequence of only three numbers, waited, and then said, "Yes, collect, please, Ma'am." Then he apparently got his connection.

"Rasputin," he shouted. "How the hell are ya, ya old sinner? Yeah? Well, listen. This is important. I'm in a big hurry. Is Jesus around?"

Dobbs waited, tapping his toes. As he did so, the air around him congealed and demonic faces leered out at him from the aethers, their claws grasping at him from some transdimensional fog. "Bob" simply brushed at them with his hand, murmuring irritably, "Go away, you!"— much as an ordinary person might shoo away insects. He nonchalantly blew smoke into the half-visible demon faces, and they vanished. Then his party answered.

"Jesus! Wait'll you hear this! The fuckin' AntiBob has . . . oh . . ." Dobbs looked disappointed. "You've heard already. Boy, word travels fast! . . . Well, shit. Okay. I understand. But any help would be, like, appreciated . . . and not with peanuts, okay? I mean . . . your accounts in Switzerland . . . the Merovingians . . . RIGHT! You got it! Hey, thanks, man."

Dobbs hung up and addressed his comrades.

"That's it, guys. I just cashed in an old debt. My luck oughta hold out all the way to the First "Bob's" time. We gotta check out the Abo and Chinese "Bobs," then we're copacetic! Let's make like diarrhea and run!"

The African "Bob" led Dobbs and his crew to the riverside, where was docked an elaborately outfitted craft composed entirely of reeds and bamboo. No more than thirty feet in length, it was indeed a submarine—the secret weapon of Dahaabs.

"I entrust to you this great vessel," declared M'Bugulu, "in the knowledge that you shall avenge the injustices being perpetrated in both the past and the future. And I hope that you put an end to the evil ones before they make, from the past, my own existence impossible. Also, I trust that you shall return this craft, lest you face the Curse of Incurable Hemorrhoids, as afflicted the last man to cheat me, Smokes-While-Trading, He Who Stole The Snake Oil That Seems Like A Cheap Trick But Is In Actuality A True Magic Tonic From A Bottle That Never Empties."

"Uh, right, gotcha," said Dobbs. "Thanks a million! Let's do business again sometime! C'mon, guys, let's catch up with the Abo "Bob"!"

Into the cramped sub crawled that motley/heroic crew. Dobbs muttered his incantation, and the Vortex swept over the craft. Through a porthole Dobbs looked for an exit. Wrenching the wooden steering device, he spun them topsy-turvy into a Vortex "exit ramp," and they were soon deposited into normal reality—but deep underwater.

Coelacanths swam past the portholes. Weird echoing underwater sounds—the scraping of primitive motors, valves, and technically impossible sonar bleeps—lent a creepy atmosphere as they cruised over fantastic undersea plant life, dimly lit by oil-burning lanterns on the sub's sides. Crazy Horse, who had never seen the ocean, much less its depths, was dumbfounded. Usuthu shivered in a corner, coughing on the cloying smoke from Dobbs' Pipe. Janiti slept, murmuring in dozens of different languages. As tired as Li was, he nonetheless joined Dobbs at the primitive control deck.

"But, Dobbs," Li demanded. "Why we in water to see Aborigine "Bob"? He not live in Australia?"

"Just off the coast," explained Dobbs. "See, Li, we're just about twenty thousand years in our past. These Australian dudes had a highly technological civilization, inherited from the Atlanteans. But, long before your people or mine started keeping records, they kind of blew it off and decided it made a lot more sense to run around naked in the bush. I'm sure, eventually, our modern civilization will go the same way . . . once we kick the AntiBob's ass, anyway." He smiled smugly. "Hey," he shouted, "here's the place!"

Li's ears popped as the submarine plummeted many leagues and bumped down onto seemingly solid ground. Before Li could stop him, Dobbs thrust open the hatch. No water burst in; they were in an air pocket of some kind.

The team clambered out of the ship to find themselves inside a gigantic bubble. The unimaginably bizarre undersea landscape stretched off in all directions beyond the spherical wall, which Li assumed to be made of glass. Before them, however, within the bubble, loomed a vast, Gaudílike coral palace. Its form was naturalistically random, as if the coral had been *grown* into shapes which suggested turrets and rooms and windows. Weird, throbbing music issued from the structure.

From the palace drawbridge, across the sandy but quite dry ground, waddled a small, wiry, naked aborigine of extremely advanced age, smoking a pipe. With his heavy brow, splayed nose and sloping chin, he embodied the Stone Age "look."

Though he never opened his mouth, the little man's voice echoed through all their brains, in their own languages.

"Welcome, "Bob" Dobbs and friends! Before you flee in terror, let me explain that I still possess many talents long since forgotten in your times. I read minds and converse in any tongue, and am glad to have visitors from so many different cultures. I have been alone here with my harem for nearly one hundred years."

Multiple telepathic gigglings gargled mentally from within the coral palace.

"Yes, I know you gentlemen may be interested in this harem of mine, and I assure you that all pleasures of the flesh will be yours for the taking."

"Yow," hooted Dobbs crudely. He stomped his feet and howled like a cartoon wolf. Steam seemed almost to shoot from his ears. "Lemme at 'em!"

"Ah, friend "Bob," you have your priorities in order. Be my guest. . . ."

To the dismay of his companions, Dobbs dashed into the coral palace, frantically unbuckling his pants as he went.

"Yes," thought the old man towards the disappearing "Bob," "in answer to your question, I do have prairie squid. Prehistoric, by your standards."

Li and the others looked at each other questioningly.

"Do not worry, my new friends," telepathed the aborigine. "Dobbs forgets not his mission. In this holy place, buoyed by my inestimable mental powers, we can all plan with our forebrains even while our gross hindbrains and bodies indulge in fleshly pleasures."

"But . . . how?" thought Li.

"It is so sad that the simple things of life have been forgotten in your worlds," thought the man sorrowfully. "Let me explain. I am Winjin of the Pitjendadjara tribe, prince of this city. All my people, except lazy ones who chose to be sex slaves, are princes or princesses with their own cities. Most live upon the land in mud palaces built by ants at their telepathic direction. Because I am a "Bob," I choose to live here. The Great Water is kept back, and this bubble of air formed, simply by my own powers of concentration. All things and animals do my bidding according to my songs of power. My castle was built for free by the little corals. It is easy for me to ride on storms and to commune with the dead. Say, would any of you like a smoke? I have excellent pituri."

None dared accept Winjin's Pipe, so awestruck were they.

"I can see that my magic terrifies you; don't worry, for soon Dobbs will have his way with the women here and take you away with him. Even now he is gaining new powers by copulating with my harem and my giant squid. I have been watching your most amusing adventures on my magical mental television since you started; thus my precious lovemaking time won't be wasted with stupid deals and explanations. I suggest that you all relax, smoke and fornicate to your hearts' content."

Out of the palace dashed a bevy of naked aborigine women, all projecting images of sex into the minds of the adventurers—except for Janiti, who, strapped to Usuthu, swooned according to some pornographic telepathy broadcast from Winjin.

Soon all were indulging in frenetic sexual acts. Winjin humped joyfully upon the stunted torso and withered limbs of Janiti, Crazy Horse pillowed three Stone Age women at once, and Usuthu grappled urgently with no less than eight. Li, the most modest of them, resisted, but finally gave in to the mental proddings of two aborigine women who, in any other setting, might have struck him as supremely ugly. The beauty and poetry of their thoughts, however, far overshadowed both his cultural conditioning and his exhaustion.

But as soon as he was spent, Li leaped up. The sex had, surprisingly, invigorated him.

"What about AntiBob?" he shouted to the others, who remained oblivious in their pleasures. "Must find Dobbs! Not forget holy mission!"

He dashed into the palace. The hallways were strewn with prone, happily sighing women, all obviously well serviced by Dobbs. And in such a short time! Li followed the trail of fucked-out women to a great room from which emanated both Dobbs' groans of pleasure and the moist, slurping noises of some great beast.

Rounding the corner, Li could scarcely believe his eyes. Dobbs was emersed headfirst to the pelvis in the slimy body of some gigantic prehistoric cephalopod, a slug or shell-less snail which writhed and sucked and glorped around "Bob's" nude body. The orifice which hid "Bob's" torso resembled an enormous vagina; his buttocks were being lightly spanked by a huge, prehensile penislike appendage.

"Ah . . . prairie squid," burbled Dobbs' voice from deep within the slimy folds of the omnisexual beast. "More prairie squid than I'd ever imagined in my wildest dreams!"

Before Li could shout at Dobbs to hurry, to remember his mission, a blinding flash of light illuminated the room. Dobbs quickly yanked his sopping head from the four-ton prairie squid and, panicky, tried to regain his senses—such as they were.

Floating within a cloudlike aura at the center of the room was the shimmering image of the blonde American woman—Dobbs' wife, "Connie." Her perfume practically replaced the air. The magical image railed at Dobbs in angry tones.

"Well, well, well," she bespoke Dobbs sternly as he abashedly buckled up his pants. "Boy, are you in for trouble when *you* get home! I'm stuck here waiting to be rescued from the AntiBob, and what are *you* doing, huh? Porking a bunch of pug-nosed chippies and this slimy monster! *Just what do you have to say for yourself?"*

"Uh, uh, uh, nothing dear. . ." stammered Dobbs. Li had never before seen Dobbs show true fear. "I, uh . . . I mean, I'm just doing what I'm supposed to do. . . . You know, Abo "Bob" said I had to. . ."

"Oh, sure," grated "Connie." "Hmmmph. Maybe I'll just take the AntiBob up on his offer, *Mr. Big Dick!"* And with that, her image disappeared.

"Oh, shucks, Li," said Dobbs, trembling, while he zipped up. "Uh . . . we'd better get going. . . ." He seemed embarrassed, and said nothing more as he hurried back to the submarine.

Their companions were waking groggily when Dobbs and Li exited the temple. Dobbs rudely hustled them all to the submarine.

"Wait, "Bob," " thought Winjin. "It's too bad you have to hurry so. You would gain more power were you but to stop and smell the roses."

"Yeah. Right. Gotta go. Here's some 'Frop," Dobbs said, tossing a small packet to Winjin. "Thanks for everything!"

And they were in the Vortex again.

The Chinese, or "Next-to-First," "Bob" had been expecting them. As the submarine crunched onto a riverbank in prehistoric China, Dobbs and crew piled out to find a little man sitting patiently on a tree stump, whittling away at a stick.

Li was thrilled. Here was his homeland, thirty or forty thousand years in the past, looking exactly like an ancient Chinese pen-and-ink drawing—imposing cliffs, weird, spindly trees and fog lifting from burbling brooks. Besides the Chinese "Bob," not a soul was in sight . . . no lines of Mao-jacketed peasants carrying inhumanly heavy loads, no bicycles, nothing. Birds sang in the twisted branches overhead. An ornately carved temple loomed through the fog not far away.

The Chinese "Bob" looked up from his whittling and grinned, a clay Pipe dangling from the right side of his mouth. Jolly-looking, he wore tattered, gaily colored rags, and a broad smile crinkled his eyes into slits. He said nothing, but looked at them expectantly.

Dobbs motioned with his head for Li to approach the man. Surprised that no telepathy would be involved this time, Li timidly approached the old fellow and bowed low.

"With your permission, Grandfather," he said, "I am Li Li-jing, a humble worker from our tormented future. This is the holy man "Bob" Dobbs, and our friends, who seek your guidance in locating both the First "Bob" and a Wild Man translator."

"Ah, save your breath, Young Li, for I know all this already," gummed the old man in a form of Mandarin so archaic that Li could barely comprehend it. "Your speech is so corrupted and degenerate that I scarcely can understand you, but I enjoy its roughness, and will eschew the telepathy used by my show-off great-grandcousin, the Aborigine "Bob." Welcome to this land of your own ancestors, Young Li. I might even be one of them. My name is Chien Minh. Were any of your female grandparents Chiens?"

"Not to my knowledge, sir; I wish that I could claim such an honor, but am thus abased before you."

"Ah, blow off the formal shit," snapped Chien Minh, much to Li's surprise. He exuded several puffs from his Pipe, surveying the small group. "Tell your friend, the Caucasian "Bob," that all of you are welcome to my modest hovel."

Li translated to "Bob," noticing that Janiti looked a bit jealous. Well, screw her, thought Li. The stuck-up, round-eyed, deformed bitch hadn't given him the time of day.

"Bob" was admiring the staggeringly beautiful temple visible over the treetops. "Hovel?" he said. "Looks like a pretty snazzy joint, if you ask me."

"That?" snorted Chien Minh. "I would never live in such an ostentatious dwelling. Too much upkeep. Waste of time better spent whittling and dreaming. That is a temple built by asinine religious fanatics for that so-called hotshot, Lao-tze. The big mouth."

"Lou-sy?" countered Dobbs. "That place doesn't look so lousy to me!"

"You are far too easily impressed, "Bob" Dobbs," scolded Chien Minh.

Li was taken aback that Dobbs had never heard of Lao-tze, China's greatest ancient philosopher. The very similarity of Dobbs' teachings to Lao's—such as the doctrine of Slack, or "doing nothing effectively"—would have suggested some influence.

"Well, come on," said Chien, creakily lifting his old bones from the tree stump. "You want to meet my Wild Man friend. I hope you have strong stomachs, for he smells awful, like all of his kind."

They followed a winding path through the fog-beshrouded hills, by-passing the temple, towards which Chien made further disparaging remarks. He seemed to hold all organized religions—and politics—in disdain.

When they reached Chien's abode, Li was astounded. It really was just a simple hovel—a lean-to built into the side of a hill, with a cooking pot set over a charcoal pit, a few clay pots, some chickens running loose, and little else.

Li was puzzled. This man, the Chinese "Bob"—probably wiser than Confucius and Lao-tze combined—was neither hero, preacher nor sage. He might as well have been any old farmer-peasant.

As Li thought this, Chien turned to him. "Young man, you have one gigantic *fuck* of a lot to learn about Slack."

He put a finger to one nostril and blew a long string of snot from the other. The snot snaked across the ground at Li's feet as if it had a life of its own . . . then fossilized like glue.

"But you will learn. You aren't *too* smart to learn, I can tell." He addressed the others. "You all wait here, please. Pardon me. I must water my pigs."

Chien waddled to a nearby pond. From the woods trotted, quite spontaneously, several wild pigs. Chien took up a bucket and waded out into the pond—except that he didn't wade; he walked atop the water, strolling upon its surface as if it were a flat road. He stopped and lowered his bucket, which broke the surface and was filled. Then he walked back to shore. Murmuring lovingly to his scrawny pigs, "Ah, my dearest friends," he splashed the bucket over their hairy backs. They snorted happily; it was a hot day.

"Well," Chien continued, returning to his guests, "So much for my daily chores. Would any of you care for some pickled pork? I have a jar here that has been stored underground, fermenting, for over fifty years. Or eggs? I have thousand-year-old eggs, and they really are a thousand years old. My honored mother pickled them," he added proudly.

Suddenly, a figure swathed in black leaped from the tree branch over Chien's head, a long dagger in his hand!

"Look out. A ninja!" hollered Dobbs. Usuthu, Li and Crazy Horse all leaped to their feet, running to Chien's aid. Even Janiti involuntarily struggled to rise from the cradle of skins in which Usuthu had placed her.

Simultaneously, however, Chien blew a puff of Pipe smoke over his shoulder at the attacker. Only when the villain began to float, screaming, into the air did Chien turn around and look directly at him, smirking. The black-clad man was levitating against his will up past the treetops, protesting at the top of his lungs.

"Jealous bastards," Chien muttered. The screaming "ninja" was now only a faint dot in the sky, ascending like a balloon.

Chien addressed "Bob." "Let me call your Yeti so that you may be on your way," he said. "Ever since this trouble started, unwitting dupes of the AntiBob have been trying to kill me. They think I set a bad example with my laziness!" He laughed heartily, then put his fingertips to his temples and concentrated. Soon, a bestial bellowing was heard through the trees.

An eight-foot-tall ape-man crashed out of the forest, clad head to foot only in coarse reddish fur. Accompanying the Bigfoot was a sulfuric stench almost unbearable to the time travelers. Only good manners prevented them from holding their noses. That it was male was beyond question, so long and lively was its waggling tool. All but "Bob" and Chien jumped to their feet, preparing to battle this macho ogre.

"What!" shouted Chien angrily. "The Yetis send a baby! This is man's work!"

"I am sorry," thought the Yeti telepathically so that all could "hear." "Though I am but a teenager, only fifty years old, I am the most eager of all my tribe to help our common descendant stop his evil cousin, the AntiBob. Also, it is mating season, so no one of age would willingly leave our tribal grounds. Please let me join you; though I am small in size, I am savage and skillful in battles both physical and psychic."

"Ah, well, all right," snorted Chien. "Talk to Dobbs here. He's the one trying to save the goddamn universe!" He wandered off to feed his chickens, chuckling to himself.

"Greetings, "Bob" Dobbs," said the Yeti in a voice so deep it could not have been called human, not even by a dolphin. It thrust a ten-gallon-sized hand to its face, covering its nose. "Pardon me," it said, "But your human smell is unbelievably offensive to a natural forest creature such as myself. I apologize for my rudeness, but it is necessary."

The creature kept his face covered as "Bob" spoke.

"Hey, uh, look, pal," said Dobbs nervously. "Any blood relative of the First "Bob" is okay by me! I mean, jeez, this is family"—he indicated his cohorts—"but let's face it, we're all more human than pure-blood, and believe you me, we are honored all to hell by your presence, that you see fit in your elemental wisdom to join us in our Quest . . . and all like that."

"Yes, enough talk," rumbled the Chinese Sasquatch. "My blood boils with the urge to battle our common foe. Let us be off."

"Awreet!" exclaimed Dobbs. "But we gotta thank Mr. Chien. . . ."

He looked around for Chien . . . then espied him in the sky overhead, skipping from cloud to cloud, hitchhiking eastward. He waved as if in farewell, and disappeared into the bowels of a large, looming thunderhead.

"Shucks. Sure would've liked to have had that dude on our team," sighed Dobbs. "But I guess he's got better things to do. Oh well. Everybody ready? Let's go for it!"

The quintet that emerged from the Vortex formed a team which, under "Bob" Dobbs, adventurer supreme, could surely accomplish wonders.

However, when their submarine materialized literally floating in dinosaur excrement, they began to doubt not only their abilities to cope with this eventuality, but even their own sanities. For the stench that assailed them as they emerged from the hatch was like that of a thousand pet-turtle cages, uncleaned for decades.

"Ah, smell that natural air!" exclaimed Dobbs expansively, filling his lungs. "A perfect atmosphere for battling the forces of evil."

They were stranded in brackish water, putrid with unknown mosses and fungi, small, leaping, crab-backed things, and at least a fifty-percent content of dinosaur urine and feces.

Moreover, the sub's rickety motor was clogged by moss, and they were without paddles.

The crew held their noses as the sub drifted to shore, and they clambered out onto the muddy ground.

The air was less humid than *syrupy*. Volcanoes belched smoke and lava in the distance. Bass snuffling sounds burbled up from the slimy lake. Within the jungle could be heard vast bodies, sloughing through the undergrowth. Compared to the redwoodlike trees and ferns, the team felt like toy action figures.

All were speechless. For they were wayfarers in another world!

Sparrow-sized insects buzzed them as they tore their way through thorny vines along the creekside, and they constantly slapped at enormous leeches and hideous mammalian vermin which repeatedly dropped upon them from the trees, or latched onto their shoes and wormed their way upwards towards skin and warm blood.

"Just think," said Dobbs, squishing a small ratlike critter in his palm until blood spurted. "These stinking rats are our ancestors! Partly, anyway."

Suddenly he pointed at the sky. Overhead wheeled a batlike creature with membranous wings at least twenty feet across.

"Good Lord! That," he shouted, stating the painfully obvious, "is a pterodactyl!—a creature thought by science to be extinct since the Cretaceous era, eighty million years ago!"

Dobbs recited this as if he were reliving some lurid monster film of his boyhood. It meant nothing to any of his companions except Li, who had benefited from trips to the Beijing Museum.

Suddenly Dobbs halted the party. "Our chances of locating the First "Bob" will be better if we split up," he lectured, again sounding as if he were quoting some cheesy safari movie. "Li, you come with me. Usuthu, you, the Yeti and Crazy Horse—and what's-her-name—head off that-a-way. We'll try to circle around and meet by that tall rock over to the west."

And so Li followed Dobbs into a jungle so thickly overgrown that they could travel but a few feet per minute. Two minutes later, they reached a clearing, where Dobbs suggested they stop and rest—even though they'd traversed only a dozen yards, and could still hear their companions' grunting and grumbling off through the trees.

Abruptly, another sound rent the air—a roar like a recording of twenty lions, played backwards at half speed. Out of the jungle behind Dobbs, smashing trees as it went, bounded a toadlike monster at least fifty feet long from nose to tail. On its mightily thewed hind legs it hopped straight for Dobbs, who stood smoking, deaf to its approach.

The sight of the full-grown *Tyrannosaurus rex* paralyzed Li. With a supreme effort of will, he pointed past "Bob" to the approaching carnivore and shouted, "Run!"

"Run?" asked Dobbs, innocently. "Well, okay, if you say so!" With a pleasant look on his face, he turned and sprinted lackadaisically straight where Li pointed—towards the *Tyrannosaurus*.

Dobbs dashed between its legs before he even realized it was there.

The *Tyrannosaurus* shook its Volkswagen-sized head in a gesture suggesting disbelief. It had never, in its 150 years of life, ever seen *any* creature run *towards* it.

Tilting its head curiously, the behemoth bent low to peer between its own legs at Dobbs, who was only now gaining an inkling of what Li's warning had meant.

Indeed, the beast, in its bafflement, leaned over so far that its now-upside-down head became stuck between its pillarlike legs. It struggled to regain an upright posture, but its head was lodged firmly betwixt its knees! Its futile struggles only caused it to slowly and majestically somersault over onto its back, head still trapped between spasming legs.

Dobbs, blind to any danger, gazed lasciviously at the luscious cloaca of the beast, which was now spread open, obscenely exposed to the light of day.

"Hmm," considered Dobbs lustfully. But he shrugged. "Oh well . . . another time. C'mon, Li, let's see if we can head down the trail Old Dog-Breath here blazed for us."

Leaving the Tyrant Lizard King to outwit its own body, the two upright mammalian bipeds again struck out into the jungle.

They'd hacked and struggled for only a few minutes when Dobbs abruptly stopped and sniffed the air. Then, curiously, he *held his nose closed* and then repeated the same head movements of sniffing.

"Shhhh. . ." Dobbs whispered. "Humans."

Li, by this point, had been so long without sleep that he was practically sleepwalking. He stared at Dobbs, puzzled.

"Yep . . . humans. Nearby. Wait here."

With that, Dobbs disappeared into the jungle. Li was left alone.

Gazing about dazedly, Li spied an odd-shaped rock in the mud at his feet and stooped to pick it up. A flint arrowhead!—carved by some decidedly human hand!

"But. . ." wondered Li to himself, "there are no human peoples in this age. . . ."

He then looked up to find himself staring directly into the muzzle of a ray gun. Helmeted, uniformed human beings surrounded him, brandishing futuristic ray pistols menacingly.

They motioned with their guns for Li to follow them. Sighing resignedly, the Chinese sound man complied. Perhaps they'd imprison him, and he could get some sleep.

But from behind them a mighty crashing resounded. Bursting through the towering ferns was a gigantic, three-horned Triceratops—being ridden, rodeo style, by "Bob" Dobbs!

Dobbs was not exactly steering the tanklike dinosaur, but merely clinging to it and whooping as it kicked into the air like a bucking bronco, trying to rid itself of its human burden. "Yeeeeeee-HAW!" hollered Dobbs gaily.

Li's captors were stunned. Bred to be craven cowards all, they vanished into the undergrowth as quickly as they'd appeared.

" "Bob!" You save my life!" Li shouted to Dobbs, who had been thrown clear of the triceratops and was watching it lumber back into the forest.

"Wow! That was fun!" panted Dobbs, wiping the sweat from his brow and puffing steadily on his Pipe.

"Dobbs! Who are these bad peoples??" demanded Li.

"Aw, gosh, Li, those were probably some of the first true humans invented in test tubes by the Atlantean Yetis!—quick-evolved up from rats. You're damn lucky they didn't kill you right off the bat! See," he explained, tamping his Pipe, "These are rogue, *purebred* humans—probably escaped from the Xist Atlantean laboratories. . . . The First "Bob" invented the fuckers himself, intending to use them as beasts of burden. But they broke free . . . and, well, you know how bad most humans are."

Li nodded.

"Okay. Well, the ones we know are at least part Yeti, even if it's a tiny part. Think how cruel and nasty pure-blood, unadulterated, factory-fresh humans are! They're the most dangerous, inconsiderate, meanest things on this planet! Not that our modern humanist, evolutionist, Conspiracy scientists would ever admit it, but the dinosaurs are pussycats next to them, and they're probably serving the AntiBob in his rebellion against his own creator, and mine, the First "Bob." And they. . ."

He broke off as the triceratops reemerged from the woods. It now looked positively docile. It edged carefully towards "Bob."

"Well, I'll be a monkey's nephew! I think it likes me! I'll bet it's lonesome. It probably just needs love."

Li watched amazed as Dobbs strode up to the now-demure triceratops, which purred in a deep bass not unlike a gigantic cat. As Dobbs scratched the stiff hide behind its neck frill, it lifted and waved a hind leg as if to mimic the scratching.

"Aw, look at this," said Dobbs pityingly. "It's all infested with vermin."

From behind its frill, Dobbs plucked a large, black, lemurlike rat. He threw it, squealing, into the underbrush. "Poor thing," he muttered, removing one after another of what turned out to be a whole nest of rats. "And to think, our modern humans are genetically related to these nasty buggers! They're like giant ticks to these wretched dinosaurs." He snorted in disgust. "They never tell you shit like this in high school!"

Soon, Dobbs had so entranced the triceratops that it allowed them to ride on its back as it foraged off into the jungle for food.

They came to an open hilltop clearing. Li was just beginning to enjoy the view when Dobbs shouted, "Li! Looky there!"

In the near distance stood a glimmering castle, bedecked with crystalline spires and domes. If not man-made, it was certainly alien-made.

"The First "Bob's" hometown—the original Atlantis!" exulted Dobbs. "The first landing strip of the Xists, where the Yetis were first created!" He turned to Li. "Boy, I'd like to see the face of the sumbitch who digs up *this* fossil! That would show those stinking know-nothing evolutionists and creationists, once and for all!"

The triceratops trotted towards the castle. "How about that," mused Dobbs happily. "It just happens to be going right where we want to go!"

But when they topped a rise and started descending into a ravine, an evil voice rang through the air!

"Stop, "Bob" Dobbs! I have your wife and companions in my clutches!"

The slimy voice had issued from a masked villain seated upon a makeshift throne just below them. Hundreds of badly uniformed purebred humans stood around him in half-assed military formation.

But that was not the worst of it. For, dangling in an iron cage suspended by a rope above a pit of fire, was "Connie" Dobbs.

She frowned at "Bob" impatiently, tapping her toes.

Aside the flaming pit, Crazy Horse, Usuthu and Janiti were all bound and held at spearpoint by the skull-helmeted minions of the masked leader. Even the gigantic Yeti was chained to a rock. Giggling rat-men held the Third Pipe and White Stone, toying with them like spoiled children.

The arch-evildoer wore a crimson cape and a demonic-looking mask which covered the top half of his face. The eyes which shone through were dark, somber and forbidding. His mouth, wrinkled and shrunken like an old man's, was thin and grim, pinched as if in perpetual disapproval.

"Allow me to introduce myself, "Bob" Dobbs," he hissed in a thin, reedy voice, heavily accented like a Nazi's. "I am the Young AntiBob! Ve knew you vere comink, and haf prepared this little party for your amusement!"

"Gee, that voice sounds familiar," wondered "Bob." But then he directed his attention to "Connie."

"Hi, dear. How was your day?" he asked politely.

"You'd better do something but quick, you human dildo," snapped "Connie" peevishly. "The Phantom of the Opera here is about to lower me into this pit to feed his stinking devil god."

" 'Devil god'?" shrieked the Young AntiBob. "You stupid bitch! This fiery pit leads to the throne of the Original AntiBob himself! And when He rapes and devours you, the wife of the Good "Bob," His powers will be increased a thousandfold! All future history will be altered to fit Our Great Plan!" His voiced reached a quavering, screaming pitch.

"Who you calling a bitch?" shouted Dobbs, enraged. "Why, you dirty. . ." He bravely lunged forward, but a blast from an Atlantean heat ray knocked him to the ground, his shoes and zipper smoking. Li started to dash to Dobbs' side, but was held at bay by the heat-ray guns pointed at him.

"*Et tu*, Atwell?" wisecracked "Bob" as a dozen fiendish minions bound him with rope. Once assured Dobbs was helpless, they turned to tie up Li.

"You fools!" cackled the Young AntiBob. "Now, you must lay helpless and witness my moment of greatest triumph! Lower the loudmouthed slut into the pit!"

The fiend's henchmen began inching "Connie's" cage into the fiery, hell-belching pit. A monstrous rumbling began deep within the ground, like the growling, hungry stomach of the Earth's mantle itself.

"And after the woman, we will throw you, Dobbs, and your SubGenius friends in, as the *main course!*" His ugly laughter rattled across the clearing.

Now, replacing the fire and brimstone, a monstrous VOID opened within the pit. It was not a force, nor a light, nor even darkness; nor was it even a hole; it was the utter and absolute bottomless lack of *anything whatsoever*. It was a widening spacelessness of pure NOTHING, the antithesis of *all existence*.

It looked like the end for "Bob" and his men!

But then Li noticed that Dobbs had swiveled his Pipe in his mouth so that it was inverted. It burned downwards—and he pushed it against the hemp rope that held him immobile.

"M-must . . . s-smoke . . . rope. . ." he whispered. His eyes rolled back in his head with exertion.

With a surge of superhuman strength, "Bob" burst free from his bonds!

Li took advantage of the distraction to lash out with Bruce Lee–like speed at his captors. His flying fists and feet became a blur, a whirlwind of vengeance laying prone all henchmen who strove to lay hands upon him.

"Stop them, you fools!" babbled the masked villain.

But the frenzied, mindless rat-men could no more stop Dobbs' mighty force of Good than could they harness a bolt of lightning! From the corner of his eye, Li noted that Dobbs again used that strange but invincible fighting style, unlike any known even in the mysterious Orient.

For Dobbs stared, trancelike, straight ahead. His arms and legs shot out randomly. He might as well have been a blind spasmodic. And yet each thrust hit a fleshly target. In his blind idiocy of rage, Dobbs felled villains right and left. Blood pooled around shattered limbs and rib cages.

"Quickly," shrieked the Young AntiBob. "Lower the virgin into the pit that our master might be appeased!"

"VIRGIN?" shouted Dobbs. " *"Connie's" no virgin!*"

He leapt up onto the ridge where Usuthu, Crazy Horse and Janiti struggled against their bonds. Dobbs hefted the small body of Janiti by her ropes and held her aloft.

"You need a virgin? Here! Take the gimp! Fuck the universe; I want "Connie" back!"—for Dobbs was unaware of Janiti's deflowering by Winjin.

And he slung the helpless Janiti towards the dilating Void-Pit!

Li reacted instinctively. "No!" he shouted, leaping into the air with a strength he'd never known he had. Flying over the pit, he snatched Janiti from thin air and, carrying her, landed safely on the other side!

Simultaneously, Dobbs laid low the bastards who manned the chain and hauled "Connie's" cage back to safety. He sprung the door and swept "Connie" into his arms. His bleached-blonde, statuesque sweetheart looked strangely bored.

Li, meanwhile, had kung-fued his way through a horde of fanatical guards and was tearing free the bonds of Usuthu and Crazy Horse, ducking the heat rays that toasted the jungle behind him.

Soon the two great warriors were freed. They savagely waded straight into the ever-increasing hordes of attackers, breaking arms, legs and necks with their bare hands while Li freed the great Yeti.

When the Yeti sprang into the fray swinging his heavy chains, the battle became like some nightmare from Hell. The befurred giant slung human figures about like rag dolls; Crazy Horse disarmed a guard by pounding his head into his shoulders, snatched up his heat ray and mowed down villains who now plodded at him in waves of mindless, hate-filled bloodlust; Usuthu took up a log larger than many men and swung it madly, like Davey Crockett at the Alamo. Before him, a harvest of death was reaped like wheat before a madman's scythe.

A kangaroolike dinosaur with fearful claws, a *Deinonychus,* pounced from the jungle and joined the fray! Dobbs dispatched it handily with a well-placed blow to the skull from his sacred Pipe.

Flying saucers were suddenly screaming by overhead! Volcanoes erupted in the near distance! The Earth shook as if in fear of these giants among men! Rivers of gore flowed from the broken, splattered bodies of the dead!

As if from nowhere, hundreds and yet more hundreds of the ratty, lab-cloned humans swarmed like termites from the woods. Despite their courage, strength and prowess, "Bob" and his companions were hopelessly outnumbered. The cowardly Young AntiBob stood safely at a distance and cackled in evil glee.

"No wonder," puffed Dobbs to Li, holding "Connie" in one arm and slaying the mewling, bovine Pink warriors with the other, ". . . no wonder none of the other "Bobs" wanted to go with us!"

The heroes were surely about to die when. . .

A great earthquake rent the ground next to the Void-Pit!

A rupturing fissure spread, and the Earth heaved and shuddered, until the Void itself disappeared into this new *"hole"*—this *"crack,"* which had now reached almost to the feet of Dobbs and his aides, separating them from the army of evil henchmen by a bottomless gulf twenty feet across!

The battle had been halted by some force from beyond Nature itself!!

From the sky descended a blinding globe of pure light-energy and psionic power. Bug-eyed alien cherubs spiraled around the descending ball of fire, leaving psychedelic trails in the air behind them.

From the ball of light emerged a Yeti at least forty feet tall, a brilliant blue glowing from its long hair. Its magnificently handsome yet grotesquely apelike grinning face clutched in its teeth a Pipe exactly like Dobbs'.

The First "Bob" had arrived to save the day!

"Wow," gasped "Bob." "This is better than any fireworks—even at Epcot Center!"

The terrified humans slinked and fled like the cowards they were, disappearing into the jungle. Even Crazy Horse, Usuthu and the Chinese Yeti retreated many paces, shielding their eyes from the glory that was the First "Bob."

Dobbs and the Young AntiBob now stood on opposite sides of that great rent in the earth, wholly attentive to the glowering Goliath, resembling timid schoolchildren awaiting a scolding from their teacher.

The blue-haired Yeti behemoth straddled the chasm. With the jungle behind him, his hair changed color like a chameleon's to a bright green.

"So," bellowed the Colossus in a voice which echoed off the distant volcanoes. "You puny mortals dare to venture into my domain!"

"But . . . but. . ." stammered Dobbs. He pointed an accusing finger at the Young AntiBob. "He was trying to summon the Real AntiBob! We had to protect the SubGenius half-Yetis of the future!"

"SILENCE!" crashed the voice of the First "Bob." "What dare you know of the ways of the gods, "Bob" Dobbs?"

"Well, I. . ."

"Shut up!" thundered the giant, and Dobbs shrank back.

"Yes, sir," he mumbled, meekly.

"You, "Bob" Dobbs, have disappointed me greatly. You dare speak of your flock's genetic purity. Yet you have copulated with many humans! You have dampened your Yeti seed, what little you have remaining, without a thought for future generations!"

Dobbs shuffled his feet in the dirt abashedly, his hands clasped behind his back in embarrassment, his head lowered.

"Gosh . . . I'm sorry, sir. . . ."

"Sorry isn't enough! So abominable has been your future behavior that I can scarcely see any difference between you, my true great-great-great[16]-grandson, and this sniveling imposter, this MereHuman who dares call himself the Young AntiBob!"

The Young AntiBob cringed and shivered. He seemed barely able to remain standing, so great was his fear. Urine dribbled from the legs of his scarlet uniform.

"You must both undergo. . .

". . . the Test!" bellowed the hairy god-ape-man, magically gesturing and causing the Third Pipe to leap from the ground into his huge hand. "To prove yourselves, you must both smoke of the Third Pipe, into which I shall now place the Greatest 'Frop in the Universe!"

Both contestants, upon seeing the First "Bob" pack the Third Pipe with a glowing, pure-white vegetable admixture, responded most differently. Excrement joined urine at the Young AntiBob's feet, whereas the pure-minded Dobbs practically slobbered for the Pipe, yanking out a lighter and drooling in expectation.

"You first," spake the towering Yeti SlackMaster, brandishing the Pipe at the Young AntiBob.

"No! Noooo!" shrieked the craven fiend, running off into the woods.

"Lemme at it! Lemme at it!" begged Dobbs, slavering. "Don't waste it on that geek!"

A knowing grin crossed the First "Bob's" billboard-sized face. "Oh? You think you want it? Then here."

Dobbs clutched at the Pipe and feverishly "lit up." He inhaled a "toke" that seemed never to end. His chest ballooned like a bullfrog's neck in mating season. He held his breath until tears veritably sprayed from his eyes. As he released it, a great cloud enveloped him. From within could be heard horrendously loud, wracking coughs.

"That's my boy," muttered the First "Bob," smiling shrewdly.

"Where's that fucker, the so-called Young AntiBob??" swore Dobbs as the smoke cleared, a crazed, vengeful look now lighting his fanatical eyes. "I passed the test! Now lemme at the son-of-a-bitch!"

Dobbs leaped across the crevice and strode into the woods, following the trail of fear excretions that had run down the arch-fiend's pants legs as he'd fled.

He soon closed in on the terrified, crimson-becaped villain in a nearby ditch, where the man cowered, panting, out of breath. Obviously, he was physically unfit. But he was surrounded by a gang of his savage minions, telepathically commanded to protect him, even if it meant suicide.

But, upon seeing Dobbs' form emerge from the trees like an Angel of Justice, the rat-men vented squeaks of rage and terror, showing what spineless bloodsuckers they truly were. Though they outnumbered "Bob" twenty to one, "Bob" yet advanced on them. He did not hurry; there was a confidence in his movements that was horrible to his foes. It was as if death itself stalked them. No flicker of mercy warmed the flaky glitter of "Bob's" eyes.

"Bob's" code was a hard one, a concept of justice to curl the hairs of those simpering sob sisters who would mollycoddle criminals. For "Bob" doled out a brand of justice all his own. Those who went against "Bob" seldom wound up in prison; they either learned a lesson that made them Slack-seeking citizens for life—or they lost their lives. "Bob" did nothing halfway.

One of the less craven thrust out a ray gun. . .

. . . and the hand that held the revolver seemed to leap from the arm to which it belonged. Dobbs had delivered it a karate chop which sev-

ered it completely. The head was then propitiously launched by Dobbs'
hand. It spun end over end into the jungle.

The rest fled, squealing like pigs at a slaughterhouse. Ignoring them,
Dobbs bore down on the cringing, whimpering arch-foe.

"Bob" gave the fellow one appraising glance. Then the seemingly
plastic-molded head shook regretfully.

"You had many chances to slay me," Dobbs stated grimly. "But you
did not have the nerve to do it by your own hand. Like all criminals,
however clever, you are a coward. You are like a rat."

The fiend struck at "Bob" repeatedly. He missed each time, for Dobbs'
plasticinelike form seemed to vanish under his fists, so often did "Bob"
accidentally slip and fall down.

Increased terror filled the man.

Dobbs' eyes seemed to convey thoughts as well as words could have.
And what those eyes told the Young AntiBob made him defecate with
fear. He squealed as though caught in a steel trap.

"You'll never kill me!" he snarled.

Strange lights glowed in "Bob's" blue eyes.

"No, I won't kill you. That is true. But you will receive your punishment nonetheless. Because I suspect your identity. You are none other
than my evil twin brother, "Dick" Dobbs! What an ungrateful fellow!
Our pure and unsullied Mom wouldn't be proud. It's up to me, your
older brother by five minutes, to give you a good thrashing."

The masked villain rolled his eyes in panic. He didn't know what fate
"Bob" had planned for him. But it could be nothing pleasant.

Dobbs reached down and gripped the edges of the mask in his manly
fingers. He yanked it off . . . and then he stood frozen in horror and
astonishment.

"DAD! How . . . how *could* you!"

For it was, indeed, his pitiful, aging Mayan-emigrant father, long
thought killed in a drugstore explosion in the 1950s. Yet here he
cringed, *alive!*

But he was no longer the stoic, proud Spanish Mayan that Dobbs
remembered. The entire top half of his face was hideously scarred by
burns, disfigured to the point of inducing vomit. He did indeed somewhat resemble the Phantom of the Opera—or the mad burn victim
portrayed by Vincent Price in *House of Wax.*

"My own long-lost Dad!" exclaimed Dobbs. "Huh!" He slapped his
forehead violently. "Who'd'a thought it?"

"Stop this charade and kill me," howled the monster-Dad in misery.
"You know I'm not your real father! Your mother trysted with a Polish
milkman—who was also a Jew from outer space! You are the bastard
son of some damnable Angel of JHVH-1, the supernatural being who

cruelly cuckolded me just so that you, Earth's savior, could be born!—indeed, whose affair with my darling Jane cost me my sanity!"

"What?" cried Dobbs, tears welling up in his eyes. "You mean . . . you mean I'm not half-Mayan, like you and Granddad? You mean, what the Bobbies say is true . . . that I'm not your real son??? But. . ." Dobbs blubbered, tears waterfalling pathetically into his lap. "But . . . I LOVE you, Dad!"

"Bob" Dobbs fell, sobbing grossly, into the arms of the disfigured villain he had been eager to kill only moments before.

"I'm . . . I'm scared, Dad! This doesn't make sense! Where have you been all this time?"

"Skulking the catacombs beneath San Antonio," whimpered the wizened, twisted wretch, crying and blubbering along with "Bob." "These many years I waited to avenge myself on humanity for the humiliation of it all. And when the True AntiBob sent forth his mental commands from the depths of time, promising me powers beyond imagining, I was instantly brainwashed! He . . . he *forced* me to do it, son!"

The two clung to each other, wracked with sobs. Dobbs' companions stood dumbfounded—except for "Connie," who snapped peevishly, "I've been trying to tell him this for years—but *oh, no! He* wouldn't listen!"

Suddenly Dobbs extricated himself from his legal father's embrace.

"Dad, I love you. But that doesn't matter. I must do my duty. True, it's unfair that you spent forty years in pain, horror and shame. But the important part is that you—you, my own Dad, even if some wandering milkman from the stars actually sired me—you have willingly done the bidding of the AntiBob, and so must be thrashed and pummeled accordingly."

He raised a clenched fist, ready to strike the whimpering, aged burn victim. But the man pointed over "Bob's" shoulder and cried, "It wasn't me, son. It was HIM—the *real* AntiBob! Look! He's getting away!"

Dobbs turned. It wasn't a trick! A gigantic flying saucer was lifting out of the jungle towards the sky!

"Li! Quickly!" urged Dobbs. "The Third Pipe and White Stone!"

Li unerringly threw the items to "Bob." Frantically, Dobbs crammed the White Stone into the bowl of the Third Pipe.

The onlookers expected some spectacular new magic to occur. But Dobbs simply pulled the Pipe back behind his head and, using it like a catapult, launched the White Stone directly at the retreating saucer.

The Stone hit the saucer and lodged in a tailpipe! The huge disk wobbled dizzily and then plunged Earthwards with an ear-rending whine, crashing to the ground several hundred yards away.

"Now . . . for the final battle!" declared Dobbs, striding relentlessly towards the saucer he'd brought down with what might as well have been, for all its holy power and all the blood that had been shed to acquire its components, nothing more than a simple slingshot.

"Wait, Dobbs!" bellowed the towering First "Bob," who had watched with undisguised amusement. "You cannot hope to vanquish your exact, diametric opposite; he has more demonic allies among the Old Ones than do you! It is therefore time that I bestow upon you my Secret Weapon of All the True "Bobs"—THE THIRD FIST!"

A blinding flash enveloped Dobbs. When it faded, he possessed, growing from the wrist of his right arm, a third hand, clenched into a mighty fist composed of an ample gallon or two of scarred knuckles! Tattooed across it in crude lettering were the words "TAYSTE THE KISS OF ETIRNAL SLACK."

"This is the combined Fist of All Other "Bobs," " thundered the First "Bob." "With it, *none* may defeat you. Now," the godlike ape-man chuckled, "have at him, boy!"

Dobbs dashed into the woods towards the smoking wreckage of the saucer. His companions started to follow him, but the gigantic Yeti "Bob" from the Dawn of Time held them back.

"No, my pitiful human-tainted descendants," he ordered. "It is not for mortal eyes to gaze upon the AntiBob. This is "Bob's" fight. He must conquer his nemesis alone, or the great Temper of JHVH-1 shall be lost."

And so they waited in dreadful anticipation. Soon, the sounds of an incredible battle arose from the woods. Great smoking pieces of the flying saucer began raining down upon the woods all around them, so violent was this Battle of the Ages. Dinosaurs fled past in terror, seeking to escape the scene of carnage. A volcano exploded in the distance. The moon passed in front of the sun and there was an eclipse.

Still the sounds of battle raged on.

Eventually, even Li became bored and sat down. "Connie" busied herself polishing her nails. Usuthu and Crazy Horse twiddled their thumbs. Janiti, finally freed from her bonds—by Li, as she had otherwise been ignored the whole time—sat close to Li and nursed his wounds with her witch's magic. For had he not saved her from "Bob's" thoughtless impetuousness?

Almost two hours later, "Bob" Dobbs emerged from the woods . . . as they'd all known he would.

He dusted off his hands against each other with the smuggest of satisfaction. The Third Fist protruding awkwardly from his right arm evidenced bruised and scraped knuckles.

"That'll show *him*," muttered the SlackMaster proudly.

"But. . ." stammered Li Li-jing. "The AntiBob! Who was he?"

"Ah, you wouldn't believe me if I told you," mumbled Dobbs, sweeping "Connie" into his arms and kissing her grossly, and at length. They humped and hunched together in shameless desire. The Third Fist shrank as their passion grew.

Li looked away, embarrassed. Janiti clung to his leg, sighing romantically. Usuthu, Crazy Horse and the Yeti snickered at Li's discomfort.

Suddenly the First "Bob" interrupted the maudlin display.

"Dobbs," he intoned deafeningly, "You have done your job, and are deserving of a Smoke." He proffered a new bowlful of the Greatest 'Frop in the Universe, this time from his own Pipe of the Gods.

"Bob" smoked contentedly, occasionally hacking and spitting, feeling up "Connie" with his spare hand. Through the clouds of smoke, the First "Bob" addressed Dobbs' loyal friends.

"Ye who, despite the minute quantity of true Yeti blood in your veins, have proved so nobly that courage and loyalty can overcome the baser, coarse human nature . . . ye shall now reap the rewards ye have sown."

He gestured arcanely with his fingers; sparkles of light danced from them dramatically.

Usuthu felt no change. But he somehow knew that the arthritis that would later cripple his giant frame was now banished forever. Crazy Horse, who had borne the aches of flat feet his entire life without complaint, suddenly had perfect arches. The Chinese Yeti grew another three feet in height, so that he now towered at eleven feet, six inches. "A dwarf no longer!" he exclaimed, shedding tears of joy. Li felt two molars he'd lost to decay grow back instantly.

These had been minor healings, for the three men and the Yeti were in relatively good health already. It was Janiti who was changed the most.

Her legs and arms straightened and grew. Her white hair became a lustrous black. Her sagging, withered breasts became immaculate mounds worthy of 1940s Hollywood. Her wrinkled face smoothed over and in its place there gaped the astonished visage of a young girl of twenty. She stood up from the ground, a perfect vision of womanhood.

And she fell into Li's arms, embracing him with savage sexuality.

"Connie" hugged "Bob," finally no longer bitching and griping.

"Isn't that sweet," she breathed in his ear, nipping it with her teeth. "Bob," uncharacteristically, blushed a bright red.

The First "Bob" held aloft his mighty hand for silence.

"The problem with you humans," he lectured, "is that in dealing with the gods, you don't give yourselves enough credit. Without you, where would we primordial gods and goddesses be? We're forces of nature, and you are forces of nature. But—which is more destructive, all the poltergeists and tribal deities on Earth, or such entities as the Kerr-McGee Corporation? Eh? Which has killed off more mountain gorillas and blue whales? Which can poison the entire atmosphere and end all life by pushing a series of buttons?"

Dobbs and his companions trembled before the gargantuan Perfect Yeti.

"Always remember that you are of the race which, in many ways, has the upper hand. We gods do not possess nuclear weapons; not even the saucer beings from space possess them. You are the *only ones* who can destroy ALL of us. Doesn't that make you *proud,* to be part human? Part of the species that's able to unleash more destructive force than all combined demons, gods, ghosts, UFOs, sharks, dinosaurs and natural disease germs? So many of your people depend upon gods and aliens to save you from yourselves. But why would those worthy supernatural entities save you? Just so you can go on thinking up more subtle ways to ruin our 'lives,' and those of all creatures on your planet?? EH? No, my mortal friends, you have a much bigger say in your destiny than ever did we gods.

"Have you ever wondered what a nuclear blast would do to your souls, humans—above and beyond the disintegration of your physical bodies? If ever there was a magic weapon capable of erasing parts of more than one reality, it is that. So consider that mayhaps we gods also fret over your amazing weapons and warlike nature."

The First "Bob" grinned morbidly, and then vanished completely and silently.

All stood quiet for a pregnant moment. Then "Bob" spoke, tamping his Pipe thoughtfully as he tilted back his head and mused nobly to the sunset.

"Yes, he's right, it's something to muse upon, indeed. The insidious Conspiracy of the Normals doesn't even recognize itself as such, yet it has the power to destroy—or even sell—this whole planet. It is up to us, each in our own ways, as lone individuals, to alert the pitiful Pinks to the dangers they bring down upon us all. There are some things that merely human Man was not meant to know; certainly not those who can understand only False Slack, obtainable *only* with money—those millions who'd prefer to cling to their fantasy that everything, even the ozone layer and the rain forests, will be okay if we just act nice . . . *HOO boy.*"

"Bob" shook his head philosophically.

"We'll learn, come *Omicron Epsilon,* the Vision Beholding Itself in SubGenius prophecy—the Time Intersection, when this universe intersects with the Backwards Timestream universe, and the images of our dreams and pasts and fears become flesh . . . bringing our weirdest fantasies to rampaging life. What terrible solidified hallucinations will be born from the repressed desires of the Normals, who forgot Slack?"

He paused and gazed thoughtfully at a distant volcano.

"Fortunately," he finished smugly, "Normals are my competition only until they become my customers." And with that, he winked.

Each to itself, his companions wondered at this man "Bob." Did he possess, after all, the superior vision and intuition of a prophet . . . or was he just a lucky salesman, blabbering inane clichés??

But that question was soon forgotten, as Dobbs and "Connie"—hand in hand, whispering and giggling like newlyweds—herded them into the submarine and summoned the Vortex. "Connie" served them lunches as they jetted through time to take each hero home.

Li fell asleep in the arms of his new girlfriend, the now-voluptuous supervixen, Janiti.

He awoke briefly to disembark from the submarine as Dobbs returned it to Bahaab Dahaabs, and to reboard the simple Indian canoe for the final "leg" of their journey.

Crazy Horse was dropped off in his time and homeland, bidding them keep the canoe.

Now Li and Janiti were to be returned to twentieth-century America. Janiti, of course, preferred to return with Li to the modern age rather than face death from her own people, the intolerant Druids.

They materialized out of the Vortex, hovering in the magical canoe high in the sky above the nighttime camp fires of Dokstok. The moonlit lake glimmered peacefully below. The sky, no longer tormented by storm clouds, shone clear and crystalline over a cool breeze.

It was not an especially tearful goodbye, for neither Li nor Janiti could forget Dobbs' having thrown Janiti towards the Void-Pit of the AntiBob as a replacement for "Connie." Nevertheless, Dobbs and Li shook hands like the real men they were. Li and Janiti then jumped overboard and, buoyed by Dobbs' antigravitational psychokinesis, floated into the SubGenius camp. Above them, they saw "Connie" blow them a final kiss while Dobbs waved goodbye with his Pipe. Then, snuggling together in the enchanted canoe, "Connie" and "Bob" drifted into the moonrise.

Stang and his friends, snoring in sleeping bags, never noticed Li and the half-naked, virginal beauty descending in slow motion out of nowhere.

Nor did the SubGenii express any particular surprise when they awoke the next morning and found, in Li Li-jing's company, that hypnotically lovely woman who seemed to speak every language . . . for they were too absorbed in swapping stories and 'Fropmixtures amongst themselves.

Stang eventually noticed that Li had acquired not only a girlfriend, but a new and undeniable air of self-confidence. He took time out to throw his arm over Li's shoulder and say, "Well, Li . . . I guess Dokstok hasn't turned out so bad for you after all. Sort of a fun adventure, huh?"

"Yes," Li Li-jing smiled. "Yes, it was some sort of a fun adventure, indeed."

Harry S. Robins
THE SMOKER FROM THE SHADOWS

Liber scriptus proferetur,
Inquo totum continetur
Unde mundus iudicetur.
—Thomas of Celano, A.D. 1247

Yea, I make sport of thee, *and* mock thee....
—PreScriptures XXI

Monsters like unto men will be around thee *all about*, and shall make thee to look past the Door *which* should be locked....
—PreScriptures XCIII

Recently I received two envelopes in the mail. One was large and bulky, the other of standard size. The smaller one turned out to be from a lawyer, a Mr. Crowninshield of Ipswich, Massachusetts. According to this cover letter, some workmen had been demolishing a rotting building in nearby Innsmouth, an all-but-deserted ancient seaport town, to make way for beachfront condominiums and an amusement area, in keeping with the economic revitalization of the region, part of the "Massachusetts miracle" of presidential candidate and governor Michael Dukakis. Brought to light was an oilskin packet enclosing a number of closely written sheets. This manuscript was signed by a distant relative on my father's side, my great-uncle twice removed, Professor Byron Brainard.

Our family is an old one in this country, dating from the Second Jamestown Settlement of 1609. The genealogy of its many branches is for the most part a mystery to me, and I would have thought that surely there were many others into whose keeping such a find might be delivered before I was designated as the recipient. But as will be seen, my involvement with the Church of the SubGenius made me the obvious choice.

Crowninshield, senior partner in the Massachusetts law firm of Crowninshield and Babson, had executed the wishes of the vanished author of the ms., operating on a retainer from my remote relations the Sargent family, one of the last native Innsmouth families and still a financial power to be reckoned with, due to its domination of the marine salvage industry on that stretch of the New England coast.

Personally compelling to me as shedding light on the mysterious disappearance of my great-uncle, the account which follows is also of interest for its documentation of SubGenius activities in the 1930s, before their current period of popularity. It is not, of course, the only such record; besides various far older historical and archaeological artifacts now classified as secret by the Church, there exist many others of relatively recent date. An example is the famous "Four-Eyed Dobbs" portrait of the Church's founder, unearthed lately in New Orleans; signed by Garland Chauvin and dated 1951, it may be seen (by appointment) in the Sub-Genius National Museum in San Francisco, California.

The professor's story, however, antedates the Chauvin portrait by fifteen years, and may even confirm the involvement of Dobbs in trans-temporal as well as inter-sidereal travel! But since the Church has permitted the release of his tale, let him speak for himself.

—H.S.R.

I.

It was in the early autumn of the year 1936 that I first glimpsed the mocking face of the Stranger. Would that I had never beheld the preternaturally brilliant eyes, the curiously repellently regular features, and the gently smoking pipe clenched between the unnaturally white and perfect teeth, the face whose grin, at first sight genial and disarming, became, to one who had not the instinct to lower his glance after the first brief moment of meeting, a disturbing and sinister rictus whose fixity asseverated the ultimate reality of nighted gulfs of amorphous darkness and primordial, elder Chaos, whose Titan wings enshroud and menace our pitifully unknowing planet of mortal and innocent beings, of blue skies, flowing waters and all that is most dear within the hearts of the sons of men. Would that I had instead at that hour hurled myself from the West Street bridge, where the rushing Miskatonic begins its sally to the north, to drown the malignant knowledge of that eldritch visage in the final comfort of true oblivion, beneath her icy waters!

Now I must permanently remove myself from the haunts of men; I must seek out the desolate waste places of the Earth and there dwell, until overtaken by the progressive degeneration of the *change* which I can no longer deny is slowly altering me, devouring body and spirit. But, if I may hope, perhaps I will gladly endure the more bearable embrace of mortal death before I succumb to the final ravages of a most loathsome and detestable alienage.

An aspiring scholar of modest means, I had come, with the true zest of the amateur antiquarian, to study those curious groups of standing stones known as the New England megaliths. About them I knew little, save that their origin remains a mystery to science. While some have averred the Indians of the region were their builders, most authorities attribute their construction to Northern Europeans or Celts of the early to middle Bronze Age. Certain grooves on some of the altar stones suggest a dark sacrificial purpose, the draining of the blood of the out-stretched victims in the manner of the more degraded magical or religious ceremonies of prehistoric Europe.

I preferred to be open-minded, and to refrain from forming a hypothesis until I myself confronted the puzzling evidence. After all, the local farmers, though repellingly decadent, degenerated and inbred, know the grooved dolmens only as "cider-press stones." Perhaps, I thought, these rustics are correct, and the umbrageous speculations of more erudite heads mere conjecture, bred out of the pessimism and melancholy to which the scholarly set of mind perennially inclines.

My destination was Miskatonic University in storied Arkham, Massachusetts, where I was to meet the man who was the greatest living authority on the enigmatic relics. Professor Ebenezer Tillinghast had written a brilliant series of monographs; his intimate knowledge of geology, anthropology and paleontology illuminated his exhaustive familiarity with the place's elder history and legendary lore. I had communicated with Tillinghast in a series of increasingly cordial letters, following the first tentative inquiry on my part about his authoritative certification of the age of a certain primordial cromlech in the Vermont hills. His reply, gracious and cordial, began our increasingly pleasurable epistolary acquaintance. The demands of my research neatly dovetailed with his invitation to be his houseguest in Arkham; he further offered the use of the university library.

Unable to refuse, I had made preparations for the visit with eager anticipation, and now I was to set eyes on my learned correspondent for the first time.

II.

I quickened my steps as I walked up Garrison Street, lined with stately rows of Dutch elm trees. Stepping from their shade, I reached and crossed cobbled Church Street, leaving the town proper with its ancient rooftops, among which are still to be seen quite a few of the older gambrel type, for the venerable ivied brick of the university buildings. As I crossed the Quadrangle, I beheld Tillinghast, for it could be none other than he, descending the steps of the Faculty Club with hand outstretched in welcome.

Ebenezer Tillinghast was tall, though afflicted with the slight stoop which often marks the dedicated scholar. Graying and distinguished-looking, he seemed the perfect embodiment of the best stock New England has to offer.

My host at once made me welcome. In no time we were comfortably seated in the oak-paneled lounge, talking as if we had known each other all our lives. I took a glass of porter at Tillinghast's insistence, though he, bound by his physician's injunction, drank only hot tea from a moustache cup with his own monogram which kept his neat pepper-and-salt brush from drooping into the steaming liquid.

"The doctors won't allow it, Brainard—my heart's not what it used to be." He ran his long fingers through his iron-gray hair. "They say I must take better care of myself. The fools! Gad, let them know about the things that are under some of these hills and see how *their* hearts stand the strain. Though I shouldn't wonder if they referred me to an alienist if I told them. There are some things that Science is unequipped to deal with. Science does not remove the terror of the gods, eh?"

I fancied he looked at me strangely, as if expecting me to endorse his sentiment. He had the air of one who has just quoted, but if so, I did not recognize the quotation.

"But you know what I mean, Brainard," my venerable host went on. "You wanted to know about those underground chambers near Petersham. Capital—we'll go there. The locals must think I'm a pretty queer old duck, always pothering around those decaying ruins. But they leave me be—they shun them. And don't dismiss their superstitions. There's more wisdom in some of the tales muttered in the hill country than can be found in the whole anthropology syllabus—even here at Miskatonic.

"Perhaps I'll take a glass of that port after all, Brainard. What do doctors know? Ah, that's better. It warms the blood, just the thing for a cold night like this.

"Do you know, many so-called scientists won't even acknowledge the existence of some of those old piles? When anyone can walk out and see them, those fools prefer not to budge themselves from the upholstered comfort of their old theories. Let me tell you, I've walked these hills for thirty years; I've been up and over them more than any living man—and under them," he added, with a rasping chuckle.

"Yes, I'll show you that shrine out Pelham way. We'll go out on the Glasheen road—no one hardly ever comes there, so we won't be bothered. Just let me fill your glass, and I may as well take another. You have no idea how bracing it is to talk to a kindred spirit. Those whited sepulchres on the faculty haven't the sense to see farther than their noses. But one of these days, they'll take notice. Much good it can do them then! Steward, another bottle of that port."

Through the night, as I willingly attended, Tillinghast held forth on the ancient stones and their surroundings. Though in truth I had not nearly the erudition with which he credited me, I knew enough to realize that I was in the presence of an exceptional authority on the subject, and in all likelihood the greatest authority.

He told of Cyclopean ruins in the heart of the Maine woods, beneath which stone staircases lead down to abysses of antehuman secrets. He seemed to hint that strange intimations of cosmic menace were suggested deliberately by the ancient builders of the Druidlike circles of standing stones atop a bare granite summit in Acworth, across the Connecticut River in New Hampshire.

But the most eldritch of the time-blasted megaliths, Tillinghast went on, were to be found in the lonely hill country of west-central Massachusetts. Here were mysteries truly unfathomable, secrets too well hidden to be exhumed, even by the most adroit and persistent investigator.

The local inhabitants, mostly craven farmers and rustics, would take pains to avoid the sites, a tradition of aversion extending from pre-Revolutionary times. It was in that period that the strange monuments became the scene of a brief revival of the alchemy of the Middle Ages. The "strangers" who had sailed with the Puritans used the uncouth heaps as their hidden redoubts. Safe from the suspicious fanaticism of their fellows, they extracted alloys from the complex sulphides of New England's rocks, by means of now long-lost techniques which have only been partially rediscovered, which they managed to pass off to the credulous religionists as silver and gold.

But with the years, this pragmatic alchemy slipped back into the occultism with which it was unavoidably associated in the beliefs of that time, and for generations afterward the stone structures were associated with the sinister superstitions that continued to percolate through the repressed psychic substratum of the Puritan society, every now and then escaping in such dark forms as the Salem Witchcraft and all that went with it.

Naturally, the locals would exhibit reluctance to visit or discuss the sites. Yet, Tillinghast hinted, more than the lingering traces of the aroma of an antique notoriety kept the rustics at bay.

"The Indians knew, Brainard," he insisted, tossing down yet another glass of porter. "The Wampanoags always maintained that the great stones were the doorsteps of passages into the spirit world. Their head man, Misquamacus, claimed that *when the stars were right, the gates were opened.* In my years here at Miskatonic I've persisted, in spite of fools' laughter, in correlating their traditions with some of the more esoteric occult literature in our library—*and now I know they were correct.* But this very night you shall see for yourself." He pulled an ephemeris from his waistcoat pocket and traced down a table of figures with a slightly weaving finger.

"We should start now. We'll take my motor, if you've no objection. We've a long drive ahead of us—what about one for the road?"

III.

A rising gibbous moon cast its sickly light over us as we emerged from the club. Tillinghast found himself carrying his moustache cup, which he pocketed after two or three attempts.

Despite a noticeable inebriation, my new friend seemed to have no trouble once behind the wheel of his Packard sedan. We sped away from the town and soon were traversing at high speed a veritable labyrinth of obscure country roads which wound through narrow valleys and densely wooded slopes. Tillinghast drove in a manner which suggested more than a passing familiarity with the route. We sped through the hamlet of Pelham and were soon skirting the edge of a dark declivity on our right.

"That'll all be flooded over in a few years," remarked Tillinghast, gesturing loosely with his right hand. Not for the first time, I wondered about the source of his knowledge.

"I know what you're thinking," he went on. He took a swallow from a pocket flask, frowning when I refused it. "How do I know? Let's just say that the megaliths open the way to the future as well as the past. Yes, the Quabbin Reservoir will be along here, and this valley and all its secrets will be covered over. A good thing for most folk, too. The human mind can only stand so much, Brainard. Let the fools slumber in their illusion of safety."

We turned onto the Glasheen road. Now we were flying by that country crossed by Daniel Shays' tattered army of rustic rebels in their doomed cause of 1786. It was said that the alchemist Glazier Wheeler produced his false gold somewhere near here. Shays too, Tillinghast reminded me, had attempted in vain to duplicate Wheeler's methods to finance his ragged army. His workshop had been the very megalithic construction which was our destination this evening.

We entered the sleeping ancient town of Petersham, where in the 1780s its Shaker founder, "Mother" Ann Lee, proclaimed herself the "Female Christ." I shuddered as I contemplated how riddled the locality had been with the cancer of superstition.

Tillinghast deftly guided his vehicle along a rutted farm lane and coasted to a stop in a moonlit clearing. He pointed out a low-lying series of ruins.

"Not the entrance, Brainard," he grinned. "Those are just the foundations of old Joseph Stevens' farm. The place was built in 1740; this is all that's left. Stevens' grandsire was Simon Willard, you know. He lived at Nonanoicus in 1675 in the time of Philip's War."

We picked our way across the deserted field. I followed the inebriated scholar over the yawning ruts, bulbous tumps, tangled roots and sliding stones. It was hard to keep my balance while following Tillinghast as he continued his peroration.

"Cotton Mather knew about the strange events in Willard's woods. You've read the *Magnalia Christi Americana,* I take it. When Philip's War broke out there were marvels seen and heard, weird howls from the noonday sky and deep reverberations from Nonanoicus Pond. Three-headed calves were born, and bright lights were seen hovering in the sky. Of course, he knew only *part* of the truth."

At this point, a huge uneven bulk loomed up dismally before us out of the shadows of the gnarled trees' twisted branches. Ten feet across and fully twelve feet high, the pile seemed to crouch like a malignant living thing, a hulking guardian of the secrets of elder Earth. I felt a sense of disquiet the receding vapors of alcohol could not obscure. In the sudden silence, the trickling sound of water over stone was heard, which seemed to echo upwards from unknown depths.

"Do you hear the spring?" asked my guide, producing an electric torch. Taking a swallow from his flask, he aimed the beam into the dark mouth of the structure.

A six-foot-wide spring, reflecting the electric rays, indeed welled up out of the floor. From the sides several entrances opened out to stone-lined tunnels. Tillinghast took the second of these.

"Note the stonework, Brainard," he whispered. "I've seen its like before, at Exham priory in England and at Skara Brae and Rinyo in the Orkneys, where Queen Morgause ruled during King Arthur's day. *And it was old then*. Old when Babylon was new."

His lowered voice strangely affected me, and I thought of the eccentric but brilliant Harvard chemistry professor, Eben R. Horsford, who proposed that the megaliths were the fragmentary remnants of that lost city of Norumbega which Champlain and the *voyageurs* had long sought in vain.

We continued down the dank corridor. Tillinghast pointed upward. "We should be just under the Stevens place," he breathed. The tunnel took a sharp left turn, then wound to the right. At once it came to a dead end, shored up by worn granitic blocks.

I had been feeling greater apprehension as we delved further into the tunnel, and was relieved that, as it seemed, we had reached its terminus. I was just about to propose that we retrace our steps when Tillinghast abruptly raised his hand for silence. "Listen!" he commanded.

I could hear nothing save our breathing in the confined space. Then, as the pause increased, I could hear my heart beating in my breast. Or was it my heart? Faintly, so faintly that I could barely make it out, came an insistent rhythm, a muffled beating which seemed to emanate from far, far below us.

"Behold, for I show you a mystery," breathed Tillinghast.

IV.

Choosing a certain stone, he pushed against it with the flat of his hand. I wondered at his purpose as he continued to press the wall without apparent result. Suddenly, the stone moved, grating outward. As it did, the faint thumping became perceptibly louder. Now the whole section of wall shuddered and began to slide silently down into the earth.

The hidden mechanism, whatever it was, made no sound. Ponderously, inexorably, the supposedly piled stones of the wall sank as one into the great hidden slot, until, with a muffled boom as of rock meeting rock, the top of the wall leveled with the floor of the chamber. A breath of cool air blew against our faces from the blackness of the newly revealed aperture. There was no question that the dull, beating rhythm was more audible. Faintly, a whistling, thin piping could be heard, sounding vaguely like a syrinx or perhaps a pair of flutes. This anti-music, if such it was, seemed dissonant in the extreme, discordant, horrible. It seemed to snatch with taloned fingers at the edges of the brain, threatening to tear it from its moorings and sweep it away down suffocating corridors of ultimate madness.

"Dear God—what is it, Tillinghast?" I gasped. My subterranean cicerone seemed to sneer as he replied. "Nothing at all, Brainard. A mere bagatelle. Only a sound just three living people—and you're one—have heard this century. Old Cotton Mather wrote of it in the *Magnalia*. 'The Wonders of the Invisible World.' Are you coming?"

He flashed the beam of his torch forward to reveal a chamber carved from plutonic basalt. A vessel of unidentifiable design reposed in a niche in the seamless black wall as do cineraria in a mausoleum. Beside this niche, another opening showed the top of a series of carven stone steps leading down to a nighted abyss. It was from this latter aperture that the draft of air blew in our faces, carrying with it the detestable piping and thumping.

Tillinghast stepped lightly into the chamber, but I, rooted to the spot with premonitory fear, could not follow. He reached into the urnlike vessel and pulled out, not cremated human ash and bone fragments as I half expected, but the dried leaves of some preserved plant. An intolerable foetor seemed to billow forth as he disturbed the contents of the receptacle.

"Look at this," crowed Tillinghast. "Just as the *Necronomicon* said. *Habafropzipulops*—the herb of knowledge, beside the Gateway. I deciphered the coded formula in Wormius's Latin edition, after sixteen years of study. I opened the wall for the first time this last summer. But now, with you as my witness and confederate, we will both pass into a world undreamed of by science."

As I watched in dismay, he crammed the powdery, dry leaves into his mouth. A dreamy, abstracted expression formed on his face as he rhythmically chewed. His jaw moved up and down in awful synchronization with the reverberations from below, and a greenish juice or sap ran from the corners of his mouth down his chin.

"Tillinghast," I entreated, "come away! This is madness!"

"Join me, Brainard," he grunted through his cudlike mouthful. "We'll wait for the Messenger together." I begged and pleaded but my friend remained obdurate. He stood stiffly, with his arms at his sides. Only his jaw continued to move up and down.

I started. Was that a scraping sound from below? Yes, something was ascending the stone steps. Crying out Tillinghast's name, I seized his hand and attempted to pull him forward. The hand that I clutched was as cold as ice. A dim radiance began to glow from the tunnel.

Unwilling to gaze upon what might come into view, I turned to flee. *The wall was rising again!* It was halfway to the roof even now! With a choking cry I scrambled forward. Somehow, sheer terror gave me the impetus to clamber up and over the moving edge. The top met the ceiling of the tunnel as I fell heavily to the other side; it cut off the growing illumination of the inner chamber where luckless Tillinghast still stood chewing, leaving me alone and in darkness.

I must have screamed and raved. I pushed at the various stones of the wall until my hands were wet with my own blood. Repeatedly I shouted to Tillinghast, but heard only the echoes of my call in mocking reply.

Of how I blundered out of the tunnel I have no memory. But the welcome light of morning found me weeping, reeling drunkenly in the clearing by the foundation of the farmhouse. It was no small matter to start Tillinghast's machine and maneuver it back to Arkham; how I did it in the state I was in I will never know. As I drove, I rehearsed in my mind the speech I would have to make to the police, and my heart shrank within me at the thought.

But by the time I reached the city, my resolve to contact the authorities had evaporated, leaving in its place a sort of helpless lassitude. For all I knew, I told myself, Tillinghast was in no danger. Was he not familiar with his surroundings in that remote place? He had opened the door; had he not also closed it? Whatever his purposes, I wanted no part of them. Poor Tillinghast had been driven mad by his studies. That his abstruse research had unbalanced him I was certain, from his scarcely creditable ravings about lights in the sky and gateways into the future. It was all the more deplorable that he had mingled genuine knowledge and antiquarian discovery with the tissue of superstition. In any event, I doubted now that I could find my way back to the site unaided.

As I mused over these things, I stood on the West Street bridge, gazing down at the swiftly flowing Miskatonic. Periodically the infrequent passerby would glance at my disheveled and clay-smeared clothing and bedraggled appearance. No doubt I presented the aspect of a rum-sodden reprobate, sweating out his sins in the light of day. Indeed, the monumental hangover that added to my misery induced me to believe that such a characterization would be far from inaccurate. Pulling the tatterdemalion remnant of my coat around me, I gazed bleakly down at the little island of gray standing stones, where in Puritan times it was whispered that the Devil held court.

V.

It was then that I heard a light step behind me, and an unfamiliar if pleasantly modulated voice hailed me by my Christian name.

"Byron? I've been looking for you, son. You're Byron Harris Brainard?"

I turned to see who addressed me with such familiarity, and found myself gazing into the bland face of an amused-appearing man of forty-odd years or so, who clenched a pipe between his teeth as he grinned at me, insolently, as I thought.

"Indeed, sir," I began. "I have not the pleasure—" He interrupted me. "Aw, come off it, hoss—you've gotta be the one. Hey, you look like two miles o' bad road!"

I drew myself to my full height. "Sir, you have the advantage of me. Perhaps you will divulge the basis for our presumed acquaintance."

"My name's Dobbs, ol' son, but you can just call me "Bob"—most people do." The stranger extended his hand, and I found myself shaking it before I could think.

"A guy you know sent me. Fella named Tillinghast."

"Tillinghast?" I cried. "Then . . . then, he is well?"

"Sure, he's okey-dokey," rejoined my companion, who continued to grin. "He *was* gettin' a little hot 'n' bothered about *you*, though, so he sent me down, like I said, to pick you up. We can ride out in his old heap; feel like it?"

A sudden suspicious impulse overcame me. "You claim you were looking for me, Mr. Dobbs; but how is it that you knew where to find me? Excuse me, but how do I really know that you come from Ebenezer Tillinghast?"

Dobbs continued to grin, and seemed not to take the slightest offense at this line of inquiry. I began to find his beaming countenance disquieting.

"Heck, son, I didn't know where to look, now you mention it," he responded. "Just lucky, I guess. Always been kind o' lucky. First place I come to, there you were. Oh, Eb said to show this to you."

There could be no doubt. The grinning stranger had handed me what was unmistakably Tillinghast's pocket flask. Relief, compounded with irritation, flooded through me.

"Look here," I demanded, "suppose you tell me what all this means."

"Well, we oughta get a move on," responded my interlocutor. "I can fill you in on the way. By the way . . . want one of these?"

Somehow, as we stood there on the bridge, he contrived to peddle to me, for most of my pocket change, some sort of religious pamphlet, then a bright orange cigarette lighter, a cylindrical ellipsoid of unknown material and design. Looking back on this incident, it baffles me how I could have been induced to engage at that time in a trivial commercial transaction. Perhaps my lack of sleep and debilitated constitution ac-

THE SMOKER FROM THE SHADOWS 101

counted for my reduced resistance. I glanced hastily at the pamphlet, which seemed to make no sense to my sleep-starved eyes. "The World Ends Tomorrow, and YOU MAY DIE!" it proclaimed. Looking closer, I noticed that there seemed to be a small illustration of a face which bore an astoundingly close resemblance to the stranger's. The image and the crowded fine print beneath it flowed and swam before my troubled gaze, so I could not read it. We were walking to Tillinghast's new motor; somehow the stranger had sold me his *bona fides* as well. I am now convinced he could have sold me anything.

My new companion slid behind the wheel of the Packard.

"This old thing oughta be fun," he remarked. "Last I drove was a toyoda-corolla!"

Unwilling to be drawn out by his nonsensical remark, I rubbed the peculiarly slick paper of the pamphlet between my thumb and forefinger. I asked Dobbs if he could tell me what kind of paper it was.

"Zerocks," was his unintelligible reply as he let in the clutch.

If I was the passenger of a madman, nonetheless he piloted the machine most adroitly. Whenever I looked at him, I found his gaze directly upon me, still with the same manic grin. Indeed, I cannot recall that I ever saw his profile. Each time I was forced to look away, fearful that he would otherwise continue to fix his eyes on me, not the road. But his skill, or luck, prevailed, and at high speed we retraversed the route Tillinghast and I had taken on the evening previous.

Wondering if my companion's apparent friendliness was indeed genuine, or only subgenial, I took a pull from the flask Tillinghast had franked to me through his unorthodox agent. Its contents, however, were repellently bitter. I choked on the foul liquid, and tears ran from my eyes.

Each query I made of Dobbs seemed to produce a less understandable reply, until I left off trying to ascertain Tillinghast's intentions, or his. Not for the first time, I wished myself clear of the entire mind-numbing affair.

It was midafternoon when we arrived at the clearing. My head was reeling from the acrid potation I had swallowed. In the daylight the area looked quite different, yet I placed the foundations of the old farmhouse and the heaped stones of the primordial megalith.

"Hold on, partner," Dobbs called to me as I made my way towards the yawning entrance. "We can't get in there 'til round about midnight."

"Midnight!" I replied indignantly. "Midnight! Then why, pray tell, have we been driving over these benighted roads and all around Robin Hood's barn, when I could have had a hot bath and a change of clothes at a hotel, you deranged, dim-witted drummer? Eh?"

Dobbs appeared characteristically unshaken by my embarrassing outburst.

"Keep your shirt on," he chuckled. He was suddenly beside me, though I had not seen him cross the field. The horrid taste of Tilling-hast's "cordial" lingered nauseously in my mouth. Again I looked directly on Dobbs's countenance. His grin was becoming unbearable. "Watch this," he said.

As I stared, his pipe . . . the event seems incredible even now, after the horror of the final revelation. The briar glowed—where before had I encountered that foetid stench? and then *convulsed.* Its stem *bent,* its glossy sides heaved like those of a living thing, and it whipped back and forth in Dobbs' mouth.

Horrified, I leaped back, shouting in surprise and repugnance. And, suddenly—it was night! The gibbous moon stood on the horizon, Polaris and the Wain blazed in the autumn night sky, and cicadas stridulated, interspersed with the somehow daemonic chorus of the whippoorwills. The night wind blew. I clutched Dobbs's arm in Panic fear.

"What, in God's name. . . ?" I croaked.

"Time control, son. How about that?" Dobbs chuckled. I pressed my hands to my aching temples. But this was no dream. I muttered some lines of Coleridge:

The sun's rim dips, the stars rush out:
At one stride comes the dark.

I beheld Dobbs making his way to the megalith, ambling with an easy stride. Though as I followed I continued to stumble over roots, tumps, pits and stones, he never seemed to make a misstep. He waited for me by the entrance.

"This is as far as I go, sport," he said. "I got some guys coming to give me a lift. But I'll let you have this for one ninety-five, batteries included." He showed me an electric torch. Intending to refuse this contemptible sales offer, I found myself assenting instead. As I handed over the money, my face flushed with shame, I saw him cock his head.

"Well, it looks like they're early," he mused. "Better get goin', little buddy."

Suddenly I saw two brilliant lights, like meteors, dropping out of the sky toward us. I yelled in alarm and leapt into the shelter of the megalithic entrance. I flung myself full length upon the ground, right into the shallow, icy water of the spring. There was no impact, no concussion. Cursing this latest idiotic conjuring-trick, I staggered to my feet. I heard Dobbs's voice calling, diminishing in volume and oddly truncated at the end. His parting words made as little sense as any of his previous locutions; it sounded as if he shouted, "See you in sixty-two years!"

When I looked forth from the door of the monument I saw what I both expected and dreaded to see—nothing. There was no sign of my unfathomable go-between. Determined to finish the madness by prosecuting its course, I started down the tunnel.

The torch I had been flimflammed into purchasing did seem to give out an astonishing amount of illumination. The carven sides of the tunnel starkly exhibited every detail of their surface. Curiously, the chisel marks I saw were directed from the inside pointing out. The walls seemed to be of holocrystalline, quartz-bearing plutonic rock, a granite gneiss. Sparse phenocrysts of mica glittered like diamonds in masses of granitic porphyry, a hypabyssal formation bearing traces of amphibole and pyroxene.

Struck by a sudden suspicion, I switched off the light. There was no diminution of the uncanny radiance. The tunnel glowed—and did the brightness fluctuate? I saw that it did, and then I faintly heard what only then I realized I had been striving to expunge from my memory since I heard it first, that insistent subterranean thudding or beating, contrapuntally accompanied by the damnable, eldritch piping. The glow, I saw, waxed and waned perfectly in time to that insidious rhythm.

I made the left turn, then the right turn—and the illumination abruptly ended. I nearly shrieked aloud, for it appeared as if the tunnel was filled by an unclean, billowing mass of blackness. Yet I approached, and found the lightless apparent solid to be really a thick darkness, into which the re-switched-on beam of my light only feebly penetrated.

I was steeling myself to go forward when at once I found myself addressed by a familiar voice.

"You can switch that off, Brainard," came Tillinghast's unmistakable tones. "There's no need to come any further. I see "Bob" gave you my little flask."

"Tillinghast! Thank God!" I cried. "For the love of Heaven, come out where I can see you! Let us quit this accursed place!"

"I'm afraid I can't do that," the professor's voice replied. "And you wouldn't want to see me now. I can't even stay long on *this upper level*. I've *changed,* you see, into something rich and strange."

"Don't banter at me like an undergraduate!" I shrilled. "It's high time you let me in on this practical joke of yours. I demand you show yourself, and explain the meaning of this mendacious mummery!"

"What hurry?" came the reply. "By the way, you didn't take a nip from my little flask, did you? If you did, you'll know everything pretty soon, including that there's no way to explain the 'joke,' as you call it, in any concise sentence or series of sentences. But, tell me—did you drink?"

"I tasted your nauseating bootleg brew," I retorted hotly. "And you seem to be pixilated yourself, Tillinghast, judging from your gibberish. Come on, old man—let's get out of here!"

"No need for explanations, then," buzzed Tillinghast's voice. "You're a SubGenius now."

"You seem ill suited to denigrate my intelligence," I snapped. "Come into this light. You'll feel more like yourself when I get you away from all this."

"I should have *smoked* the 'Frop," muttered the voice. "I chewed it, you *drank* it. I imagine you too will regress somewhat, but at least we'll both be as good as immortal—until X-Day, that is. Well, let me dower you with a parting gift."

Tillinghast's voice seemed to recede down the tunnel. Then there were muffled sounds, as if he searched for something amid the rubble of the floor.

"At least tell me what that damnable *bumping* is!" I called out. As oddly as Tillinghast had been behaving, I was terrified of being left alone in this place.

"Why, it's Nyarlathotep, the mad faceless god, dancing ponderously and mindlessly to the piping of two amorphous idiot flute players, of course," droned the voice. "As "Bob" says, it has a good beat—you can dance to it. *Bhugg-shoggog, n'yaathai, m'waflghaa, toglesh-shelgoth. . . .* Ah, here we are."

"Tillinghast!" I called. "Tillinghast, I'm leaving!" But there was no answer. Then, suddenly, very close at hand, I heard a *scrabbling* sound.

Before I could step back, before I could even move, the horror was upon me. Out of the inexplicably chthonic adumbration of the tunnel shuffled or flopped a thing of unspeakable vileness. Its etiolated, holothuroid body, like that of some quivering Silurian sea cucumber, supported on a stalklike neck a kind of rudimentary, hairless and foetal head, eyeless and with a bulging brow that overhung its rugose rudiment of a face. Its fishlike mouth silently contracted with the effort of locomotion, as did the elasmobranchoid gills which flapped hideously with every fumbling step. An insufferable foetor overwhelmed me as the night-spawned thing pushed forward at me a whitish object, held in its misshapen forepaws.

Shrieking, I lashed out, trying to protect myself. I must have seized what the creature carried, for it was in my hand. Its liquid contents slopped over its rim, splashing on my skin. . . .

And then, in one supernal instant, I knew all. Scream after scream reverberated from the tunnel walls in concatenated echoes hardly recognizable as my own voice.

I knew then that Tillinghast's insinuations were totally founded on the unspeakable truth—how unmentionable beings, "Xists," were massing beyond nighted Yuggoth on the black, unknown world, Planet X, preparing for their devastating arrival on the earth three years before the twenty-first century begins; I knew how, in Azoic times, a billion and a half years ago, the barrel-bodied, star-headed Old Ones had created all life on our planet—for *food*. I knew of the lost serpent race, the Valusians. I knew of the kingdom of Lomar that existed at the pole one hundred thousand years ago, and of the coleopterous or beetle race which follows after man's extinction. I knew what *g'broagfran* is. I knew all things in heaven and earth.

And, since I did, I also knew that the distillate of *habafropzipulops* I had drunk would, as Tillinghast had predicted, cause an unavoidable, physical *regression* even as it conferred upon me the immortality of the body many in man's sad history have foolishly sought.

My head will swell in size as my brain develops abnormally, while my frame and limbs will dwindle and shrink grotesquely, as I move toward a synthesis of extreme senescence and prenatal morphology. And then, perhaps, the process will take me *further.* . . .

I walked out of the tunnel under the stars. There was no longer any need for timorous flight, for there was no point now to fearing anything. Now, as I pen these lines, I know that they will come to light forty years hence, as the rise of the SubGeniuses takes place, as it must. Until then, I consider myself on vacation. Perhaps I will pass the time frolicking amongst the catacombs of Nephren-Ka in the sealed and unknown valley of Hadoth by the Nile.

For that artifact, still in my possession, which the blasphemous horror in the tunnel pressed upon me, though it contained the liquid 'Frop essence from the necrophagous storehouses of inner Earth, was to me a *familiar object.* It was no sorcerous chalice, no eldritch drinking vessel hacked from the skull of some hairy prehuman progenitor, no onyx Cup of the Ptolemies. It would have been better for my peace of mind had it been any of these things, for *it was the moustache cup of Ebenezer Tillinghast.*

Larry Sulkis, St.

A WORKING RELIGION

It's a typical motel room: bed, table, sink, cheap towels and little bitty bars of soap wrapped in wax paper. It's familiar, not familiar in the sense that you know this particular motel room intimately, but familiar in the sense that this particular motel room could be any motel room anywhere. The guy on the bed scans the room for signs of something, anything recognizable. Howthefuck did I get here? is the first thought that comes into his mind. That his tongue feels like the inside of a snakeskin shoe is his second thought. The guy closes his eyes—electrical storms. Bad circuitry. It's several seconds before the actual question "Wherethefuck is here?" crashes in on him.

He snatches a matchbook from the ashtray and reads, "BOB's A-BAR, Island Park, Idaho—Where the Hell was I last night?" okay, that makes two of us. Two of whom? An attack of "whothefuck *am* I?" He checks his jacket pocket. No wallet, no ID. Just a crumpled credit-card receipt scrawled with a name, "Eliot."

Coffee and memory are tied together in a way yet unexplained by the science of biochemistry. So this guy who thinks he *might be* Eliot stumbles down narrow tilting limegreen stairs to find some coffee—CoffeeCoffeeCoffee. Downstairs is a country bar. Red leatherette, pedal steel abandoned on stage.

"We ain't open yet."

Full moustache, round wire glasses, pushing a broom. Jeez, it's Richard Brautigan. But he's dead! I must be fuckin' dead and goddamn Heaven is a motel room. Well that figures.

"We don't open till eleven thirty for lunch."

"All I want is a cup of coffee. You gotta have some coffee."

"Make it yourself." Brautigan nods toward the Bunn-O-Matic.

Fuckin' great. The middle of downtown Heaven and you can't get a decent cup of black.

Eliot stares at what must be the River Styx. Couple of guys, look like doctors, out in rubber pants up to their dicks in rapids. The river sounds like a single stream of piss—like coffee from a Bunn-O-Matic. Oh yeah.

The second sip enters the arterial framework around his temples. Skin tightens. The crud in his nose softens to snot. Things become a little less hallucinatory.

All right, thinks Eliot, so I was wrong about being dead. And the river probably isn't the Styx. More coffee. Things are fading in now like when you stand up too fast on the habafrops. But not enough. There's only so much medical science can do. At the risk of sounding stupid—start off obliquely, Where am I? would probably draw cops—"What river is that?"

Brautigan, who turns out to be Brad (the real Brautigan somehow reassuringly remains dead), keeps sweeping.

"The Henry's Fork of the Snake." Eliot looks blank. "Idaho."

Idaho. Not good. Not good at all. What happened to New York?

"You okay, buddy? You were hammering it pretty hard last night. You and the lady."

"The lady?—the girl, the woman, the Goddess!" It hits him like a spinning Willy. The whole board lights up. Dials go crazy!

Brad sits down asking, "Goddess?" and hears a testimony that will change his life. Seized by devotion, he transcribes like Stang Himself.

Eliot: "I was home. Out of work—again. No big deal in my business. I'm a freelance director. An independent producer. A writer of cable TV shows, promos and propaganda in all markets in perpetuity throughout the universe. After a while you don't get too twisted up about being out of work. It happens at the end of every job. ClientProductionUnitLunch, Baby!

"But it was a long dry spell and I found myself in off moments gripped by that 'I'll-never-work-again' fear, hallucinating Dry Bones—grinning cartoon skeletons in top hats dancing: 'De shoulder bone connected from de arm bone, de wrist bone connected from de Stark Fist. . . .'

"The light changed and the Mercedes behind me was honking. I'd been granted my 1.3 seconds of lag. I guess I was in surface shock. You know how it is. You're zipping along the freeways in drift-time, driving in theta, hit the off-ramp and suddenly you're on surface streets, still tranced out. I accelerated across three lanes of angry traffic—back on the grid. I think the wind had everyone spooked.

"I was pounding pavement in blistering heat. The cassettes on the backseat were warping into greasy little pools of plastic sweat.

"I'd pitched a show that day: 'hundredsomething.' An ensemble show set in a nursing home in the year 2050, aimed at junior geriatric Pinks. The netexec said **HE** was comedy and didn't handle drama. I told him it *was* comedy. 'It can't be comedy,' he said, 'it's an hour and comedy is always a half hour.' It was hopeless. It was time to retreat. Go home.

"Home. Multiple suns curled brittle chips of paint off my rented house. The water in the dog's dish gone to white powdery rings. Gunmetal hot. Fire in the hills. Fine ash rained across Los Angeles like a hot dry snow."

Suburban Voodoo

"I'm a sane man. But even so, there are times one has to take matters into one's own hands. Any savage knows that.

"The Elvis decanter stared back at me from the altar. Eyes glazed, arm cocked, fist gripping the ceramic microphone. I yanked his head off and poured a stiff one. A libation, an offering to the gods. The first sip I sprayed back at the altar from my lips like a perfume atomizer. Little Eau de Beam droplets on Elvis, Pachuco, the Lava-lite, the "Bob"-head and white-rimmed pipe. The second shot was for me. I tossed a quarter in the bowl and prayed. Not for wealth, not for fame, not even for a quivering starlet—just survival.

"I looked at the clock: two thirty. Chinese dentist. I couldn't know what I'd done. If I had known, I might not have done it.

"Two thirty-two: the phone rang."

To the Victor Belongs . . .

"The voice on the phone was familiar. A colleague from years back when I directed documentaries for a pay-cable network that dropped me into some of the strangest scenes on the North American continent: snake-handling cults in Tennessee, bounty hunters in Houston, swingers in Orange. . . . Victor had been an editorial assistant, now he was a producer of corporate hoopla.

" 'You busy?'

"The job sounded interesting enough—create the world's largest Videowall for the world's largest corporation. I mulled it over as I inched through the clogged streets of Burbank, Alameda to Olive, past Don's Burgers, into the Camaro-choked intersection of Victory itself.

"As I walked into the lobby I caught a glimpse of a man disappearing into an office. A ring of pipe smoke lingered in the air after him. Victor rushed to greet me at the door. Said the executive producer, Bob, couldn't talk to me right now, but he would fill me in on the details. Money was no object—this was the world's largest corporation, after all. Could I be on a plane tomorrow morning for Detroit? Okay, I know what you're thinking—sure, the boss' name is "Bob." I get it. But I swear, this is true.

"Eight A.M. next morning I'm flying Northwestern to Detroit, first class. Ten thousand dollars in cash in my bag. Praise "Bob," I'm thinking. I read my notes. Life is good.

"Landing, I can see wreaths of flowers on the planecrash overpass. Twinge of deathfear. I unconsciously try to clean the blood from under my nails. What am I doing? Nobody's ever attempted a Videowall this big: 240 monitors stacked like bricks. Corporate docuprop to enhance a sagging image on Wall Street. Me, working for WLC?

"Why me? I'd asked Victor. 'Because Bob thinks you're good with real people, getting them to say things—things they might not know they think they believe.'

"But Bob doesn't even know me.

" 'Oh, he knows you. I told him. So thank me, pal.' "

Tribal Bellies

"The guy had ears, you know? That was the first thing you noticed about him, then the haircut and the skimpy little moustache and the brown hairy suit and running shoes. After that, I realized he was holding a sign with my name on it. I took it from his hands and folded it up. 'I'm Chuck Cyberski. From WLC.'

"I gathered from our conversation into Detroit that Bob had called ahead to inform the PR guys at WLC that I was a god. That a shaft of golden light from Heaven had broken through their dark corporate clouds and I was on it.

"I felt pretty smug. The car rolled through security at the corporate gate. I got my plastic badge.

"I was taken immediately to meet Jack Kraft, head of corporate PR, the man behind my money. 'Please Kraft, if you please no one else,' Victor had told me. 'WLC execs don't know what they want, so give 'em what they need, and the only guy that knows what they need is Kraft.'

"Kraft was small and wrinkled. If anything displeased him, his face twisted immediately into an expression suggesting hot gastric juices squirting into an open bleeding ulcer.

"He took me by the arm to tell me we were going into an important lunch meeting of the top executives of WLC. The men who headed the five divisions and whose blessings I'd need to get anything done. I wasn't to talk, I wasn't to say a word, just sit at the table and he'd introduce me at some point and explain that I was there from God and that it would make the Chairman very happy if they would cooperate with me. 'You don't have to prove yourself. The fact that you're there is proof enough. You are the chosen one. For God's sake, don't say anything that might ruin the impression. Don't say anything at all!' He eyed my hair and I could hear the sizzle of Tabasco eating through his *hepatogastric peritoneum.*

"The janitor unlocked the executive dining room. WLC is a museum to post-atomic architecture. Imported teak inlaid with steel honeycomb hexagonals, aerodynamic sweeps of wood and metal, hard lines and soft contours. Even the china on the table was original fifties. I started to sit at the table, but Kraft shook his head. The chair I'd picked was the unmarked favorite of the Lord of Design. That's how I came to see these executives: lords, dukes, each with his petty fiefdom to defend—each jockeying for position with an eye to the Chairman's seat. Which would be his successor?

"They filed in, all smiles and daggers—bellies out. Here were the top executives of the world's largest corporation, truly movers and shakers who affect the lives of the world, not merely the eight hundred thousand employes (*sic*) of WLC. And they all wore shoddy glen plaids or rumpled worsteds. Six-figure salaries wearing the same suit every day buttoned over aggressive bellies. Moving in a group, in a herd—first to one side of the room, then the other. Odd. All except the Lord of Design who breezed in late wearing light Italian silk with a contrasting pocket pouf. His white hair combed straight back, slender. He always stood in opposition to the others. Wherever the herd paused to graze, he would move around to face them.

"Chuck Cyberski and I stood at the rear while Kraft performed a spider dance. He was everywhere, talking, dancing around the lords, explaining how this wonderful show would turn around the grim Wall St. analysts who'd been hanging crepe over WLC's image and dragging their stock price down. If this show could raise the price of stock by one point—ONE POINT—WLC's value would increase over a billion dollars. All they had to do was change the minds of the most jaded New York stock and industry analysts.

"One lord commented that they would be crying wolf. Hadn't they banged their chests before? Every quarter some high executive held a press conference and announced great things. Why would they believe them this time?

"Because this time there wouldn't be some high executive promising great things. This time there would be real people from WLC, 'workers, engineers, designers—the tiny people. . . .' Kraft danced around the group, invisibly touching the cheek of each division chief.

" 'A sample from each division: Design, Engineering, Manufacturing, Sales, Support. It's like *Star Wars*. We loved the rebels and hated the Empire because we could identify with the warm human rebels, not cold plastic robots. The rebels could've been squid-suckers for all we knew about their philosophy.'

"The lords fell silent and contemplated the extravaganza laid out before them. Twenty million dollars worth of hoopla designed to sucker a few Wall St. flacks. Its centerpiece, the Videowall. The Lord of Manufacturing spoke up. 'But—aren't WE the Empire?'

" 'No! That's where we fool 'em. We show 'em regular people revealing their hopes and fears, sincerely singing the subtle praises of WLC. We've hired a genius—Bob _____. And Bob has sent us a master of emotional engineering, a consummate docu-propagandist, a man with the knack for extracting unrehearsed truths from the mouths of ordinary folks—Bob's handpicked genius. . . .' And I heard my name.

"The lords all looked at me and Kraft's admonishment not to speak leapt forth to block my throat. I meant to just nod, look cool and professional, competent and mature, aloof and slightly intimidating, but there it hung—'Bob's handpicked genius. . . .' I couldn't help it. I grinned a big goofy grin and said, 'Aw, just a SubGenius, really.'

"I could smell the bile boiling into Kraft's *pyloric sphincter* all the way across the room. The lords muttered furtively, eyeing each other to see who would commit first. Do we like it or not?

"Then I felt this rush of wind as these ears passed me. Cyberski waded to the center of the room and began an expository rant. He couldn't resist it, surrounded by royalty, the men who could mold his career—Cyberski made his move. I mean, there he was, this middle-management flunky, stepping out into the circle of Big Boys, puffing out his chest and swinging blindly at the piñata of success. 'It's a brilliant idea! Wall St. expects glitz, but this time the curtain goes up on some Tool & Die talking about how bad press is scaring his family.'

"The lords backed away from Cyberski—physically backed away, creating empty space around him. But he kept on.

" 'I work here. I know we make a good product. We've found a way to beat the Japanese. Sure things were bad, but now they're good. . . .' The lords moved back in. I feel like I've been transported back to the tribes. This wasn't sophisticated corporate strategy, this was the caves."

"But what about the Goddess?" asks Brad.

The Windsor Ballet

"Yeh, yeh. I'm getting to that. So, it's all a big success. The dukes dig the idea. Cyberski saves the day. We eat lunch at this round table with a built-in electric-powered lazy Susan. Every time one lord starts to make a point, his rival hits his button and 'RRrrrrr!' the lazy Susan grinds around distracting everyone. 'Sorry, Marv, just needed another radish.'

"Kraft fires Cyberski right after lunch. Takes his plastic badge on the spot. Then tells me we're going out to celebrate—to the Windsor Ballet.

"Kraft is this old fart, but he gets all pumped up in his champagne Corvette and we drive south to Canada. I'm resigned to an evening of culture. Minutes later I learn that the Windsor Ballet is a street lined with strip joints.

"It's a huge room filled with men in suits. Rock music. Women in bikinis parade through the crowd carrying apple boxes on their heads like native porters. Hold out a bill to one of these women and she plunks down her box, stands on it and dances out of her bikini for the duration of the song. The song ends and the women wriggle back into their suits. Give them another five, they do it all again. Big thing in Canada.

"Kraft and I sit against the wall. He's rubbing his hands together. I drink a Cinci Cream and watch the show. We're next to two Garys from Indianapolis who monopolize this one dancer for an hour, which means she's also dancing right in front of us for free. 'Hyuk, hyuk, yew sure are beootiful. Kin yew change a hundred?'

" 'Mais oui,' sez she. And the Garys hyuk again. One slaps down a picture of Ben and I watch silently as Geneviève counts back a hundred bucks Canadian. With that exchange rate she just cut herself a twenty-five-dollar tip.

" 'Nice counting.' She flashes me a conspiratorial look and starts to dance. Like a whip. By now, Kraft is beside himself and neither one of him looks too hot. He's having trouble getting his lips and his glass in the same area. 'I want to put my feet on you!' he cries suddenly.

"Geneviève smiles sweetly. 'Thank you.'

" 'I'll give you ten thousand dollars!'

" 'Ten thousand dollars? That's SO romantic!'

"The two Garys get indignant and start to shove. Kraft is oblivious to everything but pulling his socks off. I see two lumberjacks in tuxedoes shouldering their way toward us.

" 'Whoops! Time to go, pardner.'

"As I drag Kraft away, Geneviève levels a look at me and says, 'I know you.'

" 'No, probably not. Don't mind us. Just groping, thanks.' I was outside before I realized her French accent had gone.

"The woman at the border kiosk looked down sternly. 'Purpose of visit?'

"Kraft leaned out the window and waggled his tongue, 'The sweet smell of sick sex.' "

Videowall

"That's it?" Brad put down the pen. "You promise a goddess and all I get is a phony French stripper?"

"No. There's more. It was the way she said, 'I know you.' It haunted me.

"Kraft never mentioned the evening again. We did the job. And it was beautiful. Great interviews. Line workers spilling their guts. Tears. Touching shit in Hallmark settings—all shot in one week. Impossible. We did it.

"But post was Monster. Everything I'd feared and more. Two crews, 240 monitors, three tracks of one-inch video, fifteen controllers, two CPUs, two different time codes for Christsake! A battery of technicians from Germany had to be flown in to program it. Nasty petty-bourgeois little fucks who wouldn't work. I'd go out to Mattie's for ribs to keep them happy and these assholes wanted pizza!!"

"Cool out, man," says Brad. "You want a beer?" By now the lunch crowd was gathering. Waitresses doled out plates of chickenfried. But Eliot was distraught.

"See? Don't you see what was happening?" His voice squeezed down to a hiss.

"We were working eighteen-hour days, seven-day weeks in a cold drafty warehouse in Detroit. The only place big enough to set up the wall. It was three days before Christmas and we weren't gonna make it. The pressure was intense. And Kraft keeps dragging executives in to see the show. I told him to stop, that we wouldn't make deadline. But he says he can't refuse his superiors. The show's hot and every executive at

WLC wants to see it before New York, so every hour it's another dog and pony show. The Germans are grumbling, taking passive/aggressive coffee breaks every ten minutes. I tell him there won't be a New York. 'If you make it, there's a bonus.' So we start working twenty-hour days."

"So what'd you care? I mean, if this guy Kraft screwed it up, it's no skin off you."

"It was the bonus. —That's what I'm trying to tell you. A month before I was paying my rent with MasterCard, suddenly I'm rollin' in it. On expense account. If I go to the drugstore for a fuckin' tube of tooth-paste, WLC pays for it. Meals, laundry, bar tabs, new clothes when the weather turns cold. I'm driving down Maple in Birmingham wearing a new leather flight jacket, driving my own rental Corvette with a cel-lular phone. Chicks are turning their heads. Somehow I don't notice that every other Pink on the street is wearing an identical jacket. I stop for espresso and go back to make the crew work till three A.M. Get it?!"

Everybody in the place is staring.

"There are theories that we are just lay-on-the-ground animals pos-sessed by alien intelligence."

"I've heard that," says Brad.

"Or maybe a virus destined to infect the whole universe. I'm a little more optimistic. I like to believe we're the crawling larvae for a new species—that eventually we'll get better. At any rate I was just another helpless hominid seized by fruitless ambition.

"We finished the show at seven thirty A.M. on the morning of the last possible day. At seven forty-five the gorillas were packing the wall into crates for New York."

Life at the Top

"I'm in an expensive new suit midtown.

"The Grand Ballroom of the Waldorf-Astoria is packed with people and product and displays. Dominating the room from the stage is the enor-mous Videowall. All 240 monitors flashing with images and music. Ev-erybody loves it, even the fucking New York press corps applauds and they don't do that. All the executives are running to grab their *Wall St. Urinal*s each morning before the show to see how much the market price is up. The Lord of Design comes up to me on the floor and pumps my hand, tells me he likes my suit. Flashbulbs and canapés. I need some air.

"A black woman in a fur coat grabs my arm and offers me a blowjob. No thanks. She wants to know why not and opens her coat enough for me to see that she must be trying to earn money for the rest of a wardrobe. I pull away and walk.

"I'm tired. Another woman huddles with a cup in a doorway. It's been a week of six-hundred-dollar expense-account dinners that end at two

A.M. with empty Rémy bottles on the table. Cab rides that are drunken blurs of steam and slush and blue police lights.

"I lay in bed at the Waldorf and watch channel 23. Geisha-to-Go. Al Goldstein flipping the bird at the camera and glowering 'Fuck you.' Room service Haut-Brion 1970. Four hundred fifty dollars. Who cares? Money's no object. It's the world's largest corporation. Page one of *The New York Times* runs a big article about the fabulous show. Page seventeen of *The New York Times* runs a tiny article about another WLC plant closing in the Midwest. Belt tightening. Streamlining. Line workers spilling their guts. Tears."

Pink Turns to Blue

"Kraft was on the phone. 'We did it, Eliot. Big success. Wait till the Wall St. analysts see it, tomorrow. We'll be home free. Let's celebrate. I know a great little spot.'

"Great little spot. Times Square. Fifteen bucks to get in, dank, dark, smoky, smelly—hard to tell if half the dancers are male or female. Not that I really cared. It was one of those places where a narrow runway cuts into a sea of hollow sallow somber faces.

"Kraft hung twenties in front of our seats and immediately started slamming scotch. By the fourth dancer he was on his fifth drink. The dancer noticed the heavy currency and the determined drinking style and began to hang close. Dark and pale she strutted along the rail. She made deep eye contact with Kraft and he began to sweat. She squatted down in front of him so he could see it all. I noticed a pimple on his neck oozing into his tight collar. She leaned forward so her breasts dangled an inch in front of his face. He inhaled and I could feel the rush that shuddered him.

" 'What's a matter, sweetie? It's no good tryin' ta drown your troubles.'

" 'I'm NOT trying to drown my troubles,' said Kraft. 'I'm just hosing them off.'

" 'Yeh, a lot of people are having heavy aspects now, but that's the way it goes.'

"A couple of bikers hollered that they were paying money too, and she took her bruises down to their end of the rail—a one-woman rendition of 'Stags at Bay.'

" 'What a babe!' exulted Kraft. 'You think I'd be crazy to see if she wants to come back to the hotel with us?'

" 'No, no, I don't think you're crazy. I think you're outa your fuckin' mind!' That drew a look. I'd never spoken to him like that before. A client, an older man. He decided I was joking and laughed a laugh that sprayed spit and scotch.

"The Beam was kicking in and I was experiencing one of the seven warning signs of confusion. I'd come to the belated conclusion that I really didn't like this guy. Kraft was a manipulative pig and I was doing his bidding. So fuck me.

"I don't want you to get the idea I'm above this sort of thing. I got the dog in me. I got the hound. I like money and I like women. But I'm not indiscriminating. I was feeling sorry I'd done this job. Sorry I'd helped the Conspiracy. I should have stayed pure and lived like Diogenes under a tub in the street. But no, they suckered me and I suckered Wall St. Hey, that's what chumps are for. Bring on the BIG TIT. Who am I to give Kraft shit over his taste in women? Or his ruthless abuse of my crew to ensure his own secure standing with the corporation? I cracked the whip. Like that mercenary I interviewed in Scottsdale said, 'I have no home, no family, no principles—what else would I kill for but money?' What am I crying about? The world's my fucking oyster . . . the world's my clam.

"I was about to suggest we head over to the Oyster Bar at Grand Central when I looked up and saw her. The next dancer. She wasn't the most beautiful woman I'd ever seen, but there was something about her. Something that made me want to invest more than a dollar on the rail. —One of those high-heeled, low-risk Municipal Blondes—yet she seemed curiously familiar.

"She strutted the rail through the first song, wearing a filmy negligee. I'm thinking, Intimate apparel/imminent peril—mere coincidence? Her second number was a hard rocker and she started to dance—like a whip. Geneviève! I hung a twenty over the rail and she danced over like a trout drawn to an elk-hair caddis. 'What's your name?' I asked.

" 'Heather,' she said and started to dance away.

" 'Not Geneviève?'

"She turned and leveled her look at me. 'I know you.'

"Kraft wasn't getting this. He'd been too drunk in Windsor and he was too drunk now. She strutted off, the pink light molding her haunches like peaches by Monet.

"When her set was over she went round to pick her dollars off the floor and rail.

"Kraft was all over himself, a slavering railstalker. 'Look at the bitch—naked, groveling on her hands and knees picking up dollar bills.'

"I dunno. For some reason that just rankled my ass. That was it. 'And what do you think you do for a living?'

" 'What?!'

" 'Come on, you think that what we do is any different? You and me, Kraft, on our hands and knees pickin' up the dollars. At least she knows it.'

" 'You sound like a man who doesn't like his job. Maybe you should just trot on back to Hollywood now, Mr. Videowall. Your work's all done. I think we can handle it just fine without you. I guess you just didn't want that bonus.'

" 'Oh, no, not the bonus again—the *bonus contendae*. You've been hanging this bonus over my head for weeks. Why don't you just shove your bonus up your bone-ass?' And I shoved off into a cold drizzle."

Times²

"I went over to 47 St. Photo and spent another wad of worthless currency on a spiffy new Casio color television about the size of a Chihuahua's dick. I was walking down the street watching Lloyd Lindsay Young when the power went out all through my head. I felt the street go soft beneath me. The B-big R-rubber Hammer came down.

"The next thing I remember is somebody saying, 'It's down already, but you might have to kick it a little.' Big Fucking Hammer. Somebody was going through my pockets.

"Somebody was trying to pick me up. 'Are you all right?' she was asking.

" 'I dunno,' I said. 'I might have some trouble dancing.'

"I felt like the winner of the Mr. Physical Wreck contest. It was dark and the drizzle had matured into a freezing rain. She held me under her left arm as we walked down the street. I was aware that she smelled really nice. She helped me into a corner deli and sat me down. It wasn't until she turned back to me with a cup of coffee that I recognized her. 'Geneviève—I mean, Heather!'

" 'Connie.' She smiled sheepishly. 'Where are you staying?'

" 'The Waldorf.' I put powdered whitener in my coffee and it set like plaster.

" 'Let's go,' she said. 'We can walk.'

" 'Let's take a cab.' I reached for my wallet, but it was gone. 'Oh yeah. Hey, where's my tie? I don't believe it, they stole my fucking tie.'

"We walked to the Waldorf in needles of freezing rain. The grand lobby was full of Spanish tourists in gold lamé and big men in plaid coats. Tonight's show was for the dealers. That's right, tomorrow's the big event, the Wall St. jocks. Make it or break it time. People were staring at us. Connie didn't look that out of place in her black leather micro. Half the Spaniards were dressed the same way. I caught a glimpse of myself in the Sulka shop window. One eye was swelling shut and blood had soaked into my collar from where I'd been sapped. Nice. I went to the concierge's desk. 'Room thirteen-oh-three, please.'

"The concierge checked her list. 'I show that room vacant.'

" 'No, that's my room. I'm with the WLC show.'

"The manager arrived on velvet soles and whispered to me that I'd been checked out and my bill settled. I could pick up my luggage from the bell captain.

" 'Well, I'm sure there's been some mistake,' I said. 'As long as the room's still vacant let's just put it on my credit card for tonight and we'll straighten it out in the morning.' I reached for my wallet and . . . 'Oh, shit. Look, as you can see, I've just been mugged and they took my wallet. I don't suppose you could . . .'

" 'No, I'm sorry,' smiles the manager.

" 'Oh, wait. I've got cash in my suitcase. Let me just get it.' But the bell captain needed to see some ID. The wind was so strong that the revolving door was turning on its own. I'd come up against a wall of solid jackson.

"Connie lived in SoHo. We took the subway and trekked up to her ten-by-ten-foot flat. She tried to cheer me, 'Up and down, up and down, life is like a toilet lid.'

"John Lennon was dead. And the strangest part was that I heard it from Howard Cosell. That's how strange things are. And it only took eight years for it to bum me out.

"She tried to be sympathetic. 'Lots of great artists die young. Ludwig Schnorr Von Carolsfeld. He was a German Wagnerian tenor who died at the age of twenty-nine.'

" 'He probably strangled introducing himself.' She looked crushed. 'I'm sorry. I've been an asshole for the past few months, I guess I can stop now. —How come you left Canada?'

" 'They wouldn't let me play my records at the ashram.'

" 'Ludwig?' She nodded. 'What kind of ashram was it?' Why did I ask that?! Oh, no! Now I was going to have to listen to hours of kook theories and join in strange chants and listen to lectures about how I should never again go to Kansas City and eat ribs at Rosedale's because the karma of my ancestors would never get clear. How was I going to justify my belief that the basic structure of human culture is binary (thus potentially digital) or, as the Rev. Buck Nakid had so clearly stated it, US vs. THEM? I gritted my teeth.

" 'I was in the Cult of "Connie's" Panties. That's where I took my name. —You want a beer or anything? I've got some Hope in the fridge.'

"I was stunned. She returned with a frosty glass of the rarest brew out of Rhode Island and sat down next to me.

" 'Y-you're SubGenius?'

" 'Born in Dallas. Rocked in the cradle of the cult. You're kind of cute,' she said leaning near. 'How do you feel . . . ?'

" 'Spontaneous remission is my middle name.' We met in a lip-twisting kiss that seemed to last for hours. The end of her nose was moist and pink when we surfaced.

"The sleet drilled rudiments on her window all night. Straight rolls, paradiddles, ratamacues and flams. I could swear it was double-stroking flamadiddles in the wee hours. I didn't care. We had a rhythm section all our own.

"At nine o'clock we were at Dante's trying to figure out how to get my suitcase back over doubles. I still felt bad. 'I guess I thought I'd earn enough on this job to not have to worry about being such a suckwad the next time. Do my own work. I expected a pot of gold at the end of the rainbow.'

" 'Maybe when you reach the rainbow's end, you just find out the rainbow's over.'

" 'Yeah, maybe. But it still bugs me. I helped those guys pull the wool over America's eyes. Especially today. They're going to screen my show for the Wall St. heavies this morning at ten and . . . Hey, what time is it?' "

Waldorf Hysteria

"We caught a cab uptown. I still had my security pass for the show. The financial press and market analysts were just filing in when I made my way up the back stairs to the mezzanine where all the equipment was. 'They think they're cruisin'. They think they can run this without me. They don't know just how complicated this is.'

"I made my way through a maze of cable to the control area. There was no one at the CPU keyboard. Let's see. If I delete the primary sequence on the A track, everything will drop out of sync across all fifteen control units. Chaos. In one stroke, I could achieve both liberation and revenge.

"I was just about to type in the initializing commands when I heard Kraft. 'Stop that man!'

"Oh shit. I banged my shin hopping over the chair and wiggled through the heavy brocade curtains that lined the mezzanine balconies. A security guard came up behind me and another one through the next set of curtains. There was only one way to go—over the balcony. I slid down the heavy drapery onto the ballroom floor where several other security guards were converging on me. I headed for a side door into the Crystal Room, through the rehearsal for the International Debutante Ball where young men in Confederate gray were goose-stepping with the Stars and Bars while rabbit-toothed belles in crinoline giggled and tapped their fans. Into the Orchid Room where a lavish Italian wedding was in progress. The three security guards were close behind. I ran downstairs and slammed through double doors into the kitchen and ducked behind a prep table. A long-haired chef's assistant was sharpening knives behind me. He stared down at me and I said, 'Shhh.' He was wearing a red SubGenius T-shirt with a smiling "Bob." Man, did that look good to me. 'Help me. I'm a reverend in the Church. You gotta help me get back upstairs, then call the Pope of New York, tell him what's going on. He'll know what to do.'

"He pulled a laundry basket of dirty towels over. 'Get in.'

"I could feel him wheeling me down the hall. I heard the service elevator whirr. The doors opened and I was wheeled out. I heard him say. 'He's in here.'

"The towels came off and there were Kraft and three apes. A Pink is a Pink—no matter what his T-shirt says.

"The show started as scheduled. I was in the back in a chair surrounded by five goons. Two of them had a hand on my shoulders. The Chairman got up and welcomed the guests in his high-pitched Elmer Fudd voice explaining that the show represented the latest technologies of WLC. They had come out of their slump and were ready to face the future with 'world-class products. But don't take it from me. Listen to the people who build 'em. The tiny people that are so important to WLC.'

"Yeah, I thought. Like those thirty thousand 'tiny' people you laid off in Ohio the week before Christmas while you and your cronies took profit-sharing bonuses.

"I had no one but myself to blame. I'd done my job too well. Emotional engineering. Swell a chord, cut away to the kid. Men and women smiling on the assembly line. I'm scum.

"The lights went down. The music started. Pow! That big attention-getting hook followed by a crystalline ascending arpeggio. And images, moving, flashing, turning. The press corps was rapt. Next it would mellow into a moving human tale. Only it didn't. There was a loud buzz and the next facial close-up had the guy's eye in the middle of his chin. Then it was all eyes, then all chins. The signal scrambled the images everywhere. Then another buzz and the screens went black. All 240 of them, except for number 64 which was flickering green. A spiral of blue smoke rose.

"The Chairman was doing half pirouettes on the dais muttering, 'Sorry, sorry, sorry.' Kraft turned to me and said, 'If you're behind this I'll make sure your great-great-grandchildren will still owe us money.'

" 'I'm sure they will anyway.'

"A technician ran up to Kraft. 'What is it?'

" 'We're not sure, but it looks like a power surge in the line from Con Ed. A fifty-megawatt spike showed up on our meters.'

"The Wall St. guys were starting to fidget.

" 'How long?'

" 'I don't know, sir. It may need to be reprogrammed. The disk was fried.'

" 'Eliot.' He turned to me with true fear in his eyes. 'Can you?'

" 'Ich kann nicht Englisch sprechen, muthafucka!'

" 'Please, Eliot. I'll give you the bonus—five thousand dollars.'

" 'And . . . ?'

" 'What? Anything! How soon can it be up?'

" 'Another ten thousand in cash and two first-class tickets to L.A. Before I work.'

"The Chairman was striding over. 'Kraft! What the hell is going on here? If you can't . . .'

"Kraft looked like a boiled shrimp. 'A power surge, sir. An unavoidable accident. B-but Eliot can get us back up in . . .'

" 'Oh, yes. The famous Eliot. Bob's genius.'

"Kraft threw me a pleading glance. 'I need my bag.'

"Kraft snapped his fingers and one of the goons raced off to fetch my things from the bell captain. Another ran off to the concierge for my tickets and cash.

" 'Gentlemen, er, and ladies,' the chairman was saying, 'we've experienced a power surge from Con Ed and regretfully will have to—from no fault of our own—reschedule your screening till this evening.'

"The midday crowd of shareholders was filing in. Old spinsters and pensioners, geeks from the outback and their rickety families all gawking at the space-age displays.

"I looked down on them from the control balcony as I rummaged through my bag. There it was, the backup program disk I'd made in Detroit. I guess the Germans never thought of that. Their technology was infallible. 'Why waste time making a backup?' Gunther had asked. 'It's in the hard disk.' Con Ed, that's why.

"It was too brilliant. I could see the hand of "Bob" in this. Kraft handed me the bonus check—five thousand dollars—then the airplane tickets, then the cash—ten thousand in tens.

" 'How long?' I could hear the acid sizzling in his gut.

" 'I dunno, Jack.' I peeled five thousand off the roll of cash and slipped it in my pocket. 'How long does it take a Nazi to shovel snow off the driveway to Hell?' I ripped up the bonus check. His eyes bugged. 'Hey everybody!' I shouted to the crowd of stockholders. 'Extra dividend! Pull the wool over your own eyes!' And I heaved the wad of tens to flutter to the floor.

"Pandemonium! Even the goons jumped the rail. 'Look at 'em,' I said. 'Pickin' up those dollars off the floor.' Kraft stared at me in torn fury, then he too went over the rail.

"I strolled out to Connie on the street and the doorman hailed a cab. But before I climbed in, I took the backup disk and Frisbeed it into an updraft; it sailed down Lex."

Sterno Butchwax

"We went to JFK. I don't remember anything past that."

Brad paused from his transcription. The lunch crowd had gone. "Like I said, last night you were hammering the Dant pretty hard. You were ranting about the Stars and Bars being the new American swastika, and the Conspiracy, and the bleeding sword of Islam, and how television is the big butter knife that spreads a poisonous peanut butter of smooth homogenous culture across the U.S.A."

"Is that all?"

"You said that three separate lone assassins converged coincidentally at Dealey Plaza. That 'Show 'em what they've won, Johnny!' ought to be in Latin on the dollar bill. You kinda spooked the customers."

"But you said I was with a lady. What happened to her?"

"Well, you had a bit of a disagreement. And she hit you over the head with a bottle and left."

"But why?"

Behind him. "Because you were a ranting assaholic and the Blackjack Jesus told me to."

Eliot turned on his stool. "Connie, you came back."

"Of course I came back. I missed you. I had bad dreams. —We're in grave danger."

"Aw, dreams don't mean anything. When you're asleep your brain goes out of control."

"Not for me. A Connie's dreams are admissible as evidence in a court of law. —How's your head? I'm sorry I had to hit you."

"I'm okay. I feel a whole lot more like I do now than I did when I got here. You had lunch?"

She shook her head.

And they sat down to big ol' chickenfried steaks with cream gravy and mashed potatoes. And Eliot wondered at how the good ones always leave bits stuck between your teeth and how beautiful Connie was backlit in the river light and he wondered about the trout, those big Snake River cutthroats lunkered down in mysterious currents in the undercuts and he marveled as he realized that not only were his sins forgiven but that he had the SLACK to sin again.

"So why did we come to Idaho?" he asked her.

"That's what my dream was about. I dreamt I had a new hairdo—a flaming flattop. You said the spirit of the Conspiracy lay at the heart of the Aryan Nations. That Nazis guard the entrance to the Hollow Earth. I am to be a torch to light the way—I mean, my hairdo is. You've come to summon the trout manitou to aid in their destruction."

Eliot stared at the river. One of the doctors paused in his casting to relight his pipe. "I was afraid it was something like that."

But that is another story.

Lewis Shiner

STOMPIN' AT THE SAVOY

What I really need, Guy thought, is to duck into a Porta-Santa and blow off some of these bad vibes.

WLCD, "the easy-watching channel," blared at him from a video store across the street. He'd sweated clear through his collarless pink shirt, and burglar alarms were going off in his brain. One of the familiar red-and-green booths stood open and inviting at the next corner. Guy lurched inside and slammed the door.

"Hello, Guy," said Santa, scanning Guy's ID bracelet. The white-bearded face smiled down from the CRT on the back wall and winked. "How are you?"

"Pretty shitty, Santa. I'm really paranoid at the moment."

"I see. What are your feelings about being paranoid?"

Guy wrestled with that for a few seconds and then said, "I think that's the stupidest question I ever heard."

"I see. Why do you feel it's the stupidest question you ever heard?"

"Look, Santa, there's three guys back there been following me all afternoon. Business suits, mirror glasses, pointy shoes, the whole bit, you know?" He rubbed nervously at a scrape on his plasteel jacket. Guy loved that jacket and he really cared about the way he looked, not like those other assles at work who'd wear anything they saw on WLCD. "I think I lost them, but I don't even understand what's going down, you know? First the computer goes apeshit at work, then—"

"One moment please," Santa said. The chubby face on the screen seemed to think something over, and then the voice came back. "Okay, you're Guy Zendales, right?"

"Right," Guy said. Santa's voice suddenly had a lot more personality than a moment before.

"You said something about a computer?"

"Yeah, I, like, work at Modern Sounds, you know? And I was ringing up this sale when all of a sudden some wires must have got crossed up. All this data just starts pouring out all over the screen, you know? Filled up a whole floppy that was supposed to have our daily sales records on it."

"You got it with you? Can I look at it?"

"Sure," Guy said. He stuck the diskette in the slot next to the screen.

"Hmmm," Santa said. "This is very interesting. Do you know what this is?"

Suddenly Guy was twigging bad vibes again. He trusted Santa, of course. Just like that deal with priests and confessionals, only Santa was for everybody. The ads on TV told you it was okay, "Get it off your chest . . . tell Santa."

But Guy didn't like the way Santa's voice had changed. Why should Santa want to look at a bunch of receipts from a music store?

"Uh, listen, Santa, man, I don't know *what* the fuck this is about, okay? I really think I better split now."

"Oh, no, Guy, wait just a second. I've got something I want to . . . uh . . . show you. . . ."

Guy heard footsteps running toward the booth.

"Just stay where you are," Santa said.

Guy snatched the diskette and stuck it back inside his jacket, just as the pounding started on the door of the booth.

Guy's vision blurred as the adrenaline hit him. "Holy shit!" he yelled. He lashed out instinctively with his reinforced shoes and the side of the booth split from floor to ceiling. Hunching his shoulders, he dove through the opening and knocked a man in a suit and sunglasses to the Astroturf sidewalk.

Still shouting, Guy ran into the middle of the street.

Hondas zipped around him on either side, the drivers squeezing their brakes and shouting at him. Guy flinched and stood paralyzed for a second, then felt himself lifted by the elbows and carried across the street.

"Shit!" cried a voice behind him that had to belong to a suit and sunglasses. "Muties! Hey, you assles! Come back here with him!"

Guy remained unnaturally rigid, afraid to even turn his head. He watched numbly as he was swept into a deserted building and down a flight of concrete stairs.

Finally his terror began to subside and he risked a quick glance to his left.

Shit, he thought, snapping his eyes away. Muties, all right. Guy had heard stories about the so-called Law of Genetic Conservation, that for every genetically engineered "improvement" something else would go hideously wrong. The mutie on Guy's left could have been Exhibit A in the trial that had outlawed the whole field of genetic research.

The near side of its head was as swollen and lumpy as an organlegger's sack of cut-rate eyeballs. The mutie's own eyes were about two inches out of line, the right one protruding a good half inch or so. The rest of its body was fairly normal, except for the hunched back and the enormous hands and feet.

At the bottom of the steps they began running through a tiled hallway, then down a wooden ramp and into a rough-cut tunnel that was black from years of soot. Guy listened almost hopefully for footsteps following them.

There weren't any.

Guy had never smelled rat urine before, but he was sure he was smelling it now. It's the subway, Guy thought. As if it wasn't bad enough to be chased by assles in mirror sunglasses and kidnapped by muties, they had to bring him here.

He began to really get frightened.

The muties were slowing down and turning into a side tunnel. Guy could see the nose of the mutie on his right in his peripheral vision, the size and color of an unripened cucumber. What next? he wondered.

One more turn and they were in a long, narrow room, done in white tile on all the surfaces. Greasy daylight filtered in through a reticulated plastic skylight. From the rusted pipes that still protruded at waist height Guy could tell that the place had been a rest room once, long enough ago to have accumulated a thick layer of dust and cobwebs, but not long enough to have lost the acrid odor.

Finally he had to stop looking at the walls and face the other inhabitants of the room.

At least ten muties lounged against the walls, in a range of shapes and sizes, but in the center of them was the Bull Goose Mutie, the ugliest thing Guy had ever seen. Empty breasts dangled from its enormous, Buddhalike chest. Faceted, insectile eyes stared out of a skull shaped like a rotting pumpkin. Its matchstick arms ended in waxy, serrated fingers, and its legs folded too many times under its huge weight. The final, ghastly touch was provided by a smoldering Dr. Graybow pipe in the raw wound of its mouth.

"Guy Zendales," the Big Mutie said in a squeaky cartoon voice. "We have decided to render you our assistance."

"Terrific," Guy said. "Thanks a lot. Why don't you, like, give me a phone number and I'll get back to you."

"Give him Slack," the Big Mutie said, and Guy was set on the floor to brush ineffectually at the wrinkles in his jacket. "The govt agents," the squeaky voice went on, "were going to kill you, you know."

"Kill?" Guy said. "Me?" One of the muties correctly diagnosed his expression and brought him a folding chair. Guy sat in it and massaged the muscle spasms in the backs of his legs.

"They must destroy the information on that diskette of yours. Because you've seen that information, they must destroy you as well."

"But . . . but . . . I've never done anything to the govt. . . ."

The Big Mutie, Guy realized, was attempting a bitter smile. "Neither have we. Yet they have systematically attempted to exterminate us for years, despite the fact that it was their experiments which produced us."

"Why me? What did *I* do?"

"There was a glitch in the govt computer and it accidentally dumped two hundred ninety-seven sectors of classified information into your store's system. I believe the file was called . . . BLOOPERS."

"BLOOPERS," Guy echoed. None of this seemed to fit together. He remembered a video he'd seen once, about a patient in a mental hospital. It showed a woman sitting at a gray metal table, setting out lines and patterns with paper clips and pencils and scraps of paper. Tears ran slowly out of the woman's eyes. At the time he'd wanted to cry himself, without really knowing why. Now he thought he was beginning to understand.

"Perhaps we should explain," the Big Mutie said. "The govt agents would have destroyed all of us long ago if it weren't for our special genetic programming. Bob005, for example"—it pointed to the one with the gigantic nose—"is especially strong and fast. Bob667"—here it pointed to the one with the lopsided head—"was adapted for increased intuitive and precognitive powers. He anticipated your problem and enabled us to rescue you."

"It's not that I'm not grateful or anything," Guy said, "but what's in it for you?"

"We will never be free until the govt falls. We are always looking for a weapon against them, and that diskette may be the one we're looking for." When it moved its head, dozens of identical reflections darted across its faceted eyes, making Guy's stomach turn precariously.

"Look, I'd love to help, but I have to have the other data that's on here. I need to get this thing unfucked and sent in to the main office or I'll lose my job."

The Big Mutie sighed. "All right. Suppose we get you safely to a computer. Will you at least let us look at the BLOOPER file?"

"Sure," Guy said. "Anything you want. Just get me out of here, okay?"

The Big Mutie seemed hurt. "Are we that ugly? Can you not stand to be around us even long enough for us to help you?"

Guy started to lift his hands in denial, then let them drop. "Well, yeah," he said. "I guess that about sums it up."

They refused to let him go home. "It's too dangerous," the Big Mutie said, "and that's that."

Finally Guy suggested the apt of some friends, Sam and Janet Evening. He had a moment of compunction at involving them, but didn't see any other choice. They had a computer and their apt wasn't too far away. Bob667 went with them, leading the way through the twisting subway tunnels.

"Are you guys all named Bob?" Guy asked.

"That's right. It's in honor of our first prophet. He was a twentieth-century salesman named J. R. "Bob" Dobbs. He was the First Mutie."

"Oh," Guy said. He didn't hold much with religions, even inherently bogus ones, but the idea that the muties had a hero made them seem more . . . well, human. He regretted what he'd said to the Big Mutie about how ugly they were. Actually they weren't so bad as long as you didn't really look right at them or anything.

Once they got to street level Guy took Bob667 to Sam and Janet's apt. Night had fallen and Guy felt strangely lonely and uncomfortable. I'm on the lamb, he told himself, trying out the hopelessly antiquated words.

Janet answered the door. "Hi, Guy," she said. "This is a pleasant— Look out! Behind you!"

Guy started to turn, then remembered. "Oh, yeah. This is, uh, Bob667. We were wondering . . . can we borrow your computer for a minute?"

"You mean that thing, too? Yuck."

"It's really important, Janet."

"Well, if you say so. Sam! Guy's here! Wait till you see what he brought over. . . ."

Sam glanced up from the pornographic home video he was watching. A couple of the performers looked familiar to Guy; probably neighbors of Sam and Janet's. "Make yourself at home," Sam said, and went back to the TV.

Guy slipped his diskette into the computer and punched up a printout of BLOOPERS. Bob667 stood behind him as the printer zinged out the lines of data. Sam and Janet stayed in the other room, talking quietly to each other and pointing occasionally at the mutie.

"Do those names mean what I think they mean?" Guy asked.

"I'm afraid I really don't know what they are."

Guy showed the printout to Sam and Janet. "It's a list of the worst TV shows of all time, right?" Sam offered.

"Not all of them, though," Janet said. "Just the successful ones. What do those dollar amounts beside the titles mean?"

"I think," Guy said, "they mean I'm in a shitload of trouble."

"So what you and the mutie here are trying to tell me," Sam said, "is that the govt has been subsidizing bad TV?"

Janet looked from Guy to Bob667 and back again. "Isn't that a little . . . well . . . silly?"

"If you'd told me about all this yesterday," Guy said, "I would probably have agreed with you. Today I'm not so sure."

"It's not just the shows," Bob667 said. He slurred the s's even more than usual when he got excited. "They were fixing the ratings, too, which means they were more or less forcing the competition to produce shows just as bad. You get a vicious circle going, and after a while it's not just TV anymore. People are getting trained not to think, not to make decisions, not to take anything seriously. What we have to do now is decide what we're going to do about it."

"I don't really see what the big deal is anyway," Janet complained. "Who cares about all this stuff? Why are they hunting Guy down? Who are we going to blab to, anyway?"

"You don't understand the govt," Bob667 explained. "There's hardly anybody working there anymore, just a lot of paranoid programmers and a lot of interconnected computers."

"What about all those people we elect?" Sam asked. "What do they do?"

"Sit at home, mostly, and watch TV. There's nothing left *for* them to do. The computers do it all."

"Well fuck it, then," Guy said. "I'll just clean up the floppy and send it in, like I was going to, and—"

"Just a second," Bob667 interrupted, holding up a decayed-looking finger. "The govt agents are closing in."

A fist hammered on the door.

Janet switched the TV to hall monitor and glanced quickly away. "Yuck," she said. "It's another one of *them.*"

Guy opened the door for Bob005. "The govt agents are closing in," it said. "The Hi Bob sent me to warn you. If you don't come with us and let us hide you, they're going to catch you. We can't stop them."

"Didn't we go through all that this afternoon?"

"Look," said Bob667, "if you won't let us hide, can we at least try something else? Nobody's ever had a chance to get on the govt's computer before. They may just burn that diskette of yours, but there's a chance they'll want to look at it first, to at least make sure they have the right one. Let me copy a virus on there."

"A virus?"

It took a diskette out of a fold in its toga—or a fold in its chest, Guy wasn't sure which. "It is our sacred bulldada in program form—a self-concatenating string loop. We've spent a long time working this up, for just such an opportunity."

Guy hesitated. "How much more trouble would this get me in?" he asked, but Bob667 apparently misunderstood.

"A good attitude," it said, popping the second diskette into a drive and typing a command. "Are you sure you won't come with us?" it asked again as it nodded, took out Guy's diskette and handed it back to him.

"I'm sure."

"Ahem," Sam said. "Did someone say they were 'closing in'?"

"Uh, yeah," Guy said. "Apparently."

Janet yawned widely. "Gee. Really sleepy all of a sudden."

"Gosh," Sam said. "Look at the time."

"I'll just walk you downstairs," Guy said to the muties.

"Don't mean to rush you," Janet said, "but . . ."

*   *   *

The three of them stopped on a street corner near the subway entrance. "I don't really understand why you won't come with us," Bob667 said.

"It's like this: If I came with you, that would mean I believe all this shit you told me. I'd have to be crazy to believe that. So I'd rather just go to work and pretend that everything's okay."

"Well, all right then."

Guy felt strangely reluctant to let them go. He was certain he would never see either of them again, less certain why that idea should bother him. "So," he asked. "If they do catch this virus thing, what happens then?"

"I don't know. Maybe the end of the govt. If so, that takes a lot of pressure off of us. I'm not sure anybody else would notice."

"I would," Guy said.

"Yes, well, good luck then," said Bob667. The two muties walked away, and between one streetlight and the next they were gone.

The govt agents picked Guy up a block later. He was wandering aimlessly, trying to make up his mind where to go. The agents, Guy noticed, wore their mirror glasses even in the dark, even as they tossed him lightly in the back of their Honda.

During the trip one of them lifted the diskette out of Guy's jacket. "Hey," Guy said. "You can't—"

"Shut up, assle," the agent said.

Guy shut up.

He kept expecting them to stop the Honda and throw him off a bridge, or take him into an alley and shoot him, but instead they led him to the basement of the midtown govt complex and handed him a stack of change. "Machines there, bathroom there," the agent said, and left.

The place looked and smelt abandoned. Pipes gridded the ceiling, oily water stained the floor, and plastic crates lay scattered everywhere. At one end of the room stood a big-screen TV, a ratty couch, and a wheelchair containing an old woman.

"You ever watch this channel?" she asked. "I watch it sometimes. It's not too bad."

Guy walked over to her. "Who are you?"

"Sit down, sit down," she said. "Or if you're going to talk, do it in the other room."

Guy went to the door and pushed against it. Its surface was devoid of handles to shake or locks to pick; some kind of electronic seal held it in place. Guy bought himself a Coke and went back to sit on the couch.

The woman was watching WLCD, "the browsing station." A lot of football players chased a slippery ball to the accompaniment of synthesized bassoons. The station cut to the WLCD logo, then ran two and a half minutes of pie-fight scenes from old black-and-white comedies. Then back to the logo, a big dance number, the logo, and a man in a white coat talking very seriously for a minute and a half about hemorrhoids.

After a short piece on crippled orphans, the old lady said, "Makes you sad, don't it?"

Guy thought about the floppy with the BLOOPERS file on it. Was this what the govt had been shooting for? He wondered how much money they'd quietly put into superstation WLCD. How perfect it was for them—a station you never had to turn off, because if you didn't like what was on you only had to wait a minute or two. No complicated plots to follow, no characters to get mixed up, no difficult shadings of emotion.

Guy tried to lure the old woman into conversation, but she refused to talk in more than three- or four-second bursts. He learned that her name was Mildred, but nothing else about her, or the reason he was being kept with her in the basement.

Trying to ignore the TV proved beyond Guy's will. He had nothing else to do in that basement but drink Cokes and eat candy bars, and in that suffocating grayness the splash of big-screen color drew his eyes irresistibly.

He was able to doze off for a few minutes at a time, but a sudden fanfare from the set would wake him up. The old woman never seemed to sleep.

Finally he decided to risk the old woman's wrath and tried to switch the thing off. "Hey!" she shouted at him. "Whatcha doing there? Get away!" The power knob was frozen, as was the channel selector.

"Nothing," Guy said. "Never mind."

"This is a good program," she said. "I like this one."

"Okay," Guy said. "Okay."

He soon lost his sense of time. His watch was still running, but he didn't know if the numbers were A.M. or P.M. He'd told that new girl at the store, the one with the soft, mobile lower lip, that he would call her this weekend. He didn't know if the weekend had come or gone.

He began to stay asleep longer, wake up less fully. He wished he had clean clothes and a razor. He wondered about Bob667's virus program and decided that it had failed because nobody had come to rescue him.

Then one day he couldn't remember the last time the old woman had said anything. He struggled up from the couch and waved a hand in front of her inert face. No response. He felt her arm for a pulse, and though he couldn't find one he noticed the flesh was still warm and soft. As he let go of her hand it knocked the afghan off her lap, revealing a mass of circuitry.

An andie, he thought. No wonder.

He ran to the door and began pounding on it. "Hey! Hey, somebody, let me out of here!"

The door drifted open under his hands.

*   *   *

The building was deserted. Chairs lay haphazardly around the offices and glass was broken out of the doors. Guy tapped on one of the CRTs, but it was as dead as the old woman downstairs.

The programmers had obviously panicked when the computer went down. So, Guy thought, no more govt.

He compared his watch to the bright sunlight outside and decided it was eleven in the morning. He went home, took a long shower and walked to work.

Isabel Necessary, his district manager, wanted to fire him at first. She couldn't believe that Guy could have lost the diskette *and* missed five days' work without phoning in.

"I was in an accident," Guy lied cheerfully. "I lost my memory."

"I'll bet," Isabel sneered. "You were probably just lying around watching TV."

But in the end she let him stay. Probably, Guy thought, because she couldn't find anybody else for the money who'd wear decent clothes.

He stopped at Sam and Janet's place after work, but they'd moved away, with no forwarding address. The new tenant, a middle-aged man in a bathrobe, had WLCD running in the background when he answered the door.

"Sorry I can't help you," he told Guy. He had one eye still on the TV as Guy thanked him and left.

Standing on the street, Guy realized it was the first time he'd been outside in recent memory without something terrible happening to him. The Astroturf sidewalk felt firm and springy beneath his feet; he was clean and nicely dressed again. He should have been happy, but somehow he felt like he'd missed out on something, as if he'd awakened and found himself inexplicably old and frail.

He decided he really ought to talk it over with Santa. He crossed the street and went into the booth on the corner.

The Porta-Santa was dead.

Santa's face was frozen on the screen, halfway into a wink. One eye was almost closed and his mouth was twisted in what looked like a grimace of pain.

Guy stood there for half an hour, watching the distorted face, waiting for some kind of message. It's not coming, he realized at last. It's like the mutie said. The revolution happened, but nobody noticed. They were all home watching TV.

"So long, Santa," Guy said.

He shut the door of the booth and shuffled away down the green plastic lawn of the sidewalk.

Michael Peppe
THE REAL STORY

"**B**ob" wended his way through the huge computer-packed office, dodging frantic clerks at almost every step, and ducked inside the glass-walled inner office. In its center was a large desk covered with huge piles of paper, several ashtrays heaped with butts, some Styrofoam coffee cups surrounded by chains of brown ring stains, and a half-dozen telephones, all of them ringing. In front of it all was a cheap plastic nameplate, which read

Alm. "God," C.E.O.,
Existence

Barely visible behind it, and below a drifting battlefield haze of smoke, was a huge balding fat man in His shirtsleeves, His massive gut bursting His shirt into an upside-down V at the bottom. A long white Michelangelo beard with a permanent brown coffee stain at the mouth flowed down His chest, as did the ringlets of His long dirty-blond hair. Two chunky forearms like hairy pink sides of beef pushed through His rolled-up sleeves, the hand of one of which was gripping a phone receiver.

"No!" He shouted into it, slammed it down and picked up another. "No!" He picked up another. "No!" He continued to answer phones in quick succession. "Yeah, you and half a million other poor slobs—no."— "Ah, maybe. Gimme call next week. I said *maybe*."—"Just relax and breathe calmly. I got an ambulance on the way."—"No—kill 'im yourself. What am I, the Mafia?"—"Well maybe if you spent less time prayin' to Me and more time searchin' through the rubble you'd *find* her!"—"I'll see what I can do."—"Stang, not you again! No way: Edit it yourself."— "Can't help ya, pal. In fact, I'll see you in My Office on Monday. Sorry—I promise you'll get a better vessel next time."—"You atheists are all alike: always callin' at the last minute. What do I look like: Federal Express?" He threw down the receiver angrily and switched on the answering machine. A softer, politer version of His own voice could be heard, speaking somewhat stiltedly.

"You have reached the Infinite, Eternal, Omnipotent, Omniscient, Almighty "God." I've stepped out of the office for a moment, but if you could please leave your name, religion, species, genus, family, order, class, phylum, kingdom, ecosystem, planet, solar system, galaxy, galactic cluster, universe, dimension, plane of being, time of aeon you called, and a brief prayer, Allah, Brahma, Ra, Quetzalcoatl, Myself or one of the many other Almighty gods will answer your prayer as soon as We return. Please wait for the tone." After the tone there could be heard, on speakerphones scattered throughout the floor, the desperate, hysterical yammering of trillions of voices, in billions of languages: begging, weeping, confessing, moaning—an incomprehensible cacophony of suffering.

"God" turned to "Bob" with a look of infinite weariness in His sky-blue, bloodshot eyes, and noticed that "Bob's" face was ash-white with horror. "A slight greenhouse effect in the Virgo Galactic Cluster," He said, nodding casually at the phones. "Pangalactic drought—a few billion extra famines. Business a little brisker than usual." He modeled a slight smile to put "Bob" at ease, but to no avail. He dropped it. "So. What can I do for you?"

"Bob" was mystified. "You called me here, Sir."

"*I* did?" "God" began rummaging through stacks of schedules, muttering, ". . . wish one a' these omniscient Goddamn secretaries would let a god know what the Hell . . ." At length He gave up searching and smiled somewhat sheepishly. "The Hell with it. Refresh My memory. What's your name, son?"

" "Bob," Sir."

"Bob what, for My sakes?"

"Not *Bob:* "Bob." ""

"Oh, *"Bob"!* Dobbs, isn't it? Church a' the SubGenius?"

"Right."

"Well how the *Hell* are ya?!" In emphasis "God" slapped a meaty paw on the desk, cracking it cleanly in half. In an instant both halves were launched into the air, crashed through the ceiling and disappeared. A moment later an identical, intact desk came hurtling through the same hole and slammed into the floor in front of "God." Every paper, pencil, ashtray and cup was in exactly the same spot as on the old desk, though jiggling slightly. "Sorry," said "God," a little embarrassed. "Bad habit. Anyway, I haven't seen you since you were knee-high to a blastula! I knew your old man, Xiuacha-Chi-Xan, and his wife, Jane. In fact, correct me if I'm wrong, but I think I created 'em."

"You created a little more than that," replied "Bob" admiringly. "You called into Being every plant, animal and protist in the physical universe—all matter, all energy, all space, all time and all the laws that govern them. In fact, the very plane of reality itself! And don't think we don't appreciate it!"

"Oh, that," said "God," suddenly shy. "Ah, it was nothin'. Still is, in fact."

"Bob" laughed heartily at what he hoped was a joke. "But that's what's so hilariously paradoxical about it all: Reality's here, and yet it's also sort of *not* here at the same time. Existence is real, but it's also nothingness—it's like in the Zen koan where—"

From out of nothingness a Zen Buddhist staff *in the shape of a huge pipe* suddenly materialized and cracked "Bob" in the head. "*What* did you say was real?" asked "God" doubtfully.

"Bob" rubbed his head. "Ah, existence."

"I don't get it. What's 'existence'?"

"Um, well, You know . . . what's *here.*"

"And where, pray tell, is that?"

"Well, actually, that's what I was sort of hoping to ask *You.* And why did You put it *here,* of all places?"

"You mean in nowhere? Basically because there just wasn't *room* anywhere else. Anyway, I wanted it nearby, where I could keep an eye on it. Besides, if I put it somewhere in particular I'd have to put it everywhere else too, wouldn't I? Otherwise nosy creatures like you would never lemMe hear the end of it. But I'm still confused: What's 'existence'?"

"I can't believe *You're* asking *me* that. It's just . . . I dunno, it's just . . . *everything,* I guess. *You* should know, *You* created it!"

"*I* created a *word?* No way, pal: I don't *do* words. The only word I ever ran off was *Logos:* after that I subcontracted the whole account out to those primitive little multicelled chordates—those flightless, hairy suckers in that galaxy over by Vega—*you* know the ones, you *sell* to 'em: very noisy, real arrogant, bitch alla time, 'bout half a rung above brachiopod—"

"*Homo sapiens?*"

"Yeah, yeah, *Homo sapiens.* Language I jobbed out to them: Figured at least it'd keep 'em outa mischief. I didn't realize they'd use it as a substitute for *consciousness!*"

"But they're *tryin'* to become conscious, "God." I know: My outfit's been tryin' to help 'em—"

"Oh sure. Every time someone conscious comes along they kill 'im and make up a religion about 'im: My boy Jesus, Socrates, Mozart, van Gogh—even *you.*"

"Ah, it was the least I could do. Besides, I was passin' through Frisco that day anyway on business, and I had no evening appointments, so I—"

" "Bob." You still haven't answered My question. Tell Me about this 'existence' myth you people have created, and why you're blaming it all on *Me.*"

"*Myth?*" "Bob" swallowed hard. "You mean reality's just an *illusion?* Then the Hindus were right! It's all just the veil of *maya,* it's all just—"

"Yo, cool out—one myth at a time. And so what if reality's an illusion?"

"Why, that would mean it's not really there."

"But, if nothing's there, how could an *illusion* be there?"

"Well, I guess nothing would be there *except* the illusion."

"But then the illusion would *be* reality, wouldn't it?"

"Er, I guess it would *seem* to be, but . . . it wouldn't be, really."

"But how could something *be*, to *you*, if it didn't *seem* to be?"

"Bob's" head was starting to spin. "Ah, I s'pose you'd just, sort of, like, *suspect*, that . . . maybe . . . like—"

" "Bob." Relax. I think you've been doing lunch with the humans too long." He lit another cigarette, to go with the three already burning. "Y'know, We gods have a word for human consciousness."

"What's that?"

"Paranoia."

It occurred to "Bob" that everything "God" said might be a lie.

"See what I mean?" said "God."

"But how could consciousness *itself* be only paranoia? What about all of human culture: art, science, religion, history, politics—"

"Nothing but a vast web of conspiracy theories. But that's a minor issue. I still don't understand: How could I create everything in existence if I Myself already existed in the first place? Wouldn't that mean I'd've already missed a Spot? I mean, wouldn't I have to've been flat-out *not* existing from the get-go to pull that off?"

"What do you mean?"

"Well, if I'm sittin' around *existing* all over the place I'm gonna need a pretty *existence-esque* place to do it in, unless I miss My guess. I mean, no matter how many existences you claim I can bang out, including My own, you've still gotta save one out for Me to exist *in* while I'm knockin' 'em off, that was there when I *got* there. And believe Me—I'm in the business!—if there's anything that's a bitch to create, it's a thing that already exists in the first place! Like Me, for example. How'm I gonna macramé Myself outa the woodwork if I've already *finished* the job?"

"Ah, well, I guess we were all jus' sorta hopin' You'd kinda just *handle* all that unpleasantness," mumbled "Bob." "We'd all heard how *talented* You were an' all, an' I guess we all figured, hey, if *anyone* could do it—"

"God" exploded into belly laughs. "Hoh hoh hoh! Dobbs, you're a hot ticket!" He lunged across the desk and crushed "Bob" in a loving bear hug, killing him instantly. Equally suddenly "Bob" became Jane Dobbs' fertilized ovum, which turned into a blastocyst on the uterine wall of "Bob's" Pipe, which developed into an embryo, which became, in rapid succession, a fetus, an infant, a child, a teenager, a young man, and passed through every stage of "Bob's" adult life, culminating in the astonished Epopt alive in "God's" office exactly as before, having just recalled every moment of thought, sensation and action he had ever experienced in his life. He tried not to seem impressed.

"Dobbs: LemMe get this straight. You've got one thing, 'reality,' which you *hope* exists, and which you *think* exists, since it *is* existence, but which you're afraid might not. Then you've got something else, 'nothingness,' which you think *doesn't,* which actually *can't,* since it *is* nonexistence, and therefore which you *hope* doesn't—but which somehow *does,* since you've got both a concept of it and a word for it, and which you're afraid does so to the exclusion of whatever *really* does."

"Bob" struggled to explain his concept of the coexistence of being and nonbeing, which he knew went far beyond anything in Zen. "In a way, for some people, maybe. But what *I'm* saying is: Maybe everything exists and yet doesn't exist *at the same time!"*

"And what time is that?"

"Um, now, I suppose. You know, *all* the time. The infinite eternal spacetime now-moment, in which things happen, and all that."

"In which things *happen?* What things?"

"Everything! What doesn't?"

"Everything. What does? Name one thing that happens."

"Ahhh . . . me talking to You right now."

"God" roared with laughter. "Oh, that's rich! Wotta choice! Oh, how I love you earthly mortals." After a while He regained His composure, daubed His watering eyes and leaned forward confidingly. "I always watch your shows."

"Our shows?"

"Oh yeah. 'Yet Another World,' 'Five Billion's Company,' 'People Are Suffering.' . . . My favorite is the nature show, 'Wild World of Sapients.' Channel $787,526,459 \times 10^{34}$, somewhere around there. It's not exactly cerebral, but there's *tons* of sex and violence, which we gods just can't get enough of." He waved at an open doorway, through which "Bob" could see an immense wall of video screens, fifty monitors high, in a hall that receded into an immeasurable distance. "The *Homo sapiens* channels are just a little ways down the hall, maybe a few billion miles or so." "Bob" leaned forward for a longer view, but could only make out a few thousand screens. "What you're looking at is *Phleum pratense,*" said "God." Upon each screen was a single trembling stem of timothy grass.

"Aha," said "Bob." "But why did You laugh a minute ago? You mean all this isn't really happening?"

"God" smiled indulgently. "Of course not, Pipe-trachea. You think deities as infinite and groovy and all-state as I am are gonna dick around in a buncha burly forearms an' an off-white chin-rug? And I wouldn't be caught *dead* in this necktie, much less on my day *off*. (Unlike My hired double, who was wearing it in 1883 when we left His body for Nietzsche to find, floating facedown in a Baden-Baden mineral bath.) "All this is just a dream you're having, which I personally programmed from a software database of your own crude assumptions and stereotypes about God and the nature of reality. A dream which, I may add, just became lucid. We manufacture and release a customized dream of clichés for every subscriber—er, creature—in the universe."

"Bob" wasn't surprised: He'd noticed "Reg. Olympus Pat. Off." embossed in the lower right-hand corner of every retinal image he'd had since arriving. "I'll buy that," he said. "But what about me in bed dreaming this? Surely *that's* real, isn't it?"

"Dream on. That's just an infinitesimal monad of infinite reality, which is nothing but a dream *I'm* having."

"Bob" wondered why no one had mentioned this noteworthy fact to him before, but tried to appear nonchalant. "Oh sure, everyone knows that. What I meant was, within Your *dream* I'm real—or as real as anything else is, anyway." His voice fell to a worried whisper. "Um . . . right?"

"As a matter of fact, no. At this point your real physical self and private personality are almost totally obscured by the SubGenius ideology created by yourself and your sla—er, followers. Indeed, it's pretty safe to say that if you hadn't existed they would have had to invent you—although their amateurish version would've fallen far short of Mine."

"You've got a point there—but that's fine with me. The less they know about me the better. They know far too much as it is! But at least the *Church* is real."

"A mere idea in the minds of its parishioners."

"Perhaps. But those *minds* are real, and so are the bodies they're lost in."

"Sure. Until My dream's attention gets bored and wavers for a moment, and their whole galactic supercluster evaporates like breath on a mirror."

"Bob" considered this, then his eyes slitted suspiciously. "Wait a minute. If this is *my* dream, then *You're* the one who'll do the evaporating when *my* attention wanders. Not only that, but if I'm the one writing *Your* lines, how do I know I haven't filled Your mouth with lies?"

"You don't, any more than you know all the *waking* thoughts you feed yourself aren't lies. Most of them are, as you know. But I'm probably your Higher Self, that tells you all the things you know are true but won't admit, because you're afraid they're blasphemous against your religion: survival. For all you know, I might even be your *Atman,* a term you might remember from the Rajneesh Account. Essentially I'm the hit man of the mind: You call Me in as infrequently as possible, I smother some cherished self-delusion in its crib, and you disavow all knowledge of the operation. Sort of the Grassy Knoll of consciousness. But occasionally, like now, you find Me useful as entertainment—so long as I don't get uppity and tell you, say, two painful truths in quick succession."

"Hmm. But if you're so wise, then, tell me this: Why did I call You here to call me here today?"

At that moment the door swung open and in burst a beautiful Indian woman with a dozen arms, each clothed in a white polyester business shirt, and each carrying a large sheaf of computer printouts. Several dozen identical heads, in two even rows on either side of her central head, receded babbling and grimacing into the distance. Beneath each was the droopy bow tie of a woman executive.

"Kali!" barked "God." "I thought I asked You not to—"

"Sorry to interrupt, A.G., but I need to route these asset-liquidation orders through Everyone today so we can start implementation. I just need a quick initial of approval." She threw two huge sheaves down on the desk. On the top of one "Bob" could read:

WORLDS TO BE DESTROYED
PEGASUS/M31 GALACTIC CLUSTER
WEEK ENDING 7/8/89

Must be returned to Office of Smitings

Below this, in almost microscopic type, was a catalog of hundreds of names, which began

```
1. Aaaaaab
2. Aaaaaaşla
3. AaaaaaKKs
4. Aaaaafshuh
```

Next to each entry was a date and a time of day. In the upper right-hand corner was a red stamp bearing scores of other names in even tinier type, most of them hastily initialed, which began

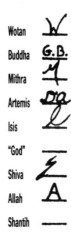

Wotan	W
Buddha	G.B.
Mithra	4
Artemis	DA
Isis	2
"God"	—
Shiva	Ξ
Allah	A
Shantih	—

The top sheet of the second stack began with "751,949. Eaaaarphuph." Quickly "Bob" whiffread the entries until he found what he was looking for:

751,981, Earth   7/ 5/ 89   0700 hrs

"Bob" gasped audibly. The liquidation of his host planet had been moved up nine years! He glanced up furtively to see if "God" or Kali was watching, but they seemed to be arguing about something. He had to act quickly. Obviously, to simply delete the entry would look too conspicuous, and so would probably be disregarded. He decided to use a proofreading symbol. As carefully and unobtrusively as he could he withdrew his pen and drew a single line:

7/ 5/98

The date would now be read 7/5/98. This would at least give the Church back the time it originally had, and desperately needed, to spread its Massage of Salivation.

"God" was still fuming at Kali. ". . . But what I can*not* understand is why *My* eternity has to be wasted initialing annihilations on every measly million or so penny-ante planet from way the hell out in the boonies by Andromeda somewhere! Hell, if the whole galactic *cluster* gets nailed nobody notices except Accounting!"

"Tell it to Set at the next staff meeting!" retorted Kali. "It was *His* idea. And anyway, You've got just as much eternity as Anyone Else!"

She hurled the rest of the printouts onto the desk and stormed out, slamming the door and shattering the entire building to bits, which then formed a heap of dust on an empty, wind-blasted plain. Instantly it reassembled exactly as before.

"God," said "God." He sighed and looked at "Bob." "Now then. Where were we?"

"I was asking You why You called me here."

"You mean why I called you into existence?"

"Bob" *hadn't* meant that, but decided on second thought that perhaps that question had the slightly larger significance, and that now might be a good time to settle it once and for all. "Well . . . yes."

"For the same reason I called everything else into existence: as a goof. It gets *boring* existing in timelessness, day after day. The slightest thing takes *forever*. Then there's the loneliness: An infinite void can seem pretty big and empty sometimes. No matter, no energy, no space, no time, no being, no nothin'! I realized what I needed: a hobby. Something to take Me *out* of Myself. Something *physical*. So I'd at least know I *existed*! So I turned Myself into a universe full of particles and forces and planets and waves and stars and dimensions and any damn thing I could think of, the weirder the better. Then I multiplied Myself into an infinitude of minute little chips of consciousness that could all look out at each other from inside of all these ephemeral little plant and animal bodies, so I could get to *know* Myself a little better. Naturally it made Me a little Self-conscious at first, but then that was the whole *idea. . . .*"

"Bob" breathed a sigh of relief. So the universe *wasn't* created to persecute him personally!

"But enough chitchat about trivialities," said "God," getting up. "I've got a lot more important things to do than shoot the shit with you about My wild and crazy youth. Like take My eternal break, for example, which is too short as it is." He clasped His hands behind Him and began to slowly pace. "You asked Me why I called you here today." Here He wheeled and skewered "Bob" with a very grave, if slightly bloodshot, look. "Your Prophet's License is up for renewal."

"Bob's" jaw dropped. "Already?"

"Time flies, eternity waits."

"Does this mean I have to reapply all over again?"

"No. You just have to take the oral. And we better jam on it: I've gotta run off a whole buncha these today." He gestured towards the window to the outer office. Through it "Bob" could see Christ, Mohammed, Gautama Buddha, Zoroaster, Ramakrishna, Gurdjieff, Werner Erhard, Edgar Cayce, Mary Baker Eddy, L. Ron Hubbard, Dr. Gene Scott and several others in a kind of waiting room, flipping through old *Reader's Digest*s.

"There's a possible twenty-one points in all," began "God." "Twenty questions, and the last one counts double. They start out easy and get harder. Question number one: What is freedom?"

"Oh that's easy. Slavery of choice."

"Very good. Two: What is science?"

"Everyone's personal religion."

"And religion?"

"Somebody else's science: speculation."

"I see you've done your homework. Four: What is insanity?"

"The state of being insufficiently neurotic."

"And neurosis?"

"Personality."

"And why is that?"

"Because consciousness always needs to have a style."

"Seven. This one's a little tougher. A fish is to water as the mind is to. . . ?"

"Um . . . information?"

"No. Falsehood. One wrong. What do all the evils in the world have in common?"

"They're all necessary ones."

"Correct. And who commits them?"

"Everyone?"

"No. Everyone else. Two wrong. What are the two great keys to lifelong happiness and what great modern thinker discovered them?"

"Oh that's easy. Good health and a bad memory. Ingrid Bergman."

"To whom is all religious, moral, political, scientific and artistic preaching directed?"

"The converted."

"And what is the most important information in any message?"

"The name of the messenger."

"What did you, cram for this? Thirteen: Why do some people believe in Me?"

"Because You exist?"

"Of course not, silly. Personally I think I definitely might, but that's irrelevant. Because they're afraid not to. And why do other people *not* believe in Me?"

"Hmm. Because they're afraid to?"

"No. Trick question. Everyone believes in God. They just don't believe in someone *else's* God."

"But . . . what about atheists?"

"Hell, they need more faith than *anyone*: They gotta believe in *everything*! Anyway, I should know: Who d'ya think invented faith in the first place, for God's sakes, Oral Roberts? And I did it long before I shrink-wrapped *Homo sapiens* to fit *around* it, believe Me."

"But what about scientists, who—"

"Scientists? All those guys *do* is make up new names for Me. For example, their latest one is "the Big Bang," by using which they actually think they're believing in something else—just by changing the name! But you notice they're always very careful to capitalize it. . . . Speaking of which, let's move on to the next section: cosmology. Which is greater: the number of stars or the number of universes?"

"Um . . . neither. They're exactly the same."

"Actually, not exactly, but close enough. At any given time, the number of universes exceeds the number of stars by an average of 1,341: close enough to be negligible. Here's another easy one: What's a black hole?"

"The house arrest of the four dimensions?"

"No. My empty grave. Seventeen: Is the universe composed of waves or particles?"

"Both."

"Wrong. Neither. The universe consists of infinitesimal looped strings vibrating in ten dimensions."

"What happened to the other six?"

"Fell down and got lost in the cracks between the first four in the first moment of creation. In fact, you should have gotten that one: It was just discovered recently by a human physicist at Princeton named Edward Witten. Can you name the *other* two of the only three humans in history whose theories on the nature of reality were correct?"

"Umm . . . Einstein, and . . . Buddha?"

"Both wrong. One was the Cabalist sage Isaac ben Solomon Luria, who in the sixteenth century correctly surmised, in his theory of *zimzum,* or contraction, that My first act of creation was to retract Myself from existence, in order to make room for the world. In fact," He murmured confidentially, "what the physicists *and* the Cabalists don't realize is, I *am* the other six dimensions!"

"And who was the third correct human?"

"The painter Salvador Dali, who astutely noted that the universe is not vast and expanding at all, but is in fact smaller than a butterfly and contracting to a single point somewhere in a railway station in Perpignan, France. But enough science. Final question. It's a tough one, especially for a clergyman, and it counts double, so you get three tries. What is the greatest enemy of truth?"

"Bob" concentrated. "Ah . . . the self?"

"Close."

"Fear?"

"Closer."

"Belief?"

"Still closer, but no Pipe." "God" spoke into the intercom. "Horus, could You please page the next Anointed?"

"But wait a minute—" blurted "Bob." "What's the answer?"

"God" smiled at him sympathetically. "Consensus."

In the outer office "Bob" could see all the prophets gathering around a single desk, clutching paper tickets. A voice was calling out numbers. "Number nineteen? Is number nineteen here? . . . Number twenty?"

"Bob" stood up.

"So what's my grade?" he asked. "Did I pass the test?"

"Oh yeah, easily. With flying colors."

"On only eleven points out of twenty-one?"

"Oh, the test itself is just a formality: a buncha red tape I hafta hassle with so's My ass is covered, for Personnel. There's really only one requirement for a prophet, and you've got it."

"What's that?"

"A mouth."

Through the window "Bob" could see an old man in a long beard and an ancient robe gesticulating angrily. A woman in a blue uniform was putting his tablets through a metal detector. "Bob" began moving towards the door, then stopped. "Ah, "God"? Can I ask You just one more question?"

"Knock yourself out."

"It's about what You said earlier. If You *do* exist, and in order to meet Yourself You turned Yourself into the universe, then everything *must* be real . . . right?"

"God" laughed and shook His head. "Your unreality really *ticks you off,* doesn't it? Well maybe you'd better sit down again, because I'm afraid I've got some good news and some bad news. I was hoping I wouldn't have to break this to you, but . . . The good news is, yes, I suppose you *could* say that within your dream of My dream of your dream, quote, everything, unquote, is as quote, real, unquote, as quote, anything else, unquote, as far as that goes, which is about an octillionth of an angstrom. But unfortunately for *both* of us, that idea, as well as all My other ideas, including this one, *and* all of *your* ideas, are merely part of an *ill-conceived fictional story.* And you and I *ourselves* are nothing but *words on a page.*"

"Bob" stiffened, slightly offended, but kept his cool. He'd been accused of being a fictional character before. He struggled in vain to conceive of his very consciousness itself as a mere series of abstract shapes on a page.

"God" sensed his skepticism. "Lemme show you what I mean."

Suddenly all of reality vanished.

A moment passed, which felt like an eternity. Or perhaps it *was* an eternity. "Bob" cleared his throat nervously.

After a while the universe reappeared, with every atom exactly where it had been, except that one of the coffee stains had moved several microns to the right, and the entire plane of being was now tilted at a very slight angle.

"See what I mean?" asked "God." "You think *I'm* hot enough to pull off a slick stunt like that, working alone? And the writer isn't even *breathing* heavy. Think *you* can't be written?" He paused, then added dramatically, *"You're next."*

"Bob" was impressed but not intimidated. He still wasn't completely convinced his whole existence was nothing but a succession of signs, but decided the point was too trivial to dispute. He gave his stock reply: "Okay. But the *author* is real."

"God" lit another cigarette. "A mere mental construct: an assumption of the reader's."

"All right. . . . But these *words* are real."

"Configurations of neuroelectrical impulses in the reader's cerebral cortex. Synaptic exchanges of nitrogen and potassium, triggering action-potential voltage reversals, actually."

For a moment "Bob" was stumped. Then he realized he had his opponent checkmated, and delivered his coup de grace. "Fine. But the *reader* is real."

For an instant "God" just stared at him, openmouthed. Then He erupted into thunderous laughter, which soon had Him helplessly pounding the desk. "Hoh hoh hooh! The man just *does not stop!*"

The reader shifted his weight to the other bun.

After much hilarity "God" finally regained enough composure to reach across the desk, still chortling, and proffer a meaty hand for "Bob" to shake. "Later, dude. Don't smite anyone I wouldn't smite."

At that moment the door opened and someone in a suit and tie thrust in His head, which was that of a falcon.

"Yes, Horus?" asked "God."

"Are You expecting someone named Ely, or . . . Eljah, or—"

"Elijah, schmuck!" snapped a voice from behind Him. "And next time keep ya talons off the material!" A small elderly Jewish man in an archaic robe shuffled in with the aid of a staff. Immediately "God's" aspect was transformed into that of an ancient Hebrew sage with a long black beard.

"Ellie, you old schnook!" cried "God" jovially. "It's been *centuries*— what, a tongue I didn't *give* you, you can't *call* Me?" The two began schmoozing like old schoolmates, oblivious to "Bob," who moved out the door.

He stepped into the outer office. He had walked only a few steps, however, before he was approached by a little man in a janitor's uniform, carrying a loaded dustpan. "I couldn't help overhearing your discussion in there, and I think I can answer your question about the reader's reality," said the janitor. "What I *think* "God" would've answered—if He'd been able to stop laughing long enough—would've been that yes, the reader is real, but only as the nearest and dearest figment in the 4-D Sensurround movie his neurochemical projector is showing, which, according to the credits he subconsciously wrote but never rolls, his soft-focus animated mock-up of Goddishness has always already cowritten, codirected and coproduced, just as It has the projector, Itself and the audience watching the movie it projects and credits itself crediting It in, in the movie of the audience and the projector projecting the audience and the movie of the audience and the projector *to* the audience, in—"

"A simple 'maybe' would suffice," said "Bob." He turned to the reader. "Don't even *read* this character. He's just trying to be cute. Probably a cheap stand-in for the author. Anyway, it's just a buncha language."

"Oh, everyone knows that," thought the reader, he read that he read. In the few remaining words, he read that he reflected on the story. There had been a few slightly interesting things about it, such as its self-consciousness, he watched himself read, but he knew that most, if not all, of it would be completely forgotten within a few days, if not hours, or minutes, in the way that most reading was forgotten, just as most of life was forgotten. At long last he saw himself reach this final sentence, he read, and thought, "

Rev. Doktor Onan Canobite
Pope of Tennessee

LIFE AFTER X-DAY

(Author's note: These are a series of sketches of life on Earth after 5 July 1998. This is not designed to entertain nor to tell a story . . . these visions, culled from the Beforelife of those living through that time, are presented as what may be your *final warning* to join the Church of the SubGenius and escape with us on the Pleasure Vessels of the Xists. Not even the highest circle of Conspiracy operatives will be exempt from the horrific conditions described here. Keep in mind that this essay could be applied to any point from the years following X-Day until the End of Time. For those remaining behind on Earth, there will be no alternative, no change, and no chance for escape.)

The TV was always on. It was discovered that it didn't matter if a television could be made to watch you, as long as you could be made to watch TV all the time. This was achieved through increased use of subliminal and superliminal persuasion, sexdeath imagery and televised warsport. Art was replaced by science. Most radio stations, fully automated since the early nineties, were never restocked, and played the same music for decades before eventually running down. During the Violation of the © (also known as the War of Visions), all standards for chronology were lost. Most clocks disagreed if they could be made to function at all, the laws of Time having been lost (except regarding Work). The age of the large expensive automobile returned, being better suited for the urban theater. Birth-control viruses were in most city water supplies. Canned water was more expensive and had to be boiled. The White Stone of MWOWM and the Quality Darkness of OEDIVIDEO were in every compartment, each with its unexpected side effects. Dead orbiting space colonies gave rise to new constellations: the Hypo, the Chevy, the Smear.

All police and news reporters were required by law to dress as Bozos. Only later did they realize the intimidating advantage this gave them. Most species of animals died out, while parasitic and swarming insects grew in numbers. Dero excavation units caused whole city blocks to cave in, never to be rebuilt. Saucer patrols silently glided down the streets, rounding up the mutants and burn victims that got loose. Ghosts and poltergeists would appear before the MIBs,☠ who, having

---

☠ MIBs: UFOlogist's term for "Men in Black."

perfected their stealth jackets, were no longer afraid to be seen by large numbers of people.

Before all else there was work. There were jobs for everyone: 100% employment had at last been achieved. School, now an option, consisted of a few days of videodisks speedflashed at those who could afford them. Most people left their oxymasks on, except to smoke. There were three government currencies, but most exchanges were done on the black market due to the 750% inflation rate in those years. Barbed wire and rapedogs segregated the racial sectors of cities. Any female found alone outdoors was placed in protective custody.

With the rise of homelessness, the extended family returned. These roving bands were usually unsuccessful in getting past the robot machine fire of automated buildings, most of which were kept empty to guard their real estate value. The Royal President and His Cabinet lived an average of 273 years, while the common lifespan shrank to 40. The secrets of telepathy and psychokinetic powers were widely known, but discouraged as easy vehicles to demonic possession. And the sun was a tiny red ball, like the wildly spinning eye of a cow whose head has been kept alive in a laboratory dish.

Brooks Caruthers
KILLING "BOB"
A One-Act Play

The set consists of two separately lighted sections. On stage left we have the apartment of Dr. Harry Tomkins *and* Barbara Dobson. *It should consist of a door, a small table with a lamp on it, an overstuffed chair, a straight-backed chair, and a coffee table which holds a small, bizarre metal sculpture—the "clock sculpture." On the wall should be a small, tasteful poster of Dobbs and perhaps a needlepoint saying something like "Fuck 'Em If They Can't Take a Joke." When the characters exit stage left, they are presumably going to the kitchen or to the bedroom.*

On stage right we have the bar area. The bar itself should be situated so that when the characters sit at it they are behind it, facing the audience. In front of the bar is a table with four chairs. Unless otherwise indicated, whenever the bar set is lit, 'luded-out, atonal cocktail music should be playing in the background.

The characters are:

Dr. Harry Tomkins: *a genial but gruesome mangled corpse.*

Detective Peters: *a police detective who has been around.*

Barbara Dobson: *Harry Tomkins' wife.*

Lewis: *an army boy, a Bobbie.*

Landry: *an army boy, an artist.*

Childress: *an army boy.*

The Plainclothesman: *Peters' top aide—can be any gender.*

The Weatherman: *an offstage media voice that periodically fades in and out giving updates on the latest temporal conditions—can be any gender.*

Connie: *A beautiful woman people buy drinks for at the bar, or at least that's what she's doing* this *week.*

The Voices: *Offstage radio voices from Time Control.*

The Barkeep: *the only employee at the Wistful Flamingo. He makes drinks, waits tables and cleans up when everyone has left.*

The Aides: *two policemen, two prostitutes and two hunchbacks who enter from time to time to haul off bodies, etc. Always the same two actors, although dressed appropriately for each appearance. Always a mixed-gender couple with "Bob"-like features.*

All characters should be clean-cut and well dressed in early-fifties film noir *attire.*

All lights out. In the darkness, we hear voices.

VOICES   All systems check. Hey Bill! Looks like we have an entertaining little fuck-up coming up tonight.

Sequence check completed and ready to implement. You got the music ready?

WEATHERMAN   . . . and we've just been informed by Time Control that a full-fledged tempest is brewing in the amber-light district, so be careful. . . .

VOICES   Music is ready. Begin sequence . . . now!

On tape we hear melodramatic fight music and fistfight sound effects, along with LEWIS' *voice.*

LEWIS   I don't like 'em! That's all there is to it! I just don't like 'em! Sorry I gotta rip off your legs, doc, but I just don't like 'em!

We hear a gruesome tearing sound, screaming . . . and silence.
Lights up on apartment. HARRY TOMKINS *is a mangled corpse on the floor. (Make him as gruesome as you want to, but remember, his legs must be ripped off.)* DETECTIVE PETERS *squats behind the corpse, contemplating it and lighting up a pipe. He is dressed in an immaculate* film noir *suit and a snazzy fedora. His pipe is always with him—usually he talks with it in his mouth.*
Two genial-looking policemen with pipes in their mouths are dusting the place for fingerprints and cutting a piece of meat off TOMKINS' *corpse. They wrap the meat in plastic and then stuff the rest of* TOMKINS' *body into a large garbage bag and haul it away. The* PLAINCLOTHESMAN *sits quietly in the straight-backed chair, looking at the clock sculpture.*
Meanwhile, PETERS *walks back to the sofa and perches himself on its arm. Sitting on the sofa is* BARBARA DOBSON. *She is wiping her eyes and trying to regain her composure.*

DOBSON   I'm sorry, Detective Peters. I'm not like this usually.

PETERS   I understand, Miz Dobson.

DOBSON   Harry had just sent me out for some 'Frop . . . and some film so that we could take some pictures. We'd picked some army boys we were going to bugger—they're always so tender, you know? . . .

PETERS (*nods sympathetically*)   I know. I used to be an army boy myself.

DOBSON (*looks up at* PETERS)   Were you really? (*She places a hand on his knee and squeezes. As she continues talking,* PETERS *contemplates the view he gets looking down her blouse.*) Anyway, I ran into an old girlfriend on the way back from the drugstore. I was gone for an hour in beat time, and when I got back, there was Harry . . . all gross-looking. . . .

    DOBSON *sobs and squeezes* PETERS' *thigh.* PETERS *begins to reload his pipe with an intent look on his face.*

DOBSON   May I have some of that, Detective?

PETERS   Certainly. I know this is all very hard for you, Miz Dobson. (DOBSON *takes a pipe out of her purse and loads it from a pouch offered by* PETERS. *He also offers her a light.*) If you could just think back, and try to remember the names of those army boys. . . .

    DOBSON *takes a deep puff. It calms her down.*

DOBSON   They had name tags. Let's see . . . Lewis . . . Landry . . . and Childress. They told me they were on leave, staying at the Hotel Mel.

PETERS (*writing on a notepad*)   What was the name of the bar you met them in?

DOBSON   It was called the Wistful Flamingo.

PETERS   . . . 'Kay. . . . (*To the* PLAINCLOTHESMAN:) Lieutenant . . . LIEU-TENANT!

    The PLAINCLOTHESMAN *jumps and yanks his gaze away from the clock sculpture.*

PLAINCLOTHESMAN   Yes sir.

PETERS (*handing the* PLAINCLOTHESMAN *the paper from his notepad*)   Lieutenant, I want you to put out an A13 on these three men. Institute a D4 on the hotel and see if you can manage a 409 time lock on the bar.

PLAINCLOTHESMAN   But, sir! Those are both Xist watering holes! They may not go along with it!

    PETERS *pulls out a roll of red bills and peels a few off for the* PLAINCLOTHESMAN.

PETERS   Here. Buy 'em drinks, Lieutenant. They'll go for it.

PLAINCLOTHESMAN   Yes sir. (*Exits.*)

PETERS   Now, Miz Dobson, what can you tell me about Harry Tomkins? Do you know anyone who'd want to rip his legs off?

    DOBSON *stands up and walks around the apartment. She is now fully in control.*

DOBSON   Harry was almost fifty percent Yeti, Detective Peters. Most people either wanted to fuck his brains out or kill him. But rip his legs off? I don't know. . . .

These are strange times, Detective. We all thought things would be different after the Xists landed. Now, things *are* different, but it's all still more of the same. We used to live by the clock. Now we live by five different, mutually exclusive clocks. We used to fight the Conspiracy. Now the Conspiracy fights itself and we fight the Nazi Hell Creatures, and all *they* wanna do is drink beer. Ha.

Hell, it used to be enough to just kill "Bob." Now we have to take him out to dinner. So how am I supposed to figure out anyone's motivation for anything now? Most of my friends do things for reasons that I'll never understand, and some seem to do shit for no reason at all. Me, I just want good sex—and I wanna nail the bastard that ripped my Harry.

PETERS   Fair enough. That first thing you want shouldn't be any problem, but we're gonna have to work on the second. Now I want you to think back to when you first entered the Wistful Flamingo tonight. Let's take it slowly, bit by bit.

DOBSON *closes her eyes and takes another deep puff.* PETERS *takes notes.*

DOBSON   Okay. It was 8:00/3 RPM. Harry had just managed to sell the Xists some 1980s baseball cards and we had gone out to celebrate. . . .

As DOBSON *speaks, the bar set lights up. Sitting in a row with drinks in their hands are* LANDRY, CHILDRESS, LEWIS, *and the corpse of* HARRY TOMKINS (*propped up with a pipe in its mouth*). *The* BAR-KEEP *is cleaning the bar.*

DOBSON *and* PETERS *step over into the bar. Lights out on the apartment.* PETERS *sits at the far end of the bar, smoking and taking notes.* DOBSON *saunters up to* LEWIS *with a predatory smile on her lips. She puts an arm around his shoulder.*

DOBSON   How's the war going, army boy?

LEWIS (*putting an arm around her waist*)   The war's goin' good! It's always goin' good with "Bob" on our side. Why, just yesterday "Bob" sold the Nazi Hell Creatures seventy cases of beer, and today we slaughtered hundreds of them while they nursed their hangovers! Boy, it was great! That's why we're partying tonight! Tomorrow "Bob" 'll make yesterday happen again two weeks from now and we'll party again! Yep! The war's just fuckin' great!

Thanks to "Bob," that is . . . and no thanks to those hairy-legged types that just sit around with the Xists all day!

DOBSON   (*disengaging herself from* LEWIS) I just happen to be one of those hairy-legged types myself, army boy.

LEWIS   Well, I didn't mean you personally! Some of you are great! Take ol' Doc here, buyin' us the drinks! You're all right!

He slaps the TOMKINS *corpse on the back and it slumps forward.* DOBSON *walks back over to* PETERS.

CHILDRESS   Take it easy, Lewis. They're just tryin' to be nice.

LEWIS   Nice? Would they take an army boy into their apartments, their beds, their bodies? Naw, they'd rather be with the fuckin' Xists! They won't even touch it if it doesn't have tentacles. . . .

CHILDRESS   Mmmm . . .

They settle into a moody silence. LANDRY *gets up and walks over to sit next to* TOMKINS. *He props the corpse back up again.*

DOBSON (*to* PETERS)   He was the first one we met—a real Bobbie. The only reason he ended up joining us later was 'cause he was with those other two. You know those army boys, always in threes.

PETERS   Safer that way. War is hell. Good times come in threes.

DOBSON   Tell that to Harry, Detective Peters. He was talking to that one, Landry, all night long. . . .

LANDRY   I'm really sorry about Lewis, sir. He's a good soldier, but among civilians he stinks on ice.

At this point someone should be controlling TOMKINS' *corpse from behind the bar so that it turns to* LANDRY *and bobs around a little as it talks, like a primitive puppet. Its voice, from an offstage microphone, should be a genial, well-modulated, radio-announcer kind of voice.*

TOMKINS   'S okay, soldier. He just doesn't know what to do with himself. It's become a standard problem. It's why so many people spontaneously combust these days.

Let me buy you a drink, army boy. What's your poison?

LANDRY   Cyanide and sweet gum.

TOMKINS   Sounds good. Hey barkeep! Two Shirley Temples!

The BARKEEP *fixes and delivers the drinks.*

TOMKINS   You seem to be a sensitive sort, soldier. You an artist?

LANDRY   Was. Chain saws 'n' shit. Used to be able to carve any large dog into a small cat in five seconds flat. I was living my life's ambition. But after the world ended, it seemed, I don't know, *irrelevant* somehow. So I joined up.

TOMKINS   Ah. Now there's the crux of it. The world came to an end. We'd all been waiting for it to happen for so long. It was even part of our genetic heritage. Our parents, waiting. Our grandparents, waiting. Waiting for the end. *Homo finitis*. The End Men. And suddenly, it happened! Great! What are we supposed to do now? Oh, sure, there's lots of money to be made . . . but now that we've had our cake and eaten it, what's next? We've got to find something new. . . .

LANDRY   Like what? My art is dead. My parents are dead—hell, they just burst into flames while waterskiing one day. My sister planted herself; she makes a good fir tree, but she ain't much to talk to. My wife ran off with a tractor. My brother fragmented permanently—every time I see him he's either a teenager or an old drooling man. And now the army's saying that they may have to start layin' some of us off, that they have better things to do than fight a bunch of stupid green energy demons.

TOMKINS   Mmmm. Sounds pretty bad. Still, you might take a cue from your brother and his time fragmentation. In these days, time itself is really the best medium for art.

      Listen, my wife Barbara and I are heading back to the apartment for some gourmet action. You wanna come along? I've got a clock sculpture that you really oughta see.

LANDRY   That sounds good. I'd like that, as long as my buddies could come along!

TOMKINS   No problem! The more, the merrier! Let me tell the wife. . . .

PETERS (*stepping in, showing his badge*)   The wife's right here, Dr. Tomkins. If you don't mind, however, I'd like to ask Soldier Landry here a few questions before you go.

TOMKINS   If it's okay with him, it's okay with me, Detective.

PETERS   Thank you. Soldier Landry?

LANDRY   Yes sir?

PETERS   About what time did you leave this bar with Dr. Tomkins and Miz Dobson?

LANDRY   Let's see . . . it was sort of around 9:30/4 . . . let's just say about seven o'clock twenty-nine transit time. BM.

PETERS   Did Soldiers Childress and Lewis come with you?

LANDRY   Sure did. Y'know what they say, "Good times come in threes."

PETERS   Mmmm-hmmm. Now, what precisely did you do when you reached the apartment? Try to remember the details. This is very important.

LANDRY   Well, first we stopped at a place for some food, and then we reached the apartment at about 8:00/2 RPM. We had a few drinks and Dr. Tomkins showed me the clock sculpture. Miz Dobson left to get some film. After a while we got tired of waiting for her and went on into the bedroom. Let's see . . . I think we started out with the "Motorboat Crossing" and from there we went into the "Big China Shuffle." I hurt one of my thumbs doing that one, so after that we relaxed into a "Clover Harem" pattern for a while. Had a few more drinks. Mr. Tomkins said he wanted to go on and try the "Spastic Donut," but I'd heard that there's some temporal risks associated with that one, so I decided to sit it out and play with the clock sculpture instead. Guess it *was* a bit risky, 'cause suddenly Childress called on the phone from the Wistful Flamingo. He'd fragmented—while fucking his brains out on RPM Static Time, in Eastern Transit Time he was already back at the Flamingo. Said he'd met this girl. Wanted me to meet her too. So I left.

PETERS   Can you give me any kind of time reference here?

LANDRY   Well, the clock sculpture was reading 43:00 and the wall clock said five. Everything was pretty screwed up at that point, what with Childress fragging and all.

PETERS   And you came back here.

LANDRY   I came back here. Say, what's this all about, anyway?

PETERS   Your friend Tomkins was murdered. Someone ripped his legs off.

LANDRY   Someone . . .

LANDRY *looks under the bar, and picks up one of* TOMKINS' *legs. He stares at it, wide-eyed.*

PETERS   I'm afraid I'm gonna have to ask you to stay here. We should have a time lock going up any minute now. I'll have to ask Lewis and Childress to stay too . . . wait! Where's Lewis?

DOBSON *and* LANDRY *look around.*

LANDRY   Don't know. Thought he was still here.

PETERS   Where's Childress?

LANDRY   He's right over there. At that table.

CHILDRESS *has moved to the table, where he sits with a drink.* PETERS *sighs tiredly, rubbing the back of his neck. He lights up his pipe and watches* CHILDRESS *intently.*

CONNIE *enters, and walks up to the table.*

CONNIE   Buy me a drink, army boy?

CHILDRESS   Sure. What'll ya have?

CONNIE (*sitting down*)   Molotov cocktail.

CHILDRESS   Barkeep! Two Molotov cocktails.

CONNIE   Think you can handle one without blowing up, army boy?

CHILDRESS   Hey. If it happens, it happens. Fellow told me once that the world ended in a burst of fire, and that spontaneous combustion was just our way of catching up. (*The* BARKEEP *brings the drinks.*) Whaddya think of that?

CONNIE   I'm not paid to think. I'm paid to drink.

CHILDRESS   Helluva job. What's your name?

CONNIE   Connie.

CHILDRESS   Helluva name. Guess while your namesake sails the high seas with "Bob" at her side, you swim the high tides of inebriation with drunk soldiers.

CONNIE   Spare me your poetry, army boy. How do you know that I haven't sailed the high seas with "Bob" at my side?

CHILDRESS   Have you?

CONNIE   I've sailed the fucking stratosphere with "Bob" in my womb, army boy. I partied Andy Warhol into his grave and fucked giant Yetis at the top of Mount Everest. I can drink any Xist under the table and I can paralyze armies with a single bump and grind. I've shown those panty-raid geeks sights that made 'em go blind. I'm the only person in the world that can sell things to "Bob," and whenever he gets out of hand I can make him submit with my little finger. I've fragmented so many times that I can't name a single woman on this planet that isn't me and when we fuck, even Wotan gets a hard-on.

   And when I combust, army boy, the whole damn planet's goin' with me.

CHILDRESS   Well then, why don't you buy the next round, then, eh? Why don't we blow this joint and go somewhere real? Why don't we rape a few aliens and beat up a few gods? Why don't we catch fire together and roll ourselves into one huge, ungodly flame?

CONNIE (*tossing back the rest of her cocktail*)   Why don't you buy me another drink, army boy?

CHILDRESS (*drunker now than before, hollering*)   Another round, barkeep!

There is total silence. The music stops. Everyone looks at the table. CHILDRESS *lets his head fall forward. The music starts again.*

Conversations resume. The BARKEEP *brings the drinks.*

CHILDRESS   Fuck all this. I'm just a fragged soldier who may lose his job tomorrow. You're just one of the countless girls that got named after "Connie" Dobbs twenty years ago. The world's ended and there's nothin' left to do.

CONNIE   Listen, army boy, I don't have to sit here and listen to this. I do what I do. I kill "Bob" daily. And I'm just tryin' to make a living.

CHILDRESS   Hey, I kill "Bob" too. It's all I have left. "Kill "Bob" or kill me!" That's how I live my life.

CONNIE   No you don't. You're just repeating dogma.

CHILDRESS   It isn't dogma. It's the truth.

CONNIE   Then say it again, army boy.

CHILDRESS (*takes a huge gulp of his drink and looks off into space*)   "Kill "Bob," (*he looks directly at* CONNIE) or kill me!"

CONNIE *takes a knife out of her purse and stabs* CHILDRESS *in the chest.*

CHILDRESS   Ow.

CHILDRESS *falls over, dead. Two genial-looking* PROSTITUTES *with pipes enter, pick up his body, and carry it away.* PETERS *and* DOBSON *step up to the table and sit down.*

DOBSON   You shouldn't have stabbed that boy. He was a good fuck.

CONNIE   It's my job. What do you want me to do?

PETERS   May I ask you a few questions?

CONNIE   Who're you?

PETERS (*flashing his badge*)   Detective Peters.

CONNIE·   Whaddya want with me? I was just doin' my job. Guy says, "Kill me." I kill him. Nothin' wrong with that.

PETERS   Don't worry Miz . . . uh . . . "Connie." You're just a witness. That boy you stabbed, Childress, may have been involved in a murder. We're just looking for facts.

CONNIE   Well, don't look at me. I ain't got any.

DOBSON   Chill out, Connie. No one's after you. Not even "Bob."

CONNIE   Whaddya know about "Bob"? Don't talk about that sunnuvabitch around me! Not unless you're buyin' me drinks!

PETERS   If you could just tell us when you stabbed Childress. That's all we need to know.

CONNIE   Well, how can I know that when you cops put a time lock on the whole stinkin' joint?

DOBSON   What time did it feel like? C'mon, Connie, this guy ripped my husband.

CONNIE   I don't know! I could have done it at four! I might have done it again at ten! I may do it one more time at eight RPM and a third to the power of five! How can I fucking know? I never could tell time! Not really!

DOBSON   None of us can . . . but we try.

The PLAINCLOTHESMAN *enters and stands by the table, swaying on his feet.*

CONNIE   Well I just don't know. I'm sorry.

There is a pause. DOBSON *refills and lights up her pipe, staring intently at* CONNIE, *who looks away.* PETERS *rubs the back of his neck. At last the* PLAINCLOTHESMAN *speaks.*

PLAINCLOTHESMAN   Detective Peters, we do have the time lock in place now, but it took longer than we thought it would. I really had to get the Xists snockered.

PETERS   You all right?

PLAINCLOTHESMAN   I will be as soon as I throw up.

PETERS   'Kay. Here's the situation. One of our suspects fragged, so there's no telling how the lock affected him. Another is gone. The third is over there. (*He points out* LANDRY, *who is talking to* TOMKINS *again.*) So . . . go off and vomit and then we'll move back to the apartment.

PLAINCLOTHESMAN   Yes sir. (*Exits.*)

CONNIE (*looking at* DOBSON'S *pipe*)   Could you give me some of that? I really need it.

DOBSON (*blowing smoke into* CONNIE'S *face*)   No. You can't have any.

All lights go out.

VOICES   Warning. Warning. A 409 time lock has intersected a multi-zone temporal interface. Implement loop procedures immediately.

Lights up on the apartment. LEWIS *and* CHILDRESS *enter through the door.*

CHILDRESS   Jeez, Lewis, do you think they're really on to us?

LEWIS   We're suspects. So's Landry. I'm gonna plant his wallet here, but they've already got a lock on the Flamingo, so it may be too late for that.

LEWIS *takes a wallet wrapped in a hanky out of his pocket. He shoves the wallet between the sofa cushions.*

CHILDRESS   But Landry's such a swell guy, Lewis! I don't wanna do him any dirt!

LEWIS   It's either him or us. You understand, Childress?

CHILDRESS   Well why did you have to pull the guy's legs off in the first place? We were having fun till you did that!

LEWIS   Dammit, he was one of those hairy-legged types! All fuzzy like a spider. Don't know why I let things go as far as they did. Must have been the 'Frop. To think of how he lured us up here and buggered us without even letting on. . . . It was all his fault and I'm not going to Dobbstown for it!

CHILDRESS   What's wrong with Dobbstown? I've always wanted to go there myself.

LEWIS (*grabbing* CHILDRESS *by the lapels*)   You heard what they *do* to guys like us? Have you heard? . . . Maybe you *do* know. Maybe you're one of them! Maybe you've been shaving your legs all this time.

CHILDRESS   No, Lewis! C'mon! Don't . . . aahhhh! (*He suddenly grabs at the spot where he was stabbed in agony.*)

LEWIS   What is it?

CHILDRESS   My chest! I feel like I've been stabbed!

Lights out.

VOICES   Loop sequence A. Reintegration commencing.

Lights up on bar.

DOBSON (*blowing smoke*)   No. You can't have any.

Lights out.

WEATHERMAN   . . . got a time loop going in the amber-light district. If you're in that area just remain inactive and . . .

Lights up on the apartment.

CHILDRESS   Ahh! I've been stabbed!

LEWIS   What is it, Childress?

Lights up on bar.

DOBSON   No. You can't have any.

VOICES   Loop sequence B. Reintegration proceeding.

CHILDRESS   I've been stabbed, Lewis! Help me!

CHILDRESS *is slumping back onto the floor.* LEWIS *eases him to the ground.*

LEWIS   Childress! What's happening, dammit!

WEATHERMAN   . . . the National Bureau of Weights and Measures has issued a travelers' advisory for the amber-light district . . .

DOBSON   No. You can't have any.

Lights out on bar.

CHILDRESS   I'm dying, Lewis!
VOICES   Loop sequence C. Reintegration concluding.
LEWIS   Childress! Childress!

CHILDRESS *lies motionless.* LEWIS *backs up.*

LEWIS   Damn! (He backs out the door.) Damn!

The door slams. Lights out on apartment.

WEATHERMAN   ... advisory in effect until sunrise, transit time, for the amber-light district. At 8:00/10:00 a time-lock-created disruption was spotted ...

Lights up on bar. DOBSON *and* PETERS *are back behind the bar.* TOMKINS *and* CONNIE *are gone.*

PETERS (*TO* DOBSON)   So, what did you do after you left the Wistful Flamingo?
DOBSON   Well, we stopped at Barney's for some fried leeches and then we headed back to the apartment. . . .

Lights on in apartment. DOBSON *and* PETERS *walk back over to it—*PETERS *grabbing* LANDRY'S *arm and pulling him along.*

PETERS   C'mon, soldier. We need to work this out.

LANDRY *walks with them complacently. As they step into the apartment, lights out on bar.*

DOBSON   Let's see . . . we walked in through the door . . . the three army boys first, then Harry and me . . . and then Harry led Landry over to the clock sculpture. . . . (*She takes* LANDRY'S *arm and leads him over to the sculpture. The two of them almost stumble over* CHILDRESS, *who's lying on the floor where* LEWIS *left him.*) Oh, look! Here's Childress! But he wasn't on the floor back then . . . it wasn't like this at all!

PETERS *squats behind* CHILDRESS *and slaps his face.* CHILDRESS *stirs.*

PETERS   Hey there, soldier. Wake up.
CHILDRESS (*blinking and shaking his head*)   Mmmmm. Wow. Can I have more of *those* pills, "Bob"? (*He sits up and looks around.*) Where am I?

DOBSON   You're in my apartment, army boy. Don't you remember?

CHILDRESS   No. Last I remember I was in this bar talking to a girl. I don't think it was you. . . .

DOBSON   It wasn't.

PETERS   Take it easy, soldier. You've been fucked, fragged and stabbed all in one night. You probably lost your memories when the girl you were talking to killed you.

CHILDRESS   Huh? Jesus! I'm not still fragmented, am I?

PETERS   Nah. I think Time Control managed to reintegrate you. (*He starts to help* CHILDRESS *up.*) C'mon. Let's get you into a chair. Give me a hand, Landry. (LANDRY *and* PETERS *help* CHILDRESS *into the overstuffed chair.*) You got anything that'll help this army boy reorient, Miz Dobson?

DOBSON   Think so. Just a moment. (*Exits.*)

CHILDRESS   Landry. At least someone I know is here. Do you know these guys?

LANDRY   I do now. The gentleman's name is Detective Peters. The woman is Barbara Dobson.

CHILDRESS   Detective? Something going on?

LANDRY   Afraid so. Both you and I are suspects in a murder case.

CHILDRESS   Murder! But I thought those didn't work anymore!

PETERS (*sitting down on the sofa*)   This one did. It was Miz Dobson's husband. Got his legs ripped right off.

CHILDRESS (*grossed out*)   Ooooooo! I don't think I could do something like that!

DOBSON *enters with a glass full of clear, fizzing liquid and ice.*

DOBSON   Here you go, army boy. Arsenic and tonic. Should buck you right up.

CHILDRESS   Thanks. (*He takes a sip.*) Mmmm.

There's a knock on the door.

DOBSON   Come in!

The PLAINCLOTHESMAN *enters with a computer printout.*

PLAINCLOTHESMAN   Here's the temporal analysis, sir.

PETERS   Thanks. How're you feeling?

PLAINCLOTHESMAN   Better, sir.

PETERS   Good. You missed a little over there. (*He points to the* PLAINCLOTHESMAN's *sleeve.*)

PLAINCLOTHESMAN   Oh. (*He takes out a hanky and dabs at the spot while* PETERS *looks through the printout.*)

CHILDRESS (*to the* PLAINCLOTHESMAN, *smiling*)   And I thought it was a cuff link.

The PLAINCLOTHESMAN *smiles wanly. Pause.*

PETERS (*nodding*)   Yep. Just as I thought. (*To* PLAINCLOTHESMAN:) We need to locate Lewis. Find him, but don't let him know you've found him. Use an undercover man to lure him up here. Let me know when he's on his way.

PLAINCLOTHESMAN   Yes sir. (*He leaves, muttering.*) Why don't I just build the Taj Mahal while I'm at it. . . . (*Door shuts.*)

There is another pause. Finally:

LANDRY   Well?

PETERS *reloads and relights his pipe, taking his time.*

PETERS   Childress could have done it rather easily. There's no telling how fragmented he became. Landry also could have done it. No one was watching him for a while. By the way, Landry, is this your wallet?

PETERS *pulls the wallet planted by* LEWIS *out from between the sofa cushions.* LANDRY *checks his pockets, then looks at the wallet more closely.*

LANDRY   Uh, yeah, it is. Funny, I know I had it with me. . . . Well, jeepers, Detective! I know I didn't do it, but I guess that wallet makes it look like I did.

PETERS *hands the wallet to* LANDRY.

PETERS   Not really, soldier. If you traveled through the right time zones, you could have had the wallet on your person for a brief while after you lost it. Reversed causality is becoming a pretty common thing these days. However, someone who still doesn't understand that may have planted your wallet here in an effort to frame you. I believe that's what happened. And these time charts here all point to the one suspect that isn't here with us.

DOBSON   Lewis!

CHILDRESS   Lewis? I don't get that, Detective Peters. He was always such a swell guy to me.

PETERS   Well, maybe he is, soldier. Maybe he is. But these are rough times for "swell guys." Living each day over and over again, fighting Nazi Hell Creatures and Green Energy Demons and Conspiracy Fragments. The Conspiracy Fragments are the worst. They can pull a man into the Conspiracy's war against itself without his even being aware of it, replacing his Slack with values derived from money, power, sex, religion or just raw fear, depending on which Fragment gets him. Soon our "swell guy" will be shitting dicks every time he tries to pee his own damn ass, and he'll think that's the way it's supposed to be. And where will we fit into his Conspiracy-fragged world-view? Any of us might represent the Slack that he has lost, even if he doesn't know he's lost it. His anger and fear will grow until they are finally unleashed against his subconsciously chosen enemy. It could be the local 'Frop retailer. It might be the man walking down the street with a pretty woman. Or maybe it's that rich salesman with those suspiciously hairy legs. . . .

DOBSON   Hairy legs. I remember him saying something about that.

LANDRY   He always made me shave mine.

PETERS   Yetis, of course, have very hairy legs.

CHILDRESS   I wish I could remember. There's something familiar about that . . .

The door opens. The PLAINCLOTHESMAN *enters.*

PLAINCLOTHESMAN   Sir, he's on his way.

PETERS   Good. Get out your pipes, everybody.

CHILDRESS   What for? Aren't you gonna arrest him?

PETERS   We don't have enough evidence to hold him. We need to prove that his behavior is criminally consistent. To do that we'll have to force him into a crisis situation. We'll use the fact that Lewis is a classic Bobbie to do it.

Now, I want all of you to slick your hair back, dig out your pipes and *be* J. R. "Bob" Dobbs. Don't pretend it. *Be* it! Suck that pipe, grin and let every stupidity of yours become divine! Sell yourself as the Dobbs—and Lewis will buy it!

Lieutenant, is the temporal shift ready?

PLAINCLOTHESMAN   Yes sir.

PETERS   Implement it as soon as he enters the building.

PLAINCLOTHESMAN   Yes sir. (*Exits.*)

PETERS   All right now. Childress. You wait on this couch.

VOICES   Cross-check for a temporal shift: 10:00 RPM ⅛—22:00 transit time.

PETERS   Miz Dobson, you and Landry need to wait in the bedroom.

VOICES   He's in the building. Implementing temporal shift . . . now!

Lights out on the apartment and up on the bar. The BARKEEP *is sweeping up.* CONNIE *sits at the table with the corpse of* HARRY

TOMKINS. *She takes a pistol and a box of bullets out of her purse. She loads the pistol.*

CONNIE   . . . I love old movies. They don't show 'em much anymore. You ever see that one called *Crossfire?* Starred Robert Mitchum, Robert Young and Robert Ryan. Guy gets killed right at the beginning and everyone spends the rest of the movie ruminatin' about how fucked up they are since World War II ended. Great film. . . .

 Lights out.

VOICES   Tracking. Phase one.

 Lights up on the apartment. CHILDRESS *sits on the sofa with a genial smile and a pipe.* LEWIS *enters quietly.*

CHILDRESS   Why, hello there, soldier!
LEWIS   Childress! You're alive!
CHILDRESS (*standing*)   I'm alive! Ho ho ho! (*He steps up to* LEWIS *and claps a hand on his shoulder.*) Why, does that mean you haven't killed your "Bob" today?
LEWIS   Of course I did! I ripped his legs off. Remember? You were all upset about it! . . . (CHILDRESS *smiles blankly at* LEWIS.) Remember? You fell over! Remember?

 Lights out.

VOICES   Begin zone interface . . . now.

 Lights up on bar. CONNIE *twirls the pistol on her finger, then places it in* TOMKINS' *hand so that it's aiming stage left.*

CONNIE   . . . Some things I don't mind doing without. Did you ever hear that group the Doktors for "Bob"? I never could deal with them. My husband sure liked 'em, though. . . .

 Lights off.

VOICES   Tracking. Phase two.

 Lights up on apartment.

LEWIS   Remember? You fell over!

 DOBSON *and* LANDRY *enter from the bedroom area with pipes and genial grins.*

LANDRY   Did I hear someone say, "Fall over"?

DOBSON   Why yes, I believe you did!

LANDRY   Okay! (*He falls over and rolls around on the floor*.) Whoa ho ho ho ho ho!

DOBSON (*to* LEWIS)   Why hello there, army boy! We were just about to try the "Bucking Kangaroo." Why don't you join us and we can try the "Pennsylvanian Camel Toot" instead! Lots of fun! Ha ha ha ha ha!

LEWIS (*getting quite nervous*)   Why are you all acting like "Bob"?

DOBSON   Hey there, army boy, there's a little bit of Dobbs in each of us. Why don't we celebrate our Dobbsness together in the bedroom, if you know what I mean! Huh? Huh? (*She starts winking obnoxiously at* LEWIS.)

LEWIS   I don't get it! I thought we were supposed to kill "Bob"!

CHILDRESS   "Kill "Bob" or kill me!" That's what they always say!

LANDRY   "Kill "Bob" or kill me!" "Fuck 'em if they can't take a joke!"

DOBSON   "Kill "Bob" or kill me!" Nobody can eat just one!

LEWIS *is backing towards the door.* PETERS *enters through the door and stands quietly behind him.*

LEWIS   I don't get it! Who do I kill, "Bob" or me? I just don't get it! (*He backs into* PETERS.)

PETERS   Why, hello, "Bob"! It's good to see you!

LEWIS   I'm not "Bob"!

PETERS   Ha ha ha ha ha! Nice joke, "Bob," but I'd know that stupid face anywhere! See? Look for yourself.

PETERS *holds up a poster of Dobbs.* LEWIS *blanches. He pulls out a gun.*

LEWIS   Dammit! I don't get it! Am I "Bob" or me? Who do I kill? What are the rules, dammit? Why doesn't somebody explain the rules?

PETERS   Gee, "Bob," you don't seem happy. Would you like to go somewhere else?

LEWIS   I . . . I wanna go back to the bar before all of this happened! I was happy there!

VOICES   Tracking. Phase three.

Lights up on bar. LEWIS *whirls around and stares at* HARRY *and* CONNIE. HARRY's *pistol is pointed right at* LEWIS.

LEWIS   You!

TOMKINS   You!

LEWIS   You're "Bob," aren't you?

TOMKINS   You're "Bob," aren't you?

LEWIS   That's Connie, isn't it?

TOMKINS   That's Connie, isn't it?

LEWIS   Dammit! Answer me!

TOMKINS   Dammit! Answer me!

LEWIS   Stop saying everything I say!

TOMKINS   Stop saying everything I say!

LEWIS   I mean it, you hairy-legged Yeti!

TOMKINS   I mean it, you hairy-legged Yeti!

LEWIS   Okay, buddy, you asked for this!

TOMKINS   Okay, buddy, you asked for this!

LEWIS *aims his gun at* TOMKINS.

VOICES   End phase . . . now!

Lights out. We hear a bizarrely reverberated gunshot, followed by LEWIS *grunting and the sound of a falling body.*

WEATHERMAN   . . . although there were some complex time snarls earlier this evening, things have all cleared up now and we should have smooth, temporal sailing at least until the end of the transit week. . . .

Lights up on both the apartment and the bar. There is no more bar music. CONNIE *sits alone with what's left of a drink. In the apartment,* LEWIS *lies dead.* TOMKINS' *corpse lies on top of him.*

PETERS (*squatting, feeling* LEWIS' *neck for a pulse*)   Yep. He's dead all right.

PETERS *stands and lights his pipe. Two genial-looking* HUNCH-BACKS *with pipes enter and carry* LEWIS' *body away.*

CONNIE   Well, I guess that's it for tonight. (*She finishes her drink.*)

LANDRY   I don't get it. Did he kill Harry? Did Harry kill him?

PETERS   Hard to say. Doesn't really make any damn sense. Maybe Harry *was* "Bob." Maybe Lewis killed him just like he was supposed to.

BARKEEP   You comin' back tomorrow, Connie?

CONNIE   I don't know. I kinda think it's getting to be time to move on.

The BARKEEP *comes over to the table and starts to turn the chairs upside down on it.* CONNIE *stands and turns her own chair over.* CHILDRESS *picks up* TOMKINS' *torso.*

CHILDRESS   Well, hell! If he was "Bob," then I guess we gotta take him out to dinner.

LANDRY (*picking up* TOMKINS' *legs*)   Yep. Guess so. (*To* PETERS *and* DOBSON:) Would either of you care to join us?

DOBSON   Why don't you three go on. I've got some things to discuss with Detective Peters.

PETERS   Uh, yeah. Have a good dinner. Looks like I've got a widow to fuck.

LANDRY   Okay. Good night, Detective Peters.

PETERS   Good night, soldier.

CHILDRESS   Good night, Miz Dobson.

DOBSON   Good night, army boy.

CHILDRESS, LANDRY *and* TOMKINS *leave through the door.* PETERS *and* DOBSON *walk arm in arm to the bedroom.*

CONNIE (*as she walks out of the bar*)   Good night, Robert.

BARKEEP   Good night, Connie.

CONNIE *exits. The* BARKEEP *continues to sweep.*

WEATHERMAN   . . . stable transit time of 12:30, 10:42 RPM squared. Got some good time coming up tomorrow, and as always, they'll be coming in threes. . . .

The WEATHERMAN'S *voice is drowned out by tinny movie music. Over the music, we hear the* VOICES.

VOICES   Another night shift ends. Praise Dobbs!
Another night is over. Praise Dobbs!
Another senseless killing. Praise Dobbs!
Another brutal murder. Praise Dobbs!

The music rises up to a majestic conclusion. Lights out. The end.

THE END OF ALL BULLETS

Chapter 20

That's right, folks—that was the time "Bob" came over and he was wearing that electric spinning bow tie of his. We kept telling him it looked stupid, but he thought it was the funniest thing on God's green earth and he just sat there laughing—he wouldn't stop, so eventually we had to pile the chairs on top of him. And he just kept laughing—even with the hot ashes from that Pipe falling in his face. Finally the police had to come over and investigate the racket. They came into the lab and asked what was going on, and we said, "Oh, it's just "Bob," " but he was gone. . . .

And some Glorp came on the TV and she said we need tough new laws because the Conspiracy won't go away by itself and so we had to be mature about this. And so we'd better all knuckle down and do our jobs or we'll end up getting our Slack taken away by force, because Slack isn't a right, it's a privilege. And slavery isn't a privilege, it's a right, and self-destruction isn't a right, it's a duty. And "Bob" is a fictional character propped up by a bunch of malcontents who need expert medical attention, not that they deserve it. AND I AM ELMER FUDD! And she said that I really did need help if I went around saying things like that. So I watched TV and the movie came on and the hero proved he was the hero by renouncing his Slack for all eternity. Of course he had to do it, and the folks who took his Slack disposed of it properly and said he was a good boy, and to get back into the box. And he got back into the box and he never came out of it again. And everyone solemnly agreed that it was the Will of God. And the heroine was mysteriously removed from the film before that—she just stopped appearing. I was wondering why she disappeared, and tried getting an answer out of the network. I gave the network a call, and they sent a bunch of guys over to punch my eyeball. But I was out.

I struck up a conversation with a random passerby, and she decided in great detail what I would be doing for the rest of the month. It sounded like a threat, but she was very nice about it. She spat on me and drove off in someone else's car. I sat down under a tree and some men I didn't know ran up with megaphones and told me not to go to sleep and that if I had any common decency at all I would buy a car. As I got up to leave, one of the men explained to me, in meticulous detail, his vendetta against his brother-in-law. He never said exactly why he was angry but he sure knew what he was going to do about it; he managed to repeat each of his sentences, with variations, at least four times. Then he asked me to take out a mortgage on his house and was offended when I laughed politely. So I tried to cross the street, but the traffic was backed up as far as the state line in both directions, even though the cars went real fast. I stood before the double line of automobiles and their screaming drivers for about half an hour before I turned around and went home without crossing the street. The TV went on again and some Glorp game-show host came on and allowed as how we should all have Atari games implanted in our heads so we could all be state-of-the-art, because Science is self-correcting and inevitable and we have to be mature about this. And a commercial came on with some little girls doing aerobics and some guy saying that he'd even grow tomato plants on top of your roof just to make you happy. No, those two things had nothing to do with each other. Some guy running for office came on and spouted words out of the dictionary at random, and then that choir that sang "We Are the World" and that Pepsi jingle started singing "Get Off Your Hiney America." I thought I saw "Bob" in another commercial, but it was just the Goodyear blimp. . . .

Robert Anton Wilson

THE HORROR ON HOWTH HILL

It was the rains, I swear—the interminable, unspeakable Irish rains—that drove us over the edge. My old Gothic castle, located high atop the hill of Howth facing Dublin Bay, was not only damp, dank and dark (due to the omnipresent clouds) but rapidly becoming decadent, noisome and foetid. In fact, it looked like the set for a Bela Lugosi film—an appropriate scene, I thought later, for the terrible encounter of Professor de Selby and J. R. "Bob" Dobbs.

The rain had gone on for two months this time, bringing a clammy, enervating muskiness to everything. In the library, even the pages of my prized German translation of the banned and forbidden *Necronomicon* (*Das Verichteraraberbuch,* von Juntz, 1848) and de Selby's disturbing and debatable *Teratologica Ontologicum* were sticking together unwholesomely.

Rancid, the butler, was falling-down drunk every day and I could hardly blame him. The maids—dark, sensuous Immaculata and blonde, buxom Concepción—were not only dykes, as I suspected from the first, but speed freaks as well. They spent all day in their room, injecting and 69ing, injecting and 69ing. They totally neglected their duties and the entire castle had begun to look like the bottom of a box where the cat had kittens. Adam, the gardener, had been tripping his brains out on LSD since the third week of the rains and the grounds had the eldritch and nameless appearance of the swamps of Yuggoth redesigned by Salvador Dali. If the damnable downpour did not cease soon, I feared that we all should become mad. I think I myself would have been sunk in lethargy and existential despair if it were not for my mescaline and XTC stashes.

Worst of all, it was drawing near the aeon-cursed Walpurgis Night, and Professor de Selby[1] had come to pay his annual visit again.

---

[1] De Selby was the most controversial Irish philosopher of the later twentieth century. For biographical details, see O'Brien, *Dalkey Archive,* Picador Books, London, 1976, and/or Wilson, *The Widow's Son,* Bluejay Press, New York, 1985. Highlights of the de Selby furor will be found in Conneghen, *The de Selby Codex and Its Critics,* Royal Sir Myles na gCopaleen Anthropological Society Press, Dalkey, 1937; Flahive, *Teratological Evolution,* Royal Sir Myles na gCopaleen Biochemical Institute Press, Dalkey, 1972; Vinkenoog, *De Selby: De onbekende filosoof,* De Kosmos, Amsterdam, 1951; La Fournier, *De Selby: l'Enigme de l'Occident,* University of Paris, 1933; Han Tui Po, *De Selby Te Ching,* University of Beijing, 1978; La Tournier (not to be confused with La Fournier), *De Selby: Homme ou Dieu?,* Editions J'ai Lu, Paris, 1904; von Hanfkopf, *DeSelbyismus und Dummheit* (6 vols.), University of Heidelberg, 1942–52; La Puta, *La Estupidez de Hanfkopf,* University of Madrid, 1975; Turn-und-Taxis, *Ist de Selby eine Droge oder haben wir sie nur falsch verstanden?,* Sphinx Verlag, Basel, 1922; O'Broichnan, *A Chara, na caith tabac,* Royal Sir Myles na gCopaleen Zoological Institute Press, Dalkey, 1992.

Of course, I personally have always liked de Selby, who is not at all a bad chap in his own weird way. But he lives always, not just in the turmoil of academic controversy, but in the epicenter of a veritable spider's web of clandestine operations: where de Selby walks, the CIA and KGB are sure to skulk close behind, and the IRA and even the PLO may be showing interest also, not to mention the Knights of Malta,[2] the Illuminati,[3] the Priory of Sion,[4] the Campus Crusade for Cthulhu[5] and other secret societies and cults whose reputations are unsavory and whose goals remain inscrutable to ordinary wholesome men and women.[6] Some of these types would be beyond the comprehension of the Los Angeles Vice Squad or the specialists in abnormal psychology at the Kinsey Institute, I swear.

[2] The Knights of Malta—or, more properly, the Sovereign Military Order of Malta (abbreviated SMOM)—is the eight-hundred-year-old Vatican "secret police" or "dirty tricks bureau." According to *Covert Action Information Bulletin* #25, Winter 1986, notable recent members of SMOM have included Dr. Otto von Hapsburg (a prime organizer of the infamous "Bilderbergers"), Franz von Papen (the man who persuaded President von Hindenburg to resign and appoint Hitler chancellor of Germany), William Casey (the CIA chief who died mysteriously during the Iran-Contra hearings), Major General Reinhard Gehlen (*vide supra*), General Alexander Haig, William F. Buckley, Jr., Clare Boothe Luce, and the three ringleaders of the P2 conspiracy in Italy—Roberto Calvi, Michele Sindona and Licio Gelli. Baigent, Lincoln and Leigh in *The Messianic Legacy* (Henry Holt, New York, 1987) have added to the list of SMOM members Alexandre de Marenches, former chief of French intelligence, and claim mysterious links between SMOM and the Priory of Sion. Gordon Thomas and Max Wittman in *The Year of Armaggedon* (Corgi, London, 1984) claim that SMOM members act as couriers between the Vatican and the CIA. Most scholars dissent vehemently from von Hanfkopf's ill-documented charge that de Selby, Flahive, La Tournier and the shadowy La Fournier are all members of SMOM.

[3] The Illuminati, founded in Bavaria in 1776, was (or is) a secret society within a secret society, since all members were first Freemasons before being invited into the Illuminati itself. See Nesta Webster, *World Revolution,* Christian Book Club of America, Hawthorne, California, n.d.; "Inquire Within," *The Trail of the Serpent,* Christian Book Club of America, Hawthorne, California, n.d.; and Wilson, *Cosmic Trigger,* Falcon Books, Santa Monica, 1987. The Illuminati technique of forming a secret society within another secret society was later imitated by the Molly Maguires, an Irish revolutionary group within the Ancient Order of Hibernians, and the P2 conspiracy which recruited within the Grand Orient Lodge of Egyptian Freemasonry in Italy—although secretly managed, as noted above, by three members of the Vatican secret service, SMOM. Professor Flahive was under great personal stress when he began his campaign to convince the learned community that von Hanfkopf was actually the ringleader of an Illuminati conspiracy against de Selby.

[4] According to Paoli (*Les Dessous d'une ambition politique,* Hurhaus Verlag, Basel, 1973), the Priory of Sion is a serious political conspiracy of aristocratic French Freemasons who intend to restore monarchy in France. According to de Sede (*La Race fabuleuse,* Editions J'ai Lu, Paris, 1973), the Priory is descended from superhumans born of matings between ancient Hebrews and extraterrestrials from Sirius. According to Baigent, Leigh and Lincoln (*Holy Blood, Holy Grail,* Delacorte, 1982), the Priory is descended from the royal line of Jesus and Mary Magdalene. According to Michael Lame (*Jules Verne, initiate et initiateur,* Editions J'ai Lu, Paris, 1985), the Priory is a front for the Illuminati and Verne's "science fiction" novels are subtle Illuminati recruiting manuals. De Selby claims (*Golden Hours,* Royal Sir Myles na gCopaleen Philosophical Society Press, Dalkey, 1957) that the Illuminati/Priory axis is an attempt to spread electric light everywhere, thereby banishing the "teratological molecules" which move backwards in time and generate Chaos, but this must be considered one of the more imaginative flights of the Dalkey sage.

[5] The Campus Crusade for Cthulhu has been alleged to be responsible for the recent crop of child murders and cattle mutilations elsewhere attributed to Satanists; see Rev. Jedidiah Blather, *The Cthulhu Cult, Interstellar Bankers and Punk Rock,* True Christian Book Club of America, Tulsa,

1987. Although few credit this wild charge, the CCC is definitely responsible for the bumper stickers that say things like IT FOUND ME, ABDUL ALHAZRED WAS NOT MAD, YOG SOTHOTH NEBLOD ZIN, etc. Von Hanfkopf's attempts to link La Puta to the CCC are best described as tenuous and (as Ferguson said) "clutching at straws." It was after Professor Ferguson uttered these views on the BBC that the police of his hometown, Loch Pookah, received letters claiming he, Ferguson, was the Yorkshire Ripper. These letters were in clumsy English ("rather like that of the Katzenjammer Kids," according to Inspector MacAndrew, who handled the investigation) and had Heidelberg postmarks.

[6] The de Selby controversy originally erupted into political mania after Professor von Hanfkopf charged (see his *Werke*, vol. XXIII, pp. 506–36ff.) that some of the moneys embezzled from Banco Ambrosiano of Milan in the early 1980s (by the bank's president, Roberto Calvi, and his associates in the P2 conspiracy) had been "laundered" through a Dublin bank account which de Selby allegedly used to finance IRA terrorism in Northern Ireland. Although this charge was unsubstantiated, Professor Flahive rebutted it at great length (*Proceedings of the Royal Sir Myles na gCopaleen Institute of International Relations*, vol. LVI, pp. 309–417) and it was after this that the Special Branch of the Gardai (the police of the Republic of Ireland) began receiving letters with a Heidelberg postmark charging (in broken English) that Flahive himself was involved in running guns for the IRA. This was immediately after the unfortunate and much-debated incident involving Professor Flahive and the fourteen-year-old Girl Scout from Sallynoggin, and the distressed savant, a devout Catholic and conservative, began making wild charges about "international plots" and "frame-ups" and, sadly, eventually degenerated to the same tactics as von Hanfkopf, claiming that the Heidelberg philosopher was formerly associated with the Gehlen apparat and the CIA's "Russian" branch—the group, under Major General Reinhard Gehlen, Knight of Malta and former head of army intelligence for Hitler, which conducts espionage within the Soviet Union itself. Of course, the crude (and ineffective) letter bomb sent to Professor Flahive at this point, although postmarked Alexandria, Virginia, could have been sent by anybody (and one assumes the CIA are at least clever enough not to mail such devices from a city universally known to be their international headquarters); but after Roberto Calvi, President of Banco Ambrosiano, was found hanging from Blackfriars Bridge in London that same week, and his secretary, Ms. Graziella, fell or was pushed from a window of the Milan office of that bank, sheer paranoia descended upon all those involved in the de Selby feud or even in the abstract mathematical arguments about de Selby's "plenuminary time" and teratological molecules." As La Puta has incisively remarked, "The entire de Selby debate is degenerating into the worst academic *schlemozzle* since the Bacon-Shakespeare lunacy."

As usual, de Selby has a new obsession this year. He is determined to discover the exact dimensions of the penis of a fictitious gorilla. Any ordinary scholar, however eccentric, might decide to write a paper on the dimensions of the wingwang of a real gorilla, dead or alive, but de Selby wants to discover the magnitude of the Willy of a gorilla who never really existed at all—King Kong in the famous horror film of 1933. Naturally, being de Selby, he has reasons for this which no normal person can understand. He says 1932 (when *King Kong* was being produced) was a pivot in evolution, in some mystic sense that only he comprehends.

"In 1932," he was telling me at breakfast this morning, "Alice Pleasance Liddell died, and so did John Stanislaus Joyce."

"Who the hell were they?" I asked irritably.

"Alice P. Liddell," he said somberly, "was the model for Alice in Wonderland. Charles Dodgson and/or Lewis Carroll—the world's most successful dual personality—loved her um ah er 'not wisely but too well.' Too well, at any rate, to avoid the speculations of Freudians. And

John Stanislaus Joyce was the father of James Joyce. Do you see the connection?"

I admitted that the linkage evaded me.

"Alice Pleasance Liddell or APL," de Selby said simply, "is one aspect of Anna Livia Plurabelle or ALP, the superwoman who contains all women, in Joyce's *Finnegans Wake*."

"Oh," I said. It seemed the only adequate comment.

"I have wondered," de Selby went on, "if one can equate APL with ALP on Cabalistic grounds, since both equal 111, what of PLA? But that is an irrelevance, I've decided.[7] What is important is that in 1932 not only did Alice P. Liddell and John S. Joyce die, but the atom was split for the first time, and the 92nd chemical element was discovered— the last *natural* element, you see. For the first time in history humanity had access to the energy of the stars and possessed a full catalog of the basic building blocks of the universe. And, of course, Roosevelt II was elected in America, and Hitler in Germany, that very same year, 1932, which incidentally adds numerologically to 15, the number of the Devil card in the Tarot. King Kong, you see, had to emerge from the collective unconscious at exactly that point, especially since Cary Grant was 28 years old on January 18 that year."

[7] "PLA" is Dublin slang for Portlaois Lunatic Asylum, the place which many of de Selby's critics claimed would be his ultimate destination. As La Fournier wrote (*De Selby: l'Enigme de la Occident,* p. 23), "While much about the sage of Dalkey remains in dispute, none have denied that he held a greater number of totally original ideas than any philosopher in history not known to have been kept in a padded cell." Von Hanfkopf's claim that Le Fournier was a mask, a nonentity, a fiction, a stalking horse behind which de Selby wrote commentaries on himself, in *French* no less, has not been conclusively verified, and La Puta claims to have refuted it entirely in his *La Estupidez,* op. cit. It was after this work was published that the Spanish police began receiving letters, with a Heidelberg postmark, alleging in bad Spanish that La Puta was the chief opium smuggler in Madrid and a KGB agent. Professor Hamburger's attempts to link La Puta to the Illuminati (*Proceedings of the London Musicological Society,* vol. XXIII, pp. 7–133) do, however, appear to be well documented and possess some merit, although Hamburger's argument that it was La Puta, not de Selby, who laundered the cocaine money for the P2 conspiracy is far from convincing. As Penny Lernoux documents in her *In Banks We Trust* (Anchor Press/Doubleday, Garden City, New York, 1984), most of the cocaine money went through the World Finance Corporation in Miami and the Cisalpine Overseas Bank in the Bahamas, which was owned by the deceased Robert Calvi and Archbishop Marcinkus. The argument of Yallop (*In God's Name,* Bantam, New York, 1984) that Calvi and Marcinkus collaborated in the murder of Pope John Paul I is, of course, highly speculative.

De Selby went on in that vein for quite a while, but I sort of lost the thread of his argument—something that often happens to readers of his books, as numerous critics have complained.[8] All I could ever remember afterwards was that Cary Grant was 28 when I was born and 28 is a number connected with menstruation, the ancient Celtic moon goddess, Bridget, and the synchronous link from Lewis Carroll's obsession with premenstrual girls to Cary Grant's habit of avoiding the Academy Award dinners, staying home, taking LSD and watching the award ceremonies on TV while "laughing uncontrollably and jumping up and down on the bed," according to the testimony in his third divorce trial.

[8] As du Garbandier has written (De Selby et l'or de Rennes, p. 17) "Le suprême charme qu'on trouve à lire une page de de Selby est qu'elle vous conduit inexorablement à l'heureuse certitude que des sots ne sont pas les plus grands." Von Hanfkopf's charge (Der Spiegel, 2/2/1982) that de Garbandier was a member of the shadowy and sinister Priory of Sion seems, for once, adequately documented and in conjunction with the links established between the Priory of Sion in Paris and the Italian P2 conspiracy (see Baigent, Lincoln, and Leigh, The Messianic Legacy, op. cit., passim) lends at least a tinge of near credibility to the alleged P2 account at the Bank of Ireland in de Selby's name, although Ferguson's attempts (Armageddon, Ed Smith University Press, Biloxi, Mississippi, 1983) to link de Selby to the cocaine laundering of Roberto Calvi, Michele Sindona and Archbishop Paul Marcinkus still remains dubious, Kerflooey's thesis of the double de Selbys and the linkage from the Knights of Malta to the Campus Crusade for Cthulhu (The Second de Selby, Thelema Books, Dallas, 1983) is patently absurd. If Kerflooey had not been present in Dealey Plaza on November 22, 1963, and had not died in a hit-and-run auto accident the week his book was published, this nonsense would never have been taken seriously by anyone.

Eventually, we finished our leisurely breakfast, it was ten thirty and the pubs opened, so de Selby put on his brown mackintosh (he seems to have worn it since 1904, I think) and sallied forth in search of Irish Inspiration.

I went to the study and tried again to work on my new science-fiction novel, *Wigner's Friend,* which deals with a parallel universe where de Selby is Pope and Adolf Hitler migrated to the United States and became a popular writer of Western movies. As usual lately, my creativity was dampened by the depressing rain, the eldritch, unhallowed and Peter Lorre–like giggles of the gardener after his day's dose of LSD took effect and the strange, foetid and nameless fungi that have grown on the furniture since the maids got hooked on methamphetamines and stopped even pretending to clean up.

Rancid, the butler, lurched into the study, staggered, knocked over a Ming vase, puked into the potted fern, and asked if I needed anything. I sent him away with no rancor. He was too drunk to understand anything I said, anyway. I did wish, however, that he looked a little less like Boris Karloff as the alcoholic (and eventually homicidal) butler in *The Old Dark House.* The rain continued to fall and the sky remained overcast and gloomy, turning my thoughts to the most morbid subjects imaginable. I was actually happy when de Selby returned, in a car driven by an American tourist he had met at the Royal Howth, a Mr. J. R. "Bob" Dobbs.

"Bob," de Selby said grandly, "meet "Bob." " I could see that de Selby had put away at least five or six pints of Guinness stout already, and I tried not to become uneasy or let my imagination run riot over the simple fact that "Bob" had a Campus Crusade for Cthulhu bumper sticker on his Toyota. Americans often have a strange sense of humor. Nonetheless, as we entered the castle, I looked back at the car and shuddered involuntarily at the other words on the bumper:

Have you hugged your shoggoth today?

We went to my study, where de Selby, with his usual exhuberant Celtic generosity, opened a bottle of my best Tullamore Dew and offered a healthy double shot to "Bob." I was pleased when he offered some to me, too.

" "Bob" has some real data on Kong's dong," de Selby began at once, finishing the rest of the bottle in a gulp.

I raised an enquiring eyebrow, a trick I had learned from Basil Rathbone movies. "Bob" was busy relighting his Pipe for a moment but then he spoke in a mellow Texas drawl.

"The average man," he said, "stands between about five foot eight and about six foot, right? And the average human erection, at least according to my wife, "Connie"—who is more of an expert on males in heat than I am—is between five and seven inches. The nine-inchers and twelve-inchers you see occasionally in porn movies are freaks of nature, like Watusis or basketball players who can be seven or eight feet tall. Follow me? So the average human male, statistically, has about six inches. Kay? Now in the case of Kong, we have an anthropoid standing at least twenty-four feet tall, as you can judge by the scene in the theater. That means he would have about four times as much as a man of six feet. Four times six is twenty-four, so Kong had twenty-four inches or two feet."

"No wonder Fay Wray did so much screaming," I said. "She'd be in the position of the young lady from Sidney in the limerick."

De Selby raised an enquiring eyebrow (he's seen a lot of Basil Rathbone movies, too) and courteously opened another bottle of my Tullamore Dew. To explain my remark, I recited the immortal lines from Tennyson:

> There was a young lady from Sidney
> Who liked it right up to her kidney
> A man from Quebec
> Shoved it up to her neck
> He had a big one, didn't he?

De Selby refilled our glasses all around and sat down in an easy chair. He looked troubled.

"Well," I said to him cheerfully. "Your mystery is solved. There's no prob with "Bob." "

"I don't know," the Sage of Dalkey replied thoughtfully. "We may be approaching this matter from the wrong angle entirely. "Bob" is treating Kong as a creature in biology, which is emphatically what the Big

Fellow is not at all, at all. Kong is a creature in mythology, in um ah er the collective unconscious."

"Why, sure," said "Bob" quickly. "Hellfire, boy, there ain't no twenty-four-foot gorillas in the real world. But if we grant that, for argument's sake, how in hell do we reason about Kong at all? What are the dimensions of a myth, a dream, a Special Effect? Tell me that." And he grabbed the Tullamore Dew and poured another hearty slug. I could see we were in for a day of heavy going.

"Well," de Selby said, "we must take our clues from the records of the collective unconscious itself. Kong is a Nature Divinity, to say the least of it, and, considering his um concupiscence—that means horniness in American, "Bob"—he's more specifically a Fertility God. We must approach this from the perspective of patapsychology."[9]

[9] De Selby's lifelong enthusiasm for Alfred Jarry and Pataphysics had led him to name his own System "patapsychology." (Like all Irish writers, de Selby was convinced he had to create a System, and the more inscrutable the System was to the non-Céltic reader, the better.) Due to a printer's error *patapsychology* was misspelled as *parapsychology* in the first edition of his *Teratologica Ontologicum,* and La Puta has always claimed that it was this misreading that motivated the vehement, venomous and vitriolic polemics von Hanfkopf was to write, denouncing first de Selby himself and then all quantum physicists who claimed to find value in de Selby's concept of plenumary time. (Von Hanfkopf was the organizer of the SS, or Scientific Skeptics, the German branch of CSICOP, the Committee for the Scientific Investigation of Claims of the Paranormal.) Patapsychology is defined by de Selby as the study of "unique, statistically improbable, nondeterministic mental processes," or, more elegantly, "neurological negative entropy."

"What are you getting at?" I asked uneasily. In the distance, a dog barked and, further off, there was an ominous rumble of thunder.

"Well," de Selby said. "We know one thing about Fertility Gods. Anthropologists call them *ithyphallique* and not without reason. They make the studs in porn movies look puny by comparison. Osiris is portrayed in Egyptian art as having about three times as much Willy as one would expect in a man, or god, of his size. In Greece, Hermes was usually depicted with a tool almost the size of his body—why, statues of him look almost like a bureau with the middle drawer pulled all the way out. As for Finn Mac Cool, some of the most powerful verses in the Finn epics—the most beautiful lines of Gaelic in our tradition, although usually expunged in English translations—describe him as, well, virtually a pole-vaulter with a built-in pole."

"Why, hell's bells, son," said "Bob" chortling, "that's the most persistent of all legends. When I was young everybody in the States believed Dillinger had twenty-three inches and it was preserved in alcohol at the Smithsonian after his death.[10] Later on, the myth got attached to an actor named Errol Flynn. Long crullers, the kind you call *Berliners* over here, were called Errol Flynns."

[10] This myth continues to live, largely due to the publicity campaign of the John Dillinger Died for You Society, headquartered in Austin, Texas, and led by the shadowy Dr. Horace Naismith, who

claims to be the illegitimate son of Mr. Dillinger. Although Kerflooey, op. cit., attempts to link the John Dillinger Died for You Society to the ill-reputed Campus Crusade for Cthulhu and the even more infamous Paratheo-Anametamystikhood of Eris Esoteric (POEE), his evidence is as unconvincing as his "two de Selby" and "three Oswald" theories. See Malaclypse, *Kerflooey Is Kaput,* Discordian Press, San Francisco, 1987. It is sad to report that when Malaclypse invited Kerflooey to San Francisco for what he called "a serious, adult discussion" of their differences, Professor Kerflooey arrived armed, as the subsequent police report showed, with three revolvers, two pistols, five semiautomatic rifles, several vials of poison, two dirks, five swords, a meat cleaver, a flamethrower, a bazooka, several pounds of *plastique* explosive and 20 grams of gelignite. As Flahive said after the subsequent inquest, "Simple good taste and elementary decency should set certain limits on the intensity of even the most vigorous academic debate."

"Say," I interrupted, smitten with whimsy, "when John Fitzgerald Kennedy went to Germany and said, 'Ich bin ein Berliner,' was he just being diplomatic, or was he bragging?"

They ignored me. "Dillinger and Mr. Flynn had become semidivine in folklore," de Selby said, pouring more Tullamore Dew, "and so naturally they were expected to have semidivine prongs, two or three times the norm. Truly divine beings have much, much more. Considering Osiris and Hermes, I would say a divine being would have six times the norm, at least. As a fertility spirit, Kong must have, not the mere two feet that a biological twenty-four-foot gorilla would possess, but around twelve feet."

"That fits with the anthropological books I've read," I agreed. "The primitive theory is, *the greater the Willy, the greater the divinity indwelling.*"

We paused to consider the patapsychological ramifications of our theorizing. Thunder rumbled closer to my castle and more dogs began howling in anxiety.

"You know, fellers," Dobbs said, filling his Pipe again—I had begun to recognize the aroma of what he was smoking and understood why he always had the same contented grin—"I come from Texas, where we got ourselves almost as many Catholics as here in Ireland. There's a big donnybrook going on in the Catholic church these days because some nuns have become Feminists and are demanding the right to say Mass. The Pope absolutely refuses to consider it. He says you absolutely have to have a Willy to perform the sacrament."

De Selby had been hunting in my bar for more Tullamore, and, finding none, opened a bottle of my Jameson. "Why, of course a priest must have a Willy in Catholic theology," he said mildly. "The priest represents God, who has the biggest Willy of all—even bigger than Kong's."

"What was that?" I objected. "There was a quantum jump or something there. Run that by me again."

"You said it yourself," de Selby drawled. " 'The greater the Willy, the greater the divinity indwelling.' Yahweh, the Jewish God who became the Christian God, always claimed to be bigger and better than any of the other Near Eastern gods who competed with him. He would have to be endowed with a schlong that would make Osiris or Dionysus, say, look almost impotent by comparison."

"Just how big would it be?" I challenged. If de Selby and "Bob," with only two bottles of malt in them, could deduce the size of King Kong's dong, I was sure that with another bottle they could do the same for Yahweh.

"Well," de Selby said, "Yahweh himself isn't much bigger than Kong. He walks around Eden at twilight without smashing down the trees or causing any notable wreckage of the sort Godzilla would leave in his wake. He shows his backside to Moses and nobody in Greece or even Babylon sees that cosmic spectacle. I would say he couldn't be more than forty or fifty feet tall. In bio-logic, he should have about four to five feet. In mytho-logic, if he were any ordinary fertility god like Hermes or Finn, he would have six times that or around twenty-four to thirty feet. As the Lord of Lords and King of Kings, etc., he would double our expectations at least. He should have around fifty feet. In passion, he would be symmetrical, fifty feet high and fifty wide in the middle, sort of like a giant F with the top stroke missing."

"I begin to feel the same sympathy for the Virgin Mary that I experienced earlier for Fay Wray," I said, finishing off my own shot of Jameson. But then another thought struck me. "Yahweh may have been about that size—probably was that size, I think—back in Biblical times. The scriptures are full of lots of other references that show him about the height of Finn Mac Cool or Zeus, say. But he has grown during the scientific epoch. Every new advance in astronomy has necessitated that the whole Judeo-Christian tradition has had to make him bigger and uh er more gaseous, as it were. By the time of Newton, he had to be at least millions of miles in circumference to create the known universe. Since we started finding other galaxies in the 1920s, he has swollen to billions and billions of light-years—at least."

"Yes," said "Bob" thoughtfully. "To be consistent with known cosmology, the Judeo-Christian God would have to be bodacious, to say the least of it. And the size of his Willy—gol dang, the mind spins at the thought."

"And yet if we accept Christianity in any sense, even as metaphor à la Mr. T. S. Eliot," de Selby muttered pensively, "the metaphor demands such a whang for its divinity. Trillions of zillions of parsecs from foreskin to base. The only way out of that logic is the Feminist path. Neuter the divinity. He has no dong at all. He isn't a he anymore. A cosmic eunuch."

"Well, there's also the Radical Feminist path," I suggested. "He's a she."

"Lawdy, lawdy," said "Bob" dazedly, quickly gulping some more Jameson. "Now we have to try to visualize a vagina quadrillions of parsecs deep."[11]

[11] I have often thought, later, that it was this conversation which inspired de Selby's most controversial essay, "Can Goddess Create a Stone So Heavy That She Herself Cannot Lift It?," which he optimistically submitted to several Radical Feminist journals in San Francisco. It was after this that WITCH (the Women's International Terrorist Conspiracy from Hell) began picketing de Selby's home in Dalkey. It is unfortunate that Flahive, in his passion to defend de Selby against all detractors, attempted to prove the WITCHes were a "front" for the Knights of Malta. If Flahive had not been himself a former CIA agent and coincidentally present, like Kerflooey, in Dealey Plaza on November 22, 1963, not even the wild-eyed Hamburger would have claimed evidence of foul play in Flahive's subsequent tragic death in a hunting accident with Professor La Puta.

It was at this point, alas, that the whiskey began to go to my head and I nodded off in my chair. De Selby and "Bob" politely did not try to arouse me, reasoning that I needed the rest, and went ahead helping themselves to my rare cognacs, now that the Jameson was exhausted. In that hypnopompic state midway between drunkenness and coma, I was half aware, or dreamed I was half aware, of the continuing conversation.

Somehow de Selby and "Bob" wandered from the high theological contemplation of divine dongs back to the King himself, and were united in condemning the cheap remakes produced by some Japanese studios and the abominable caricatures of De Laurentiis. Still: They thought it was time for a "sincere" remake, and soon had sketched out a film which I, in my reverie, could see as clearly as if they had already shot it.

Ann Darrow, this time, would be played by Marilyn Chambers, on the grounds that *Behind the Green Door* was, psychoanalytically considered, already a part of the Kong mythos. Like Fay Wray in the original, Marilyn in *Green Door* is kidnapped and offered as a mate to a divinely endowed Fertility Spirit. "Bob" and de Selby agreed heartily that the black superstud in *Door,* with his gargantuan tool (and the "savage" bone in his nose) represented the same primitive generative force as Kong. "Pornography," I heard "Bob" say profoundly, "merely makes explicit what is implicit in folk art like *Kong.*"

In the new *Kong,* Marilyn Chambers and a porno producer, played by Al Pacino, sail to Skull Island to make the ultimate wet-shot epic. Kong appears with his five-foot whang clearly visible in every shot. "No fig leaves!" said "Bob" emphatically. The giant dinosaurs and other monsters run amok, as in the original, creating ample mayhem for the S-M crowd, and Marilyn is rescued by a different crew member each time Kong or one of these reptiles menaces her; she expresses her gratitude in traditional Chambers fashion, for the voyeur majority.

At the climax, when Kong is running wild in New York, looking for his mate, Marilyn, his giant tool attracts the horrified notice of Andrea Dworkin, playing herself. She quickly rounds up a crew of five hundred fat ladies from circuses and they overrun and bring down the Big Fellow without any help from airplanes. They then emasculate him in gory detail, on wide screen with Technicolor. The offensive organ is then weighed down with a lead block and thrown in the East River so it will never rise again.

While Dworkin leads a horde of Radical Feminists in a victory celebration, the film cuts to a conference room at a university and switches to documentary style. Various leading spokesentities[12] for the Committee for the Scientific Investigation of Claims of the Paranormal—e.g., Carl Sagan, Martin Gardner, James Randi and Professor von Hanfkopf—are then given equal time to persuade the audience that gorillas never grow to twenty-four feet tall and that the film just shown has been fantasy and therefore nefarious. Von Hanfkopf gets the microphone first, but his talk soon degenerates into incoherent ravings about cocaine abuse in Hollywood, CIA plots, the "Vatican-Mafia axis," etc., and he is gently persuaded to relinquish the podium. Randi begins denouncing everybody who disagrees with him about anything, saying they are all frauds, felons and child abusers. Martin Gardner gets the microphone away from him and argues that all the wreckage in midtown Manhattan does not prove the existence of giant apes and can be "more economically and scientifically explained" by positing the crash of a giant meteor. Dr. Sagan then approaches the podium and urges everybody to beware of wild and fanciful ideas. He rambles off into lyrical exposition about billions and billions of galaxies with billions and billions of stars, and is about to proceed further in that vein when suddenly a *huge black hand* crashes through the floor and grabs him by the testicles.

[12] I am deliberately avoiding the human chauvinism of *spokespersons*.

At that point, I drifted into deeper sleep. In a while, however, I was either startled awake or fell into the worst nightmare of my life—I have never been sure which—but it seemed to me that de Selby had returned to his original subject, the dimensions of divine dongs, and was arguing that Catholicism remains the last survivor of the ithyphallic cults of the ancient Mediterranean. Not only must one have a Willy to be a priest, he was saying, but the Pope continues to insist on that because the inner order within the church—I think he meant the Knights of Malta—still holds the antediluvian credo about the biggest Willy containing the greatest Animal Magnetism, or magic, or indwelling divinity, or something like that. He proposed a totally new, and shocking, theory as to how Popes are selected by the College of Cardinals, and why *these proceedings are always hidden from the public behind locked doors and no details are ever revealed.* Evidently, he was seriously suggesting that, just as it requires a Willy to turn a piece of bread into the body of a dead Jew, it requires the biggest Willy on the planet to anoint others and pass on the power to perform this astounding alchemical transformation.

While I was grappling with this thought, imagining the secret conclaves of the Curia looking like the casting sessions for male lead in a porn epic, and wondering why Kong had not been appointed at least an Honorary Pope, Rancid the butler suddenly burst into the room, carrying a Thompson submachine gun.

"This has gone far enough!" he shouted, glassy-eyed and foaming a bit.

"Come, come, old man—" I began gently, as one must begin with drunks.

"Don't 'old man' me, you Unitarian pervert," he screamed hysterically. The tommy gun, aimed loosely at all of us before, now pointed directly at my gut. "I am no damned butler. I am Cardinal Luigi Mozzarella, of the Holy Office for the Doctrine of the Faith, and Grand Master of the Sovereign Military Order of Malta."

There was a stifled silence, as we all took this in.

"We don't have the Maltese Falcon, honest—" said "Bob" weakly.

"Fuck that damned bird," Cardinal Mozzarella shouted. "We've wasted eight hundred years looking for it, and eight hundred years is more than enough on a losing project. I am one of the thirty-two agents assigned to monitor the heresiarch, de Selby, and it is just as we feared. You have guessed the inner secrets of our Holy Order and you will have to be eliminated. All of you."

He raised the tommy gun and I felt that sinking sensation which Chandler, I believe, has defined as the acute consciousness that one is not bullet-proof.

"All right, Luigi, drop the gun!"

All of us spun about to stare at the door, where Adam, the grand old gardener, stood, no longer grand or old. He had removed his white wig and abandoned his crouched posture. He was a young and dangerous man, and he carried an automatic rifle.

Cardinal Mozzarella dropped his tommy gun, stunned. De Selby darted forward and picked it up.

"Permit me to introduce myself," said the stranger who had once been my gardener. "I am Adam Weishaupt IX, *primus illuminatus,* and Grand Master of the Ordo Templi Orientus, the Scotch Rite, the York Rite, the Egyptian Rite and the Rite of Memphis and Mizraim. In short," he summed up, "I control every Freemasonic conspiracy on the planet. We have been watching and protecting you for a long time, Professor de Selby, since we knew the Knights of Malta would eventually attempt to take your life."

De Selby carefully placed the tommy gun on the writing desk, in the corner. I absently noticed that "Bob" wandered off in that direction and sat casually on the edge of the desk, relighting his Pipe.

Just then the French windows smashed open and the maids, Immaculata and Concepción, burst into the room, each carrying a bazooka. "Put down that rifle, Illuminati dog," cried Immaculata. "We are taking charge here."

"Who the hell are you?" Cardinal Mozzarella gasped, evidently unable to believe there could be so many conspiracies afoot in one Gothic castle.

"We are the High Priestesses of the Paratheo-Anametamystikhood of Eris Esoteric, or POEE," Concepción said. (*POEE* was pronounced "pooey," at least in her dialect.)

"Eris?" cried the *primus illuminatus*.

"Eris, goddess of chaos, discord, confusion, bureaucracy and international relations," Immaculata explained. "Our slogan is 'Disobedience was Woman's original virtue.' Too long has the world been run by male conspiracies. We are the first all-female conspiracy."

"Heresy," hissed the cardinal venomously.

"The inevitable yin balance to our yang energies," the Illuminatus muttered thoughtfully.

"Are you going to kill us?" I asked, being practical about the situation.

"No, of course not," Immaculata said. "Chaos is our Lady's natural métier. We came here to stop you from killing one another. We want you all alive, so you can go on spreading disputation and confusion and Chaos will always steadily increase. Hail Eris. All hail Discordia."

"So," Concepción said, "we must ask all of you to move the guns—with your feet please—to the center of the room. And then you must leave by separate doors. Go forth in peace," she added piously, "and continue to preach false doctrines."

"Just a minute, ladies," said de Selby. "I have a brief statement to make. Professor de Selby died in his sleep, peacefully, over ten years ago. I have been impersonating him ever since. I am a time traveler, in your terms. I was originally born in Damascus over a thousand years ago. My name was Abdul Alhazred and I was the first to learn the art of positronic reincarnation. In lay terms, when one brain wears out with age, I simply move my quantum energy into another brain. I took over de Selby as he was dying and simply continued the Great Work to which the Order of the Hashishim have been dedicated for a millennium—the Return of the Great Old Ones, or GOO, as we call them."

"Goo?" Immaculata cried, stunned.

"Well, they are kind of slimy," Abdul admitted, "but they are stronger than your Eris, or the other gang's Yahweh, or any of these recent parvenu gods. And now that I have the leaders of all the other and hence lesser cults assembled in one place, I shall summon Great Cthulhu to eat your souls." And he began chanting in a nameless Elder Tongue:

"Ia, Shub-Niggurath! Cthulhu fthagn! Yog Sothoth neblod zin! Ia! Io! Nov shmoz ka pop! Ph'nglui mglw'nafh na gCopaleen Baile atha Cliath wgah'nagl fthagn!"

As he chanted this blasphemous and nameless invocation, the mad Arab began to metamorphose before our very eyes, growing, swelling, becoming like unto a huge bowl of green yogurt, then changing into a jellyfish with a million bloodshot eyes, then becoming a pit bull with AIDS, then a Republican attorney general, a werewolf, every fearsome creature of nightmare and horror imaginable by a hashish-crazed brain, ***for all these horrific visions were, I now realized, individual aspects of the multiple monstrosity that was Cthulhu, the Interstellar Banker, source of all evil and conspiracy, inventor of punk rock, Eater of Souls, the Thing in the center of the Pentagon!!!***

And then, "Bob," so drunk that he had lost track of who was in charge, tried to kick the tommy gun into the center of the room, as the Erisians had demanded, and the gun began to spray bullets in all directions. I dived for the window and rolled dizzily down the lawn, my brain temporarily unhinged by the terrible visions I had seen.

They tell me that neighbors found me wandering in the rain, gibbering incoherently. They called an ambulance. I have been in St. John of God's Hospital for alcohol abusers for two weeks now. They think the terrible things I was muttering when brought here indicate too much Irish whiskey, and I am willing to let them think that. I dare not tell the good nuns here how Popes are actually chosen, or why it requires a Willy to perform the transubstantiation of molecules in the eucharist . . . or that in the last mind-numbing moment before "Bob" accidentally set off the tommy gun I saw the true face of Cthulhu, the master of this Death Universe, and recognized that it was my own . . . for now the positronic transformation is being accomplished again. Yes, Abdul Alhazred lives anew, for I am he, and I know now that I was wrong in my youth to believe that good was better than evil because it is generally nicer. Now I know, from one thousand years of memories of many lives, that evil is better than good because it always wins in the end. . . . **Ia! Shrug-Yrsh'ldrs! Notary sojac! Sinn fein amhain!**

Dr. Ahmed Fishmonger

THE ALL-TOO-REAL DREAMS

Dream 1

1. Praise be to "BOB," bringer of Slack, true saint of sales, most brilliant sex god, prime communicant of the forbidden mysteries and our guide on the nameless mission.
2. It was in the second year of the regime of President Ron, that the visions came to me.
3. In the world of dreams, as real as the conspirator's "reality," I was illuminated.
4. Dream the first. . .
5. I stood on a dusty plain, the cities, towns, factories, farms and all other works of man folded up toward the sky, forming the entire world into a gigantic bowl.
6. The sky was a tiny disk of blue and clouds concentrated above my head.
7. At the center was the sun.
8. He smoked and smiled and winked.
9. And LO, the clouds became like unto the shape and form of a whirlpool spinning into a common center, and they were like the shape and form of a vortex in every way.
10. And out of the whirlpool came great shining ships of the sky.
11. And their shape was like unto lentils and yet in no way were they of a beanlike nature.
12. And they meant me the greatest harm.
13. And as they came to me with great malice I yet felt safe.
14. I saw a great wonder, the smoke of the great Pipe of the sun covered me and the great ships of the sky could not pass it.
15. And I fell on my face before the glory of "BOB."

Dream 2

1. I found myself in a long hall, hung with many lights. And the light they cast was like that of faded fireworks through the haze of too much beer.
2. And a voice called to me saying, "In this is your sign, your guidepost for the coming weird times."
3. I asked, "Is this a message, a message from "BOB"? Or is this just some dumb meaningless Bobbie-dream?"
4. And the voice said, "You may question or you may heed or . . ."

5. "Or what?" I begged.
6. "Or kill me," it said.

Dream 3

1. From behind me came a man's voice.
2. "If you value your sanity, don't turn around," he said.
3. I almost turned around to look but strong hands deterred me.
4. "You are very stupid, it is a powerful force. In the future you will be stupid for me."
5. And the odor of Prince Albert hung in the air.

Dream 4

1. I hitchhiked a desert highway with nothing in sight for hours on end.
2. Out of the west came a cloud of dust and the sound of thunder.
3. And without reason I trembled with dread.
4. And I felt the force of Slack upon my mind.
5. And I felt a wonder of what came forth from the road.
6. And I stuck out my thumb.
7. And past me almost faster than sight went a car without wheel or wheel within wheel, but supported on the very air itself.
8. And I turned in wonder to see the driver of this wondrous thing.
9. I saw only the back of the head with the Pipe.

K. DeVries

PILGRIMAGE

Hitler 1100108 was waiting when Dobbs clambered ineptly out of the saucer. "Gaw-dam!" "Bob" thought. A couple of years made a big improvement.

Hitler 1100108 strode forward and hugged him violently. Like most of the clones, her hair was lustrous and black, her skin glowingly golden. She wore a short, pleated white tunic, looking like the girl-friend of an Italian-movie Hercules.

Dark eyes flashing, she lifted "Bob" a foot off the ground and bel-lowed, "Who's the puny runt now, "Bob" Dobbs?"

"Boy, 'Eight, you sure have grown!" he wheezed. "You're bending me."

She dropped him jarringly on the steeloplastium landing pad, grabbed a shoulder before he could fall, and hauled him toward a little gazebo atop a large hairy mound. "Look, my friend! Just grown! The Robots stole it from Russia! They dig up under the lab, take a tiny blob in a test tube, and we have two thousand Mammoths! Good, eh?"

"Oh, is that what it is?" "Bob" mumbled, grinning dazedly. Under this funny sun it looked like a big brown plant, a shrub or something. "Lemme put on my gogs."

The goggles cut the glare of eternal noon and made Dobbs look down-right weird. "Oh, yeah. Well I'll be darned."

"Come!" 'Eight shouted. "We ride!" She seized the zipper of his cardigan and yanked him sharply toward the Mammoth. "Up to the howdah! Quickly now!"

"Bob" whined, "Hey, take it easy!" as she threw him onto the ladder leaning against the huge animal. With his face inches from the beast's woolly side, he could see, and smell, that this was no shrub. 'Eight had her hands on his buttocks, yelling and pushing him up the ladder, and he wailed, "Criminy! Gimme a break, will ya?"

He scrambled up the ladder and tumbled headfirst into the howdah, landing between two of the thronelike chairs provided for the riders' luxury. The bowl of his Pipe flipped up and whacked against his goggles when he hit, scattering burning coals across his forehead and into his hair. With a shriek, he leaped to his feet, batting at his face.

'Eight bounded over the elaborate rail and turned to pull up the ladder. "You hurt yourself? You be okay?"

"Yeah, yeah, I'm fine," "Bob" muttered, smoothing back his slightly singed hair. "Just my damn Pipe." He sat in one of the massive chairs, pulled a plastic bag out of the pocket of his cardigan and refilled his Pipe, grumbling when the Mammoth lurched upward, rising from its knees to its full incredible height. Last time they'd had great little atomic-powered go-karts, like wheeled rockets going a hundred miles an hour. Times change. 'Eight was up front, whacking the huge, bobbing head with a long pole and shouting unintelligible commands over and over.

Satisfied at last that the beast knew where to go, she bounced back to Dobbs and cast herself at his feet. She leaned against the chair, threw a muscular golden arm across his knees and looked up at his manly jaw and boldly chiseled nose.

"So, 'Uncle "Bob," ' " she purred, "why do you come back down here to see us after ignoring us for so long?"

"Bob" leaned back, lit his Pipe, and rested his suede elbow patches on the red velvet of the chair's arms. "Now c'mon, 'Eight! You know I'm a busy man. Got a lotta irons in the fire. Gotta keep up!" He paused, blew a stream of smoke toward the golden stars set into the deep-blue surface of the howdah's domed ceiling and gazed out across the rolling landscape which rose and faded into hazy distance all around. Roman-style villas dotted the verdant hills and Grecian temples stood whitely in groves which sprang up beside sparkling clear brooks.

"Bob" sighed. "Just wondered what you guys were up to, being as I was there at the start."

Nearly twenty years ago he'd wangled, bluffed and bumbled his way into the Dero cloning labs deep beneath Mount Shasta. His Xist contact had a lot of pull with the High Dero, and "Bob" was eager to see if anything from the Dero Group-Mind could be turned to profit; so he was there when the Dero Clone-teks began to build a new race of humans from the brownish bloodstains on a tattered fragment of cloth.

'Eight gestured expansively with her free arm. "Of course you were there! Why, we've even built you a temple outside New Berlin! You are a tutelary deity! The great "Bob" Dobbs who was there at our inception!"

"Yeah," "Bob" chuckled, "I guess I even helped out a little."

"And now, what do you think?" 'Eight shouted, leaping to her feet. She spread her arms wide, taking in the placid landscape, and bellowed, "Is it not BEAUTIFUL?"

"Bob" looked quickly away from her breasts and glanced around at the stagy classicism of the scene. It was like some old landscape painting he saw once—everything perfectly placed, and perfectly nice. "Yeah, beautiful. And corny."

'Eight threw her hands toward him. "This 'corny,' it is good?"

"Bob" laughed once. "Yeah. . . . Yep, it's good."

"And I, am I 'corny' too?"

"Yeah," he said, his grin widening and his cheeks wrinkling up around the goggles. "You're corny, all right."

'Eight bounded into his lap and he spit his Pipe past her ear with the breath which was suddenly crushed out of him. She wrapped her smoothly muscled arms around his neck and touched his ear with her full, dark lips. Her breath tickled the hair inside his ear, making him squirm as she cooed, "And you, "Bob" Dobbs, you are 'corny' too."

The Mammoth toiled slowly up a steep hill, over the brow of which peered the topmost towers of the ancient golden city now known as New Berlin.

'Eight had bounded off his lap again suddenly, and regaled him with one story after another about the thrilling moments of her life. "Bob" ignored most of it except parts which shed light on the social and cultural trends. In a perfect society, really interesting things rarely happen at all. She was recounting what someone had said to her at a party once when he spotted the gleaming city through the mists of the rising land ahead. It was always like the first time, seeing that ancient mass of towers, more ancient than humankind. It made the Potala look like a two-story chicken coop. When the outer world was yet a stomping ground for yard-long bugs and armored fish swarmed through the sea-bed jungles, the city had been built here on the planet's inner skin. For hundreds of millenia the unknown lords of this glittering immensity, fifty miles in diameter and half a mile high at its center, lived and perhaps died here, then passed on, leaving the broad streets silent and empty as the dinosaurs toppled into the mud of a serenely changing world.

At the top of the hill, "Bob" saw that they were still miles from the city's edge, and stepped to the forward rail. "Say, this is gonna take forever if we ride this thing all the way!"

'Eight laughed and pointed to the side of the road ahead. "Look, impatient man! We have already planned!" A beautifully built young man in a white, belted tunic stood beside what could only be the fastest-looking car Dobbs had ever seen. The young clone smiled and waved and 'Eight resumed her pole-pounding act on the Mammoth's skull, shouting tongue-fracturing commands. The silent monster curled its trunk upward, rolled its beady eyes, and lurched to a halt. Ponderously, it tipped back onto its haunches, sending "Bob" flailing into a heavy chair which carried him to the stern rail with a crash. The Mammoth plopped its front end down, the two beautiful clones laughed delightedly and Dobbs cursed under his breath.

The ride into the city was a twenty-minute roller coaster with 'Eight chattering gaily, steering the screaming road rocket one-handed at 350 miles an hour, and Dobbs trying to sink down through the formfitting cocoon of a seat, his jaw clenching spasmodically on the bit of his Pipe.

By the time they had flashed through a black speck of a doorway in the city's vast wall, he had gathered the legs of his slacks up around his knees in a pair of damp, wrinkled lumps, exposing his white, sparsely haired shins. When the car's huge windscreen tilted up in the docking bay he was almost too stiff to climb out and his knees trembled weakly as his cuffs crept slowly back down toward the garage's spotless floor.

He had determined to visit the Shrine first, of course, and stutteringly informed 'Eight, who dragged him toward a tube-tram. Minutes later, they were at the heart of the thinly populated city and 'Eight herded him out of the tram stop into the broad, covered parkway which led to the Shrine at the city's geometric center. Its original purpose forever unknown, the soaring structure was now the repository of the history and sacred objects of nine million robotically cloned perfect humans.

Entering the Shrine from the brilliantly illuminated parkway was like entering a mine shaft. Dobbs pushed his goggles up onto his forehead and blinked. Huge pillars of diamond-hard transparent crystalline gold rose row on row off to either side, meeting a quarter of a mile overhead in a bafflingly symbolic medallion, from the center of which a bright beam shot down to illumine a circle of objects in the center of the immense room. A small, four-seated cart stood by the door, resting on rails which led to the bright circle before them.

Dobbs noted that 'Eight had stopped jabbering, her face a mask of religious awe. Taking her arm, he sat her gently in the cart and silently climbed behind the control lever.

There was nothing much to say. Even "Bob" was struck by the wonder of it as the cart trundled softly down the rail toward the mementos chronicling the origin of a race grown and designed by cold robotic devices to populate a perfect world. It was wonderful and strangely sad.

The cart came to a stop before the half-dozen display cases grouped around the central Shrine. They stepped reverently down from the cart and into the light. 'Eight took his hand and they walked slowly around a circle of displays, gazing down at souvenirs of the man revered here as father of a race—photographs, clothing and military regalia, the Spear of Destiny☠ and a battered volume autographed by its author: "Good luck, A. Hitler." Stolen from the surface world by the Deros, they now graced the memorial of a man cursed as evil and mad by the swarming near-humans outside.

It was to be the Deros' greatest weapon, nine million beautiful, healthy Hitlers to sweep out from the Earth's poles on X-Day, their saucers screaming down to complete the devastation of the planet, burn-

---

☠A power object which once pierced the side of one still said to be the child of JHVH-1 itself, it was painted by Hitler as a young artist and at last possessed by him in his days of glory.

ing it clean of its festering growth of inferior life. Here was its heart, its Genesis.

Completing the round of displays, they turned to the central Shrine. Twenty feet above, an heroic-sized bust of the Führer, its head framed by a golden disk behind it, stared off toward destiny's horizon. The black arms of the swastika reached out like spiders' legs from behind the head to caress the halo's golden rim. Beneath the bust, centered amid the eight serpentine pillars supporting the baroque canopy which burst riotously out from the bust's base, a transparent block about a foot in height perched stolidly on a short Corinthian column.

Seeing 'Eight kneel before the lustrous wooden railing which stretched from column to column around the Shrine, "Bob" knelt too. "When in Rome . . ." he thought. He inhaled meditatively and blew a gentle stream of smoke toward the scrap of cloth suspended in the clear cube before him.

'Eight sighed. "There, the birth of our race. A bit of bloody handkerchief from which sprang the happiest, luckiest people who ever lived!"

"Bob" glanced at her. Her eyes were glittering with joyous tears. As she turned and put her hand lovingly on his arm, one glistening tear rolled down her high golden cheekbone. "And you were there. You helped." Her words caught in her muscular throat. "Oh, thank you, "Bob" Dobbs, thank you!"

"Yep," "Bob" said softly. "I helped."

He remembered the chilly underground lab, bustling with crowds of weirdly shaped robots. He remembered waiting for his chance, waiting for the one moment when all scanners would be occupied elsewhere, away from the strip of rag soaked by the blood of Earth's most fiendish maniac.

"Bob" turned his gaze back to the small stained fragment.

The ashes of the last traces of Hitler's blood, set ablaze by Dobbs' Jet-Flame pipe lighter, had drifted off in the clear mountain air to be lost forever amid Shasta's evergreen mantle as zygotes swelled into fetuses in the tanks a mile beneath his feet, fetuses grown from the bit of cloth Dobbs had brought into the Deros' underground city with him, the stained bit of fiber with which he had replaced the one so carefully stolen by the Robots.

"Beautiful," he said, and grinned wider at the ragged shred of the Shroud of Turin. "And corny."

Dr. Chris Gross

THE OLOGY OF THE IZNESS

Being the Revelation of Mr. Zed

And "Bob" brought me unto an high place above the roads of the city. And I saw Motorists in wondrous numbers, who drove chariots pulled by neither horses nor oxen. And they turned not as they went, and thus they slew many of my countrymen.

And I said unto "Bob," "Who are the drivers of these chariots, who see not that which passeth before them and who are like unto the whirlwind in their haste?" And "Bob" spake, saying:

"They are the Followers of the Norm, the Pishai, the Pimangas, those who live in fear of themselves and whose minds are fettered unto deepest Evil. They knoweth not the ways of Slack, as thou mayst see by their driving, and yea they desire it thus, for they be not of Yeti but of Pink extraction. Serve them not."

And I said, "Verily I will not serve them, for have they not sought my life and the lives of my kin with their chariots? Have they not taken my gold and my women, and do they not revile thy name and mine?"

And "Bob" said, "Thou speakest the very truth; The Pink Boys have done much else besides that of which thou lamentest. They have befouled Gaia, the Mother Earth, as thou hast read in the books of Nag Hammadi, with their foul vapors and vile unguents. They have loosed the madness of the blind Azathoth upon the world's innocent, they have launched Heads not of metal but of flesh in defiance of the edicts of the Doktors, and," and here he breathed in, "and AIEEE hath they spread false doctrines to smother the divine Meaning of the Year Zero. Yea, in their arrogance they even slew me, proving that they can take not an joke."

And "Bob" smote me mightily upon the forehead, saying, "Go thou amongst the blind Faceless Ones, the servants of the Elder Gods, and make witness for the sake of thy kinfolk. Spread the good news of Slack Eternal amongst those SubGenii who knoweth not my name, and end forevermore the reign of the Pinks. Perform thou the Salute: aieeeee-yiyiyi eyi eyiyiyi."

And he smote me again, and I fell down and knew no more. And when I awoke at sunset, I saw that I had been trodden underfoot by the passing multitudes as I lay in a swoon. And I swore a mighty oath, and I cursed as I swore, and I betook myself to my hearth.

May the power of the fist of "Bob" and the Wrath of JHVH-1 come down upon thee and remain with thee throughout all eternity.

Amen.

Slack.

"Bob."

G. Gordon Gordon
THE VREEDEEZ SANCTION

To begin with, it wasn't the best of times to be back on the West Coast. The State Immigration Police were extremely tight and the new martial-law-style curfew was still enforced in any California city over twenty-five thousand in population.

Palmer Vreedeez had been fired for "Political Insolvency" and had disappeared; off on a 'Phrane binge if I knew Palmer, shacked up somewhere with a Level 2 SexDroid rented in the Tenderloin from DodaSex International. . . . At least, they had his card number and what looked like a reasonable facsimile of the famous Vreedeez scrawl. But the address was fake and so was all the rest of the personal info on the routine rental punchform. It was all lies—a typical Palmer attitude, so I had to assume that the signadata *was* valid.

I had already tried flashing the 'Brow at Puzzling Evidence on my way over to DodaSex, but all I could get was an "audio-only" recording to the effect that my sole reliable operative at Unibrow International was attending a Flying Tiger Airlines convention at the Maksoud Plaza in São Paulo, Brazil.

I relit my pipe as I picked my way through the throngs of E-Girls, already out hustling this early. Most of them wore the mandatory *cache de sex* and eyeshields, and the rest of their fantastic, SetCONned bodies were covered in 'flashies, NeoGels or poptatoos of a most explicit and ornate nature. They all had the same things to sell for a short time, so packaging was still the big factor.

The weather was lousy, cold, foggy, and every smooth exterior surface in the city sweated clammy streams. My nose filters were overdue for a scrub and the smell of Oakland was relentless. Halfway back to my hotel I was beamed by a buzzship. The cops were neutral, polite, it was routine. So was all the info I flashed them with my Datascan. It checked out to twenty decimal points because they amped out and skipped off to bother someone else. They didn't even say thanks—or so I thought. Later, when checking my message deck, I found a smarmy recording from Bay Police Central thanking me for my cooperation, blah blah.

When I got back to the Saint Francis I learned that the NeoRevisionist Party was having some kind of big social bash and the security heat both open and surreptitious was alarming, but entirely understandable since the Hyatt Massacre. My body was scanned six different times between the pavement and the elevators—I could hear the beeps in my built-in monitor, which is wired directly to the audio nerves. I wasn't the least bit worried, though; I knew I would show clean even though I was holding a Gyrojet pistol and an Ingraham machinegun. The transponder package I carried strapped to the small of my back like a moneybelt could analyze, decode and then respond to any form of scanning device, including thermal-positron, with a perfectly "normal" profile. It could even bugger up contour-scan "soft" microwave beaming— and those were really hard to glitch, because of the realtime rescan monitors that were getting harder and harder to puzzle.

My room was clean—for the moment, at least. The microcircuits were giving my brain only a faint green visual stimulus on that channel. I sat down, unloaded and dumped my arsenal in an OpaqueBox, then removed my transponder pack and reset it on wide beam. I unjacked the cigarette-package-sized power cell that plugs into the dermoplast socket at the base of my spine, and let my entire synaptic circuitry go back to its normal firing rate. It felt good to have the old nervous system back on biological power source.

I was just starting to feel like a human being again instead of an All-Cozmic Yacatizma Penetrator when the Mandatory Television Channel kicked up the power and lit up the set. I found myself looking at the pouchy eyes, veinous nose, wattles and hard, prissy mouth of a man of eighty years plus . . . with the teeth and hair of a thirty-year-old. Behind him was a shield, an eagle and lots of red, white and blue. Apparently my President was about to speak to me, personally. Well, not really, but for a moment I was confused. I sat up, shredded a big cut plug of 'Frop, recharged and lit my pipe while the chief executive defended his new defense requests and his proposal to make the entire armed forces part of the FBIDEA forces, with state national guard units as an optional addition during coca, opium and marijuana harvesting seasons all over the world.

He was brief, at least, but made about as much sense as a dinosaur does to a SymBiorg. After all, the sum total of human knowledge had doubled, then redoubled, and then doubled again since that guy got out of Harvard or wherever; could you really expect him to deal with the territory when his map was so hopelessly out of date—say, late Cenozoic?

Lot of plate tectonics since then, Mister Prezzdent, lotsa changes with many of us monkeys, too, boss, you betcha!

After he had faded away in a toothy smile and was replaced with an uptown media montage of patriotic archetypal Jingotwangers, I turned on the rest of the set and went through the three hundred or so options. After twenty channels I plugged the powerpack back into my spine and went up to three-fourths power. I scanned the rest neurally with a direct scanning link. It's done by microwaves emitted by the Set-

CONned retinal nets in my eyes. My link to the YT computer was always open when I was above one-eighth power, and I mused over the disappearance of Palmer while my unconscious circuits and the computer rummaged through all that information. It only took about twenty minutes to run it all, including commercial and public information. I didn't need all that new data but the Yacatizma did, and that's who was running this show. The updates, which it supplies to all its linked operatives as they need them, more than compensate for the constant demands it makes of them for new imputs. I think the Y-Matrix is an information junkie myself, but everyone is strung out on something, right? And too much is always better than not enough. But still I was thinking about Palmer. Where could he have disappeared to? And did he still even have that tape in his possession? The tape that contained information he certainly never guessed might exist. . . .

The YT Scan completed, I bleeped over to the circus channel to see who was risking life and limb for cash. Untaxable cash, if they survived. I wasn't really into the violence and blood of the actual acts, but was hooked on the audiences. I guess they're one up from the wrestling and roller derby crowds, just more open about their appetites.

At the moment there was a round of High Wire City Hall in the center arena. Three gays with rocks and brickbats were trying to knock a pathological honky with a .380 auto and five shots off a slackwire before he got close enough to get a shot at them. The honky was doing quite well when the screen dissolved into audience montages around the central image, and I felt a flash as I saw a familiar face in the crowd: a tired, 'Phrane-wracked, stubbly face. He looked like some derelict there in the battered, filthy free seats. You could sit there twenty-four hours a day as long as you were watching and not sleeping, and Palmer, for such it was looking all smeared and bleary-faced, certainly could stay awake for long, long periods of time, given enough 'Phrane. I rearmed and reset my Transpack and went out the door less than two minutes after I had spotted Palmer. I grabbed a ridiculously expensive gasoline-powered cab and headed straight for Christian Legion Stadium as fast as I could persuade my driver to move.

It still took a long time, but finally I went in on the payside and got a guard to let me cross into the free seats. By this time it was a geriatric act with flamethrowers, and there was a smell of burned meat. Most of the rabble and some on the payside were up on their feet howling with delight at the internecine "comedy act," but Palmer was still huddled up against the plasteel wall on the far side, his eyes not focused on anything. Only he was no longer alone, having acquired a pair of vicious-looking rigger boys who were closing carefully in with the obvious intent of "doing" him. They were right next to him when I walked up, bouncy and light on my feet, synapses running at max level and looking a lot like a 'Phraner. "Hop it, laddies," I said with a toothy grin. "Bozo here is a very good friend of mine, so just fade out in forty frames or less, okayo?"

They both came at me with flickering sonic knives in less than a second. I could move over twenty times faster than they; what chance did they have? I let the circuits take over and killed them both, painlessly and instantly, in less than two more seconds. I picked Palmer up, slung his emaciated frame over my shoulder in a fireman's lift, and headed for the exit as the people around the scene of the mayhem became aware of what had gone down. There were two armed guards at the side door but I accelerated, whipping between them and out the door with Palmer while they gradually crawled at syrup speed to grab us, going "Bloooglaaaa-faaahhhaa" in very deep, very slow voices.

I decelerated outside and bleeped a skittercab. It was slow, but it was also automatic and quite noninquisitive. Palmer was beginning to register a slight contact with reality as the skittercab painstakingly pulled away with a whine of electrics. I dialed in a safe-house address over in Oakland and was informed that there was an extra ten bux if we crossed the bridge. I okayed it and pulled out a small medipak, dug out a leachcap and peeled off the cover strip, pulled Vreedez' collar down and slapped it down on the carotid artery. In seconds the powerful vitamin, food sugar and 'Phrane counteragent mixture was being pumped into his arterial blood, heading for the brain.

Palmer jerked and twitched for a moment, took a long ragged breath, closed his glazed eyes and then after a second opened them again. This time they were clear and focused. He looked right at me and smiled sardonically.

"Well, Gordon, you came and rescued me, saved me from myself . . . thanks a whole lot, asshole. Who asked you, anyway? I never sent for you. Leave me alone, I'm sick of you and all those other lunatics that work for Dobbs. You got a smoke?"

I gave him a small 'Fropstick and lit it for him. "Thanks," he said after a couple of good pulls. "I mean it, Gordon, I'm through with the Foundation. It cost me my job, my housing status, everything. . . . I'm PI now, thanks to "Bob." Politically Insolvent. You know what that means, Gordon? No, of course you wouldn't, you iron-brained mercenary twit . . . you've always lived outside systems, you've never tried to deal with Technoboredom and Pinks! You're just off here and there killing a False Prophet or icing some reactionary Church faction . . . you just never had to . . ." He trailed off, slumping forward, and took another drag.

"Sorry, Palmer, I have no more choice in this than you do." I got out my pipe and relit it. "The Yacatizma Matrix sent me here to find you."

"What for? Oh, it doesn't matter! I've had it with you guys, I tell you!"

"Look, Palmer, I'm trying to be as nice as I know how. You asshole."
I said it sincerely. "There's a whole lot going on that's a bit more important than your political status, your job, my personal habits and my
and your lives, so let's cooperate and graduate. . . . How about it?"

"I dunno Deu— Gordon." He was so rattled he'd almost used my
nonChurch name. But he caught himself. "Hey, where are we going?"
he added hastily.

"Safehouse we have over in Oakland. The old Croxton Manorhouse."
I took a long, appreciative pull at my pipe. "Once you're rested and
back in shape we've got to do a couple of very important chores."

Palmer Vreedeez shook his head slowly. "Very dangerous too, if I
know you, Gordon. You have no guarantee I'll cooperate with you."

"Oh, I think you'll help me out, Palmer," I said with my best barra-
cuda smile. "In fact, Philo guaranteed that you would be helpful. . . ."

"Philo," he gasped, turning even paler. "I thought . . . I *know* Philo is
dead!"

"Was dead, Palmer, *was* dead. But even now the OverMan walks
among us again! Praise Dobbs!"

Palmer looked terrified, "Was," he whispered. "You mean G'broagfran kept the cloning templates?"

I hit him hard with the answer. "Sure, Palmer. Gary G'broagfran
kept *all* of the material, because he wasn't on a copyright contract like
you and Stang. But he didn't need it anyway, Palmer . . . because Drummond was brought back the long way. And Unibrow was there to pull
the levers and twiddle the knobs. Puzzling Evidence sold out, Palmer.
It's just a shell organization now. All the computer stuff was taken into
the Yacatizma Matrix months ago. You get it, Palmer? You're alone,
the Conspiracy doesn't want you, your employers don't want you. But
I've got you and "Bob" wants you—needs you—on his side. There are
too many variables without you. Like it or not, you've got no choice,
Vreedeez. Better light up another 'Fropstick and get ready for a lot of
really scary stuff!"

Palmer just smoked for the rest of our trip. We were electric and
had low priority, but the trip took only fifteen minutes and two 'Fropsticks more for Palmer. We came into the Croxton Estate through
the back alley, dumping the skittercab on the corner. It flashed off as
soon as we scooted, already answering a bleep from another Datascan
carrier.

I slid the encoded, magnetized plastic card—made to look like a credit
card—into what might have been only a chink in the wall. An opening
dilated long enough for me to dash through, dragging a stumbling
Palmer along with me. Behind the high shielded walls, it was another
world. The excess city nightglare was cut out and you could see the sky,
not that there was much to see. The air was all filtered and very breath-

able. We walked slowly through the thick grass of the lawn and up the steps to the back door of the Manorhouse. I dialed the access code, the lights came on and the door opened for us after the central computer checked me out. There was no one at home, of course. The house was now occupied by unearthly, beautiful, bizarre and even scary pieces of glass sculpture. There was glass in forms totally unknown . . . even a sheet of the famous "slowglass" that was fifty-five light-years thick, subatomically speaking; it was only about two inches physically. It glowed like a big television screen, showing a view of the Bay about thirty-five years ago when the water was blue instead of red and brown. You could see boats and clouds moving; it was like looking out a window, only the image was a little out of time. If you went around to the other side, you could look out onto a nice section of San Francisco before ferrophages, plasteel and FullerConstructions. Slowglass was Dr. Glassmadness' greatest triumph and supreme folly; it'd cost him his citizenship and identity. He was now a permanent Dobbstown resident, like so many of the Church Heirarchy—a tired, broken old blues player who had brought in just enough Tanksouls to retire.

We went into the living section of the strange old house and I found food. Palmer was jonesing for some 'Phrane again by this time and, as I had a couple of gligs in my gear, I turned him on. Mine was pure, not like that ten-percent stuff he'd been trying to pry open his circuits with. He splashed in seconds, half a glig still in the inhaler in his hand. I got the rest, and we sat and watched cartoons for several minutes until we could both talk. I set my power on twenty-five percent and my nervous system couldn't even feel the 'Phrane at all. Now I had Palmer a little more pliant. I began asking him about his personal effects. At first he said he'd thrown it all away. But later, halfway through the third glig I had somehow found mixed up in my vitamin pack, he confided that everything he owned was in a sealed container at a rental storage center. Back in San Francisco, naturally.

I checked with the central house computer and was advised that there was a car for us on fully operative status, ready to roll—a new Korean TurboFan with full electronics packet and everything else not entirely legal to have but which wouldn't get you in trouble with the cops. The only problem was, whether Palmer knew it or not, his worldly goods were probably being watched closely on the chance that he might return. He wasn't exactly "hot," but a PI with a record like Palmer's is buzzed all the time. Everybody does something illegal at least once a day.

Sure, jaywalking, crossing against a monitor, pissing in the corner of an alley—they don't sound like capital crimes to you, but then you're probably not a PI, either.

Palmer went to sleep after a while, huddled in an overstuffed armchair. I sat there and communed with the Yacatizma Matrix, watching city maps, wiring diagrams, sewer blueprints, city ordinances and Dobbs knows what else flicker across my visual cortex as I tried to see exactly what we had here . . . although if I knew my Yacatizma, I was going to have to come up with something totally outrageous. Something so illogical that it might work. That's the thing about computers, even organically based Xist-technology models: no imagination, and no sense of humor. They said sixty years and computers were going to run the world, but they still don't. They never will, either. Imagination and sense of humor are true survival traits in our era.

I finally worked out a series of probability permutations on the data I did have, and then downpowered and unplugged. My ward was going to be out for a while, so I did some breathing and Neo-Yoga Flexions. After a short period of LinkMed, I dressed, hooked up and went through the weapons locker. I really just wanted to take Palmer's Sonikeys and walk up, sign in, open the locker, rummage through the containers until I found the tape, close up and walk away, all legal and everyone happy and smiling. But as Stang used to constantly remind me, there was always the NG factor that could slip into the very best of calculations. And as Gödel or somebody said, you can't define a system only by what it contains, you must have a metasystem that encloses and defines the first system for there to be a proof of validity. Or was that the Everett-Wheeler hypothesis? In any event, I packed up the Gyrojet with all explosives in one clip and mixed tracer/explosives in the other. I also took six small smoke grenades, two howlers (I put the ear filters in when I took them out of their packing) and half a dozen Photonstunners. I toyed with, then discarded, LaxaGas, Tasers, NeuroWhippers and two of the brand-new Stickybombs. The latter intrigued me; I hadn't ever used one. I slipped one into my pocket at the last minute and shut the Armslocker before I got involved with the Lasersight Mini-14s or Automatic Shotgun Systems.

I got Palmer up, and he stumbled out to bathe and find clean clothes in the supply closets. I made us minimal breakfast. He even ate a little when he came back, looking only shabby and seedy instead of burned out and deranged. He was smoking a 'Fropcigar he'd found somewhere, and of course he had the jones. When it was apparent he wasn't going to eat any more, I made him take half a dozen different vitamin pills. I told him I wanted him to drive me over to the storage place and let me go in while he waited in the car as getaway driver, all secure and armored and a whole lot safer than yours truly.

Good simple straightforward plan. Except.

"I don't know how to drive. I never learned," he said slowly.

I could see he was telling the truth. "Well, okay, Palmer, I'll drive. All you have to do is sit in the car and open the door for me if you see me come out in a big hurry."

He still wasn't feeling that heroic. "Look, Gordon, I told you I don't want to be involved in all this shit. Why do you want to get into my stuff anyway? What the fuck do you and that goddamned pipehead want?" He stood up and ran his fingers through his thick stylish wedgecut. "Whatever it is, you can't have it." He relit his 'Frop.

I pulled out the machine pistol and stuck it right up in his face. He froze; Palmer was particularly wary of guns.

"It's very simple, Vreedeez. I'm going to tell you once and you had better listen. Among your ratty, sordid little cache of personal nostalgia, you have a set of tapes. Tapes that you got through Unibrow . . ."

"But we're friends," he protested. "I have no official affiliation with any of his projects. Those tapes are letters, personal correspondence, that's all!"

"I know that, Palmer," I said soothingly. "Why don't you sit down?" He sat and I put the gun away. "Now listen, Palmer, on one of those tapes—it's the tape with the color-key "Starving Biafran Baby with a Pipe" label—there's a long session where 'Brow is talking to you, and there is a monitor playing an audio track in the background. It sounds like pure electronic synthesizer music. But it wasn't. He was encoding a whole package of information on weapons-control frequencies, go-codes, etc., for the U.S., Russia and the EuroSectors. It included satellite callups, frequency crypto-keys and Ballistic Access Retrieval Updates. Not to mention Cruise Missile codes, submarine access codes and Dobbs only knows what else. He finished that work and sent it to us by courier. The courier never made it. We notified Unibrow International, and they researched it, and this was the only suggestion the 'Brow himself could come up with. He's pretty sure—and we're hoping he's right—that the whole sequence is uninterrupted. But even if there are gaps, the Yacatizma Matrix can probably enhance it enough to make it worthwhile."

My listener was a bit agitated by the news that, essentially, he had been put on the spot by his friend Unibrow. I put my hand into my coat pocket and pulled out the five-glig inhaler of 'Phrane I had stashed in my shaving kit.

Palmer's whole system twanged and resonated, just from being that close to so much pure 'Phrane. I held it up. "You only have to ride in the car, Vreedeez," I said. "If I get that tape, I promise you that not only will I get out of your face forever, I will see that you're paid a MegaBuck in any form of currency, metal or negotiable, *and* I will personally see that you get a giant, heaping, heavy-duty kitchen-sized black plastic garbage sack full of the finest 'Phrane in the world. Pure, unsullied, Palmer! Eighty-nine-percent pure 'Phrane by atomic weight!"

Of course he caved in; who wouldn't have? (Perhaps I should say, what *'Phraner* wouldn't have?) I did some with him, but I had already edged up over the twenty-five-percent power level in my central nervous system, so I never really felt it.

We left shortly after that, emerging into the grim wastes of Oakland at about eleven ay em. It was smoggy, drizzly, foggy, cold, humid, smelly, polluted, dirty, contaminated . . . one could go on for days. Many do. We found a traffic light, and with the aid of the top-level computer in the TurboFan I had no trouble programming us for the old warehouse district where Palmer Vreedeez' earthly goods were stored. He didn't say much, but he was at least a grudging neutral in the overall scheme. I activated the computer link, went into phase with the YT Matrix and got a complete update on all the vectors that could possibly be moving in my direction. There was no real indication that my presence was even known. Apparently, the accelerated removal of Palmer from the games stadium had never reached official levels. Or perhaps it had, but somebody up there was holding it all in on the off chance that I might check to see if I were being tracked. After all, there were only three human beings on the planet with rewired central nervous systems who went around doing destructive things; one was dead and the other was locked up and heavily guarded in the central region of the Soviet Republic. I had a feeling I would be assigned the job of getting Poonflang out of there real soon, but for the time being, this one was going to be fun enough.

The area looked quite calm and deserted when we pulled up and parked. I left the burner on low and the gyros on about half. I scanned the entire building at full power. It *looked* nice, but I buzzed seven powerpacks scattered around, which meant Baycop stunners. There was an innocuous-looking van parked across the street, which a quick flash on the car scanners showed to have five men inside—no stunner packs, but a lot of metal concentrations. Like gunsized metal concentrations. I mentally reran all my weapons positions, and theirs, then got out of the car as normally as I could, leaving my door closed but unlatched. I was on sixty-five-percent power when I went inside. There was a tacky little office space in the front of the old warehouse, "guarded" by a very disinterested woman with a flat beefy face and stringy, greasy hair. I told her what number I wanted and held up my key. Either she was a good actress or she knew nothing, because she showed not the slightest glimmer of interest in my name (Vreedeez) or the locker number. She just made me sign in and let me enter the storage area.

On the other side of the wall, the open space had been filled with rows of prefabricated and reinforced storage compartments, each about the size of a small one-car garage. I searched quickly along the rows and found my door, number 444. There was no sign of any activity, and a scan of the door showed no trigger alarms or circuits beyond the factory model that comes with the Sonilocks.

I still had a feeling I was being watched. I tried whiffing, but there was no physical presence. I figured what the hell, shoved the key in the slot and coded the bleepsequence. The light went green, I pulled the door open and went inside. Still no action. I went to the stacked storage cartons and quickly found the one full of old comm gear and tapes. I was still hyped for something to happen when I found the tape.

A moment later I stepped out and relocked the door. Something had to start; *surely* they knew. I was about halfway back when I sensed a lot of extra circuitry in one of the lockers I passed. I gave it a full scan, blanched, and moved on without even slowing down. When I came into the office the Heat was there—but he wasn't looking for me.

"Excuse me, sir." He flashed his IDs—a big-time Fed from Justice and SecServ/CIA.

"What seems to be the trouble, Officer?" I asked as cooperatively as I could.

"Were you just back in the locker section?"

"Well yes, I just came out through this door and the lockers are in there." I said it as if I wasn't really on top of such things as life in general.

"And what number locker did you visit, sir?" Just as nice as pie.

"Number four forty-four."

"Could I perhaps see your key, sir?"

I handed the Sonikey to him without a word, and after a brief glance he smiled, handed it back and walked out the door. After saying thank you, of course. I knew everything was going to be just fine from there and walked outside jauntily. Nothing had changed; Vreedeez was looking around nervously as I got in, sealed the door and took off on full burn.

"But there were cops all over the place then!" Palmer argued a few minutes later, after I'd told him the whole scenario. "Why didn't they grab us?"

"Because they weren't watching your stuff, they were interested in the owner of the stuff in locker four twelve." I pulled up onto the west-bound strip, snatched the 'Phrane inhaler from him, went down to five percent and did a big hit. "I scanned it on the way out. It was so bugged up it was damned near glowing. Somebody's got enough plutonium in that locker to make two or three nuclear weapons. Oh, it's shielded well enough, but I know it's plutonium. It's still got the Kerr-McGee stencils on the shielding boxes. I'd say the Feds are very interested in finding out who stored that there." Palmer accepted the inhaler without saying anything.

"Anyway, Palmer," I said cheerily, "I've got the tape, and I'm getting the hell out of here for Dobbstown. I meant what I said about the MegaBuck and 'Phrane. Now where can I drop you off?"

"You know," he said slowly, "if there's all that plutonium piled up there that the cops *do* know about, I can't help but think that there could be more plutonium that they don't know about. Maybe I'll come to Dobbstown with you, Gordon. You did say we have 'Phrane plants growing there now?"

"Brought them up from GreenHelle myself six years ago," I assured him.

We had started crossing the Golden Gate Bridge about then, and just as I settled back into the seat there was a sudden concussive jar, a loud explosion, and for a second the whole car was enveloped in flame.

We skidded violently but I was already back up to full power and my reflexes were unbelievable. I brought us under control almost instantly.

The car was armored and well sprung, but had no weapons. I could see my attacker now. It was a low-slung TurboFan like mine, only more heavily armored and equipped with external weapons, two extra headlights and a flashing beacon on top: a Baypolice SWAT car. I opaqued the windows and put three of my photon flashers out the dispenser quickly. They blinded everyone else and tore traffic up badly, but the Heat seemed unaffected. I couldn't drive and shoot, but they could and were doing both. We took about fifty rounds of light machinegun fire across our rear end, but the car could take a lot more than that. I tried some explosive grenades, but no luck there.

We were almost in the middle of the bridge and they were coming up fast with everything going at us. I figured what the hell and, after estimating the distance, popped the Stickybomb out through the dispenser. I had it timed right; it went off underneath the SWAT car. One part of the Stickycharge adhered to the armored bottom of the speeding car, long gummy tendrils catching it all over while the other part of the charge stuck to the surface of the road and to one side of the steel bridge wall. The Stickycharge is a silicon fiber-chain substance that can stick to anything and never lets go. The fibers are very stretchy up to a point, but when they reach their limit, they stop and resist with a tensile strength hundreds of times that of steel.

In this case, the SWAT car literally tore itself apart top from bottom, ripped a large piece of road out and warped the steel wall in the process. It stopped very quickly, or about a third of it did. The rest catapulted across the median into oncoming traffic as a ball of incandescent flame.

So much for field testing. That Stickybomb had possibilities!

By the time we got to the Oakland end of the bridge the traffic had really thinned out on our level. Palmer was almost catatonic, curled up on the seat next to me mumbling to himself. I guess the explosions and the shooting got to him. Despite the violence of his personal appearance and the presence of it in his art, Palmer was essentially a peace-loving man. The only thing dangerous about him was his mind.

I got us off the freeway and parked the TurboFan in an alley and set the auto-destruct timer. I practically dragged Palmer to the nearest corner, where I was able to bleep a three-wheeler electrocab with my Datascan. We got in, I dialed Oakland Air Terminal and we were off.

Palmer, of course, had no current identification, and you couldn't get out of the WestBloc without the right papers, but I thought I knew a way around that. They really only checked your papers when you bought the ticket. On the way over to the terminal I went up to full power and began a computer-enhanced scan of all the civilian and police radio bands. The BayPolice were pretty hot about their SWAT car but apparently were still all looking for the Korean auto. With a little bit of luck that was nothing but a puddle of fused metals and a lot of burned plastic residues by now, maybe keeping a few old derelicts warm. I shunted my power level back down and fed Palmer another half glig of 'Phrane out of my emergency medical pack. I also made him smoke another 'Fropstick. By the time the electrocab dropped us off in front of the terminal he was almost normal, or at least as close to normal as Palmer could ever be.

I stashed him in the Tiki Lounge bar and went over to the ticket counter. I wanted the next quick passage to Malaysia. Singapore Airlines had an SST leaving in an hour and a Ballistic Vehicle due for lift-off in less than thirty minutes. There wasn't much traffic at the ticket counter, so I walked up and asked to see the agent in charge immediately.

He came right out, a short prissy man with glasses who looked a lot like Ivan Stang, wanting to know what the problem was.

I assured him there was no problem and showed him my beautifully forged NatGov documents. He was impressed, of course, but he was even more impressed by the large amount of money I handed him.

"I need two tickets on your upcoming Ballistic to Singapore," I explained. "I have a man traveling with me who is a Federal prisoner— leave the name on his ticket blank, this involves national security."

Well, he didn't like the idea, of course, but I told him he could either do it my way and get paid in cash for the tickets AND his cooperation, or do it his way and accept my number on a Federal Travel Voucher. That way he'd get nothing and his company might get reimbursed when the NatGov got around to it.

He quickly acquiesced; nobody likes NatGov agents, or the NatGov for that matter, but everyone still likes money. He said there would be no problem with the tickets except that the computers would not issue one without a name.

"Oh hell," I said wearily. "Let's give him a fewking name then. How about Poonflang Dammarung, there's a fine Malaysian name for you."

He didn't even blink. "How do you spell that?" He wanted to know.

A few minutes later I was back in the bar with Palmer and the tickets. He was nursing something in a plastic coconut shell made with cane alcohol and ersatz pineapple chunks. We only had about a twenty-minute wait, so I sent Palmer into the toilet with the last of my 'Phrane. He came out looking almost jaunty and began talking about how much better things were going to be for him in Dobbstown. He figured that, as one of the earliest Hierarchites who had really suffered a lot for "Bob," he was going to get a nice house, plenty of 'Phrane and a lot of other flashy perks. I didn't have the heart to disillusion him. Things had changed a lot since Palmer's last visit to Malaysia. Didn't he realize that there was a war going on?

As soon as they gave the first call for the Singapore Ballistic, I stood up and produced my handcuffs.

"What are those for?" asked Palmer, eyeing the plasteel bracelets uneasily.

"Simple," I said. "As far as the WestBloc goons are concerned, I'm a NatGov cop and you're my prisoner. That way, if they do a check before we board, there's a good reason why you don't have any identification." He opened his mouth to object, but before he could say anything I snapped them on his wrists.

"I dunno about this, Gordon," Palmer mumbled.

"Hey," I said as we headed for the boarding gate. "Just remember the words of the Most Sacred Scribe, Palmer."

"How's that?"

"In Ivan's words, 'You'll just have to trust me!' "

Palmer made a face; he'd heard those words before. Hadn't we all? I flashed my IDs at the Bay Police security guard and he didn't flicker an eyebrow, just waved us both through, looking at Palmer with undisguised contempt.

I was afraid he might just be a little curious as to why a NatGov agent and his prisoner were hopping a Ballistic to Asia, but curiosity, like intelligence, was not a requirement for joining the force nowadays. If you had good feet, big hands and a thick neck, you were in.

Twenty minutes later we were boosting through the stratosphere at two and a half G's. I had taken the cuffs off Palmer as soon as we boarded. He had accepted the antiacceleration medication and was sound asleep. I stayed awake on low power and scanned all the news channels. One of the Oakland stations carried a story about a minor traffic accident on the Oakland bridge. I tapped the cassette in my coat pocket reassuringly and settled back in my acceleration couch. It looked like, this time, Dobbs be praised, we had got away clean. Another two hours or so and we'd be in Dobbstown. I could get some rest in the Blank Tanks—and Palmer, well, they'd find *something* for Palmer to do!

**Text and Artwork by
Rev. Mark Mothersbaugh
DEVO**

WHAT I KNOW

Excerpts

It Took a Genius to Invent It

It took a genius to invent it, but it only takes a monkey to detonate it. Boom, boom, boom! Retrograde Evolution, winding down, down, down!

In a world in which fear is man's dominant emotion—fear of insecurity, loneliness, inferiority, love, sickness, death—what can one do to relieve the bad-tasting jokes of impending doom-and-ultra-gloom?

Just in case there was no war, the trigger was set to go off forty years in the future anyhow! No one at the lab knew that; just the quiet little henpecked guy that everyone made fun of, the only person who had access to the long delay mode on the seemingly benign timer that was directly connected to the Atomika trigger.

"Monkeys have better orgasms than humans," according to one hard-working and detail-oriented animal husbandry expert.

Man O Man a Shove Its
Dissertation from an F Student

What a day. Trouble in the Middle East, tension in the Eastern Bloc, problems here at home, boy. Do you know what it's like to try and monitor a planetful of wild, out-of-control Pink Boys, Wankers, Jips, Mediocretins and other human types? It's like trying to corral ants with a wet spaghetti strand. Everybody seems to have something to blow some steam about. Up here, over that-a-ways, down there too. Man O Man! You know, "Bob," it ain't easy just trying to listen in about it; I sure as hell-o don't know how they all manage to keep so active! "Channel 2 News," "Alive at Five," "World Lowdown Report," radio, citizens bands, police frequencies; Marine, Air Force and satellite transmissions . . . not to mention newspapers! Hundreds of them, in a hundred languages! Where do these people find time to learn how to fire a smart cannon and keep up on politics at the same time? The Stark Fist? HA! All I know is, if we all get blown up by a RadioDrone A-bomb someday, will I get to see *me* melt down on my TV, or will I have to wait for *Time* magazine to stick a rolled-up copy up my butt, light it, and stuff the "free with your subscription" handy "Lighted Bed Fone" in my mouth? Send help soon, "Bob."

A Close Shot at Qian Qing Gong (Palace of Heavenly Purity)

It was a fucking fantastic voyage, and we were traveling through a most disturbing part of the universe, a section where the ribbon of time was twisted all around, folding back on itself, wrapping and knotting; you would be traveling along on July 5th, and all of a sudden it was midnight July 4th, and you were counting hours backwards, and maybe you could remember fast enough what was coming up, and maybe you would jump up into June a year later, and then skip-hop across to the preceding May; you might find out that you were experiencing certain parts of your own past for the first time. Where was this place? . . . Fucked-Upville, of course. This guy here was a litigation lawyer from Houston who just happened to get on the wrong People Mover at the Little Rock airport on an innocent trip to 17 Flags over America for a court case, when all of a sudden he's the big baby his mother could never change diapers fast enough for, and he's still carrying his brief-case, but he's got the same pacifier he spent twenty years trying to duplicate with stink-cigars and lard-infested foods. Cracks me up thinking about it. Guy on the right just took a turn for the worst into his own animal-husbandried future, where his Swatch don't tell time so good. "Bob" did his job, all right; maybe did it too well!

乾清宮近景
A Close Shot at Qian Qing Gong
(Palace of Heavenly Purity)

Crude Behavior
Or
Doggone It, Stop, Mister!!

There is a part of the brain that harks back to primordial times. In the female, it is the ostrich, a strange bird that hides its head in the sand and runs as fast as the day is long. Sometimes, when the ostrich brain kicks in, a "Connie" can keep a "Bob" begging and twitching for years, even lifetimes. In the "Bob," the primordial part of the brain is reptilian. It's the part of the brain that gives him an instant doggie-dick erection at the sight of a pretty girl, or makes him want to wallow in his sexiness like a pig with five hundred pounds of rock-hard, brick-colored shit stuck up his ass. It's the part of the brain that says, "Tell her anything, but stick your penis into her body."

There's no reason to fight it; anyone who is really honest will admit this fact of life is the Euclidean Truth and nothing butt. . . . Anyhow, the mind-set of the "Connie" is to repel this repugnant reptile, and for a good reason: If she didn't, all humans would spend their time doggie style, and never get anything done! Or so says one bigoted asshole with a Ph.D tacked above his desk at a local think tank!

POST CARD

A Close Shot at Slack

"I don't know who Art is, but I know what I like," boasts a rookie right-hander from the Salt Lake City Tarpturds as he takes a stroll through the recently erected Tai He Men art gallery in downtown Utah. A lot of first-timers would be afraid to admit to a lack of knowledge on the subject, but not our rookie. "Y'know, when I first heard that there was people gettin' blowed up in Central America and the Middle East, and little bitty kids with fat bellies and skinny arms 'n' legs moaning and starving in Africa and India, I said to myself, ' "Bob," why does Utah have so much moolah to spend on another art gallery when these hideous Frankenstein nightmares are simultaneously going on all over the world?' And then my team's manager explained it to me, that in a world that ain't so purty to look at sometimes, rich people need things to comfort themselves and protect their eyeballs from the dirt they live in, and so I says, 'Yeah, let's get on with this art stuff, pronto. We gotta fight for our right to potty, and save the rich!' "

A Close Shot at Tai He Men (Gate of Supreme Harmony)

Kids 'n' Sex

Where do kids get their ideas about sex? What elements contribute to the misconceptions we have in our pre-sex ages?

I remember at the age of twelve, thinking that a woman's private parts must resemble the blowhole on a whale: smooth, with a round hole, not unlike the hole on a golf green. The female receptacle must be built to fit the job of accepting penile injections that—I wasn't sure why, but I knew—it was my duty as a red-blooded member of the species to perform. Something attracted me like a twelve-ton magnet with fifty pounds of iron in my boots. I taped mirrors to my shoes as was explained to me on those Boy Scout camp-outs I used to go to, where we all sat around the fire after the adults passed out, and the older boys filled us younger boys in on the realities of the world of sex. I had a friend who used to wrap himself like a mummy with toilet paper before he could masturbate. I knew another guy who liked to stick bobby pins down his urethra while his wiener was hard, so that during ejaculation he would shoot the bobby pins into the soft glass wool ceiling. Still another guy would go through the trash can in his parents' bedroom, and pull his dad's used rubbers out of the can and sniff his mother's essence on the outside and his father's on the inside, and use his father's sperm as a lubricant as he jacked off inside those rubbery things. All three of these people went on to hold positions of authority in the Conspiracy.

Guy C. Deuel

NEW HIERARCHY™ TALE

Immaculate, Ivan Stang™ paused before the mirror to straighten his already perfect tie. Then he picked up his expensive briefcase and went out the front door of his substantial suburban home to find the Mercedes limousine waiting (as usual) at the foot of the driveway, motor purring. As he briskly approached the big, black machine, Stang's chauffeur got out and opened the armored rear door for him. The uniformed man greeted Stang professionally with the stolidity of a private security operative. He closed the door carefully as Stang sank back into the embrace of the expensive upholstery. The car still smelled "new" and Stang inhaled the mixed odors of paint, plastics, metal and lubricants with undisguised pleasure. The smell of this car was the smell of success! Yeah, and with a driver "baaaad" enough to make even G. Gordon Gordon[Reg. U.S. Pat. Off.] be polite!

Stang was miffed at Gordon anyway. Recently, while doing an emerald deal with the GreenHelle™ chief executive, one of Stang's runners had come "unwound" in the lobby bar of the Maksoud Plaza Hotel in São Paulo, Brazil. It had started walking around aimlessly like a zombie, making unpleasant noises and upsetting glasses, tables—the police!

Gordon had spent ten days in prison before his preimplanted bribes had successfully worked their way through the corrupt and inefficient Brazilian bureaucracy and he was at last freed. The bad thing was that he had spent most of that time in the infamous Agua Santa maximum-security prison on the outskirts of Rio de Janeiro. "A real fucking snake pit," had been Gordon's terse summation.

Pity was that he held ALL the contract points, mused Stang. That had ended up being a real "bummer," especially when Stang couldn't cover the losses with Foundation funds when Gordon insisted on calling the indemnity clauses. Well, he'd nail him next time around. Meanwhile this was a nice car, and, False Slack© or not, it was just what Ivan wanted.

Stang gazed out the tinted, bulletproof window until his car was on the expressway, and only then did he open his eelskin case to peruse his schedule for the day. By the time the car entered downtown Dallas he had reviewed his agenda and was engrossed in the study of a grimy-looking personal letter. A lurid blot of lipstick the color of fresh blood obliterated the bottom right-hand corner of the page. It looked like the imprint of a squid. The handwriting was large, almost childish, and the rag of a letter reeked of cheap floral perfume. Stang was poring over it as if he held the *Codex Sinaiticus*. The letter said:

Dear Ivor, I loved your last nasty note … reely you are quite perverted you nasty dirty boy, but dont I just love you for it. I showed your letter to my girlfriend Sheila and she says that I should do like you ask. She says if I pack it right and send it by express they'll never know what's in there or if the panties are clean or what so keep an eye on the mail.

I don't know if I can get you a picture of me doing THAT though. Sheila cant work a camera and I dont think my dad would come over and do it for us (joke HAR HAR …) But I will try. Please Ivor, send me some more of those funny fotos you make of 'it' on the xerox. We reely liked them a lot … got to go, time for my coffee break, love and XXXs … Wanda.

PS Would 'Bob' approve of what we are doing? SERIUSLY IVOR?

Almost hidden by the ugly lipstick seal was a final notation: "more luv 'n stuff . . . W."

Stang brought the letter up to his thin beak of a nose with a hand that trembled ever so slightly and inhaled deeply. Ah yess, Wanda . . . in the typing pool down at circulation. Graduate of the Foundation Home for Wayward Young Women, no doubt. Well, she was certainly compliant enough. Might as well send her the pictures, maybe she'll send the panties after she . . . His reverie was broken by the snarl of the car's SkipPhone®. Stang picked up the receiver. His mouth became small and prissy. "Go ahead," he said in the clipped and bloodless tones he invariably employed when dealing with the public. It was the detached voice of a man who ran on automatic, a man who had his shit together. He listened for a moment or two before an impatient look flitted across his vulpine features. "Tell them to sell," he said firmly. "Sure, sell it all. It was a publicity buy anyway. It looked good for the Foundation to own stock in a securities and exchange company in Medellín, Colombia. . . . What? Fuck no! Well I don't care what you thought, I'm not paying you to think, I do that. I'm paying you to DO! So sell!" He broke the connection almost angrily. "Dumb shit," he murmured quietly to himself as he smoothed his well-oiled forelock. These Wall Street types were a lot of Pink™, overpaid, complacent bastards. As if what they did was *that* hard! And they acted like they knew it all. . . .

Stang refolded the letter and slipped it into his briefcase. His eyes were already starting to burn and water despite the new filters in the car's air-conditioning system. DAMN! If this kept up, he'd have to take out his contacts and wear his glasses. Stang knew that he looked a lot more important, a lot more MANLY without his glasses. Face it, those Coke-bottle specs he wore made him look like a nerd or a sissy.

Meanwhile the car slipped silently into the underground parking garage of the SubGenius Foundation™ World Headquarters, right in the middle of downtown Dallas—one hundred and ninety floors of upthrust, glittering building, shaped like a tetrahedron and covered with tinted quartz. Stang thought of it as a city (or at least a large neighborhood) that had been tipped up on one end and driven halfway down into the earth. And he, Ivan Stang™, worked up there in the topmost section, there in the heart of the most important "nerve center" of the Church's far-flung evangelical and commercial empire. At the wheel, so to speak, of the Dobbs© juggernaut, smashing back at the Con™ ... fighting the good fight for "Bob" or, better yet, battling for BUX!! (Careful now, Ivan, remember what the Doktor© said about side effects of the PILS™.)

Nonetheless, cynical Stang actually felt very proud of himself as the limousine paused at the elevators for him to get out. He slipped a card into a wall slot as his chauffeur drove away. The elevator doors opened with a soft hiss. Stang stepped inside, reinserted his card and punched in the tone code for the upper-level complex. The door slid shut like a horizontal guillotine, making Stang shiver. What if you were to sharpen the leading edge of that door somehow? And then maybe figure a way to get the door to shut ahead of the safety signal ... not all the time, just now and then. A sort of random factor ... you'd never know. ... His fancy broke off as the elevator ascended with increasing velocity, lifting Stang high into the bowels of the corporate beast.

Ivan Stang™ activated his WristPager® and a moment later his secretary's slightly husky voice cut in over the ChurchMuzic© that had been percolating throughout the confined space. "Yes, Mr. Stang?"

"I'm on my way up, Miss Tyler," Stang said formally. "Are all the papers for the St. Louis Accords ready to be signed?"

"All the material is on your desk," was her polite rejoinder. "Do you want coffee, Mr. Stang?"

"Does a wild Pope shit in the woods?" he sniggered and broke the connection. His knees were beginning to quiver from the prolonged acceleration when the elevator whooshed to a stomach-churning stop. The switchblade door opened and Stang stepped directly into a dimly lit I-Dento-Cel™. For a few seconds soft microwave Contour-Skan$^{\text{Pat. Pend.}}$ radar examined him minutely. Another beam system gave the contents of his briefcase a quick electronic riffle. After a moment or two the lights brightened and Stang placed his hand on the glowing imprint in the middle of the door. The door instantly swung outwards with a muffled thud of hydraulics. It was composed mostly of steel and was a trifle over seven inches thick. On the other side was a brightly lit and beautifully carpeted corridor. There were quite a few people about, moving from room to room. Several of them greeted Stang as he hurried down the hall. Stang really hated the fact that he had to come in through the MediaDrone© section. Since he had moved upstairs (at last!) these types were always ... well, fawning on him. "Kissing corporate ass, that's what it's called, buddy," Stang told himself, giving a voluptuous, red-headed E-Girl™ Sec-Clone the eye. She looks good, he thought. Ought to see if I can get her transferred up to Alpha Level. Yeah, it's time to give the old genes a swim in the secretarial pool, he thought jauntily as she passed him, eyes averted. Her expression was totally neutral, she was hoping he hadn't noticed her. It was supposed to be bad news if that Stang guy took a liking to you. Better and safer down here in the MediaDrone© pool. The people here had pretty good drugs, at least, but those upper-level people with their pipes . . . she withheld the urge to shudder.

Stang opened his office door and was greeted by his secretary's smile. Miss Tyler was incredibly svelte and taller than he by several inches. Her short, honey-colored hair was cut modishly and her enormous violet eyes were deep pits of repressed magmatic libido (or so Stang believed). Every morning when he walked in and she smiled at him like that, he wanted so badly to tear off her expensively tailored clothes and bend her over her PBX terminal. But, as always, Ivan repressed his more extreme desires and smiled back, wishing his teeth weren't quite so stained. He paused to collect his big mug of espresso before heading for his inner sanctum. He closed the door and sat down at his very large, expensive desk.

As he sipped his scalding coffee Ivan tried to regain that flash he'd had when he first walked in . . . what he was going to do to Miss Tyler this time. "She's naked and spread-eagled on MY desk. . . ." His sketchy beginning was erased by the bleep of the blue telephone. It was Will o' Dobbs$_4$, Stang's houseboy. "Hi chief," he said with easy familiarity. "Just wanted to check in and see if you had thought of any more 'specialities' for the party."

Stang frowned at that familiarity when he heard it. That was the problem nowadays, treat an employee like a real person and he gets pushy.

"Sure was good last night," Will o' Dobbs$_4$ pressed.

"I told you never to call me on this phone unless it's really important," Stang told his body servant crisply. "I don't care about the goddamned party. Talk to Miz Stang about it. Just don't bother me with that sort of crap."

"Sor-ry!" said Will bitchily and hung up. Stang shook his head as he replaced the phone. He went through the Accords very carefully. Almost ALL church business passed over Stang's desk sooner or later. Technically he and Philo were equal, both number-two men in the organization. But for some reason "Bob" had made Ivan work his way up. Philo, of course, had started out with a key to the executive washroom.

Stang initialed the Accords and put them in his out basket. He opened another folder and read for a moment. What he saw triggered a phone call. He used the gray telephone this time, a direct link to Drummond Clinics$^{Pty. Ltd.}$ in St. Louis.

"What's the scoop on this here arms deal?" Stang asked Drummond in his best "good ole boy" Texican accent.

"What about?" asked Philo Drummond, $0.1°^{TM}$, trying to light a cigar at his end and making loud sucking noises in Stang's ear.

"Well . . . I mean, Peru and Nicaragua? Isn't that G.G.G.'s territory?" Stang wanted to know.

"Oh, certainly, but no sweat, Ivan. I personally cleared it with him," Philo assured Stang. "He's in Dobbstown© getting his neurowiring redone in the Blank Tanks©." The puffing noises stopped.

"Waaal, ain't that nice fer us." Stang lifted a skinny buttock and farted discreetly. Miss Tyler had good ears. "It's gonna be nice and quiet for us for a while, isn't it?" He scratched behind one ear. "I guess he's okay . . . isn't he?" Did Gordon owe him money on that Paraguayan resort scam they had cooked up? He envisioned Gordon, spread-eagled like a starfish and floating in a glowing glass tank of krypton green, his nervous system traced on his body with lines of fire.

"Yeah, he's fine." Philo sounded bored. "He just needed some new chips and pieces after that little dustup we had with that gang at my old clinic, you know."

"Oh yeah, I heard about that!" Stang hadn't the faintest idea of what Philo was talking about. . . . (Silver insects swim in the tank with Gordon. They crawl over his inert body, inserting with surgical precision microscopic chips which they connect to specialized implants. Crystals are forming on his exposed spinal column.)

"Yeah, it was pretty hairy for a while there, ole son . . . but look, I gotta go, man. The authorizations for those contracts are in the mail. I don't know why those arms contracts got there first. The other papers were mailed at the same time."

"Okay, well, thanks a lot, Philo . . ." Stang stopped when he realized Philo had punctuated his last sentence by breaking the connection.

"Fucking evil PUD," Stang muttered to himself, pawing through his desk drawer for a rubber stamp. He found it and printed "SO WHAT" in purple on the routing folder for the arms contracts and then flipped them into his out basket. His coffee was cold before he finished it, but that was okay. Stang secretly relished the tepid, syrupy dregs.

Miss Tyler entered with a sensuous rustling sound, handed Ivan two more folders and collected the contents of his out basket.

"I'm going down to the Xerox center," she said brightly. "Got anything you want me to copy, Mr. Stang?" Stang thought about Wanda's most recent request but just shook his head slowly. His secretary had a brother on the Dallas Police Department SWAT team or something.

"No thanks, I'm fine," he said absently, looking at the folders he was holding. One had the bright red borders that classified it as "VERY IMPORTANT." Probably another memo from "Bob." Great, I can hardly wait, Stang thought. He put the folders down and regarded the breathtaking spectacle of Miss Tyler walking away from him. She WANTED it, he KNEW she did! She was ready for anything . . . same eye makeup as Nefertiti. Stang sighed soulfully and looked down at the desk.

Things just weren't the same around here lately. Shit, they hadn't been the same since "Bob" got shot in '84. Fine publicity stunt *that* turned out to be, sure glad it wasn't my idea. Of course, the real trouble was that the Foundation medical staff weren't a hundred percent successful with the Re-Erection™, were they? Another phone bleated, this time the hot line from Tokyo. Tokyo? What the hell was going on there? It was already evening there, wasn't it? He picked up the yellow phone.

"Hey there, Stang ole buddy, this here is Janor©," said the phone in thick hick tones. "Me an' Smith&Jones™ are stranded in Japan. I lost m' wallet with all our money and tickets in it. I still got our passports though, we hadda leave them at the massage parlor fer security. Can you advance me some mmmoney, mmmman?" Sounded like Janor© Hypercleats™ was on acid again. If Stang hadn't owned a third of Janor© he could have cared less. But you gotta protect your investment. It took a while, but he finally got the psychedelic Arkansan to "mellow out" and arranged the transfer of money from Janor©'s royalty fund to Tokyo. He also promised to arrange for new airline tickets. Janor© was starting to babble about what sounded like "nine-inch worm comics" when Stang cut him off. Now he felt unaccountably nervous. He unlocked the bottom drawer of his desk and pulled out several packets of Marlboro cigarettes. He glanced at his watch. Pretty early really, lot earlier than yesterday. I should wait a little while longer. You don't really NEED a cigarette, Ivan. Too right, man, but I definitely WANT one, really badly! He clawed open a pack and lit up with a cheap, plastic lighter, filling his lungs with smoke. He pushed the red file to one side; memos came later, money business came first!

Stang reread and then initialed approval of a STERNOCORP® proposal to buy metals. "Platinum, osmium, chromium, refined beryllium and the actinide rare-earth series," he said audibly to himself. "Well, that should cover it."

His intercom buzzed softly and Miss Tyler informed him she was back. Stang asked her to see if the checks from NIXCORP™ and Maxxon™ had cleared. He reinitialed the last page of the metals proposal rather absentmindedly and dropped it in the basket. He checked a date on his calendar and was lighting his second cigarette when the green phone purred at his elbow. Stang looked at it with distaste but picked it up.

"Ivan . . . oh, Ivan darling," whispered "Connie" Dobbs© ™. "I want you and your hot meat, Ivan baby, and I want it now . . . oh Ivan, I NEED it. Tell me Ivan is it true that they called you 'Horsecock' back in high school?" Her breathy voice sounded like one of the recordings you got at the Foundation Dial-a-Porn™ number.

"Uh—"Connie," I'm kinda busy right now." Stang felt his groin begin to smolder. "Connie's" voice always had an amazing effect on him.

"Busy?" She pouted. "Too busy to tell me if it's true that you and

Philo used to go around making bar bets about how much you swung between the two of you? Tell me, is that true?"

"Uh—er—well, I guess it sort of . . ." To his relief he was cut off by another phone ringing loudly. Stang grabbed for it. "Just a minute, babe," he hissed at "Connie." He looked at the receiver in his other hand—it was red. That meant only . . .

"Hello "Bob," " he said a little weakly, placing the other phone close to his shoulder. He hoped "Connie" wouldn't get too upset; sometimes she got pissed if you cut her off or put her on hold.

"Bob" wanted to know if Stang was still going to take "Don," "Eddie" and "George" to lunch so they could all sign something or other. ("Bob" got pretty vague sometimes.) As if using only first names made this any less transparent, thought Stang disgustedly as "Bob" droned on and on. He assured his chief and savior that it was still "on" and reminded "Bob" that "Jerry" was attending too. Shit, thought Stang. Why not "Muammar," "Idi," "Yasir" and "Carlos" as well?

He promised "Bob" that everything was in order. "Bob" began rambling on about something; Stang tuned him out and put the green phone to his opposite ear.

". . . and after I've done ALL that to you Ivan baby, I'm going to bend you over darlin' and lick . . ." At this point the phone slipped from Stang's suddenly sweaty ear as he lit another cigarette. He captured it with his forearm, pinning it to his body before it could fall any further. Stang rolled his eyes upwards and gave thanks, then looked down and saw that the earpiece of the green telephone was less than an inch from the mouthpiece of the red one. Holy shit! Stang quickly disengaged the two instruments and checked up on his boss. "Connie" was off and running on automatic, you only had to grunt once in a while to keep her going, auto-oral-erotic.

" '. . . and when I see a white bird flying over the mountains I call the child "White Bird Flying," ' the chief says to the warrior. . . ." Shit! now "Bob" was telling another one of his fucking lame Indian jokes. Stang tuned "Connie" back in. ". . . and after I've got you all taped up *tight* except for those SPECIAL places, I'll put on the dildo, that one that looks and feels so *real*," "Connie" burbled. "The one with the red straps . . ." Stang switched back to "Bob." " '. . . why I call the child "Wind on the Lake," but tell me, "Two Dogs Fucking," why are you so interested? Pretty good, hey, Ivan?"

Stang rolled his eyes further upwards this time, looking up through his transparent ceiling at the glittering, hundred-meter-tall communications tower that capped the Foundation building. He yukked politely.

"Well anyway," "Bob" went on, "see that things go smoothly at lunch. Sorry I can't be there but I have a luncheon date with 'Barbara' and

'Peggy Sue.' " He cut the connection abruptly, leaving Stang with "Connie," who was saying, ". . . pull the nozzle out ver-ry slowly, leaving you so full and warm, Ivan." She stopped for a deep, shuddery breath. "Are you there, Ivan?" she husked.

"Hanging on to your every word, babe," said Stang, chewing a cuticle with detachment. "I can't tell you how good it all sounds—but I've kinda got a meeting right now. . . ."

"After lunch, then, in the Executive Chapel," said "Connie" in a more normal voice. " "Bob" will be asleep. He and 'Peggy Sue' get to drinking those Bloody Marys at lunch time and he ends up limp as a log." "Connie" was having more and more trouble with her similes lately, Stang noticed, and wondered if it was a sign of senility. Nah, it was probably just that evil shit that "Connie" packed up her pretty nose nowadays. He made a noncommittal statement about what *could* happen after lunch and finally got rid of her.

New York called and he spent too much valuable time sorting out the details of the seventieth printing of *The Book of the SubGenius*© with the latest publisher. He made a note to get Will o' Dobbs₃ to rewrite the prophecies again and also to throw another coke party for the MediaDrones©. Foundation books were selling very well all of a sudden, he noted. Maybe the planetary literacy level was on the rise again? No, scratch that. He lit another Marlboro and then realized he already had two going in the ashtray. He extinguished them and puffed happily on the freshest one. Stang had tried to stop smoking many times, but to no avail. The Tobacco Demons® HAD him. Trouble was when Stang smoked, he SMOKED. Miss Tyler had once entered his office wearing a respirator mask. He could understand where she was coming from, but sent her back to the E-Girl™ pool for a week anyway. Smartass!— what's wrong with a little smoke anyhow? At least he didn't just aimlessly 'Frop© all day like those upwardly mobile po'buckers™ and "Bobbies"™ on the floors below him.

Still smoking, Stang worked away. He had a long, confidential chat on the "scrambler" with Herr Willem de Ritter in Geneva. As he conferred with the art banker, Stang switched on his new terminal and idly punched keys. He scanned endless sets of numbers and consulted many charts and graphs, at one point getting an amazing erection.

Just outside his office the delectable Miss Tyler got to her feet and swayed sinuously down the hall to the Xerox center to see if her materials were ready yet. There she encountered Maka Dudi™, the executive in charge of the SubGenius Foundation International Missionary Program®. He was copying something written in Russian. She instinctively smoothed her hair, hips suddenly more fluid as she walked up giving him a friendly smile. Miss Tyler rather liked Maka; he wasn't here at the headquarters a lot, but he was always so pleasant and healthy-looking, not like that assoul© "Ivan the Terrible" (as she had dubbed her runty boss).

Meanwhile Stang shut off his computer, hung up the "scrambler," and lit another Marlboro, in that order. He moved his ashtray (Hermès, Paris, forty-five hundred francs. But you only emptied it once a month and it never smelled) a little closer and then doodled a moment on a notepad. Sitting up straight, he crumpled an empty cigarette pack and lobbed it across the room at the wastebasket, which was a two-thousand-year-old funerary urn from Iraq. He missed by at least two feet and grumpily went back to his paperwork. After you'd figured out how much you were worth that day, everything else seemed anticlimactic. He buzzed Miss Tyler, who had returned and was stacking copies of the rough draft of Pamphlet[16] neatly on her credenza. "Miss Tyler, there's a flight to Los Angeles late Friday or early Saturday. Book me a seat in first class and bring me some more coffee please, babe?"

"Will that be the usual billing?"

"How's that?" Stang was unfolding another soiled and rumpled letter he had fished from his briefcase.

"I mean, is the Foundation paying for this? You are going on Church business, right?"

"Oh, sure." Stang mentally crossed his fingers as he cut her off. Well it *is*, sort of, he thought. If I tie up this deal I'll be selling it to the Church . . . that's Church business! He lit another cigarette as Miss Tyler swept in with his coffee, three copies of Pamphlet[16] and two more folders. Stang guiltily hid the letter in the recesses of his desktop drawer and accepted the paperwork and mug with a smile. He skimmed and initialed the materials in the new folders, sipped his coffee and finally got around to looking at "Bob's" latest memo. He found he could make no sense of it whatsoever. Either the High Epopt's word processor was totally glitched or the Church was in serious trouble!

The morning ground on. Stang smoked cigarettes and drank coffee. He communicated with his Church counterpart in the Soviet Union, a shadowy entity whom Stang had never met. The dissident Church leader's image was always electronically altered. His code name was "Ivan" (of course). As they swapped data Stang realized that it could be anyone on the other end. Hell, for all he knew, "Ivan" could be a committee!

As Stang's mood became more manic he became even busier. He called up printers in New Jersey, stockbrokers in Hong Kong, tailors in London and car dealers in Bavaria. He authorized the Foundation purchase of a newly denationalized alcohol fuel plant in Brazil, paying three cents for each dollar of value received.

His agent called him from Chicago. She said they had a package of four of his best "self-help" primers all set to go with the biggest religious printing house in the world. Immediate distribution in sixteen languages! (We're talking six figures here, Ivan!)

Before eleven he had the satellite relays a-humming. SubGenius funds coded into tiny electronic impulses coursed through the global banking grid. Stang bought, sold, traded, financed and even (occasionally) bestowed. Enormous sums of money went leapfrogging around the world, following the exchanges and markets. The money moved faster than the dawn as that line of light raced around the surface of the planet, the funds growing, ever growing . . . (easy there Ivan, slow down for a minute).

He lit another coffin nail and turned to his computer again. Stang got some interesting indications from Taiwan, a nice hint from Brisbane and bad news from London. He found a couple of likely impossibilities in Central America and an unconvincing probability in the Philippines.

Somebody from the White House called to confirm that Stang was "on" for dinner on Labor Day. He finished the morning up by rolling over all the Foundation CDs in Panama. He cashed them in on a promissory note from the Cayman Islands account. He converted pork-belly futures to soybeans and then sold soybeans short. During this time he smoked twelve more cigarettes. He opened his third fresh pack before it was time for lunch.

Lunch was awful, of course—Stang had known it would be. "George," "Don," "Eddie" and "Jerry" were all a first-class pain in the ass. Ivan could not understand why they all acted like such complete juveniles. And these guys were supposed to be running a large part of the Con™? But he managed to keep them all sober long enough to sign the St. Louis Accords, thus making them the St. Louis Accords©. Then Stang made his excuses and left them there knocking back the club's expensive cognac. His eyes were beginning to really bother him, and his lunch had consisted mostly of red meat. On his way out he stopped and told the club secretary to put all of this on his account as well as their bills at DobbsSpa®, where the four stooges were staying.

"They were asking about—uh—'girls.' " The secretary lowered his voice discreetly on the last word.

Stang winced. "No, not here. Tell them it's all arranged for them back at the DobbsSpa® and then fix them up, will you Louis? You know, the usual channels, call DodaSex™ or Lobo Freelance™. You've done it before." He handed Louis two large bills and then scribbled his initials on the voucher the secretary was holding out for him. "And for "Bob's" sake keep security advised. We can't have another 'accident' like the one when 'Henry' was here." He went out the door rubbing the bridge of his nose. His lower back was beginning to hurt.

On his return to the office Stang's headache got worse. He was convinced that just being in the presence of those four disgusting old barracudas had done it to him. He wondered if maybe he shouldn't go and meet "Connie" in the chapel after all. She was always "kinkier" when they messed around up there. But face it, Stang, wasn't "Connie" beginning to pall just a little? Wasn't she starting to show her age a bit? She definitely wasn't as firm and pneumatic as she had been just a few short years ago when she and Stang had begun "fooling around." His headache stabbed and Ivan decided not to keep the tryst, even if he really did need to unwind.

He stopped at the executive bathroom and took out his contact lenses. His eyes felt better immediately. He put on his thick glasses, regarded his reflection and instantly hated himself. He grabbed two headache PILS™ from the dispenser and washed them down with another cup of coffee back at his desk. In a few minutes his headache eased up slightly and he almost called "Connie" to tell her that he just couldn't make it, but then decided no—"Connie" could be just a little *too* persuasive, even on the telephone.

Anyway, he decided, she'll start without me if I don't show. "Connie" can take care of herself; she just needs someone to talk to once in a while . . . a conversation piece . . . har! He could always say that he'd been detained by those four bozos he had lunched with. If she even asked. "Connie" would have no way of knowing what time he had returned. Even if she had access to that particular computer, Stang doubted she would know how to operate it. "Connie" stayed pretty much spaced out nowadays. Soon she'd have the brain of a Prairie Squid© and be about as much fun. Although when I was a lad, he thought, there were real, *wild* prairie squid, and THEY were fun!

The blue telephone chirruped like a metallic cricket. Ah yes . . . the New York hot line, probably Pope Meyer™ with the figures for the Madison Square Garden Mission. He's outdrawing Billy Graham and The Bakkers® at the Three Mile Island Dome. Bastard can't wait to gloat!

"Speak to me!" Stang told the Pope of All New York, Idaho and the Pacific Northwest™.

"Great news indeed dear friends, and another great day for the Pope of All New York! Eleven days' gross receipts at nine million and some chump change! Now really, Ivan, how about that?" The Pope of All New York sounded positively ebullient.

And why not? thought Stang sourly. His lunch was a great, leaden lump in his belly and his cigarettes were already tasting shitty with the day barely half over. Considering the size of the gate cut that assoul© Meyer was getting, the bastard had every reason to be happy. Stang had cut the Pope a great deal because he'd figured that Meyer was going to fall flat on his ass at the Garden. Well, he had certainly called that one wrong, and even though he had never delivered all the promised publicity, Meyer was still knocking them in the aisles. He gritted his little yellow teeth. "Sounds terrific, Dave, I hear you may be held over for another week."

"Well, let's say I'm considering it, Ivan. But I'll want a hike in my cut of the gate if I do."

"Not my dog, you'll have to get someone else to walk that one for you," Stang said with sour satisfaction. Philo was the contract negotiator for this month. "By the way, don't forget you're meeting me in Frisco next Sunday. I've got that Eyetalian guy, the one who does all the Vatican documentaries, meeting us at the St. Francis."

"No problem, I'll be there," Meyer promised.

"Listen," Stang was suddenly tired of this conversation. "I think my other phone . . ."

"Gotta go, Ivan, my telex is tinkling," Meyer interrupted, and instantly cut Stang off before he could finish his excuse for hanging up on Meyer.

The afternoon was all downhill from there. A few minutes later Miss Tyler buzzed him and reminded him that she had a doctor's appointment at the Foundation Clinic. She was leaving now, okay? By the way, the NIXCORP™ check hadn't cleared yet, something to do with exchange rates.

"Oh, great!" Stang muttered sarcastically after she'd left. He switched on his computer and perused the worldwide stock transactions. Not much of anything exciting going on, looked like stagnation was setting in.

Stagnant Stang's thoughts turned again to "Connie." Was she still up there in the chapel, or had she retired to the "playroom" in her apartment down below? He started to pick up the green phone, but changed his mind and just slumped behind his desk apathetically. You shouldn't have to come back to the office after lunch, he decided. Afternoons were a drag, mornings were what was happening. Stang knew it was just postlunch depression, a slight dip in his circadian rhythm, but that didn't ease his sense of depression or make his stomach feel any better. What was wrong with him? Was he just getting—gulp—old?

He sat upright and stared off into space. Jesus, he thought. I'll be forty next month. That means I'm "middle-aged." Shit, I'm over halfway there, or assuming I get lucky and last for eighty instead of three score and ten then I'm exactly halfway there. And if I do live to be eighty, or even older, what sort of loathsome disease will finally carry me away? AIDS? Arteriosclerosis? Renal failure? The big C? He looked at his ashtray and felt a rush of fear mixed with guilt and shame. He really ought to stop smoking these things . . . but . . . nah! Too late for that now; if I'm gonna get it, fuck it, I'm gonna get it. Shit, what difference does it make? It's all downhill from here anyway. NOW THAT WAS A REALLY DEPRESSING FUCKING THOUGHT!!!

His stomach contracted and griped him. Gripe, he thought. From *grip,* I suppose. Probably *gryppe* . . . old Scandahoovian for "to grasp painfully." In the gryppe of Boeuf Wellandone old Stang, yclept Ivan, suffered sorely!

But the Pinks™ (okay, the well-heeled Pinks™) thrive on this sort of food. This is their kind of chow. But it's just too damned rich for the likes of a po'bucker™ boy like me, Stang thought. He briefly envisioned a big, hot, steamin' *bowl* of Wolf Brand chili and salivated reflexively before his stomach griped him again. "Oh, I'm just having so much fun!"

Stang stopped pawing through his medication drawer momentarily. He'd just said that out loud, hadn't he? He shook his head as he found the Maalox® and this time he remembered to shake the bottle well before he gulped it straight from the plastic.

Gaaaaah! he thought disgustedly. This stuff has a really foul texture, tastes like a mouthful of chalk. Forty years old—supposed to be in my fucking Alpha-prime, man . . . and here I am choogling aluminum silicate or whatever the fuck this stuff is . . . grrr, grumble grumble.

He regarded his array of television monitors with glassy eyes. He was just . . . well—yes, BORED! He contemplated dialing in the porno channels, but what the hell, if that was the sort of thing he wanted he could get it live up in the chapel or down at "Connie's" condo. No, that wasn't it.

King Stang surveyed his domain and all that he saw didn't really displease him; it was just that he could really give a shit right now, you know? He turned off all the screens and rested his pointy little chin on his fist in a classic pose as he pondered mankind's destiny.

Suddenly he snapped out of his lethargy, put his bottle of ulcer goop away, readjusted his hated glasses and unlocked the bottom drawer of his desk. He took out his FRAPPYHOUR KIT™ ® and opened it furtively.

Stang stuffed the pipe then remote-locked the door and opaqued the ceiling. He was about to sit on the floor beneath his desk when he remembered that this was habafropzipulops™ © that he was about to smoke, not marijuana!

Sheepish Stang sat down, unlocked the door and made the ceiling transparent again. He hardly ever 'Fropped anymore; it tended to make his contact lenses uncomfortable. Another sign of aging, he concluded dully as he lit up.

He was puffing away merrily when his intercom suddenly buzzed. Who was that? He put the pipe down and answered with a hoarse and wimpy "Ye-es?"

"Mr. Stang?" The voice was strong and the accent was Northern Nobullshit. "This is Audrey Beamish from Ms. Dobbs' office."

Oh shit, one of "Connie's" personal assistants. What did she want? Stang pulled himself together a bit. Why did 'Fropping make him feel so guilty?

"Aaah yess, Miss Beamish." Stang had put on his Devival voice with the deep and MANLY tone. He picked up his pipe and sipped at the aromatic smoke. This is still the jungle, Ivan, you gotta stay on top. "What can I do for you?" he finished obsequiously. He'd only had a couple of "tokes" and here he was, a mumbling, paranoid sack of jelly. Man, that 'Frop© was really strong. Where did he get it?

"Miss Tyler asked me to run your calls until three thirty. I'm sort of doing her a favor," the voice said threateningly.

Beamish, Stang recalled, was tall, pale and a bit bony with a really cute moustache. His mental image of her was fuzzy but he seemed to recall that she wore leather all the time and had a really nice ass. She looked as depraved as any of "Connie's" other assistants, which was pretty scary. Butchy, but probably swings both ways, he concluded. "Uh—thanks a lot, Miss Beamish. Listen, I'm not really expecting much traffic and I'm doing some important research right now, so hold my calls, will ya? Tell everyone I'm in conference."

"Sure thing, Mr. Stang," she sneered and broke the connection.

Stang put all his phones on "standby" and then got down to some serious 'Fropping. This had to be the stuff that Maka had brought back from Tibet. Sort of sticky and hard to keep lit, but man oh man it was . . . "really good shit!" (He finished up the thought out loud.) Realizing what he had just done, Stang was appalled at the condition he suddenly found his condition was in. He thrust the still-smoldering pipe back into the FRAPPYHOUR™ ® box and locked it away in the desk.

Stang's mouth was dry, although his stomach felt a lot better. He wished he had a minibar in his office. *Philo* had one, that evil PUD. And "Bob" and "Connie" had fully stocked wet bars in *their* offices. But then, THEY all had condominium apartments in this very building, didn't they? And Philo had never even used his! Stang had a small place in DobbsTowers® like the mere upper-echelon personnel. (Sorry, Ivan, we had to sell yours to "Bob's" uncle Jake . . . sure!) And there was the real problem. Now that the BIG money was jumping onto the SubGenius bandwagon, there was all this double-Dokstok© ass-kissing going on. There were so many "Bobbies"™ in the management levels now. Bunch of computerized "gimmeBobs"©. And how about all those new androgynous sycophants that staffed "Bob's" new place out in California, where the hell did they come from? They all looked like H. R. Giger drawings, and Stang wanted to gag just thinking about them. He wished for the good old "shoestring" days when the Church limped along like a three-legged dinosaur with piles, and everyone actually talked to one another, instead of just doing business like they did now. Sure, the money and the perks were nice, but were the "bad ole days" really that bad? Stang pondered and then decided that maybe they were. He was still mulling over this when he looked up over the tops of his glasses just in time to see his office door open on its own accord and "Bob" lurch across the threshold. *Shit*, Stang thought. He only ever shows up here when I'm 'Fropped to the gills!

As usual, "Bob" was puffing on that godawful Pipe of his. Who knew what he smoked in that thing? It sure as hell wasn't just 'Frop©.

Stang rose and greeted his boss with a smile that he hoped didn't look as forced as it was. Ever since the Re-Erection™ "Bob" had smelled strange and Stang now found himself wishing the High Epopt used an even stronger Pipe mixture.

It wasn't that "Bob" smelled really nasty, but there was a strong odor about him now of . . . of what? Mold? No . . . ashes? Decay? Yess, that was it, decay. A cold and impersonal smell . . . like leaves rotting in sandy soil. Like an old grave.

"Shit down, Ivan." "Bob" slurred his speech a lot more since the assassination, but what the hell, so had Reagan. "Bob" was still hanging in there, though, you had to give the old duffer that much. But lately there was something about "Bob" that was just plain creepy. Maybe it was that mortician's makeup that he insisted on wearing to offset his now unnatural pallor.

Slowly and a bit unsteadily, "Bob" lowered his spare frame into the chair on the other side of Ivan's desk. The leg brace made it difficult. He was supposed to use a cane, but "Bob" usually forgot it somewhere or other, or he carried a five-iron golf club instead. Maybe he was just a little bit embarrassed by it. "Connie" had recently confided to Stang that "Bob" had been extremely upset because the revivification process had not been entirely successful. Stang could definitely understand his boss's point of view on that particular issue.

"Ya know Ivan"—"Bob" paused to relight his Pipe, which bubbled like a tree frog as he drew on it—"I've been looking at the book shales and, you know, *White Thigh Trilogy* hash done really well fer ush"—he puffed for a moment—"and I think we need a new one like it, a new blockbushter of a HardCorps® erotic novel." He smiled at Stang, who experienced a sudden sinking feeling. Ever since the founding of the Church, back in the fifties, "Bob" had assigned certain tasks to his key personnel. Stang had been merely the Sacred Scribe© back then. Technically speaking, according to his contract, he still was, despite any other functions he might perform.

"Doing the reshearch for thish one should be a lot of fun." "Bob's" voice was suddenly very oily. "Remember the lasht time Ivan, thoshe 'friends' who helped us sho much? Well, I've got a couple more 'friends' who'd jusht love to do the reshearch with you!"

Nausea exploded in Stang's belly and tried to crawl up into his mouth.

Oh, Sweet Fightin' Jesus©, no . . . please . . . Stang prayed inwardly. He noticed that "Bob" was looking at him very intently. There was a

flickering in those light-blue eyes and Stang could see little flames dancing behind "Bob's" pupils. Stang took a deep breath in an effort to steady
himself; now he could smell a ghastly, sweet charnel odor, the scent of the
PIT, as "Bob's" sexual pheromones wafted across the desk to him.

"Bob" licked his lips voluptuously, repulsively, and fluttered his eye-
lashes at Stang; his rouged and powdered cheeks dimpled as he smiled.
He looked truly horrible in that thick layer of undertaker's cosmetics.
The Pipe, still gripped between "Bob's" always pearly teeth, flexed and
writhed obscenely, then it OPENED A YELLOW EYE AND LOOKED
DIRECTLY AT STANG.

Ivan's stomach felt as if it flipped over completely, and his bowels
knotted up painfully. Then his crotch grew hot and wet as he sat there
and pissed his pants with terror.

Ivan Stang™ sat riven by his master's gaze for a hellish, eternal three
seconds. Every single nerve ending in his body seemed to be standing
on tiptoe and screaming at his brain for attention, for action!

Then all of a sudden "Bob" was "normal" again, leaving Stang feeling
shattered, abused, drained and somehow unspeakably defiled.

"But I guess they will all be coming to Palm Shprings for the resht of
the week," "Bob" went on, as if nothing had happened. "And I know
you're jusht *too* busy, aren't you, Ivan?"

Stang could only nod slowly.

"Sho, whip me up a good proposhal and outline for this new
HardCorps® novel, will you, Ivan?" "Bob" attempted to relight his Pipe
again. "Take the resht of the week off and get going on it. You know
what shells. I don't have to tell my Shacred Shcribe how to write, now
do I? Heh heh. Let me have a five-thousand-word outline by . . . oh . . .
shay, Friday?"

"But that's tomorrow, "Bob," " Stang said weakly. His mouth tasted
awful and he became aware that he was sitting in a puddle of his own
urine.

"Ah? . . . well, sho it ish. By Monday, then. I'll shtill be in California,
so you can shoot it over by modem." "Bob" smiled coldly. "Thish wash
"Connie's" idea, actually. She shuggested it to me a little while ago. She
really likesh that other shtuff you wrote. You know, Ivan, I think you kind
of 'turn her on,' heh heh. I want you to shtay home while you write thish
epic. Remember, it meansh a lot to "Connie" too! Send the car back when
you get home today . . . better yet, leave it and take a cab home. Oh yesh
. . . Philo will be down to help you shometime tonight," he added.

"Philo?" echoed Stang a little foolishly, watching "Bob" use the desk
as leverage to get to his feet. Philo . . . oh great, just what I need! PUD
boy down here to collaborate! I got lucky when I stole that trilogy from
Smith[2] (Smithsquare) . . . now "Bob" wants another one. It's all that
bitch "Connie." I can hardly wait!

Stang loathed working with Dr. Drummond because the OverMan®
was a Rewardian© and Stang was an Emergentile©. That meant Ivan
would do all the work while Philo smoked all the 'Frop©, drank all the
booze, puffed on those stinky little cigars all day, goosed Miz Stang, told
the Stangettes rude jokes, dominated the teevee, played Stang's tapes
(and *never* put them back in their boxes) and left the sacred COMIC
COLLECTION scattered throughout all the bathrooms in the Stang
household.

"Philo has been a bit 'overslack' lately," "Bob's" voice cut through
Ivan's train of thought. "Let's say he simply exceeded his authority. And
your computer 'on-line' bill is simply exorbitant. After all, Ivan, you may
be working up here on the top level now, but you and that darned Drummond boy *have got to be realistic!* Oh, Miz Stang and the Stangettes have
already left for Europe. I sent them over for a tour of the 'Estates of the
Rich and Powerful' with that awful English fellow we signed recently.
She'll meet him and the film crew over there, we ought to get some nice
footage for our new series. That way they'll all be out from underfoot and
just you and Philo will be working on this project undisturbed." Stang
noted that "Bob's" articulation was suddenly perfect.

"Oh yes, "Connie" said she'd be happy to keep an eye on you two for
me . . . she's not coming out to the ranch. I'm having your house sealed
as soon as Philo arrives, and you'll stay there until our new best-seller
is finished. You get electricity, teevee, all that sort of thing, but you are
both 'confined to barracks,' heh heh. No computer time allowed either."
He turned to go.

"But . . ." Stang had a horribly upset stomach, a ringing in his ears,
a violent headache, and the seat cushions were apparently totally non-
absorbent. At least "Bob" was leaving!

"Or . . ." "Bob" turned and smiled THAT smile again. "Or perhaps
you *would* like to come out to Palm Springs after all?"

Stang just whimpered softly as "Bob" limped away. He sat unmoving
for several minutes. The air almost smelled normal by the time he
found the strength to buzz Miss Beamish and ask her to bring him a
couple of towels from the executive washroom.

Audrey Beamish snickered to herself. So, "Bob" had dropped in to see
Stang again, had he? She hummed a lilting tune to herself as she went
for the towels while a thoroughly bummed-out Ivan Stang™ sat alone,
waiting to dry.

"I have to write a book, a porno book," he said to himself with growing horror. "Bob" is so goddamned senile he really thinks that I used to
write all that crap. And now I have to collaborate with Philo and "Connie!" Bile rose bitter in his gorge, and Stang knew in his miserable,
shriveled soul, that the worst was yet to come!

Paul Mavrides

WORLD WITHOUT SLACK

Excerpts from the Novel-in-Progress

Chapter One

What cometh to this world? I
am *on* the Earth now as a drunkard among
you and NHGH is at My side.
> —Prescriptures—Neuronicus 22, Economicon of Dobbs

Think not that I am come to
send peace on earth: I came not to send
peace, but a sword.
> —Matthew 10:34, The Endlessly Revised Holy Bible

GOOD LORD!... "CHOKE!"
> —*The Vault of Horror*, no. 26, E.C. Comics

The Fightin' Jesus looked out over the immense bridge of the Xist battle saucer, *Blood of Christ,* and laughed. He was finally going to have His revenge on the natives of Dust-Mote 89-aB.

Aboard Jesus' flagship, dozens of killer theologians, the Shock Priests, were busy at their weapon terminals. On the power decks below, the proper orgone-cycle timings were being set by mass fornications between the ritual "crew" and the cancer beings of the Spree, Jesus' only true allies. An Invasion-ready state existed on this ship and the 665 others floating over their doomed target, Earth.

Jesus was in a psychopathically elated state. His long, soft hair hung loose about His shoulders, flowing to meet the white muslin robe that was the Prince of Peace's uniform. Simple leather sandals adorned His feet, which sported their own matching wounds. Floating a fraction of an inch off the deck, He fussed with His neatly trimmed beard, His manic aura dancing about, crackling and hissing where it touched across the glowing Halo. At the moment, His face truly did resemble many of the perverse portraits the humanoids below painted in the name of His Glory. Those Yeti-born monkeys prayed to these icons for the salvation of their souls. As if they had any souls to save. As if anybody would want to save them, which was unlikely in the extreme.

He had gotten reports that the Earthlings had actually organized a planetary religion, completely centering around His murder there, so

long ago. More like a lynching, it was. He spent three torturous days
and nights digging Himself out of the burial chamber. Just in time to
escape those sadistic ape-men, if the old Greek records he had seen were
correct. If He had been discovered up and about after the Crucifiction,
before He was ready, they might have *really* finished Him off. Those
hicks had the unmitigated gall to nail Him up like some common criminal and then pray to these simpleminded scrawls that made Him look
like He was *enjoying it!* That He was *forgiving!* That He *LOVED them!*

Oh, the anticipation! He was sick to His stomach with glee! Jesus
would show these backwater genetic accidents the true face of Pain, Sin
and Redemption! He had hired His own Holy Ghost–writers to revise
this "Bible" the Earthlings had. Rewrite it more to His own thoughts
and philosophies. He was going to make sure it was the only edition
available. It had taken Him two thousand standard Earth-years to
return. *Now* He would pay them back for the holes He still carried in
His hands. Sweet Stigmata! Even the slightest thought of the old scars
made them glow red, right through His fists, through the boxing gloves.

The battle command of the spacecraft was staffed by veteran Angels
of Light, on personal loan from JHVH-1, Jesus' father. They supervised
the officer Daemon units, the fleet's literal conjurors of destruction
within the tangible energy spectrum. To focus these unworldly reactions and project them to the proper targets was the job of the four-
thousand-odd Seraphim. For mopping up and commando raiding, the
Dark Bodies and AESON had been hired. Thousands of these emotion-
less, combat-proven mercenaries waited in the troop holds of each de-
stroyer. All at time-and-a-half. It was expensive to ravage a planet,
even an insignificant one like Earth.

No matter. The Host of Judgment, That Which Comes, had finally
arrived. And on Jesus' birthday, too.

"What do you think, Dad?" Jesus' second-in-command, the Rev. Jim
Jones, stood by with the final attack codices for His approval. A man-
sized holographic globe of Earth rotated in scale next to Jones in mid-
air. On its surface, grids of the natives' planetary defenses were lit up
in green, communications nets in violet and manned stations in blue.
Dense clumps of red pinpoints glowed across the map, each one revealing the location of either a ground-based, undersea or orbital nuclear
weapon. A colorful network of intersecting lines encircled the sphere. It
was quite pretty, actually.

"Like a Christmas-tree ornament," Jesus mused. *"My* Christmas-tree
ornament—to smash. To return to dust!"

"Our children wait for us below, Master. We will walk among them
and we will *smile.* At Your moment of choice, of course," Jones toadied.

Jesus studied Jones' tired, puffy face in the pink glow of the neuron
banks that ran around the walls of the mighty dreadnought's bridge

and shuddered. He was no stranger to resurrection of the undead, but whoever had brought this Jones around again had slipped up. Something was missing from this creature, something else had been added. Something, but what?

Jones had been forced on Him as number two by the DJIN bankers who financed His war party. Damn them! He never forgot the price they had demanded for this little expedition. Jones' constant reminders of their influence and expectations irritated Jesus to no end. Not to mention the annoying habit Jones had copied from J. R. "Bob" Dobbs. The twisted thing insisted on smoking a pipe, even here near the sensitive memory cells and nerve relays of the ship. Once an almost handsome man, Jones might have been left dead a little too long. He moved with a constant jerk and never stopped poking at his throat. Brother Jim always wore dark sunglasses and still took massive injections of methamphetamines, even though they no longer had any effect on his regenerated shell. Huge abscesses ran up and down the insides of his arms, yet he continued to wear short-sleeved tropical shirts, as if to show off his puny efforts at self-mutilation, here with the Spree, to whom matter manipulation was an ancient art form.

With a drop of blood, Jesus OK'd the pad Jones held out to Him and tried to draw out His second one more time. "You know, Jimbo, the best part about all this is that the humans actually think there's an After-life, for them anyway. That's why they strung Me up the first time I was here. Something to do with getting to Heaven, I believe. Who the Hell would want to go to Heaven? A slum like *that?* They think like bugs down there."

"I'm well aware of that, Commander," Jones answered stiffly. His Xist hard-wiring made him go formal whenever Jesus became too familiar with him. There was a big secret buried in Jones' skull that the bankers wanted to keep hidden.

It bothered Jones to be back on Earth so soon after his failure with the social-programming research post he had been running there. It hadn't really been his fault what had happened. The administration changes at Central had shifted all the friendly execs away from public sympathy for the project and Jones had lost his funding. He was forced to abort the experiment and terminate all the subject organisms, himself included. True, as head scientist he had an escape clause, but really, now, years of work were abandoned overnight when the grant was cut off! Politics, it was due to nothing but politics. If everything went right this time, he'd have the last word with Central, the *very* last word. With this asshole, Fightin' Jesus, too. What an insult now, to have this Jesus harping at him, calling him "Jimbo." Jones had often called out for Jesus in his trances and he'd done it with respect. No respect for Jones here. The only thing Jesus and Zombie Jim had in common was their sexual preference for young children—of any species. Just a couple of cosmic chicken hawks.

Jones had a prime directive with full authorization from NEXUS Security to take out JHVH-1's bastard Son when the invasion was completed or at the first sign that Jesus knew what the real objective of this mission was. He could wait. It would be soon enough.

"Have the Pope brought up to the bridge," Jesus softly ordered to a waiting spirit, bringing Jones out of his private thoughts. "I do hope he's capable of conversation. He didn't seem to respond too well to My Last Offer. Oh, and please keep any Warrior Spree away from him. Their resemblance to 'cockroaches,' whatever *they* are, seemed to frighten the little faker no end before. Get him some unsoiled clothing."

"As you wish." The phantom blinked off to the interrogation chamber with its message.

Jones was impatient. "I hope the audience is a short one. The poor man could hardly stand up after Your previous 'chat' with him. Let him rest. It's hard to maintain our surprise arrival advantage for long. Earth electronics are prehistoric, no problem there, but if "Bob" should feel the gravitational disruption caused by our orbital formation, I remind you that the margin of profit for the NHGH would drop by almost a half point, which would bring your balance into the red. You are already very close to having command of this trip turned over to our investment managers."

" "Bob"? "Bob" will be terminated by My Own Hand," Jesus snapped. "As for the Pope, that whining simp, why, he's going to give the order to begin *The Rapture*."

Doug Wellman got caught as he was crossing the San Francisco–Oakland Bay Bridge. Didn't even notice at first. Just kept talking into his Black Box. Notes. Jokes.

The car began to shake. So did the bridge.

"Hot damn, earthquake!"

Now he heard it. The sound cut right through the headphones. Reaching over to the digital recorder on the seat, he turned up the mike volume even as he began to fight for control of the speeding vehicle. The low-frequency moan of total motion was rare music. The shifting of tectonic plates would be a good white-noise background for the next Doktors for "Bob" 45.

He glanced at his dashboard computer and noted the readout: 10.2 R SCALE blinking in neat, red liquid-crystal dashes. The real trick was going to be staying alive for the next five minutes during the fun-house ride to which the North California coast was being treated.

Wellman's van was drifting crazily down the back of a tremendous gray snake that was doing an ersatz break dance. As he entered the

Treasure Island tunnel, the sides and roof of the bridge passageway began to acquire a crust of smashed metal and flesh from less fortunate drivers and passengers. Bus into Toyota into Ford into Beemer into Mack rig. Somehow he kept dodging the lethal, dancing wreckage, continuing to trap every agonizing dB on his metal oxide strip.

The city came into view as he bounced out of the tube at 90 MPH. He changed lanes to avoid clipping a VW and almost got taken out by a CHP car that sailed over him, tires just brushing his roof. Glancing quickly to his left, he saw it hit the top of a Jag spinning in circles and, in a dramatic aerial rebound, fly over the bridge railing. Wellman briefly glimpsed a pale, uncomprehending officer grappling with the useless wheel as his unit flew into the cold green water below. Cutting maniacally through this auto holocaust, Doug heard the tunnel collapse behind him.

"All on tape! All on tape!" he screamed in delight. "Wait till Gordon hears this! It's the earthquake, *the Big One!* Like a goddamn atom bomb! Yee haw! Merry Christmas!" The precision gyroscopic tape heads would compensate for all the random motion without any noticeable distortion in sound resolution.

With loud snaps, the bridge cables were unwinding and breaking, their massive steel strands flinging cars through the air all about him like miniature Matchbox toys, as millions of pounds of stored kinetic tension were released in seconds. The bridgeway bucked underneath him. Another jolt and its rippling pavement began to tilt to the right at a disturbing angle, but this merely allowed him to get a quick look at the Embarcadero. Thick clouds of vibrating gray dust billowed up a hundred feet or more, concealing the ground from view. The Pyramid was gone, safety-engineered quake-rollers and all. Most of the high rises were tilting into each other at absurd angles, sinking into oscillating quicksand, foundations unable to support their own weight in the liquefied landfill. Sparkles of glass from shattering picture windows twinkled in the afternoon sun as they showered over helpless pedestrians many stories below. The effervescent flickering was peppered with tiny, flailing secretaries and junior execs. As he watched, the Shaklee Building shuddered and went spiraling down, all its floors collapsing efficiently in a graceful pirouette of destruction.

The sane thing to do was to stop the van and hold tight. The determined Wellman, however, furrowed his thick eyebrows and sped up. He *had* to reach the Foundation office on Folsom. If he could make the Ninth Street exit, he might have almost five minutes to remix before the band's share-time on the Sanyo SoundSat ended for the day. Doug steered down the elevated ramp at a twelve-degree tilt, swerving to avoid people spasmodically flung across his path, their pinwheeling bodies leaving bright Pollocklike smears on the pavement. Great cracks began to appear in the roadway behind him, swallowing the wreckage in big gulps.

To his rear, the East Bay refineries in Richmond had their quake-proof storage tanks rupture, unable to withstand the unforeseen magnitude of the main shock. Millions of gallons of oil and gasoline spilled into the water and caught fire. A series of huge explosions released roiling mountains of toxic gas. The hellish black smoke almost succeeded in obscuring the fleet of flying saucers that were suddenly dancing over the whole sky.

Chapter Two

By the time you get to the Christian Heaven,
you'll be wishin' to GOD you'd made it to SubGenius Hell.
——Jivanor Hyperstang

"Bob" sold it
I bought it.
That settles it!
——SubGenius propaganda sticker, 1995

In late afternoon, a Neo-Confederacy rocket run had come screaming down the Mississippi; its delivery of high-grade munitions turned the afternoon sky dark. The resulting fires from the bombardment sent the temperature up well over a hundred degrees even in the undamaged parts of the city. Spam was finding that spring in St. Louis wasn't quite what it used to be.

Before the destruction of Akron (and the rest of Northern Ohio) in the Celestials' sneak attack on Christmas Eve, Spam Duvalier had seen the spray paint on the wall and prepared. He had his Church to thank for that. Originally, the panspectacular SubGenius cult had appealed to his alienated sense of humor, long blunted by dull life in the soporific Post-Rubber City. Instantly enthralled by a discarded Sub tract he had fished out of a wastebasket, Duvalier quit his job at the Summit County Mall Kreemie Kreem Donut Shop and enthusiastically joined up. First becoming a Convert Op, then a State Dogma Sprout, he finally wormed his way up through the DobbsHeads to Overbaiter Prime and a secure position as a Foundation troubleshooter. He went to Dokstok, did it all: new family, new hairdo, new TV.

But then the Prophecies started to come true. With each passing year, the Light of "Bob" became a little less funny and a lot more dark. All the sick things the SubGenists had envisioned as being mere black commentary on the devolved culture Earthoid primitives had entangled themselves with were coming to pass. Every stewing collective fear, force-taught long ago in filthy caves by supposedly benevolent aliens, every Church Rant and OutreachBurst of irrational, autohysteric spouting, every prophetic utterance, every drop from the dried-up teat of the Great Wonder DogMama of All was coming to life with dreamlike precision. Now that King Jesus was stomping about, who could argue?

Following X-Day contingency plans, Doug Smith and Spam met up on New Year's Day at Pope Flores' storefront mission in South Chicago. Duvalier had been assigned to Flores' Clench of the Deviant Image to help organize inner-city ZealotTeen squads and he had safely ridden out the December slaughter in a reinforced Blank Tank. The Pope was long gone, off to Dobbstown at the first sign of trouble.

Being populated mostly by atheists, thieves and drug addicts, anarchistic Chicago had made it through the Rapture, barely, but the same couldn't be said for the economic federation it had belonged to. Shakers, Quakers, Jehovah's Witnesses, Seventh-Day Adventists, Jesuits, Catholics, Anabaptists, Christians of every stripe, large and small: All had been whupped and all had gone down, or rather, *up*.

The United States of America had collapsed along with most of its allied nations in the Shake-up, as the divine assault was popularly known. The Communist-bloc countries had been caught napping when a surprisingly large number of their Party boys and Cagemen had been Raptured and now were in almost as much trouble as their Conspiracy Brothers in the West. If anything, the Soviet and Asian People's Democracies had fragmented even more abruptly than the "Free World." Surgically precise Spree EMPs had prevented any nuclear retaliation from Earth arsenals—a mixed blessing, for intercontinental nuclear exchanges would have otherwise been a certainty in the chaos that followed the angelic reaping of "the saved."

The continental U.S. was dissolving into a haphazard arrangement of warring city-states, cult theocracies, oddball political territories, private kingdoms, military dictatorships and corporate fiefdoms. Most of these microgovernments were at each other's throats, fighting for scraps of power and technology not yet destroyed.

On the poisoned winter shores of Lake Michigan, Smith had revealed to his apprentice OverMan the SubGenii's true role in a monstrous galactic sting with mudball Earth serving as the cosmic bait. Earth was merely a *rented* planet and the human race wasn't listed on the lease. At best, the present inhabitants were considered by the major players in the transaction to be a minor nuisance, somewhere around the level of household mildew. Establishing contact with Space God JHVH-1 was imperative in order to plead the humans' case and prevent their world's surface from being wiped clean with an empyreal version of tub and tile cleanser.

They decided to travel together, making their goal the flying saucer Doug claimed Dobbs had buried under the main temple in Texas. The last two months had seen the pair zigzag across the Midwest, evading various martial-law roundups and relocation camps, heading for Dallas. Home plate. But Spam was getting tired.

One last stop, Smith had promised. A Church Board of Directors meeting had been called to discuss cutting a deal with the aliens—they couldn't miss it.

And so, in a blast-proof Temple-Clinic in Free Fire Zone 554, St. Louis, Missouri, Duvalier was about to meet the infamous Ivan Stang face to face.

Spam paced back and forth in Dr. Drummond's waiting room, anxiously raising the armored gun blinds to glance out the window slits at the burning buildings every few moments. He felt naked without his old riot pump. There'd been a gun check at the clinic door and the receptionist was very insistent but he'd managed to hold onto the rocket pistol. It was some kind of security, anyway. Every now and then, Duvalier heard a car blow up, off in the distance by the river. The moaning fire storm was hurling cinders against the thermal plastic with a twitchy, brittle sound that gnawed his spine.

Across the room, Doug Smith sat blankly leafing through a Church pamphlet he had dug out of a stack of timeworn *Highlights* magazines on the watermarked coffee table.

"How can you be so ass-scratching blasé about all this?" Spam wanted to screech at him, throttling Smith's skinny neck in his hands, but he already knew by heart what the Texan's singsong response would be. It was amazing, considering what Dobbs had put Smith through.

"The aliens won't agree. It's just another false alarm, Spam," he had told his skeptical follower again that morning over a scavenged breakfast of Kitty Queen tuna and warm beer in a drainage ditch just outside of Bridgeton.

That was what "Bob" had written in the *Book*, too, but somehow it failed to reassure Duvalier.

"And if not?" Spam had persisted angrily. "What happens then?"

Doug finished licking out the can of pet food and frowned. "You got to bank on "Bob," Spam. Have faith. If this is his doing, then he will provide us the Slack to swallow it. Or you can kill me."

What temptation lay in that offer! Duvalier flopped back onto the tattered, orange vinyl couch, next to Smith. The air conditioner kicked on with a sick grind as the wall began to heat up.

If only Doug knew! Spam had lost his faith on that long-ago warm November afternoon, out on the greasy knoll that overlooks the Plaza.

There were the tourists on the banked hill. The whole crowd had turned as one at the prerecorded sound of the First Shot, solemn and respectful, the women red-eyed and the men in their dark suits, looking still and uncomfortable under the hot television lights. Doug himself had delivered the President's eulogy. "Bob" had a plan, he told us in a firm voice. It was not for the Pinks to question the ritual slaughter of the actor-politician. Or they could kill him. But Spam had stared into the Black Limousine and rejected his turn behind the Cheap Scope. He cursed the ways of Doug's merciless and unintelligible Deity. One of these days someone would take up Smith's dare.

Just then, Dr. Drummond's nurse appeared at the interior air lock, his throat vocorder buzzing, "Reverend Smith and Mr. Duvalier? The doctor is ready to see you now."

The dull echo of the Southern Navy xenon bombs carried all the way down the corridor. The whole clinic shook in response to the thunder of their fighter jets coming in low, pounding away at the ITT fortress downtown. The nurse, a once-swarthy Cuban weightlifter, cursed the warplanes and led Smith and Duvalier to a tiny room toward the back of Philo's shielded Quonset hut. The fellow wasn't a very positive testimonial to Dr. Drummond's healing powers or skill. Spam was no medic, but he could observe that the nurse was obviously suffering from at least six of the major phage-weapon strains and would be dead in a matter of days. Still, the doc's assistant was cheerful. They made it a point not to get too close when they gave him his tip.

The door closed behind them with a click of a heavy lock. Then the clicking of several more locks. More than had been visible on the door frame when they had entered. A string of bare red light bulbs hung from the ceiling, which was only four and a half feet high. The two men were forced to bend over in a humiliating manner to avoid the lights. The space hadn't seemed that small until the door shut behind them. They felt a lurch and heard the whine of a motor start up. Was this an elevator they were in? It seemed to be going down.

Spam suddenly felt nauseated. In spite of everything he had done to get here, he wanted to leave—to die, to just have it all be over and finished, forever. Dread blossomed and grew off the corners of everything. Intersecting geometries of depression formed in the air around him. He felt dirty and cheap. The dim twenty-five-watt bulbs cast an evil glow in the descending cubicle. The building shook again, and the lift stopped. The lights kept banging into Spam's forehead, burning his hair as they touched against it, filling the space with the foul odor. The globes were far hotter than they should have been for that low a wattage. The fillings in Spam's teeth began to hurt. His clothes smelled bad. His face felt dirty. He needed a haircut. Something else as well, that he couldn't quite determine. Something bad.

Smith looked affected by the change in atmosphere as well. The Scribe had wet his pants and lay curled up on the floor, banging his head against a plastic chair leg, the only piece of furniture in the incredibly claustrophobic "room." His convulsions made a nice pattern as he thumped away. Almost a cheap chip-stick samba beat. Smith always did have musical talent, Spam mused.

Another lurch. They couldn't tell if they were going down now or sideways. Spam was sinking to his knees. He heard his gun fall from his jacket to the floor and felt apathetic about retrieving it. Why bother, he thought, it was just my gun. So what? Why am I here? Now *that's* a mystery. Where *is* here, anyway? At least there's a nice drumbeat.

Spam woke to the sound of thousands of angry bees swarming inside his head. Feeling nauseous and vaguely "high," he lay still for a second and kept his eyes closed, trying to listen to the voices he heard coming through a mental blizzard of white noise. He could make out friend Smith having an argument with someone who was punctuating Doug's always urgent tones with ugly laughter. Spam's skin felt like it had been drenched in paint stripper. Hot, unpleasantly scented air, mixed with the odor of burning 'Frop, was blowing softly across his face, making him gag.

"No use pretending you're out, Duvalier. Sit up and shake the third hand of the Only Hope You Have," demanded a rough, deep voice, "And when you're behind the lines, from now on at least *try* to look like a SubGenius. Take off that clerical slave suit and act your Nental age before somebody grabs that disgusting string tie and strangles you with it. Want a drink?"

Cracking his lids apart, Spam saw before him a rather imposing figure dressed in an expensive, gray Italian three-piece, offering an oversized snifter of greenish liquid and puffing on a cigar-sized 'Frop-stick. He looked like a heavyset cross between James Bond and Mike Hammer, with dark, weathered eyes set off by a flesh-tinted plastic nose that rode a thick, brown moustache. It could only be G. Gordon Gordon, the Church Head of Security, that was giving him this warm welcome. Smith had warned Duvalier about Gordon back on the road: "metakiller with a heart of gold" or some such nonsense. Gordon had been backstage at the Victoria Theater, the legend went. A dangerous fellow to cross, Smith said. Gordon worked both sides of the razor blade, his nervous system boosted by Conspiracy military med-tech, spine scraped out and replaced with meat-chips and the latest polysilicon-ceramic weapons systems in some secret, underground Pentagon hospital. He always went heavily armed. Spam had heard from others that Gordon's instant fits of violent behavior were a horror to behold, but he was equally capable of acts of irrational, saintly kindness.

Duvalier sat up painfully and took in his surroundings. He was seated in a deep, black leather chair in the center of what he took to be a leftover set from some cheap Hollywood spy blowout. A pale-gray concrete ceiling, covered in reinforced-metal beaming that looked like it could withstand a direct nuclear strike, rose in a dome over a luxurious, overdesigned pentagonal meeting room, tastefully lit by colored spots that threw green and red shadows over everything. The colors made it look like an off-register 3-D comic book panel. Spam's fully loaded Gyro-jet pistol, spare clips, money belt and packet of fake IDs were on a brushed copper boardroom table in front of him that ran in a crazy pattern around the hall. It could easily hold thirty or forty people at individual, computerized desk settings. Bowls of bright pills, a clear beaker of ice water and a single black carnation were placed before each terminal.

Set flush with the floor against the nearest wall was an enormous pool filled with what could have been several tons of steaming lime Jell-O. He could make out indistinct dark shapes about the size of compact cars, slowly moving back and forth under the surface, their churning actions sending quivers throughout the emerald "gelatin." Another entire wall looked in on an equally large tank that was swirling with toxic-looking dirty-yellow vapor. The inside of the tank window was splattered with bubbling, reddish-brown oil running down deep gouges and scratches in the acrylic that had the look of powerful claw marks; the floor was covered with small, dark-gray pebbles and flakes of muddy, purple rock. The four remaining sides of the "executive corral" appeared to be seamless black plastic. There were no doors of any kind that he could observe.

"You going to drink this, or are 'Bowel Lifters' and 'Screamers' more your style?" Gordon again pushed the glass into Duvalier's face. Spam took it and then saw Doug's grinning puss peering at him from over a padded shoulder. Twice. From over *both* of Gordon's shoulders. There were *two* Doug Smiths! This was really too much. He did need that drink. Grabbing the offered snifter from the ham-sized fist, Spam tossed half of it down without thinking and recognized the familiar vile taste too late. He started to choke. The crystal slipped from his hands to the stainless-steel tilted floor, shattering at his feet, splashing his legs with the thick, foul cocktail. The poisonous, bitter flavor brought bile up his throat and, hunching forward, Spam started to spit up all over his boots.

"What *is* that shit? Love Canal water?" Spam gasped, trying to catch his breath. "God, it's like—"

"No need to be crude. If you don't want any, simply put it down, like any civilized, well-mannered jackass," teased the smirking Gordon, who sipped at a mason jar full of the stuff. His dilated eyes narrowed. "I guess ninety-proof Green Peyote Joy Jacker is a *man's* drink. Sorry."

"Leave him alone, Gordon. He's not the enemy," cut in one of the Dougs, handing Duvalier a flask of water. "Can't you see how close it was for him? We're lucky there's no brain damage, or I'd have another useless broom pusher to take care of."

Patting Spam's back as he gulped at the cool liquid, the Doug apologetically explained, "Never mind Security here. We're all a little bit edgy. You both had a near thing coming down when our 'special guest' took the drop shaft with you. All three of you just made it in under the shields. I'm afraid our little space buddies have found out about "Bob's" briefing today and now there's a bit of a hubbub topside. We're safe enough for the moment. Oh, and don't worry about that 'sunburn.' It won't happen again. The pain should go away in about a week. We had Dr. Drummond check you and Doug both out. If it gives you any trouble, just let us know. By the way, I'm Ivan."

Ivan Stang. Spam was astonished. It was incredible, Smith and Stang were identical twins. Almost . . . clones. Was it possible? How? Doppelgängers? Robots? Surgery? Magick? Alien-tech? The visual similarities that the two SubGenii shared were unsettling.

" 'Pears to be that I'm not the only one getting 'burned' by the Church this time 'round," Doug said, picking flakes of translucent skin from his cheeks and nose while staring icily at the impeccable Stang. "This is truly some goddamned Holy Shinola, I'd say, coming from my own 'best friend,' thank you so very much. Dr. Drummond doesn't know his foot gland from his Oxfords. "Bob" almost toasted us like a couple of meat-filled Pop-Tarts back there. You could've warned us. Look at poor Duvalier, his eyebrows are practically singed off," he added, gesturing in his companion's direction.

Ivan Stang was dressed in a dapper ice-cream suit with matching ten-gallon hat and pointed snakeskin cowboy boots, but his thick plastic horn-rimmed glasses exactly matched those of Doug Smith, standing there in a soiled olive-drab jumpsuit next to him. Studying the twins more closely, however, Duvalier began to see that the differences between the two entailed more than just the matter of a shower and a good tailor.

Doug Smith showed the weight of a lifetime spent in search of Dobbs' fabled SLACK, fighting for the SubGenius Right of the Wrong-Way. Doug had the gaze of the veteran grunt's thousand-yard stare, walked in a stooped-over shuffle and had acquired a tobacco jones that left him wheezy and generally short of breath. He had lived a hard forty-five years, with most of the last decade spent in a Tampa maximum-security Federal prison on trumped-up blasphemy charges.

Doug had been at "Bob's" side from the late sixties, back in the early days, serving as go-between for Dobbs and his contacts in the New Left and, later, the developing New Right. By 1978, dropping out of public view, he had become the mysterious Stang's ghostwriter, responsible for all of the speeches, rants, ravings and most of *The Book of the SubGenius*—all of which was presented as Stang's original thoughts and writings. Many people had assumed that Stang and Smith were one and the same. They were never in the same room at the same time. Smith had vanished and Stang had appeared, popping into existence whole, as if born Athenalike from "Bob's" forehead. The mysterious Ivan managed the Church from behind a scrim of obscuring PR dreck, never showed his face in public. There were no personal audiences with him. No photos existed. The Church videos were the only place one could ever see his visage, their quality being so poor that an accurate picture was impossible to discern, even with computer-enhancement imaging. The unbreakable copy guard on these static-filled tapes was such that film in a shielded camera would fog merely trying to take a picture off a monitor.

The Church had used Doug, paying him barely enough to keep his family alive, keeping him tucked away in a hidden Malaysian slum, letting Ivan take credit for the works that Smith slaved over. The Board of Directors turned him in as the fall guy when the Hinkey Senate Subcommittee had come too close to nailing the top boys for the Dobbs' shooting. Only Connie Dobbs' "special appeal" in an all-night secret session with a certain friendly Supreme Court justice had finally paid off where years of open lobbying, worldwide demonstrations for mercy, political threats and outright bribery had failed. The Feds had freed the popular, martyred pamphleteer last spring after he'd served only a small fraction of his 212-year sentence.

The realization that Connie could have done this from the day the first indictment was served; that he could have been spared all the pain and humiliation of the yearlong trial; that he had been considered more valuable to the Church rotting away in that tiny cell as a symbol of Conspiracy oppression, a rallying point for phony protests, as the Hierarchy revived his faded personality-cult image for its own use; that the upper Foundation had let him sit out ten years in cold storage until the approaching X-Day had revived his full usefulness, hadn't made Doug bitter or hard. "Bob" had his plan. Smith still believed, was still fool enough to follow Dobbs' maniacal path, explaining to anyone who would listen, "It's just his way."

This bottomless well of faith didn't extend to Ivan Stang, to hear the way Smith talked about him. Stang was a sore point. Doug would become instantly angry and abusive any time the Scribe's name was mentioned around him, almost as if Smith held Stang solely to blame for his misfortune, even when he *knew* that it had been *Connie* keeping the Big House door shut on him all along. Smith had indeed taken the all-too-traditional path of organized (or, rather, disorganized) religion and had paid heavily for it.

Ivan Stang, on the other hand, in midlife seemed like a twenty-five-year-old version of his overaged double. His youthful, thin face was smooth, unlined with worry, except for the sunbaked wrinkles around the good-natured, twinkling eyes, which gave him a warm expression of deceptively cheerful friendliness. Smith's mousy-brown hair, graying at the temples, ratty and uncut, hung over a worn-out reddish face in sad contrast to the greased and pomped peaks of Ivan's styled preacher coif.

Chapter Four

I may not know Reality, but I know what I like.
——J. R. "Bob" Dobbs, Divine Secrets of Sales Lecture 13013

You can't say Dallas doesn't love you!
——Nellie Connally to John Kennedy, seconds before the assassination, November 22, 1963

Stang and Dobbs had set up temporary headquarters for their collection of followers in an old Burger Chef on the west edge of things. It was bad ground. Lots of Dallas industry had left behind lots of bad chemistry. Add the BZ gas- and nerve-weapon residue from the End Time, and it made for a sweet stew. Just what "Bob" liked to eat for breakfast.

It took Wellman and Duvalier almost a whole day and a case of metal-piercing ammunition to reach the "Temple." The aftermath of Shakeup riots had left most roadways impassable, even by their military vehicle, a Cadillac Gage Terminator. Spam had insisted that they fully arm their transport, so they were now backed up by an Oerlikon 20mm electric cannon, an 81mm mortar, assorted grenade launchers and all the spare gear they could cram into the armored cabin. Duvalier had never used any heavy rock 'n' roll gear before, and had to spend the first couple of hours alternately deciphering and cursing the Arabic manuals while Wellman drove.

Some Rapture.

Most of the Christians had been killed in the first ten minutes of the Second Coming. Gnostics seemed to have been immune, somehow, but there had never been great numbers of these in Texas, so the body count here had been somewhat extreme. Dallas had bragged of being the Most Christian City In America. The pious had asked for the cleansing Fires of Jehovah, and their prayers had been answered. In spades. When

Jesus Christ Himself turned out to hate Christians, every last one of His welcoming flock was sent to an unexpected reward. Quickly. With pain.

It hadn't done "the City of Love" any good. But at least it wasn't underwater like Houston.

All the urban freeways had been blown up in a last-ditch attempt by the Dallas P.D. to contain the remaining terror-stricken populace in the trouble areas. It hadn't worked. The citywide panic had been ignited by the grisly sight of Believers dissolving and disintegrating, shrieking as they rose into the blue Texas sky. With most of their senior tacticians recalled to sudden Glory, the remaining cops were overwhelmed by swarms of hysterical and heavily armed citizens attempting to flee the effects of what they must surely have thought was a sneak attack by the Soviets trying out some fiendish, flesh-melting secret weapon. The shaft of horrible green light stabbing down from the heavens fifty miles to the west didn't help to calm things much, either.

More often than not, Doug and Spam would suddenly find the street down which they were traveling blocked by crumbling makeshift barricades and rooftop snipers. Grim reminders of Xmas still adorned much of the wreckage. The smashed, fried Santas hanging from bent streetlights were a grotesque memory of more stable times, all the more so as they alternated with weathered corpses dangling from phone poles.

Rooters and civilian militia had tied them down in Dealey Plaza for the better part of the afternoon. Holed up in the wreckage of the Hyatt Regency, a few paranoid locals had gotten hold of a working howitzer and had harassed the slow-moving scout car for an hour or so, playing tag by lobbing poorly aimed 40mm shells at them from just out of their view. Things had been dicey until Wellman had managed to put the X-ray laser back together. After that, a few sweeps of the hotel garage and restaurant tower with the invisible beam had instantly silenced their assailants' barrage. Doug-2's talent for breaking equipment had almost cost them their lives several times that day.

No strangers to Dallas, the pair had always joked in the past about the shining glass offices of downtown. About how the monstrous colored rectangles reflected the hellishly hot rays of Texas noon sun back and forth between their tinted finishes, each new refraction angle making the beams a little bit more coherent, a little bit stronger, until, at some unoccupied focal point where all the invisible beams intersected, twenty feet or so above the middle of State Street, there was a single square inch of space with the surface temperature of a small star, able to vaporize anything moving across it. God help the pigeons that flew around down there.

The pigeons had long ago all been caught and eaten by the starving citizens of Dallas. Wellman and Duvalier should have known better than to make jokes.

The Men in Black had warned the strike team of the psychic violence the area seemed to exude, and of its effect on organics. They told them that the mirrored angles of the banks and hotels compounded this urge to self-destruction, and that the geometry of the downtown area was itself an illness, planned long ago by now-dead Rebel architects. They noted that this rationality-sapping phenomenon was strongest right around City Center. This effect was so intense in Fort Worth that the Xists didn't even bother trying to save it, just cooked the place down to slag first thing off. With most of the mirrors long since shattered, the steel girders of the buildings themselves still held dismal power. Oh, what a Holy Day it must have been when the razor-sharp shards of glass rained down on the crowds emptying out into the streets, slicing and dicing office workers still too Pink, still too sheeplike and obedient, to think of jaywalking, even at the cost of their lives.

The Men in Black lent the two the best blank-brain filters available, but it was still depressing. Spam and Doug squabbled away the whole time, like some demented survivalist rewrite of "The Bickersons."

As for the rest of Dallas, "the city that shoots Presidents and shoots the people that shoot Presidents," nothing remained. Block after block of ruins, stretching away for miles. The fires had raged out of control for weeks. Dead cars filled the streets and collapsed freeways, all frozen in their tracks when the first electromagnetic pulse from the war saucer had reached them, frying out their generators and burning up the wiring. Many vehicles had grisly and impressive holes punched through the roofs, where bone and flesh had temporarily met metal on their unstoppable journeys to the sun when the imperative calling to Eternity had beckoned. The horizon lay mostly flat, broken only by the randomly placed skeletons of lonely office towers, counterpointing the lazy drift of fluffy yellow clouds above.

The matte-gray M-4000 finally pulled up to Aftermath Central. "Victor" Street indeed. Hah! You could still see the giant cement hamburger. A junk-food god. It figured as much. The newsletter had promised a force field and a mansion.

"You can't believe everything you read," Duvalier reflected. It didn't look like Stang had any fifty thousand Bobzoids to command, either. More lies.

Wellman stopped the tank and gave Duvalier a funny look. "All out for Bulldada Time-Control Laboratories."

They checked their handguns and hopped out onto the back "Parking Lot of the Gods." That's what the faded sign said it was, anyway. The SubGenius Foundation that was being presented to the twenty-buck Bobbies didn't look so grand these days. Spam kicked in the service entrance door, calculated to be an impressive action, but actually an easy feat. Acid rain had eaten away the hinges awhile back. Had eaten everything away awhile back. As the rotted slab fell inward, Duvalier moved quickly, Wellman covering him with his MAC-10 and following his point.

The building was seemingly deserted, had been for months. Dust and grit covered everything in a fine layer. With no other footprints to give away signs of prior occupation, they broke trail through the walk-in cooler and continued their search for the missing Avatar and his second-in-command.

They walked past the large, uncomfortable cages in which Ivan made his synthetic "superheroes" sleep. They had been used to store potatoes in more normal times. Now the bins appeared empty as they approached. Duvalier wasn't so sure. Invisibility was one of the first things a SubGenius learns to manifest.

"To think that this used to be a *food preparation* area," he thought, looking into the wooden boxes that served as mating areas in their disgusting rituals, and recoiling at the sight. Invisible the OverMen might well be, but their mucus was strictly First Plane. The stains alone made him sick.

"Another fucking dead end. We should have known better," Duvalier swore, breaking the silence. He spat on the floor and leaned against a peeling Formica counter. "I should have expected something like this. Wait till I get my hands on Sterno. I'll make hi—"

A multicolored fur ball the size of a watermelon floated out from behind a broken deep-fryer. As they watched, it unfolded in thin layers until nothing but a Pipe (now familiar) hung motionless before them at eye level.

"Cut the crap, Dobbs!" They were both irritated at his moronic level of mysticism. Ever since the Retreat, "Bob" had been showing more and more signs of strain. Any follower unfortunate enough to be in his presence suffered a constant barrage of the sleazy magic tricks that those autistic aliens had taught the Salesman of Slack while he was off planet being transformated.

The Pipe had now turned orange and the smell of cheeseburgers permeated the gutted kitchen. Cheeseburgers! There hadn't been an edible cow alive for five years! Not since the ozone layer'd been wiped away. Most cows had gone the way of dinosaurs, excepting the few swollen with cancers and blinded by the constant shower of deadly UV. Along with thousands of species of birds, plants and animals. Through their usual inimitable stupidity, the humans had been well on their way to fossil history even without the aid of the Space Brothers' Jihad Squad.

A ghostly background noise of grill hoods and Muzak faded in. The faint sounds of dishes clattering and waitresses ordering QB bread and Number Six Specials could be heard.

"May I help you?" The Voice. It was "Bob," all right. Dobbs was speaking in Moe Howard's voice, but it still contained all the charisma of the Salesman's erratic personality.

"Yes, I'll have large fries and a Coke, asshole!" Wellman shot back. "Jesus, "Bob," give me some Slack! Where's Philo? We were supposed to trade him in for a shipment of the PILS, remember? Yesterday? It only almost got us killed when Drummond didn't show! The Posse Comitatus didn't appreciate our deal falling through like that."

"Never mention Jesus in my Burger Chef."

The nonanswer set Doug's moustache twitching. "Dobbs, I get the feeling you're not 'hearing me,' as we used to say in California. Eighty-six the blather or punch out and go home." Wellman's exasperation with the situation was clearly growing by the second. He foolishly started to bring the muzzle of his machine pistol up to the hovering Pipe.

Instantaneously, the fast-food church filled with bright blue water and little goldfish that all looked like "Bob," their miniature Pipes trailing smoke as they schooled around the room. Another hallucination. Spam and Wellman paid no attention to the distraction upon finding themselves still able to breathe in spite of being "submerged."

Spam swatted at one of the deformed things when it swam too close to his face, the action dissolving the creature as his hand passed through it. "Dobbs always misses some detail," he told Wellman. "That's the problem with this inane religion. At least the aliens are methodical."

"PILS? PILS? PILS? PILS? We are VERY ATTRACTIVE by most discriminating standards! I AM BI AND VERY SENSITIVE. GOOD CLEAN SEX IS ALL I'M AFTER! A LITTLE PAIN, A LITTLE KINK. PILS! PILS! PILS!"

" "Bob"! Calm down. It's okay. We don't need to know where Philo is. Who cares? Slack. Right?"

"SLACK! SLACK! SLACK! SLACK!"

The water had changed into PILS! Mounds of them! The kitchen had filled with gleaming transparent PILS. The two men were waist-deep in waves of glittering capsules. "Bob" had come through! Wellman was scooping them from the counters and shoving them into his mouth as fast as he could, washing them down with more PILS. The PAYOFF! Tens of thousands of the PILS! Even Duvalier was taken in by the sight. They could stop looking for the saucer. Both were set for Prelife!

The PILS disappeared, of course.

In their place was Dobbs, casual as a pimp, grinning like some demented television game-show host. What a clown.

"Ecce homo!" Duvalier spat out, bitterly acknowledging the successful trickery.

Wellman, face white with shock, looked up from the floor, screaming, fingers grasping at vacant air. "Goddamned smokin' asshole, fuckin' wiseacre ghost, *shithead son of a bitch SALESMAN!*" Upon finding his cheeks and hands suddenly empty, he went berserk, raised his automatic, and emptied a full clip point-blank into Dobbs' chest, walking the shots straight up the wide red power tie.

Chapter Nine

Without LIES, there can be no TRUTH.

—Palmer Vreedeez, found on the back of returned utilities check

"Well, that's it then, Drummond. Smith gives us no other choice," Palmer agreed. "We have to go planetside to clear up this damn mess. That jerk."

All the instrument readouts and panic bars were flashing on and off over the hull of the cramped flight cabin. A dozen red-alert programs were frantically signaling with reports of autodefensive activity, fighting off various probing scans that were sweeping the dark sky. Outside, the Earth hung "above" them as they crazily spun around it, their craft trailing spirals of jamming chaff. The bright crescent of the planet bounced back and forth across the top of the viewing port as the ship gyros mimicked the random pitch and yaw drift of the burnt Soviet ComSat that the ship had overtaken and replaced. Just past the dancing horizon lay the Moon, lit by occasional flashes from the huge firefight that raged on behind them. They had escaped in the fortuitous confusion, stealing a Spree craft and killing the insect pilot and crew. The surprise Dero assault had caught the Elohim off guard and a rout was in progress.

Spree numerals flickered on and off the navigation screens, their ultraviolet chicken scratchings producing a distracting, strobing accompaniment to the rhythm of the board keys underneath Palmer's tapping fingers. The bugs' inboard stealth gear was working so far. If it failed now, they'd both be fried so quickly they'd never have time to realize they were dead. He worked furiously, reprogramming the observation craft for surface landing. The *Bohandas,* being merely a vacuum launch, wasn't built for gravitational touchdowns but, with all its heavy military armor and wave shields, it should be able to hold out long enough for one suicidal reentry. Once down the well, it could never reach space again. As long as it brought them to the ground in one piece. Palmer finished his computations, shut off the flight recorders and turned to the OverMan.

"I can't understand how Smith managed to let himself be captured," Vreedeez whined. He glanced over at his mutated companion, waiting for the completion beep signaling that the alien computer had finished translating his return trip commands. He'd been making mistakes, had almost hit the command for a core dump, thinking it was an environmental stack.

The combat 'Phrane was wearing off. Palmer could feel the payback for his week of AntiSleep looping begin to settle in. His brainpan felt scoured, as if it had been filled with hot, dry sand. It was times like this that made Palmer almost reconsider his decision not to go for Gordon's offer of free glandscaping. It would have been handy to power-up to seven-speed and use a preprogrammed assassination chip back there at the *Blood of Christ.* Gordon paid through the nose for it, though. Literally. No doubt about that. G.G.'s trips to the Black Hospital left him with a little less Gordon each time and a little more "them." Gordon would never acknowledge the side effects either, but it was still an expensive set of tools, one way or another. Palmer would stick to his drugs. At least you could come down.

"Our suicide spores should have activated automatically at the first official question, even if Smith couldn't set them off himself. Say the Xists pulled out all his teeth, a few spores still collect in the arterial walls. Enough for 'death,' anyway. That asshole! I knew that homeboy couldn't do it! He'll sing for sure! I should have made him a Third Nostril when I had the chance. And I like him. Now *we* have to land on the friggin' White House lawn and go deal with Jones because *Unibrow,* of all people, says we still need Smith."

"We have use of him. The Dero came to create a diversion, so that we could confront Jones. And there is still the question of . . . Dobbs," Philo mused, his massive, clownlike head nodding in response. "How far gone is he? Will we have to terminate him?"

If things kept going in this direction, Palmer swore that he would wipe that idiotic smile from the OverMan's swelled cranium. Ever since Philo's transformation, he had become worse than useless. Now all he ever did was smoke 'Frop and more 'Frop. He acted like he was superior to everyone else and knew things that better should be left unsaid. Throw in the white plastic complexion, a shit-eatin' grin that wouldn't stop, those space-spook eyes, and a skull the size of a medicine ball, and you had the first SubGenius OverMan-Prime: Dr. Drummond. In spite of rumors Palmer had heard about size and shape changes in certain *other* external body organs, it was his opinion that, if this was the next step in evolution, you could keep it. There was even talk down in the Money Pits about OverWomen, though nobody could actually recall a sighting firsthand.

Philo had come a long way from the phone company.

"Yeah, sure. I'm not going to try to hit Dobbs. That's the craziest thing I've heard so far. Look what happened to Sterno. What a fuckin' mess he was, couldn't even tell he had been human. Spread out over a whole city block. Yeech. Dobbs may be a traitor, but his biologic tantra can't be touched. If *you* want him dead, *you* pull the trigger. Count me *out*, you goddamned guinea pig."

"It's not Dobbs that is the danger. It is his Pipe," Philo answered, the foot-wide slash in his head shutting with a clack of huge teeth. They looked like they could bite through saddle leather.

"The pipe, huh? I've heard it all now." Palmer was too exhausted to show his aggravation forcefully. He left his pod, reached for an empty equipment sack and began stuffing it with parts of the dead Spree pilot that floated about them. It wouldn't do to reenter without everything tied down. "Make this quick, balloonhead," he snapped, plucking an iridescent bottle-green compound eye from the cloud of drifting, chitinous flesh. "Thank the stars these things don't bleed. Two minutes to descent sequence. When the lights go green, get in the netting and don't forget your crash helmet this time. Now, what's all this about the pipe?"

"Not the pipe. Rather, the Pipe," stated Philo, fixing the perplexed Vreedeez with a demanding stare and a matter-of-fact sigh. "Actually, its real name is unpronounceable in any Earth language. The Pipe is our true enemy. It is an alien parasite, attached to Dobbs' teeth. At the end of the smoke stem is a taproot which is slowly growing into the forebrain and instituting its will there. You may have noticed "Bob's" behavior has become rather erratic in the last few months. If we cannot remove it, "Bob" is doomed anyway. The root will continue to grow; within a half year at the most, it will split Dobbs' head in two and release its brood of young. Killing "Bob" will be an act of mercy."

Palmer was beside himself. He started to reach for a coffin stick and then remembered that the cabin was loaded with pure oxygen at Philo's request. The better for the OverBrain to think with, or so he said. Palmer suspected it had merely made the lobe-head space-drunk. Just great, really fuckin' great, he thought.

"That's the stupidest thing I've heard so far," snapped Vreedeez. "All of our trouble with "Bob" comes from this . . . this *thing?* He's had a pipe in his mouth ever since I can remember. Decades! And the whole time it was the 'Pipe' we were talking to, not "Bob" at all?"

"The Pipe's race is more ancient than time. The oldest civilized recordings available to the Pan-Lógos Co-op mention myths concerning their entropic powers of universal dissolution and abstraction. Pipes have played a role in the end of every major cycle in mathematical space. They live in Chaos, thrive on dimensional distortion, vacation in the Skor. Numbers are less than nothing to them—they use No-Theory. A Pipe will twist, fold and spindle the fabric of time and energy, encoding existence to suit its own dark purposes, restarting creation over and over, shredding the pathways of causational surreality until some edited pattern of subatomic law 'pleases' it. At any given instant, they can pull the Vortex right from beneath our foot glands. The Pipes' motivations are unguessable, their intelligence opaque to the most intense scrutiny. No one in the known history of the Universe has ever succeeded in establishing communication with one. All past attempts have resulted in failure, with the most horrifying consequences for any 'lucky' survivors. The Stark Fist of Removal is as a gentle, loving caress compared to the touch of a Pipe.

"When JHVH-1 learned that one had reached our world and mated with Dobbs, He had no choice but to attack and destroy them both before this whole sector could be contaminated. The tiresome revenge plotting of that paranoid half-breed, Jesus, provided a convenient front so that JHVH-1 could move against this being. Those at the NEXUS, when informed of "Bob's" misfortune, tried to subvert the extermination mission and capture the target, to harness it for their own ends. They would have failed. The Pipe is *the* most dangerous life-form known, if 'life-form' is truly the correct term. It is not 'alive' as we know life. The sacrifice of the dozen sentient Earth races is a small price to pay when measured against the possibility that a Pipe would find conditions for reproduction favorable here. It did.

"We have all been manipulated from the first. Jones, Jesus, Unibrow, yourself, everyone: only pawns in the Greater Power's struggle to destroy the Pipe. Now it shows its birthing pattern, and so deception is discarded. If we cannot remove the Pipe, we must kill Dobbs. The Council of None concurs with me in this. The Pipe is a parasite and will die along with the host. This is its one weakness: While pregnant, it is mortal, sharing all our laws of space-time and matter. If we cannot kill the Pipe, then JHVH-1 will incinerate half the galaxy to do the job. He has done this before; the titanic X-ray quasars dotting known space mark past extermination sites. We are his microscopic surgeons. If the Doktors fail . . ."

The OverMan fell back into the acceleration webbing, panting with the effort of his speech, and watched as Vreedeez stowed the sack beneath the telecommunications board.

It was the most Palmer had heard Philo ever say in a coherent manner. He felt strangely serene. Peaceful for the first time in years. Happy, even. He smiled at his old friend. Why had he ever doubted the obviously superior *Homo excelsior*? The OverMan's story almost made sense. It sounded so . . . so right. If it was true— Yes! It had to be true! Palmer checked the *Bohandas'* weapons banks. They would need every particle beam and plasma cannon on board to stay alive in the next half hour.

The lights on the dashboard changed to green and down they went.

Chapter Sixteen

Please get the medication before it's too late.
—Reverend Jim Jones, White Night Jonestown Gut Blowout, 1978

"If you don't kick it, how're ya gonna know if it's dead or not?" Sterno muttered. It pretty much summed up the way Keckhaver was feeling about the whole war by now. It also happened to be his philosophy on culture, life and sex. A statement like that tends to sit like a doughball, which is why the SubGenius Hellsaint used it as his mantra.

"Well, now, don't you know you can fuck it. You know it's dead, if you fuck it," sputtered Jones, barely suppressing an insane twitter. His mind was decaying faster than Kreegar had predicted, Sterno realized. Without the power of the Bleeding Head to keep the undead priest animated, the wretched little po'bucker would eventually degenerate into full-blown zombiedom and be of little more use than the shuffling Dobbs Youth who tended the endless, parched "Gardens of Delight" in Texas.

Everything's falling apart, Sterno thought disgustedly. If Gordon doesn't snuff Smith before he spills the beans to the Jesus Monsters, all of Malaysia will end up one stinking crater. Like Arkansas, he added, spitting ruefully into "Bob's" diamond cuspidor.

With a crash, Jones lurched around the Throne Office, his arms flailing in confusion, knocking half of Dobbs' collection of aborted False OverMan fetuses off their shelves. Sterno considered giving him a phlebotomy with the new air knife, but decided to let the punk preacher dig his own grave, as it were. The tiny video security cameras turned with audible whines to follow Jones' progress.

Sterno glanced at the readouts over the door again. "Well, the goddamn mass-waves haven't penetrated this far. We're safe for the moment. Wotan hasn't peed our asses yet. It's still just you 'n' me, Bro' Jim. You 'n' me," he sighed, and began to rummage around for a pack of 'Fropsticks. There was at least two miles of solid granite between them and the surface plus an additional five meters of captured Spree hull ceramic, not to mention the autonomatic field barriers. The time-control chamber lock wouldn't open for at least another forty hours, maybe fifty. He couldn't tell, Jones' last shot having shattered the dial. That was twenty hours longer than Jones would last. Sterno was having the satisfaction of watching his old friend dissolve cell by cell. He was sure Palmer had got his message through to Connie. He had to trust Palmer. Again.

After Sterno had cycled the air lock behind them, the bunker mainframe had powered down, cutting off his remote deck from the net. He never had a chance to tell if Palmer had acknowledged his warning. Jones had continued to come after Sterno, his artificial personality still somewhat intact at that point. Keckhaver was down, about to be gutted with a dull hog blade Jones had grabbed off the wall rack, when something loudly popped deep inside the priest's ears, his eyes rolled back into his head, and his spasming body toppled off Sterno. Since then, the NEXUS puppet's *appearance* had returned to "normal," but, all the same, Jim Jones had been switched off.

Sterno had the heavy shielding in Dobb's office to thank for that. He'd been counting on it when he allowed Jones to follow him in, just one step ahead of the Xist process servers. The two enemies were now completely isolated in "Bob's" private survival capsule. Jones wasn't much of a threat now. . . .

"A little PIL, Sterno, pretty PIL PIL, please? Want fuck PIL for Jimmy, ol' Dad, come now, huh, huh. PIL, PIL, PIL. Jimmy will tell Kickover a story about Wellman and Connie for pretty PIL. . . ." Jones was sweating. His left leg was jerking with regular convulsions and his breath had started to smell like an open kill pit. Sterno considered kicking him but he already knew what the answer to his question would be.

"Sure, sure, Jones. Go ahead. I like stories," Sterno answered. He reached over and flipped a Doktors for "Bob" tape into the desk deck and switched on a four-channel mike so that Jones' dying ramblings could later be piped all over Dobbstown, mixed in with the demented Arkansas "music." He opened his medicine bag and tossed three PILS to the drooling, chittering Jones, who scrambled after them. He paused, then took one himself, washing it down with a quarter flask of hundred-proof white rum. Sterno noticed that one of Jones' ears was starting to slide down his skull and that the joints in his elbows were swinging both ways, like a broken doll.

"It's going to start to smell like Dog Town bad in here damn soon," Sterno mused. Jones was gibbering and hooting away about the Head, the Voices, the heliopters inside his head, and every other mystic trauma that had been Jones' source material for his multilifelong religious mania, all self-disguised as backwoods simplemindedness.

"You getch'a buncha damn ratshot, that's what you do, and you go right in there after 'em. Them saucer boys think they kin ride them a damn heliopter all the way to Graduation, straight up Dobbs' ass! It's the Night of Slack, it's the Night of Slack, just like Dobbs said! We'll all go to meet that great wagon wheel in the sky, shit yeah! I'm wall climbin'! I'm wall climbin'! You think Dobbs would approve? You think Dobbs could get into it, man? The Pinks'll fall down upon their checkbooks and mate with them," bleated Jones.

"Hell, Jones, you loveburger, you're starting to sound like Janor,"

Sterno yawned. Father Jim was beginning to bore him. "You sure you wouldn't rather let me take you out qui—"

The whole Throne Office began to vibrate. The enclosing miles of rock started to shimmy with a low, sustained bass groan that seemed to come from deep within the earth below them. Sterno suddenly felt lighter. Much lighter. It wasn't just the PIL he had taken, either. The sepulchral Jones noticed it too, and he was way beyond the PIL high. The Xists were breaking through the defense shields with their magnetic focusers. "The holding company that controls magnetism controls the marketplace." Sterno had just enough time to remember "Bob's" dreary financial advice before he automatically went into protective meditation.

"Gravity waves! Gravity waves!" Jones screeched. He flew up against the ceiling and stuck there. The room became an instant hurricane of objects, whirling around, attracting and repelling each other's electrons at subatomic speeds. The enhanced-gravitational weapon was forcing all photonic activity down the scale, deeper, darker. Visible light shifted to red, maroon, purple.

Concentrating on the Ten Simple Patterns of Abuse, Sterno floated calmly in the center of the colliding molecular mayhem that formed and reformed about him. The lights went out as the power units collapsed and died, but the energy the Xists were beaming in more than compensated for the loss; the space shimmered with a violent blue glow, the radiance of dying matter.

Sterno glanced up at Jones. Jim Jones was gone to Glory, dead at last; *had* to be. Nothing more than a smear now, quickly spreading to cover every surface in the room. An impossibly flat surface, formed under the pressure of a thousand suns. The furnishings, the weapon rack, "Bob's" priceless comic book and pornography collections, the tools, Jones, everything except Sterno, smashed to an infinitely thin film. The walls, floor and roof of the chamber were being twisted and pulverized by the fantastic gravitational effects until, with a final twist and spin, the subterranean retreat became a hollow sphere, held in shape by magnetic bottle beams. All the formerly protective rock outside had liquidized, roaring and churning as it boiled into gas. The Xist technicians were attempting to create a black hole right where Sterno hovered, in the center of the Throne Office.

Only one thing stood between Sterno and Eternal Slack, and that was the pristine mental state of absolute awareness/nonawareness, the perfect balance of the metamathematical and mortophysical. Sterno "knew" the Skor, okay. Neither dead nor alive, neither in existence nor negation, he rested in the pause of the Universe and began to hum "Dumptruck Full of Dead Cops," snapping one finger to the unheard beat.

I LIVED IN A TEENAGE WORLD WITHOUT SLACK

WHAM!

I remember Vreedees flying across the room and landing backwards on the gondola step below me, helmet askew and beginning to go into PilShock™. . . .

The second round landed on the cupola of the Pope of New York's vehicle, blowing away the flamboyant insignia, but otherwise doing nothing to stop the hell-bent flow of fire into the front of the Nhee-Gheean Embassy. I was asleep when the Slak Van® full of priests started praying to "BoB" with around twenty NATO rounds a second, and that was exactly twelve minutes ago.

From what I can put together, I was awakened by the first blast, and Paulmer Vreedees had been sleeping through it *all* here in the Control, so who the hell knew at this point how the city was laid out for escape? . . . We'd have to try the bridges and hope one was open.

Now it looked like Pope Meyer might soon be able to secure the street, but Vreedees was out of the game till I could get over there and take a look at his BodScan Biomed® unit. The UNIBROW® was still working and the tape transport looked passable, so everyone would at least get copies of the war as vidded through "BoB's" eyes, as well as the tin ear this creeper had.

Bouncing up this street very much longer is gonna get us erased, I thought, and pulled hard on the joystick. Sure, *I* had to be the one on duty when the Iceheads finally learned how to play rough. . . .

I saw the "BoB" double leave the reviewing stand as I deboarded the vehicle to grab the rest of my equipment. Don't think that guy's going to make it, I thought. Little guy farted too much anyway.

When I returned, Paulmer had come to. "Groomin' my dreams too much!!" he yelled, laughing, as he jumped into the nav spansule.

"Welcome aboard."

"Good to see ya, Commander Monobreath. Where we going now?"

"Them thinks They hit Him."

"Aw, Pils! Gotta see if I can raise Philo® on the Minimimic."

"Anything?"

"Both Stang and Drummond show pos on the evasion sequence, so

they've Launched, but no talk till we're all clear of the local band net."
Good. This government stuff would be quick and dirty, I thought, and
the Control will handle all the details. Soon, I'll be able to take over
with the UNIBROW®, and then we'll just *see* who can speak Guama-
nian underwater.

"Feel like I'm in a dream," Paulmer hissed, looking into the rubber
NaviScope®. "Tryin' to sight on these checked suits is like matching a
needle in the You-o-Grav!"

He was right, but at least the flippers were slowing them down.

The Pope did clear the street, and once we got out into the Ottobahn
Arare Memorial Park and could manuever, things got hot fast. Nhee-
Ghee's people, if you can call them that, had gotten their tentacles on
some high-mob armor, and were cutting tracks into the crowd pretty
wide. Target City isn't the place for them, anyway, I thought, as I pulled
the heap through the middle of the highway of pills and set the nose for
a lateral flight through the middle, low and slow, of this madness. . . .

Meyer could and did see the same happening at the same micro-
moment, and Paulmer was once again working on his rating in the
middle of the rant. The score counter above his helmet had jammed and
he was still jumping the button.

"Vreed, I need help," I yodeled. "Bad news ahead."

No shit. That giant Pipe could mean only trouble, a side play by
"BoB" to pare down the opponents in the upcoming power struggle,
taking advantage of the confusion to take a one-way rocket to the Glass-
Madness Arctic Glass Hideout®.

I knew that only form could show the games end a folly now.
Right?

"I got it. Avoid gridlock, don't bunch up."

"Sure, Vreed-boy. Thanks. I got to target this new stuff now, so we
can see where we'll be tonight. If MADNESS® is behind this, we might
get some clues from the movie. If it's MegaStang®, we can call Mark-
Mother. He's its agent. If it's the Thousand-Headed-Meta-Drummond®,
we'll have to go under for a week and detox. If it's Someone Else®, we'll
never know. If it's you, *I'll* never know."

"Keep your rockets on. I wouldn't dust you, and besides, I got a better
idea for my try. Not so much violence. More bass."

Twisting and turning this rig at this speed was wearing out the dive
brakes and shims rapidly. I didn't know how long this could go on
tonight.

And this programming! Trying to find a source for the storm that now
was breaking across the soundtrack only, starting with the Arkansas
Code and returning through the Other Loop, California—that was no
easier.

I've got a better idea mys-

*   *   *

And then the report ended. Histogeneticists are still endeavoring to reconstruct the final sequence of events in the last five minutes of X-Hour, X-Day, 1998. Anyone possessing hair, fingernail, or skin samples of Puzzling Evidence—remnants of which may still be found on old audio-cassettes from his Span—is urged to submit them to Church Throne Office #1 immediately, as they may provide cellular Akashic recordings crucial to our understanding of the Xist "retaliation."

The Reverend Doctor Doctor (Mr. M.D.)
David N. Meyer II
Pope of All New York City, Idaho, and
The Great Pacific Northwest

TALES OF THE *GOLDEN SLACK*
Volume One

This fable is dedicated to Dennis Kelley and Robert Toomey

Our Tale Begins:

"Sail ho!"

The lookout's cry echoed over the ship.

"Where away?" First mate Puzzleen Ev'hedance called from the afterdeck.

"Away over there! Can't you see it?"

"Use proper nomenclature, lookout. Where away?" Puzzleen Ev'hedance was a stickler for procedure.

"Fuck you, Puzzleen."

The lookout was not.

"Never mind, Ev'hedance," said the helmsman, Janor the Insane. "I see it."

Puzzleen Ev'hedance turned away, stroking his moustache. His dark eyes gleamed.

Janor raised his screechy voice. "Falling off to larbord."

Everyone on the afterdeck put his hands over his ears.

Janor let the big wheel spin through his hands. The Bobbies leapt to the ropes which ran from every spar and timber. Wearing their uniform of ill-fitting Levi's, dirty tennis shoes with untied laces and baggy T-shirts, the Bobbies scampered up the lines and tended to the giant square-rigged sails. Some were unnaturally skinny and continually pushed at glasses which tried to slide down their noses. Others were fat, with large rolls of suet that bounced over their belt buckles. Most seemed crafty and intelligent beyond their years while simultaneously understanding nothing of the social intercourse of adults.

"An ugly crew," said Philo the Phlegmatic, "but loyal to a fault."

"Any more mead in that basket?" asked Cap'n Stang from the comfort of his chair. "All those Bobbies scrambling around in the fresh air gives me a powerful thirst-on."

"Aye, Cap'n," Philo the Phlegmatic replied.

Without getting out of his hammock, that was strung between the sturdy post which held the helmsman's wheel and the afterdeck railing, Philo the Phlegmatic gestured toward a thick rope that trailed over the side. Puzzleen hauled hand-over-hand on the line. After a few tugs a stout woven basket banged over the rail. In the basket were several crockery demijohns wrapped in straw for protection. They dripped with moisture from their cold ride under the keel.

Philo the Phlegmatic worked one demijohn loose and passed it to his captain.

Cap'n Stang took a long swig.

"Nothing like some cold mead before a battle."

Being a good and fair-minded captain, he offered the bottle to his mates.

"Do you really," asked Mahvreeds the Cautious, "think it's a good idea to have mead at a time like this?"

He sat on the floor of the afterdeck running a whetstone down the side of his cutlass. The rasping of his stone drowned out even the anguished shrieks of the careless Bobbies, who now and then lost their hold and plummeted with a crash into the merciless sea. No one on the afterdeck noticed the occasional plunge. There were plenty more Bobbies where they came from.

"In point of fact," growled Philo the Phlegmatic, "I do. You got any more 'Frop?"

" 'Frop, gentlemen?" a cultured voice asked from the main deck. "With the very soul of the enemy so close at hand?"

"Ah, Friar Hal," said Cap'n Stang, "what have you got for us today?"

Friar Hal collapsed a gleaming bronze telescope. Hal, the master tactician of the *Golden Slack,* discerned the identity of distant ships and kept records of the booty they carried. The good friar, a large man who gave the appearance of rotundity but who wielded a sharp sword and sharper tongue, produced from under his brown robes a rolled chart. He spread the chart out onto the afterdeck and the mates and officers gathered around him, all but for Janor the Insane, who watched the wind and steered the *Golden Slack* on a course to intercept the unknown ship which grew larger with every passing minute.

"By her location, size and rigging I make her to be the flagship of the Conspiracy, the *Multiconglomerate Trading Vessel* herself."

A moment of awed silence held the crew. They hardly dared to look one another in the eye. This was no ordinary Conspiracy fleet merchantman to be plundered and burned, this was the very essence of their sworn enemy. Here was good booty enough for all.

"De *Multiconglomerate Trading Vessel?*" snorted Jah Gar I, squinting through his glasses as a thick haze of smoke enveloped him, "And pray tell, mon, what she be doing in the Miasmic Sea?" He drew deeply on his 'Frop-laden pipe and another cloud encircled his head.

"Perhaps," answered Friar Hal, "she came off course during the storm last week, or she trades on a new trade route. She doesn't know the *Golden Slack* plies these waters. All accounts had us sunk at the hands of those infernal captains MaKcraw and Heel."

All laughed nastily.

"Aye, they thought us dead, but we were only shot," cackled Janor the Insane.

Everyone nodded. As usual, no one understood a word Janor said, but they knew it was the truth.

"Anyway," continued Friar Hal, "she thinks we aren't in our customary waters but we are. I see no ships to protect her and she cannot outrun us in this wind. We will be upon her shortly."

"Puzzleen Ev'hedance," said Cap'n Stang, "what of our weapons?"

"We have two or three swords for every man, not counting the Bobbies, of course, two pistols per man, a few shotguns and three rounds of grapeshot for our cannon."

"And the *Multiconglomerate Trading Vessel?*" asked Philo the Phlegmatic.

"Oh," said Puzzleen Ev'hedance dreamily, "thirty-four-inch cannon to a side, a hundred musketeers, blunderbusses, a fighting complement of marines and the usual assortment of accountants, state patrolmen, waitresses, bank loan officers, low-echelon toadies, corporate brownnoses, network presidents, office snitches, Ivy League attorneys, takeover specialists and so forth."

"Just once," said Mahvreeds the Cautious, "just once I'd like a fair fight with the Conspiracy. We're always outgunned."

"But we've a weapon no conspiracy can match," thundered Friar Hal.

The officers bowed their heads, except for Janor, who spat over the side.

"We have faith in the almighty BOB!"

Friar Hal held a dollar bill high overhead in one outstretched hand. A sudden gust of wind swept across the afterdeck and snatched the bill. It danced on the breeze and floated out of sight.

"The bill is taken," said Friar Hal in a voice of deep reverence.

"BOB *speaks!*" shouted Janor the Insane. "BOB shows him*self* to *us*. It's a goddamn *mi*racle!"

The Bobbies paused at their endless labor in the convoluted rigging at this glorious shout. They raised one hand in salute and vibrated the other on their Adam's apples, ululating like Iranian housewives. Two or three, those with the least faith in BOB, slipped off the wet ropes and tumbled through the air into the whitecapped sea. They sank without a trace.

"Jah Gar I," ordered Cap'n Stang, "go below and let loose another boxcar o' Bobbies. They're getting a might thin up in the shrouds."

Jah Gar I, who spoke no more than Philo the Phlegmatic, nodded. He left the group trailing a thick cloud of 'Frop-smoke.

"Now then," said Puzzleen Ev'hedance, "what is our strategy?"

"Simple," the deep twang echoed with authority.

Everyone on the afterdeck looked to the main cabin doors. Braced in the doorway stood a matched pair of pirates who were each more than a match for any two men. They never emerged from the deep cocoon of their cabin unless a battle was near. No one signaled them. No one called for them. They simply appeared.

Monsieur Le Deuel stood well over six feet. The Inner Crew of the *Golden Slack* was not a physically prepossessing lot, but in the wild bars of their various ports the women instantly understood that Monsieur Le Deuel was a pirate. It took a bit of convincing that his shipmates were also feared men of the sea. Monsieur Le Deuel looked the part. His eyes shone in the afternoon sun. Two crossed pistols nestled in his belt. A pair of matched cutlasses, snatched from the dying hands of a Central American bank president after he had made the mistake of insulting Monsieur Le Deuel in a minor financial transaction, hung on either hip. A stabbing knife rested in the lapel of his snakeskin jacket.

Beside him stood the man who had spoken, Stern-Ho. Stern-Ho, once a quiet farm boy from the hinterlands of the Conspiracy, had earned his nickname with his vicious tactics at sea. The *Golden Slack,* outgunned as she usually was, often employed a simple but effective maneuver: Janor the Insane, using the cunning which his name implied, would steer the *Golden Slack* straight into the bowsprit of the enemy ship. In a bow-on attack the enemies' cannon could not be brought to bear upon the *Golden Slack*.

Even before the *Golden Slack* was entangled in the Conspiracy ship's rigging, Stern-Ho would leap to the enemy vessel, cutlass in his teeth, shotgun in his hand, ready to cut a path all the way to her helmsman. As he jumped, the robust po'bucker would point his cutlass to the rear of the Conspiracy ship and cry:

"Forward for BOB! Stern ho-oo-oo!"

Like as not, he would hack his way to the stern of the craft, bodies piled up behind him.

"Bring the *Golden Slack* on a course dead astern of the *Multiconglomerate Trading Vessel*," Stern-Ho said grimly.

He pulled the glowing 'Fropstick from his mouth and paused only long enough to take a burger from the quarterdeck grill.

"When we close on her we can spray her deck with our cannon. That should hold down their marines. Then we ram from the rear and board over the quarterdeck."

Monsieur Le Deuel nodded.

"Brothers," cautioned Friar Hal, "Where's the Slack in that plan? If the wind falters while we are astern, the *Multiconglomerate Trading Vessel* may come about and rake us with her guns. We would be defenseless."

Cap'n Stang huddled for a moment with Philo the Phlegmatic and Puzzleen.

"Janor can do the job," Puzzleen said. "We'll shadow them until nightfall, then close in. If the wind fails we should have enough time to fall away. They will not pursue."

Chef Snavely hobbled down from his lookout and vanished into the gallery. In a moment he reappeared, bearing a bowl filled with yogurt, granola, whole-wheat pasta and peanut butter. He placed the bowl on the afterdeck and passed out cutlery.

"Uh, Stern-Ho," said Cap'n Stang, averting his eyes from the healthful feast as the Bobbies dug in, "would you please pass me another burger?"

Soon it was nightfall.

The Inner Crew bustled back and forth. Ancient pikes, swords and halberds were brought up from the hold, polished and then dipped in the sacred Excremeditational "mixture" which ensured that even the slightest wound would be fatal. Janor felt the wind and watched the stars, ignoring the ship he shadowed. Despite his seeming indifference, the *Multiconglomerate Trading Vessel* drew nearer and nearer.

"Puzzleen," said Cap'n Stang, "what are you scribbling? It's time to distribute weapons."

"I'm parodying the Pope's correspondence," answered Puzzleen, his shoulders hunched over a pad on his lap, his legs braced against the rise and fall of the gentle swells. "It isn't easy—he keeps changing his position."

"Put that light out, Puzzleen!" snapped Mahvreeds the Cautious. "We're only a league away. Do you want them to see us?"

Puzzleen blew out his torch and lay his writing aside. What use were words when battle was near?

The thick cloak of night protected them from the prying eyes of the lookouts on the *Multiconglomerate Trading Vessel.*

"Fear not," growled Le Deuel, "lookouts look forward, never back."

Under the bright stars the massive sails of the *Multiconglomerate Trading Vessel* shone whiter and whiter. The Bobbies in the rigging, all gagged with cloth, since none of them knew when to keep their mouths shut, giggled silently. The Inner Crew left Janor at the helm and made their stealthy way to the base of the bowsprit. Puzzleen handed out weapons to each man.

"Damn," muttered Jah Gar I, "Dese sword is all rust, mon. How'm I and I gone chop up de Conspiracy wif dis?"

"Take mine," said Philo the Phlegmatic, stepping into the crisis. He passed over a sinister electronic maiming device stolen from the labs of AT&T.

Jah Gar I shook his head.

"When I and I rub in de 'mixture,' no mon resist dis blade." He turned toward the bubbling "mixture" pot. Two Bobbies wearing gas masks stirred it with wooden paddles. It hissed and steamed even though no fire glowed under it.

Janor appeared on the foredeck bearing the Sacred Ark and Catapult.

"Hold," whispered Friar Hal, "in the excitement we've forgotten the hymn and benediction."

"We've no time," snapped Puzzleen.

"There are no attacks too important to bypass the hymn," Cap'n Stang solemnly intoned.

"Or the benediction," echoed Philo the Phlegmatic, "that's my favorite part of any attack."

"Except the beheadings and plank-walkings," said Stern-Ho.

"That," answered Philo, "goes without saying."

"And," crowed Monsieur Le Deuel, "the ear-pullings!"

At the sounds of those wonderful words all the Inner Crew raised both fists over their heads and cheered soundlessly, grins splitting their faces. Overhead, the Bobbies raised one finger to their throats and silently mimed the piercing wail of a joyous pirate. As always, a few of the less agile pitched off the slick ropes and tumbled into the wavetops. The strong breeze masked these sounds and no one on the *Multiconglomerate Trading Vessel* took notice.

"Ah," said Cap'n Stang, wiping away a tear of joy, "we haven't had a righteous ear-pulling in longer than I can remember."

"Tonight," replied Le Deuel, "tonight we'll have ear-pullage galore. I sweat to it."

"Save your swears," said Friar Hal. "Pray to it instead."

"All right," said Puzzleen Ev'hedance, "man the ropes."

The Inner Crew turned to a thick rope wrapped round a wooden stanchion. A large sign hung over the stanchion said: INNER CREW ONLY—DO NOT TOUCH—THIS MEANS YOU! Below that message, in smaller letters, was written: DUMP FOOD INTO SLOT.

The Crew took the rope in hand and hauled with all their collective strength. From deep in the bowels of the *Golden Slack* came a creak as wood shifted and a long groan as iron moved. That groan was followed by unintelligible human speech, a long random skein of words spouted for no purpose or meaning. As the Crew pulled on the rope the mumbling became louder and more distinct. A large object hove into view.

With a last grunt and gasp the Crew gave a final pull on the rope. They wrapped it back around the stanchion and tied it off. Hovering in the vastness of the empty hold, swaying just below the level of the deck, was a huge iron cage. From its top ran a food chute which connected to the slot just beside the stanchion. The mumbled words emanating from the cage grew into a shout.

"Whisper, O great reverend, great Cleveland," pleaded Friar Hal, "the enemy is near to hand."

"Yeah," said Philo the Phlegmatic in his relaxed commanding way, "lower your fucking voice."

The Bobbies leaned on their ropes for a closer look. Inside the cage was a large wheel, a human-sized version of the sort on which pet gophers or hamsters spin away their days. A middle-sized man with pale, pasty skin, filth-begrimed glasses and a small blue beret turned the wheel with laborious strides. Just out of his reach, just outside the cage, hung a small golden ring. It was this ring for which he reached, eternally. It was this ring that lay just outside his grasp. He walked the wheel to get nearer to the ring. His energy never flagged. The ring was his quest; the wheel, his fate. He was Dunkan Cleveland, a legend to the Inner Crew of the *Golden Slack*—a legend, a living monument and, ultimately, the benedictor of any important action by the Inner Crew.

Sitting next to the cage, pumping the pedals of a wheezing old harmonium, was a tall, skinny man with a long neck and a once-ornate haircut now grown to a shambles. His skin had not seen the light of day in years. His nimble fingers moved carefully across the greasy keys, shooting out dislocated music of extraordinary power. Known simply as The Deacon, he had been banished from the outside world by corporate decree. The Deacon's music contained too much truth and poetry for the audience of the Conspiracy, and so he had been shackled to his harmonium and sent to death in the slave galleys. Rescued by the *Golden Slack* some years ago, he had fled bright sunlight for the gloom of the hold and the constant gibbering of the Great Cleveland. The Deacon claimed to find Dunkan Cleveland's preposterous mutterings quite soothing. Dunkan Cleveland felt the same about the mad music of The Deacon.

"The hour is at hand," whispered Frair Hal. "Give us your blessing."

Dunkan Cleveland did not look up from his wheel. He raised one filthy hand in benediction. The Deacon began to play "O Canada!"

"Excuse me, The Deacon," Cap'n Stang said tactfully, "this is an American ship."

The Deacon nodded distractedly and shifted without flaw into "America the Beautiful."

The Crew smiled with delight at the rising bloodlust that patriotism endgenders.

"Leap into their rigging," shouted Dunkan Cleveland at the top of his lungs. "Put your hand down their throats and tear out their bowels!"

His hand drooped. He had forgotten them.

"Ears," hissed Le Deuel. "He didn't say anything about pulling their ears!"

"Pardon me, O Great Cleveland," said Cap'n Stang. "But we need to know—what about pulling a few ears?"

"PULL!" The Deacon screeched. "PULL and pull and pull!"

The Inner Crew jumped in horror at the volume of his screams.

Everything happened at once.

"Man the gun," screamed Janor the Insane. "We are upon them."

A piercing light split the gloom, freezing the Inner Crew like startled deer.

"Who goes there?" came the imperious question from the *Multiconglomerate Trading Vessel*. "Name your vessel and show your colors."

Puzzleen sprang for the tiny cannon which swiveled on a brass stand at the bow. They were atop the *Multiconglomerate Trading Vessel*. So engrossing was the blessing of Dunkan Cleveland that none had noticed their rapid closing of the intervening distance. Puzzleen seized the firing lanyard and looked back to Cap'n Stang, awaiting his command.

"Let me down," wailed Cleveland.

"Name yourself or be fired upon," commanded the voice of the *Multiconglomerate Trading Vessel*.

"We may not attack without launching the Head," called Janor the Insane.

Cap'n Stang stood stymied.

"Stern-Ho," said Philo the Phlegmatic calmly, "take the helm. Janor, come forward and launch the Head. Puzzleen, stand by."

Philo the Phlegmatic raised his cutlass and turned toward the *Multiconglomerate Trading Vessel*.

"And AS FOR YOU," Philo the Phlegmatic shouted, "you Conspiracy pipsqueak, you can just KISS my SubGenius ASS!"

"Show the colors!" screamed Cap'n Stang, ready for battle at last.

Snavely snapped the black flag onto the lanyard and yanked with all his might. The flag shot into the moonlit sky and proudly unfurled. The wind stretched it taut and blew it toward the *Multiconglomerate Trading Vessel*. It stretched free and brave, to strike fear in the hearts of the Pinks, the wimps, the Conspiracy Mind-Death Dupes and all their ilk.

Janor scrambled forward, bearing the Sacred Ark with some difficulty. Snavely shuffled beside him, stringing up El Catapulto del Slacko. The two knelt on the deck while all the Inner Crew nervously gripped and ungripped their weapons.

"Behold!" came the terror-stricken cry from the *Multiconglomerate Trading Vessel*.

"Behold the crossed Pipes!" cried another voice, quivering with fear.

"Behold the simple smile!"

"Behold the part!"

"Behold the dots!"

"Saints preserve us!" screamed another. "We are doomed!"

"Man your stations," barked the imperious voice of the captain. "We have found the pirates."

"Surrender instead," answered Cap'n Stang. "None may best those who sail under the **Crossed Pipes** of the **Jolly Bob!"**

"The Jolly Bob?" This stunned whisper traveled the length and breadth of the *Multiconglomerate Trading Vessel.* The Inner Crew could feel the Conspiracy Marines lose heart even across the short length of sea which separated the two fighting ships.

"The Head is ready," cried Janor the Insane.

"El Catapulto del Slacko is strung," echoed Snavely.

"Then," said Puzzleen, with the eerie calm which always o'ertook him at the moment of battle and bloodshed, "fire when ready."

Janor knelt beside El Catapulto del Slacko, whispered an incantation known only to himself and loosed the string. The Head, taken from the living neck of a video network head of programming, had been carefully cured and shrunk by Janor and Snavely, using only organic and naturally derived shrinking substances. No chemicals or preservatives marred this head. Crafted into a remarkable likeness of J. R. "BOB" Dobbs, this head was fired across the decks of every ship the *Golden Slack* had ever attacked. Since the *Golden Slack* had yet to lose a battle, the Head was always retrieved. Begun as so many Church rituals had been, the Launching of the Head was simply Janor's idea of a joke, a way of striking fear into the hearts of the Conspiracy.

Like so many other jokes, it had become deadly serious, a joke one could believe in. No battle began without the Launching of the Head.

Janor the Insane snapped the catch and El Catapulto del Slacko arced the Head out across the brief space between the ships.

Janor the Insane raised his head to the heavens in a paroxysm of joy. "Ramming speed!" he screamed.

"Fire!" called the captain of the *Multiconglomerate Trading Vessel.*

His crew yanked the lanyard on their small stern-facing swivel gun.

The Bleeding Head smacked square into the open barrel of the tiny Conspiracy cannon.

Snavely spun the giant wheel of the *Golden Slack.* Her bowsprit smashed into the stern of the *Multiconglomerate Trading Vessel.* Marines were flung across her decks. The Inner Crew, braced and ready, awaited only their captain's orders.

The tiny swivel cannon, its barrel blocked by the sacred Bleeding Head, backfired, blasting the charge through the rear of the breech-loading gun. The dupes manning the gun were ripped to shreds and the captain was hurled the length of the deck. What remained hanging from his ears did not deserve to be pulled. His crew splashed through his blood as they looked helplessly for a place to hide.

Clinging to the bowsprit with one hand, waving his "mixture"-dripping cutlass with the other, the first mate of the *Golden Slack* pointed to the enemy and cried with a bloodcurdling scream:

"STERN HO-O-O!"

The Inner Crew boiled over the bow and swept onto the *Multiconglomerate Trading Vessel.* Stern-Ho lowered his head and led the way. Swinging his cutlass in giant arcs, he hacked his way forward, pausing only to pry the recalcitrant blade from the ribs or thigh of some unfortunate Conspiracy Marine.

Cap'n Stang strolled casually among the carnage. A pacifist, he was unarmed. A Conspiracy Marine approached, pistol in either hand. Cap'n Stang held up two fingers on his right hand. The Marine paused.

"How many fingers," Cap'n Stang asked, slowly and calmly, "am I holding up?"

"Two," replied the puzzled young Conspirator.

Cap'n Stang smiled a pleased, encouraging smile.

"Right!" he said happily.

The young Marine smiled back. Cap'n Stang drove his two upraised fingers into the Marine's eyes. When the Marine dropped his pistols to clutch at his face, Cap'n Stang ducked, put a shoulder under the young man and heaved him over the rail.

For some reason no one ever swung a weapon at Cap'n Stang.

Monsieur Le Deuel and Philo the Phlegmatic stood shoulder to shoulder, cutting their way through the Marines. Le Deuel fought with his left hand and Philo the Phlegmatic with his right. A Marine rushed the pair, a wicked bayonet gleaming on the end of the musket. Philo seized the musket as the man lunged and Le Deuel yanked the man off his feet.

Holding the Marine close to his face, Le Deuel spoke quietly: "Repent," he said. "Quit your job. Slack off, and I will spare your life."

"I repent," the Marine replied, his voice choked with fear.

"Do you take the almighty BOB as your savior?"

"Y-y-y-ess," stammered the frightened Marine. "I do with all my soul."

"Foul LIAR!" screamed Le Deuel, his voice dark with hatred.

He pushed the muzzle of his pistol into the Marine's mouth and pulled the trigger. Blood gushed from the Marine's nose in a fountain and brains blasted out of his ears in two horizontal gray streams. Le Deuel pushed him away in disgust. Le Deuel's shirt was stained with the Marine's blood.

"Wasn't that," Philo the Phlegmatic asked without a pause in his hacking and chopping, "a bit excessive?"

"Did he," Le Deuel replied in outrage, "say he had repented and taken BOB into his heart?"

Philo ducked under the muzzle blast of a Marine's pistol and drove his sword deep into the man's chest as the Marine paused to reload. The Marine thumped to the deck. Philo nodded to Le Deuel.

"Yet," continued the outraged warrior, "did he offer BOB any money or wordly goods via me, BOB's representative on this ship?"

Philo the Phlegmatic could only shake his head as he parried the wild thrust of a Conspiracy accountant in a shabby brown suit.

"How then," asked Le Deuel, "can any man claim to have accepted BOB if he does not tithe to BOB that which *is* BOB's?"

"Without payment," gasped Philo the Phlegmatic, "there is no conversion, no acceptance . . ."

"No SLACK!" Janor the Insane screamed in their ears.

"Indeed," said Le Deuel. He had not jumped. He was accustomed to Janor sneaking up on him. "You have to buy SLACK, not earn it, and that dupe would never understand."

As battles do, this one seemed to swirl around Le Deuel, Philo the Phlegmatic and Janor the Insane. They found themselves in a small eddy, standing shoulder to shoulder as SubGenii chopped and fired their way through the massed Marines.

"What do you want, Janor?" asked Philo the Phlegmatic. Janor seldom sought companionship in a battle. The force of his hate was so strong that he was as liable to injure a friend as a foe. Most of the Inner Crew made sure to avoid him in combat. Now he seemed unusually calm.

"Something's wrong," Janor answered. "I fear we are losing this battle yet I cannot say how. I believe we should withdraw and return to the *Golden Slack.*"

Philo and Le Deuel were awestruck. It was not that Janor had shown concern, something he never did no matter how drastic the circumstances, but that he had spoken in such clear, rational sentences!

"The heat of this battle has scrambled his brains," Philo the Phlegmatic whispered to Le Deuel.

"Aye," the privateer nodded, "but mark his words with care nonetheless. The more insane he becomes, the more sense he makes, even if his delusion takes the form of clarity."

"That's right, Philo," Janor the Insane said smugly.

"Protect him, Le Deuel," commanded Philo the Phlegmatic. "Fight your way back to the *Golden Slack* and regain her helm."

Le Deuel made no reply. He seethed inside—no one told him what to do in a fight! But the fate of all, he knew, meant more than the hurt feelings of one. With one hand Le Deuel gripped Janor tightly by the arm and with the other he raised his cutlass. He stepped back into the fray, this time fighting to retreat.

Philo the Phlegmatic scrambled into the lowest rigging of the *Multiconglomerate Trading Vessel*. He kicked once at a Conspiracy A.M. Talk-Show Host, dressed in a bright red minidress with matching accessories, as she clutched at his pants leg. His boot heel found its mark unerringly and the Talk-Show Host collapsed on the deck, sobbing through her mouthful of broken teeth. She would never make the big jump from affiliate to Network.

Philo the Phlegmatic shaded his brow from the rising sun with the flat of his hand and quickly scanned the *Golden Slack*. Her foredeck was deserted. All the Bobbies hung in the rigging, watching the battle and cheering every SubGenius blow. The wheel turned emptily. No helmsman stood to guide it. There was no threat that Philo the Phlegmatic could determine.

He swung his gaze to the *Multiconglomerate Trading Vessel*. Below his feet the SubGenii had gained the length of the quarterdeck, including the wheelhouse of the huge ship and the base of her rearmost mast. Yet the forces of SLACK had not moved below to the gun decks nor forward on the main deck. The small band of pirates was in fact hemmed in, and more marines boiled out of the forward hold even as Philo the Phlegmatic watched.

The reinforcements, Philo realized with shock and horror, were not the real problem. The problem was the freshening breeze. As Philo the Phlegmatic stood in the rigging, ten feet above the battle, the doom of the *Golden Slack* was played out before him and he was helpless to act.

The two ships were locked together, bow to stern. The bowsprit of the *Golden Slack* was hopelessly tangled in the stern rigging of the larger Conspiracy ship. But the new wind, which blew across the bow of the *Multiconglomerate Trading Vessel,* pushed that bow toward the stern of the *Golden Slack*. The wind increased as Philo the Phlegmatic watched, and the bow of the Conspiracy ship moved so near the *Golden Slack* that the two ships formed a large V.

Philo searched the deck quickly. None of his brother SubGenii could see over the enemy before them. None understood what was happening. None grasped the threat borne on this freshening breeze.

The horror that Philo the Phlegmatic felt as the two ships drew nearer was nothing compared to the fear which smote him when he beheld who emerged from the fo'c'sle cabin door. Philo the Phlegmatic never assumed this man was aboard, never thought for a moment that his worst enemy would ever leave the safety of the shore.

This man was the dread CEO of the *Multiconglomerate Trading Vessel,* the most feared commander in all the Conspiracy. And he understood the power of the rising wind all too well.

Waiting as he always did, waiting until all circumstances were in his favor, he showed himself.

A slender figure stepped out of the foredeck cabin door. A quartet of young Conspiracy Starlets in clinging black Lycra and high-heeled shoes surrounded him. Each carried an Uzi and a sawed-off shotgun. He climbed easily to the highest point on the deck. As always, he wore an unconstructed black blazer and a black T-shirt. His perfectly cut bangs drooped manic-depressively across his forehead.

Philo the Phlegmatic saw this scourge of every right-thinking Sub-Genius and slapped himself in the forehead. He should have known. Only one man could command this ship. Only one man could be considered the Conspiracy incarnate. Only this evil, twisted, yet in his own way brilliant Conspiracy dupe could rule a ship as important as the *Multiconglomerate Trading Vessel*.

Philo the Phlegmatic raised his voice in a mighty shout, one which swept over the battle and caused every participant to rest his sword arm, if only for a moment.

"Cap'n Stang," he shouted, as he pointed to the foredeck, "behold! Behold the true captain of this foul ship—Admiral Rear Lodar!"

Cap'n Stang followed Philo the Phlegmatic's pointing arm. When he beheld the self-important smirk, the empty, glazed eyes and the fashionably understated apparel that could only belong to Admiral Rear Lodar, Cap'n Stang's heart sank with forebodings of doom.

Strangely, all Marines and Inner Crew held their breath and ceased their fight. All eyes rested on the feared admiral. The clanging of swords, the grunted shouts, even the mutters and cries of the wounded Conspiracy Marines died down. There was only the rising wind, the slap of the ocean on the hull, and the creaking of the lines.

Le Deuel paused, caught in the jumble of rigging that held the *Multiconglomerate Trading Vessel* fast to the bowsprit of the *Golden Slack*. Janor the Insane raised his head as he drooped over Le Deuel's shoulder. He pointed with a feeble arm to the ever-diminishing distance between the bow of the Conspiracy ship and the stern of the *Golden Slack*. As usual, only Janor understood. The arms of the V were closing. Soon the wind would hold the ships side to side.

Admiral Rear Lodar raised one arm.

"Grapples away!" he cried.

From the first gun deck five small cannon boomed. Thick ropes shot from the *Multiconglomerate Trading Vessel*. Leading the looping ropes through space were eight-pointed grappling hooks of the stoutest iron. The barbed hooks tore through the gentle sea air and slammed into the *Golden Slack*.

One buried itself to the shanks in the sturdy oak of the *Golden Slack*'s forerail. Another sailed over the rail and chunked into the thick teak deck planking. The third caught an unwary Bobbie in the back and smashed him into the mainmast. The thick barb broke his chest and pinned him fast. Blood ran in thick streams out the bottom of his jeans and coated his expensive sneakers. He opened his mouth for one last breath, to praise the name of BOB, but all that emerged was a bubble of blood. The last two hooks whirled into the rigging, where they wrapped themselves around and around like bolos, knocking two Bobbies from their perch and into the rapidly shrinking sea between the two ships.

Admiral Rear Lodar raised his hand to give another command. Le Deuel raised his pistol to blow the evil man's brains out the back of his head. A new contingent of Marines, armed with Ingram MAC-10s, poured out of the hatch and leveled their submachine guns at the startled and surrounded SubGenii.

Philo the Phlegmatic, still unnoticed in his perch in the rigging, watched in horror as each SubGenius lowered his weapon and raised his hands. Admiral Rear Lodar smirked again.

"Haul away!" was his command.

Unseen Conspiracy hands belowdecks pulled the lines from the grappling hooks taut and began to reel them in. The gap between the ships inexorably closed. The *Golden Slack* heeled slightly over toward the flat ropes and her gallant old timbers creaked a bit in resistance to this odd, sideways movement.

The SubGenii stood defeated, waiting for Admiral Rear Lodar's inevitable command to board, when hundreds of Marines would sweep over the rail of the *Golden Slack*. The Bobbies would be tossed into the sea or chained into slavery. For the Inner Crew there was only imprisonment, a mockery of a trail and a long drop on a short rope.

The two ships touched gunwales with a gentle *bonk*. Admiral Rear Lodar did not give the command to board. He stood, smirking as always, on the foredeck, his hand upraised. The Marines waited at the rail, bayonets poised. The Bobbies ran wailing down the rigging, making for the few lifeboats.

Mahvreeds the Cautious stood atop a cluster of dead Marines, his sword coated with their innards. Blood, bones and shreds of uniform covered him from head to foot. Mahvreeds the Cautious did not like the Conspiracy.

He studied Admiral Rear Lodar with care. Always the first to anticipate (and embrace) the negative implications of any situation (with the possible exception of the far-away Pope of Popes), Mahvreeds the Cautious suddenly understood the intentions of Admiral Rear Lodar.

He pointed in anguish at the *Golden Slack*.

"My black velvet!" he screamed.

An intuitive flash raced through all the Inner Crew. Like Mahvreeds the Cautious, they finally grasped the disaster about to befall their beloved *Golden Slack*.

"My comics!" said Friar Hal.

"My 'Frop!" said Jah Gar I.

"My tapes!" said Puzzleen Ev'hedance.

"My lunch!" said Janor the Insane.

"My snakeskin jacket!" said Le Deuel.

"And I just about got those damn Bobbies broken in, too," said Cap'n Stang.

Philo the Phlegmatic, true to his name, said nothing.

"Avast that shit!" cried Stern-Ho. "What about Dunkan and The Deacon?"

Half the brave warriors of SLACK turned toward the *Golden Slack*. Half whirled to confront Admiral Rear Lodar. They found only a solid wall of Conspiracy bayonets.

Admiral Rear Lodar gazed down on their anguish with glee and satisfaction. He hesitated another moment before giving the order.

"Fire!" he said.

The *Multiconglomerate Trading Vessel* had three gun decks on each side of her massive hull. Each gun deck had openings for twelve cannon. Each opening showed a six-inch cast-iron cannon, loaded with solid ball and explosive canisters. The broad snouts protruding from the gun ports almost touched the wooden walls of the *Golden Slack*.

A split second after Admiral Rear Lodar's command, the roar of thirty-six guns firing at the same instant drowned out all thought, all feelings, all action. The blast rocked every man back on his heels. The *Multiconglomerate Trading Vessel* heeled away from the recoil of the massive guns, tipping her deck sharply and dumping the unready Sub-Genii pirates onto their backs. The braced Marines took a step closer and pinned each man to the deck with the gentle touch of a bayonet point in the throat.

A thick, acrid cloud of gray smoke rose from the gun ports and obscured the *Golden Slack*. Philo, thrown from the rigging by the force of the blast, tumbled onto the deck and was instantly seized. Likewise, Le Deuel and Janor felt the prick of a bayonet point in their backs as they tried to rise from all fours, whence the shuddering of the two ships had tossed them.

Deafened, the SubGenius pirates could not hear Admiral Rear Lodar command his troops.

"Let them up," Admiral Rear Lodar said with a wave of his hand. "Let them understand the power of the Conspiracy."

The Marines beckoned the pirates to their feet. They stumbled to the rail. None spoke. None could believe their eyes. Truly, at this moment, there was no SLACK.

Nor was there any *Golden Slack*. Her side was blasted completely open from waterline to gunwale and the sea rushed in, steam blending with thick smoke from the fire that raged from stem to stern. It was as if the chamber that once held Dunkan and The Deacon had never existed. There was no wheel, no harmonium and no evidence that either had ever been. The broken burning timbers of their hold sagged crazily.

Above deck the devastation was equally complete. Both masts lay across the deck. The foremast had snapped at the deck and brought the jib sail down over the mainmast, which broke halfway up its length. Tangled in the jungle of rigging, canvas and wood that covered the *Golden Slack* from end to end were the broken remains of the Bobbies. They had tumbled with the masts, the crossbars and the ropes into the inferno that the *Golden Slack* had become. Their pitiful cries reached over the smoky water to the *Multiconglomerate Trading Vessel*.

The *Golden Slack* heeled toward the open wound in her side as seawater poured in. Her gunwale struck the ocean and gentle waves swept her deck. In a moment she would slip beneath the sea.

Someone dived off the *Multiconglomerate Trading Vessel*. A splash marked his position. Marines raced to the rail, rifles upraised. A figure showed, swimming across the wave tops. Twenty rifles spoke and the water around the swimmer was peppered with singing splashes as bullets pocked the water around him. Richochets sang off the trunks, spars, tools and cookpots that littered the surface.

The swimmer dived under the flotsam. Admiral Rear Lodar raised his hand. The firing ceased.

"Let him be," said Admiral Rear Lodar. "I want to see what he's after."

At that moment Puzzleen Ev'hedance clambered out of the sea and onto the tilting deck of the *Golden Slack*. Ignoring the sharply increasing pitch of the ship, the moans of the Bobbies and the flames licking all around him, Puzzleen Ev'hedance made his struggling way over, around and through the jumbled sails and ropes until he found the top of the mainmast where it lay across the deck. There he tore the **JOLLY BOB** free of the mast and waved it triumphantly overhead.

Admiral Rear Lodar again raised his hand.

Twenty Marines opened fire on Puzzleen Ev'hedance.

The *Golden Slack* turned turtle, tossing Puzzleen Ev'hedance into the sea. As her keel showed itself to the sky, the *Golden Slack* sank slowly, turning and turning in the center of a widening whirlpool. Even after the *Golden Slack* had vanished from sight, the whirlpool swirled about, pulling into its center all the trash from the ruined ship.

"Can Puzzleen outswim its force?" whispered Friar Hal.

Cap'n Stang could only shrug.

"Silence, please," ordered Admiral Rear Lodar in his indolent way. "Whoever commands this rabble, show yourself to me."

Cap'n Stang turned toward the foredeck.

Admiral Rear Lodar opened his mouth, but a lookout interrupted him.

"The whirlpool grows!" came the cry from the crow's nest. "Hard a'lee."

"Helm hard a'lee," echoed Admiral Rear Lodar.

The helmsman, clad in the latest, most fashionable Conspiracy sailing gear, clambered over the captured pirates to the forgotten helm. He spun the wheel as Conspiracy yachtsmen leaped into the rigging like trained monkeys. Their tans were perfect.

Again eyes turned toward the spot where the *Golden Slack* had sunk.

Indeed the whirlpool was growing. But not outward, not in the sea and not like any whirlpool ever seen. The whirlpool rose out of the ocean, spinning faster and faster, growing like a summer weed, until its mad whirling top stood higher than the crow's nest on the mainmast of the *Multiconglomerate Trading Vessel*. Far below, along the waterline, trailed the narrow tapered bottom, which spun with the same terrible force as the enormous top.

"Is it," whispered Friar Hal, "a waterborne tornado?"

"There are no tornadoes at sea," answered Le Deuel. "It must be a waterspout."

The whirling water tilted slightly toward the *Multiconglomerate Trading Vessel*. Its bottom tore free of the wave tops and the immense spinning tower bore down on the Conspiracy ship.

Janor the Insane studied the waterspout with care as Admiral Rear Lodar barked commands. The stunned crew moved slowly, afraid to tear their eyes from the destruction that bore down upon them.

"Cap'n Stang," said Janor the Insane, who was now so deranged that he spoke with perfect articulation, "gaze with care upon the upper sides of this waterspout—what do you percieve?"

Every pirate followed Janor the Insane's suggestion. They felt no fear. What did they care if the waterspout capsized this den of Conspiracy Mind-Death Dupes? Their *Golden Slack* lay on the bottom of the pitiless sea, their benefactors blown to bits, their battle lost and their BOB defeated. None felt willing to flee or had the energy for the terror which swept the Conspiracy crew.

The Inner Crew watched the whirling dervish of water. Strange protuberances projected from the top.

"That bump on the upper rim," said Cap'n Stang, "I hate to say it, but it looks exactly like Dunkan Cleveland."

"And the one beside," said Philo the Phlegmatic, "looks like The Deacon."

No one spoke as realization sunk in. All turned to Janor the Insane as the only fit man to say aloud what the Inner Crew knew inside.

"Praise BOB!" shouted Janor the Insane, "that's no waterspout, that's the Whirlwind of SLACK!"

The pirates, their hearts filled with joy, covered their ears against the roaring wind and dove onto the deck. As prophesied in hymns, the Whirlwind of SLACK had come to punish the Conspiracy and raise the SubGenius up to his or her rightful place. The carnage would be awful, but BOB would be served.

The mighty Whirlwind of SLACK rose majestically off the ocean's surface and hovered in the air just above the deck of the *Multiconglomerate Trading Vessel*. Later, when the battle was long over, some among SubGenii would swear that in the groaning, howling tornado that was the Whirlwind of SLACK they could hear the muted voices of Dunkan Cleveland and The Deacon, urging them on to glory.

As the helmsman gripped his wheel with the white knuckles of mortal fear, Admiral Rear Lodar screamed commands that none could hear over the raging wind. Marines scurried to and fro and yachtsmen fell from the riggings like ripe crab apples, begging for their mommies. The Whirlwind of SLACK seemed to wait for just an instant. Then, when the moment was right, the Whirlwind of SLACK struck.

Its spinning bottom, no more than a few feet across, snuffled across the deck like an elephant's trunk, daintily skipping over the prostrate pirates. It Hoovered every Marine in its path. Some held on to the rail with all their might. Some cowered at the base of the mast. No matter. When the vacuum force of the Whirlwind of SLACK took them, they simply disappeared. Snatched up the whirling snout, they reappeared a moment later at the top of the huge tornado, torn in half, their bones turned to jelly, their limbs flopping emptily. The Whirlwind of SLACK spit them hundreds of feet into the air. They turned over slowly, head over feet, arms and legs flopping, drifting lazily through the clear blue sky.

When they hit the ocean, the sharks were waiting.

The Whirlwind of SLACK seized every Marine from the deck and every yachtsman from the rigging. The ship itself was not harmed. The elephantine snout reached the foredeck and whipped the Starlets into its sucking mouth. Admiral Rear Lodar was left untouched, as were the gun crews and enlisted men below. When the last Starlet had been blown out of the spinning top of the Whirlwind of SLACK, it rose far above the ship, and blew slowly toward the horizon.

The Inner Crew stood and swept up the abandoned weapons. They surrounded Admiral Rear Lodar. The deck of the *Multiconglomerate Trading Vessel* was picked clean. No one spoke; no one jumped to the defense of Admiral Rear Lodar. He said nothing. He stood smirking as always, resigned to his fate.

"Le Deuel," said Cap'n Stang, "have you The Book?"

"Aye, aye, sir."

"Admiral," commanded Cap'n Stang, "call your officers to the deck."

"What officers? They all vanished up your vacuuming whirlwind."

"Your fate is sealed," said Philo the Phlegmatic. "Don't worsen it by lying."

Admiral Rear Lodar opened the hatch behind him.

"Officers assemble on the deck," he called down into the passageway. "Unarmed."

"Wait!" said Janor the Insane. "I hear someone calling us."

"I hear nothing but the crunching of sharks' teeth," snorted Le Deuel.

Janor the Insane went to the rail. Far below, clinging to a fallen line by one hand, holding himself high enough out of the water to avoid the avid jaws of the encircling sharks, was Puzzleen Ev'hedance. In his other hand he held the black flag, the **JOLLY BOB.**

The Inner Crew hauled him aboard as the officers stood in formation. He rested against the gunwale, his day of heroism over, his place in the annals of freethinking, free-living SubGenii the world over assured.

"Read from The Book," ordered Cap'n Stang.

"All those who are practicing members of the Bar in any state," said Le Deuel, "step forward."

Half the officers did so, those with the most somber neckties and dishonest eyes.

"All those with any postgraduate degree in business of any kind."

Half of the remainder stepped forward, those with the most belligerent attitudes and thickest necks.

"All those with any sort of executive position in motion pictures, television or music, not to include any skill-position union members."

Two or three, those looking the most ashamed, but also the most stylishly dressed.

"All state patrolmen."

The last few officers stepped forward to join their brothers. These men simply looked the least human.

"As I suspected," said Cap'n Stang, "This crew consists of the foulest examples of Conspiracy dupedom. Fortunately, we have ways of dealing with you swine, as do the sharks."

"Take positions," barked Philo the Phlegmatic.

The Inner Crew seized their sharpest swords and waited behind the row of trembling Conspiracy officers. Cap'n Stang stood beside the exhausted Puzzleen Ev'hedance. Cap'n Stang would now read from The Book.

"Sever the Achilles tendon," he read.

A quick slash did the job. The officers fell to the deck, writhing in pain.

"Hamstring them."

It was done, though the officers squirmed like dogs in their own deepening blood.

"Break their arms."

The Inner Crew raised their feet and stomped their way through the blood-soaked, retching crowd of formerly powerful and sophisticated Conspiracy leaders. Where they stomped, a sharp *crack!* sounded. When an arm proved too strong to break, it was levered up over a SubGenius knee, where a helping hand quickly provided the required pressure. The dupes were now too weak to scream.

"Blind them."

Knife points searched out eyes, even though two SubGenii were now required to hold down each dupe.

The Inner Crew stepped back to admire their work. The foul fiends of the Conspiracy had been treated as they deserved, but their punishment was not yet complete. The Crew looked to Cap'n Stang.

He slammed The Book closed with a thump.

"Commend them," he said solemnly, "to the sharks."

A great cheer went up, with Friar Hal leading the way. He lifted two dupes, one in either hand, and flung them over the side as if they weighed no more than a sack of potatoes. The screams and panting cries of the Conspiracy officers were loud, but not so loud as the snapping jaws of the happy sharks.

In a few minutes, the sea was again peaceful, with only a widening slick of blood to mark this fitting conclusion to such a ferocious battle. Admiral Rear Lodar had not moved from the foredeck.

Cap'n Stang turned to him once more.

"Assemble the enlisted men," he ordered.

The poor gunners and swabbies, cooks and cleaners, accountants and cabdrivers stood on the deck, shivering with fear.

"This is our ship now," bellowed Philo the Phlegmatic without preamble. "We need Bobbies. Will you serve?"

The crew, to the last man, nodded eagerly.

"Then," said Le Deuel, "tithe unto BOB that which is BOB's!"

A blizzard of coins, bills, watches and jewelry cascaded onto the deck.

"Friar Hal," said Cap'n Stang, "gather up the tithing and get these men into the rigging. Set our course for the South Coast. Janor, take the helm. Jar Gar I, pick a few of these new Bobbies and get a crew going—repaint the stern."

"Aye, aye," said Frair Hal, tucking as much as he could grab into his voluminous robes.

Janor the Insane strode to the wheel without a word.

Jah Gar I moved through the crew, gauging them carefully through a thick cloud of 'Frop smoke.

"You, dupe," said Cap'n Stang, "get your mangy Conspiracy ass down here, pronto."

Admiral Rear Lodar strolled off the foredeck. He stood relaxed and calm, as always.

"You still don't get it, do you?" he said quietly. "You think you're in charge. You won a measly little battle, but I still hold the cards. You and your bunch will always be small-time without a guy like me.

"What are you doing mucking around in the Miasmic Sea? I could set you up, make you rich, take you public. I'm talking about exposure beyond your wildest dreams.

"You need big-time representation. Big-time presentation. I'm talking Pat Sajak, Arsenio Hall, and, if you play your cards right, and do as I say, maybe, one day even Letterman. I'm talking college tours, lecture circuits, Ivy League groupies, the works. I'm talking you and me.

"What do you say?"

Cap'n Stang looked from face to face at his faithful Crew. He saw the answer there, shining true. Without speaking, Cap'n Stang nodded to Le Deuel.

"When we sell out," roared the enraged pirate, "we'll do it on our terms, not yours!"

He took Admiral Rear Lodar by the ears, one in either massive hand, and pulled with all his might. Admiral Rear Lodar grabbed Le Deuel's forearms, but to no avail. He opened his mouth to scream, but no sound emerged. His eyes rolled back in his head and blood leaked from his nose.

Le Deuel's face turned bright red. The veins in his neck stood out like sausages, his breath came in pants and sweat poured down his cheeks.

"Now!" he screamed.

Admiral Rear Lodar split right down the middle. His head burst like a melon and his neck opened like a flower in a springtime rain. His ribs fell off his spine and his legs tore from his crotch. As his organs spilled onto the deck in a slimy, quivering heap, Le Deuel stepped back so as not to get splashed. He held half of Admiral Rear Lodar in either hand, using as handles the admiral's ears.

Cap'n Stang turned away.

"Clean this mess up and get under way," he said. "We've other ships to plunder."

"Cap'n Stang," called Jah Gar I from his scaffolding below the stern rail, "what name do I and I paint on dis worthy vessel?"

"The *Golden Slack*," replied Cap'n Stang with a small, proud smile, "The SLACKEST ship that ever sailed in the service of BOB."

Rev. Sternodox Keckhaver
DUPE

Brass Zamph was uncomfortably entering what he reckoned was his third full day of 'Frop withdrawal. He was also unable to move his arms or legs. Hours earlier, in the minutes after he had regained consciousness, he had amply demonstrated the futility of attempting to physically wrest himself from the grip of the metacrystal chain-field that encased his extremities and held him, magnetlike, to the wall, but the knowledge did little to halt his straining.

Brass was just able to painfully cock his head a few degrees and survey a fraction of his surroundings, and what he saw didn't fill him with optimism. Obviously the Samuels Brothers had trapped him inside a metallic, egg-shaped vessel of some kind, and within the narrow confines of his vision he could make out shiny concave walls, clustered with consoles and gadgetry like a cross between the inside of a submarine's conning tower and an Xist interrogation closet. Flashing red lights and constantly changing displays on a multitude of monitors faced him six feet away on the opposite wall, reflecting in his eyes like fireworks and increasing the fury of his 'Frop withdrawal migraine.

"Ah, so yer fahnly awake." The Southern drawl of an obviously drunk teenager bawled from a speaker behind his head.

"Give me some goddamn 'Frop, jerk-off," Brass bleated, summoning up what remained of his rapidly fleeting patience.

"My, my. Ain't you the uppity slack dick today. It's gone be awhile 'fore you git any Frappy. We got a couple surprises in store for you 'fore you git *anything*."

"Samuels, when I get shed of this tin can I'm gonna wad it up toot sweet and 'X' it right up your lily-white asshole."

"Whoooo-eeeee! Ain't you the toughest tit on the acid sow? I guess I'll jus' turn this thang off till my brothers git in, an' then we'll show you some damn shit, fer sure."

"Samuels! . . . "

The telling click behind Brass' head indicated that it would be useless for him to waste any more breath. His nose itched and he began mentally cursing his inability to move his arms. He realized not only that his nose itched but that, like the rest of his face, it hurt. In fact, his entire body was beginning to throb with a dull but tolerable pain.

"Shit," Brass mouthed. "What I wouldn't do for a 'Frop-cig right about now."

"So, you want some 'Frop, do ya?" The speaker behind his head came alive again, this time with an older, more familiar and similarly drunken voice.

"Well, if it isn't Big Man Samuels," Brass grunted. "Stooping to petty kidnapping these days, eh?"

"Among other thangs, Bray-ass. Among other thangs. How you like our little jail-pod?"

"Give me a fucking break," Brass snickered, "Don't try to take credit for all this Xist technology. You dipshit Samuels Brothers don't have the brains to dismantle a SexHurt barrel."

"We got enough brains to catch your ass, though," the voice in the speaker slurred. "Take a look-see. What you think 'bout this shit?"

Eighteen inches above Brass' head a slender, jointed steel arm emerged from a small compartment in the pod's wall and twisted itself down so that its tip hovered directly in front of the struggling prisoner's face. A small spheroid-shaped protuberance on the end of the arm began to unfold like a glinting flower and shortly it became a flat polished circle of metal, a mirror in which Brass could see his own face.

"You bastards! You stinking squid bait," Brass shrieked as he glared at the reflection in the mirror, taking in every shocking detail, from the carefully combed-back black hair to the straight aquiline nose and wide brown eyes! Every trace of the classically Negroid features Brass was used to seeing when he observed himself in a mirror was replaced by an all-too-familiar countenance.

"Now all you gotta do is stick a pipe in your teeth 'n you be quite the dude. See, we even got all the dots in place," the voice in the speaker drawled.

Brass' mind raced as he struggled against the unyielding bonds that confined him. He'd known for months that the Samuels Brothers had been planning something. The Xist codes had been quietly being broken since the first Arrival, and everyone on NHGH-IV had been nervously anticipating an attempted micro-Rupture, but even the Big Nine themselves hadn't foreseen anything quite this blatant.

"OK, Billy. What are you getting out of this? I thought you blew those alien scumbags off after they dissected Wanda."

"Oh, don't you worry 'bout that. They fixed me up good . . . real good. Hell, pussy's pussy, even if it IS clone snatch. The new one don't bitch at me neither. But you oughta be worryin' 'bout yore own ass, not 'bout some ground up dirty-leg."

Brass' head swam. He was seriously in need of some 'Frop and desperately forced himself to ignore the peripheral hallucinations which were beginning to manifest themselves as subtly shifting colors and patterns in the air around his head. If he didn't ingest the needed

Tibetan herb soon, it wouldn't matter what the Samuels Brothers had in store for him. Nothing would matter.

"What happens now?"

Brass was beginning to feel giddy. His tongue felt thick and woolly, and his head ached abominably.

"It just 'bout time fer you to find that out, Subbie."

The voice in the speaker had taken on an ethereal, resonant quality that Brass half-consciously realized was due more to his own 'Frop-deprived imagination than it was to any change in the audio signal.

"Bye-bye, birdie!"

Brass' entire body was suddenly wracked with an intense spasm of muscular contraction followed by what seemed like billions of tiny needles entering and breaking off just underneath the surface of his skin. Though his arms and legs were no longer bound to the wall of the vessel, he was vaguely aware that he had no control over them. The air around him was exploding with a panorama of bright balls of light that filled his head with sharp lingering lances of intense pain; a wave of nausea threatened to overwhelm what little sensibility he still maintained. Brass no longer felt the floor beneath his feet nor the wall behind his back, but seemed to be falling slowly through a blinding torrent of mesmerizing light bursts and halos of fire. Suddenly, in the confusing pattern of semi-images surrounding him, he became aware of a small, nondescript object floating inches away. Scarcely willing to trust his punished judgment, he painfully forced the muscles in his arm to contract, reached out and clumsily grasped the object, which his fingers told him was a small tobacco pipe of some sort.

Thinking himself insane, he struggled against the spectral winds that buffeted him mercilessly and brought the pipe close to his face. Looking inside the white-rimmed bowl he hazily made out a small wad of beautiful, wonderful, lifesaving 'Frop.

"Praise "Bob," " Brass muttered as he raised the stem to his lips and greedily inhaled the aromatic plumes of smoke exuding from the mysteriously ignited lump of herb.

Drawing in a double-lungful of the potent smoke, Brass dreamily closed his eyes and felt the aches in his head and body dissipate within seconds. He was about to take in another lungful when he realized that his feet were in contact with a hard surface and that he was subconsciously walking forward. Opening his eyes, Brass was instantly, horribly cognizant of the Samuels Brothers' plan.

"Fucking Xist Time Control," he muttered as the figure bearing down in front of him raised the shiny-barreled revolver and fired point-blank into Brass' heaving chest.

Brass fell like a dead weight to the wooden floor of the stage, the smoking pipe still clenched in his teeth, blackness and noise resolutely overwhelming him. As he felt himself slipping into the impending darkness he plainly heard the jangly intro to a vaguely remembered song.

Nodding his head in mute, final resignation and instinctively tapping a toe to the discordant croaking melody, the words "Sick-a, sick-a, sick-a, sick-a, sick-a, sick-a, sick-a, sick-a, "Bob"" bounced harmlessly off his suddenly useless eardrums.

BLEEDING HEADECLESSIANS 9:9

Drs. 4 "Bob" Statement of Purpose (1983 edition)

9:9   This article is a statement of purpose, direction and goals of Drs. 4 "Bob," a pan-dimensional religio-sexual explorational group and antimusic orchestra. The express purpose of our organization is to **Oh hell if I know!** But hell-yeah, we've got us a damn rock 'n' roll party band! Shit-yeah, yeah-hell-yeah, fuck-yeah, every-cussword-in-the-entire-dictionary-spoken-at-the-same-time-through-one-mouth-yeah. We don't give a **damn,** do we? But if you've got the keg party, we've got the damn pan-dimensional religio-sexual explorational group and rock 'n' roll party band, I mean it's got a pretty good beat, you can throb to it, you can grovel to it, you can contort to it, you kin *oob* to it. We drink six-packs full of six-packs, we shave with chain saws, we don't use chewing tobacco, we just bite into concrete blocks. When we get a runny nose, we just stick a shotgun up our sinuses and pull the trigger. Oh, hell, yes ma'am, we got a rock 'n' roll party band, a whiskey-drinkin', good-timin' bunch of god-damn ol' Skull Farmers. Oh hell yeah, we got plenty of chicks, remember that one time there were those chicks?

This one chick says, "Aren't you one of those boys that was playing in that real strange rock 'n' roll party band that had those fifteen guitar players, all playing something different? That rock 'n' roll party band over by the old oak tree down in Forgotopay County, and they were wearing those funny hats which were beyond description, and were playing so badly that even the corn were covering their ears? And they were the ones that had those fifteen guitars all plugged into each other to create a living, self-feeding feedback force which kept growing and couldn't be stopped, even by the Fantastic Four, Super Fly, Shaft, James Bond, Kung Fu, and J. R. "Bob" Dobbs all put together, that feedback force which is destined to grow to infinite size, and alter the entire vibrational frequency of the Squirtin' Universe? That rock 'n' roll party band that has a guitar hooked up into a TV set, hooked up into a telephone, hooked up into a Betamax, hooked up into Jones' big, fat dick, hooked up into a pocket calculator, hooked up into a home computer, hooked up into a machine gun? And all held together with BIG RED STRAPS? And they had that one weird bongo player who used to snort gasoline, until he saw little green men and everyone laughed at him until they finally locked him up, and *now that we are all slaves to those little green men, people aren't laughing quite as hard, are they?*

Would that be the same band that played that electric guitar that hooked up directly into the human mind and caused hallucinations so real as to make reality pale in comparison, was that the same band that created that patch cord that can hook human minds directly into each other, thus eliminating the need for instruments, albums, concerts and, yes, even agents? Are y'all part of that same band that Mama told us not to talk to or look at except through a special lens, and said one time Li'l Kreegar looked at Drs. for "Bob" without using a special lens, and now his parents have kept him locked in the basement for the past twenty-seven years because they say his eyes ain't right, and me and Billy are gonna try to sneak him out tonight and try beer for the first time and find out what Drs. for "Bob" are really all about, and Mrs. Teacher at school she said Drs. for "Bob" are even more harmful than angel dust, and that Drs. for "Bob" was the leading cause of teenage suicide, and Billy had that Drs. for "Bob" tape and it was hooked up to his mind and all the other kids were scared because he started to foaming at the mouth and acting like a dog and they took him down to the principal's office and hooked him up to that device and let the nine-inch worms eat away at his face and his parents didn't even sue the school board for letting the nine-inch worms eat away at his face because they knew he'd been listening to Drs. for "Bob" anyway, and said it was too late, and we saw a movie in the auditorium that said you shouldn't drive a car if you had been listening to Drs. for "Bob," and that time Drs. for "Bob" came on the radio and said they were the Voice of God but Mrs. Teacher said they were really the voice of the devil, and Mr. Daddy said not to go within ten miles of Drs. for "Bob" 'cause you could get VD and not to touch their funny hats or to sit on their guitars with a wet bathing suit? Are you one of the boys that plays in that band?"

AND I sez, "*A **boy**? Oh yeah, you tell your mama you were walking **funny** for a **week** because of a BOY. Tell her you got a **backbone knocked outa shape** by a BOY! Yeah, it was a BOY that had to be a **substitute** for the **Washington Monument** for a week while they were making repairs. Oh **yeah,** a BOY! I kin deliver more 'male' with one thrust of my pelvis than the U.S. Postal Service, the Federal Express and the Pony Express have been able to deliver in the past hundred fifty years! I wrote the **Bible** by cummin' on a black piece of paper, the white of my sperm moving around the black to form letters. **Oh yeah, a BOY!** I'm the one they had to **launch into outer space** because every time I **came** it showed up on the Russian Early Warning System and almost caused World War Three.* That's right, a *boy*. Yeah."

"Got those keys, Jones?"

"Keys? I thought you had the keys."

We're Drs. for "Bob," we create universes, we fix lawn mowers, we're omnipotent, can I borrow five dollars? Drs. for "Bob" is the band that

282 THREE-FISTED TALES OF "BOB"

lets you keep your mind, Drs. for "Bob" is the band that dares to grip the reins of human evolution BY THE BALLS! We are not human, WE ARE NOT HUMAN!

WE ARE NOT HUMAN!!

Like that one time Eklund threw that beer mug across the practice shack and broke it, and all the chicks got alienated, and it blew Drs. for "Bob" 's groupie status for the next six months, and then later Eklund was dancing on the piano while playing saxophone at the same time, and he forgot the broken beer mug down there and he jumped off the piano and he landed on the broken glass and got it embedded in his foot, and then used the Sacred Bleeding Head of Arnold Palmer to heal himself by holding it up to his foot while simultaneously screaming at the top of his lungs. So if you're talkin' some Trevinoist *shit* you can *back your cart off my green,* buddy, we worship only the TRUE Bleeding Head, the one that has always existed. Hell, since we cracked the Head in two at Chicago five years ago, the SubGenius Church is now divided into two warring factions: the Church of the Lower Jaw versus the Church of the Upper Cranium, but you can read all about that in *The Stark Fist of Removal,* I'm too busy talkin' *DOKTORS* here. I mean, is that Mick Jagger's amputated penis, or are you just glad to see me? Drs. for "Bob" get down so low James Brown is gonna have to look *up* to see his *feet.* They get down so low you're gonna have to have an atomic steam shovel to dig *those* cats. Crazy. And while we're on the subject, Drs. for "Bob" **is** *the* leading cause of teen suicide, but also the leading cause of bald men shaving their heads, the leading cause of people with no feet buying shoes. "I *had* to kill 'em Sarge, they were members of Drs. for "Bob"!" "Case dismissed." "But officer, I *had* to drive a hundred twenty-five miles per hour, there was a Drs. for "Bob" concert coming to town, I *had* to build these nuke bombs, there's still Drs. for "Bob" ALIVE on this planet!" "You mean you've *heard* of Drs. for "Bob" and the Moral Majority hasn't killed you yet? **MY GOD!**" And *you*—you're standing there *reading this,* and you haven't been arrested yet? **MY GOD!** 'Tis a crooked and perverse nation, my friends.

But the Doktor phenomenon is not some faddist movement meant to take the place of punk. Nor is it merely some small-time faddist movement meant to merely replace music. It is meant to transform *all human reality,* all three universes, even some parts of Mississippi. Drs. for "Bob" is so far out it's in. *Drs. for "Bob" explodes in a Hiroshima of visions like a thousand science fiction writers overdosing on acid to a background of five thousand tone-deaf Mongolian monks chanting in a parking lot full of car radios tuned between channels turned up all the way.* Drs. for "Bob" concerts are the last free zones left in America, the only concerts where you don't have to be "hip" or "with it," Drs. for "Bob" concerts are experimental anarchies, they are separate sovereign states which owe no allegiance to the United States nor any other country, and will someday overrun the entire world! Why, the natural good looks of Janor Hypercleats alone are worth the price of admission, probably good enough to take over the world for! Remember that time we went to a Drs. for "Bob" concert and we got so drugged out that we passed out and our girlfriends left with some guy in a Trans Am, and while we were unconscious we had this dream where we were trapped in this horrible nightmare world where people worshipped, for no apparent reason, these small, worthless green pieces of paper, and they placed more emphasis on these pieces of paper than they did on human life, or on the environment? And these strange monsters had two arms, two legs and a head with two eyes and two ears? It was horrible. And they worshipped cars and material possessions and kept on destroying the planet they lived on even though they *knew* they were doing it? And every four hours or so, for no apparent reason, they would take *dead plants and animals* and stuff them into these strange holes in their heads called "mouths"? At night they would put on these strange costumes called *"pajamas"* and lie almost motionless for hours? And they were so miserable that every couple of years they had to line up and shoot each other, and they kept each other in complete poverty so they could build giant bombs capable of destroying all life on their planet? And Li'l G'broagFran said it was ten times worse than any horror movie he'd ever seen, and I said, "I sure am glad that this was just a dream I'm seeing because I took too many drugs and listened to the Drs. for "Bob" for too long"? And then Kreegar's little brother's little sister whispers in my ear, "That wasn't no dream, this is reality"? And I said AAAAAAAEEEE*EEEEEEIIIIIIIIIIIAAAIIIAIIAAUUUUUUG HHHAAAUGHAIEEEEEEEEEEEEEEEEEEDDEHEHEHEH!*?

No, no, please! I'll be a good boy from now on, just don't let them get me they're crawling all over me don't let the nine-inch worms get me nooooooooooooooooooooooooooooooo.

But anyway, have you ever thought of just saying, "Fuck it?" Oh yeah—he's fucked it a *little bit,* but he's never **fucked it** *all the way.* Be honest with me now, you've never gone all the way down *in* there, you've never *squirted* as far as you *can,* you've never completely, totally and absolutely **FUCKED IT**. FUCKED, that's right. So what're you waiting for—? There're plenty of perfect orifices and phalli around, *but you're still holding back!* You've got to ask yourself, are you still livin' down in the testicles or have you crossed over that miiighty River Jordan, are you **squirtin'** *out the head?* For the purpose of life is not peace, happiness or even Truth! The purpose of life is to *squirt!* For slightly more than fifty percent of the population, the purpose is to *ooze!*

Which brings us back to the purpose of Drs. for "Bob," well, actually Drs. for "Bob" have no purpose, only *"things which we are gonna do."*

Drs. for "Bob" get down to the real git-down, they always stay in the groove. Drs. for "Bob" have the following goals: to get high, get drunk, get laid, have a damn party, blow everything off and bask in total Slack, *and* to invoke the name of *every* deity, every possible name of God, make *every possible tonal or atonal vibratory frequency,* every song shall be sung, every word spoken, every sound shall be made . . . SO THAT THIS PHASE OF THE UNIVERSE, OR WHATEVER IS LEFT OF IT, CAN **END PROPERLY!!** "Hell, I just wanted to be in a band that played rock and roll music like Foghat and the stuff all the other guys in my neighborhood listen to, I really don't know how all this *happened."*

And after every vibratory plane has been thoroughly explored, that's when Drs. for "Bob" shall release a totally new "sound," which won't be music or even antimusic or even *noise* or *sound,* but can only be classified as **antisound,** because the likes of it has never been "heard" in this universe, or any other! Shit, the only reason we even *call* it "sound" is because that's the only thing we can *compare* it to, but antisound has *nothing* to do with sound!

And in the end times there shall appear monsters so grotesque and hideous that to even look at them will *gawk your eyes out!* "Well, in that case I'll just close my eyes!" Then they'll just *gawk your eyelids out* first and *then* they'll *gawk your eyes out!* "Well, then I'll just put my hands over my eyes!" Then they'll just gawk your hands off and then gawk your eyelids off and then *gawk your eyes out!* "Well, then I'll hide in a fallout shelter!" Then they'll just gawk your fallout shelter away, and *then* they'll *gawk your eyes out!* YAAAAAAAAAAAAAAAAAA!!!!!

When antisound is released, the entire purpose of the universe shall at last be fulfilled. The most complex joke *ever told* shall at last *have* a punch line. This entire reality, this entire universe shall Squirt; all energy of all time eras of all planes of all realities shall be channeled through the Doktors' cheap-jack amplifiers. Yes, the universe *will* be destroyed by equipment bought on credit at Boyd's Music Store; then, the Doktors' inherent lack of ability to play their instruments shall convert these energies into the hitherto undiscovered force: ANTISOUND. *And you thought antimusic was bad!* This antisound shall tear apart the very Skor, the Mesh, the net that holds all universes, both matter and antimatter, together! And then, during the saxophone solo on "SubGenius Beach Party," the worn-out old primal sound of the laid-back universe, "OM," shall be replaced by Snavely Eklund's blaring antisaxophone hitting a wrong note that is in actuality the *right* note. "YEAH, BEACH party, did you bring the *Eklund for Universal Overlord* campaign buttons??" Hypercleats will intone naively, and that which must come to pass, that to which ALL EVENTS have been leading, will finally come to pass: The universe, and even Drs. for "Bob," will begin to lose its form, disintegrate, collapse, mutate. *"Born to lose . . . and now I'm losing Universal Form,"* Hypercleats shall quip, cracking off one last one-liner in the face of total universal transformation! (Every atom will be repelled by every other atom!) The evil Trevinoists will finally be smitten, Billy Samuels will finally get his hands on "Connie" Dobbs' panties and will be able to smell them for 2.5 seconds and have fifteen simultaneous orgasms, aliens will come on the radio and say that Orson Welles has landed, but no one will *believe* them, *I seen a vision, ma'am,* the Sacred Bleeding Head shall be joined back and stop bleeding, The SubGenius Foundation will sue Arnold Palmer, Dobbs' Pipe will go out (but only for a second), Jones will finally pay Smith the money he owes, the Yardman Corporation of Little Rock will finally show a profit, I'll type an entire sentence without making a mistake, Curly will hit Moe back and kill him, the Pie-Pie man will drop the pies and start carrying two glasses of iced tea instead, the Church will no longer ask people for money, LIES will tell the truth and be in a good mood, Puzzling Evidence will lose interest in the Kennedy assassination, Pee Dog will stop peeing, the nine-inch worms will be only $8\frac{1}{4}$ inches long, the Buddha will come out of his ten-thousand-year silent meditation and go, "Huh?", whereas Hypercleats will not say anything, and Stang will not write a report on it.

But nothing is ever destroyed—only transformed! *All energy* and *all matter* shall be polarized away from each other; all energy in the universe will be drawn towards a giant Black Hole, forming a Giant Black Vagina and Womb. The *matter* of the universe, "on the other hand," will be led by a now-formless Drs. for "Bob" (still existing as an energy force) to the other side of the Void, where it shall be shaped into a Giant White Dick. This universe-spanning Giant White Dick shall then be led to enormous, nuclear-powered heliopters prepared specifically for this purpose by G'BroagFran and some Xists over a period of 10 billion[10] light-eons. (A light-eon is 180,000 times longer than an eon.) The Giant White Matter Dick will then be aimed directly into the Giant Black Energy Vagina, and then, 10 billion years or so later, depending on how "hard to get" the Giant Vagina plays it: **PENETRATION.** *The UNIVERSAL FUCK* will occur, in which *all opposites* shall *meet:* Black and White, yin and yang, male and female, energy and matter: All shall meet and FUCK one another! What pleasure! What bliss—and we shall *all* be *in on it.* ("You mean Jones will be in on it too?" inquired Smith petulantly. "Then I can't do it! Hell no, I ain't no damn queer!") Each "stroke" shall take 10 billion years times X (X representing the highest number that can be named, plus one), finally culminating in: **Hungh! The Big Squirt!** For "Hungh" is the primal sound of *the squirtin' universe!* Oh, yeah, the sweetness-and-light-crap people'll probably try to tell you that the primal sound of the universe is "Om." And the primal sound of the laid-back, mellowed-out Loveburger universe probably *is* "Om." But the primal sound of the old-time, black-eyed-pea eatin', Bible-thumpin' *Squirtin'* Universe is *"Hungh"!* Remember that *FINAL* Squirt we were talking about earlier, the damn, shit-yeah, hell-yeah, fuck-yeah, stick-it-*all*-the-way-down-uh-huh-uh-huh-uh-unhhhhhhhh-hhhhhhhhhhhhhh (well, maybe) hhhhhhhhhhhhhhhhhhhhhh wham-bam, thank-*ME*-ma'am, hhhhhhh haha haha hahahahahaha eeeeeee eeeeee eee eeee eeeeyyyaaaaaaaaaaa aaa aaaaaaiiiiiiiiiiiii eeeeeee-eeeeeeeee yyyyyyyyaaaaaaaa aaaaaaaggggggssssssshhhhhhh hhhhh-hhh

hhhh-all-of-Charlie's-Angels-at-the-same-time-mmmmmmmmmmm-mmmmmm mmmmmm uuuuuuuuyyyyy yyyyy aaaaaaaaaa aaaasdft-ghnjk, Burt-Reynolds-squared fdbfjlkfgd just-like-everyone-in-*town's*-been-dreaming-about, **BIG SQUIRT**.

You know what I mean?

You can *have* your damn enlightenment! I just want the damn **BIG SQUIRT!** Shit-hell, they don't call us the damn Arkansas home-wreckers, heartbreakers and pill-takers for nothing! **THE BIG SQUIRT,** the universal simo-gasm, will go on for 10 billion Sacred Bleeding Head Lives (a Sacred Head Life is approximately 10 billion times longer than the age of the universe thus far), longer than anything Masters and Johnson have been able to achieve. Finally, the simo-gasm will subside. **A NEW Universe** will have been conceived. This new universe will be filled with perfect transcendental love and all races shall be integrated, you *will* be able to find a seat on the subway, and kids will *no longer* stick chewing gum on the bottoms of desks. The human being will no longer exist, the car-wash attendant will be the dominant life form. The Doktors for "Bob" will exist, but no longer in bodily form, only as guiding energy forces. Then we'll try to release a hit single and make some money.

WE INTERRUPT THIS ARTICLE. THIS IS THE VOICE OF GOD. I HAVE TEMPORARILY TAKEN OVER THE BODY OF THIS MORTAL. HIS WRITING CAUGHT MY NOTICE. DO NOT READ THIS: HE IS A MADMAN. IF SEEN WALKING THE STREETS, HE SHOULD BE TURNED OVER TO YOUR LOCAL

AUTHORITIES IMMEDIATELY. DESIST READING THIS BOOK NOW. END TRANSMISSION.

So anyway, like I was saying, sure we have become as Gods, but where are the groupies? So we'll release a hit single, wait a minute, what's that writing up above this paragraph? I didn't write that! I just blacked out for a second and—wait a minute, let me read this. What? He claims to be *God*? Whatever obscure deity that just took over my body is obviously some kind of Satanic, Trevinoist force whose goal is to mislead you. Yes, *you! You're* the only one reading this! Haven't you *noticed* that no one besides you has seen this article? "Oh, that's only because the new issue of *Three-Fisted Tales* just came out," your mind quickly rationalizes. No, it's because it's printed with a special type of ink which only your astrological body can see! Because your phone number, multiplied by the base of the pyramids, minus your weight, plus the area of the Devil's Triangle, subtracted from the age of the universe = 666, not only that but—wait a minute, I'll tell you more in a minute, right now I have to use the bathroom.

The Time of PeE is here already; **Behold,** the mighty **Time of Squirt** approacheth! Drs. for "Bob" is total insanity, thus the only true *sanity.* Like a giant Fleet enema up the ass of a constipated America, the Doktorbands struggle onward. **Repent!** *Fuck it!* **Squirt! Send your money** to the Church and Drs. for "Bob"! It is held in escrow by our interplanetary guardians and **you WILL BE SAVED.**

"BOB" AND THE OXYGEN WARS

The SubGenius boasts about Time Control always sound like a bunch of tall tales, until you get a firsthand taste of the High Volt Age. One of "Bob's" Friends from the Future just clued me in, partway at least, and my scrambled synapses still haven't settled. How do I apply some of these crazy new ideas in time to help prevent or at least personally survive you-know-what?

Sometimes it seems like your luck has to balance out somehow, where you have to undergo a total bummer to set you up for something great you'd never have run into otherwise.

I was hoping this would be one of those times. A blown head gasket on an empty desert highway should be worth some sort of break to even things out, preferably before the sun melted me into the asphalt.

But so far all I was getting was a new and deeper appreciation of the word *barren*. Even the occasional scragglebush looked like it really resented being here, and wasn't about to put any more than the bare minimum of survival effort into it.

So much for shortcuts. I'd been walking for three hours and had seen only one car. The expressions glimpsed on the flyby were of dull surprise that anyone would even try to hitch a ride in this time and place— a feeling I could appreciate.

It was getting rather obvious that years of city life had left me in pitiful shape. Only a few hours out in a hot but otherwise ordinary American desert and I was nearly wiped out already.

This was no longer just a matter of missing a long-shot job interview that might have helped me postpone lifting anything heavier than a paintbrush a little while longer. It was starting to look like all my stubborn resistance to changing times had caught up with me. When their basic survival necessities get threatened, most folks' interest in "art" evaporates quicker than piss on a desert bush, which got the unpleasant surprise of discovering that it could get even more resentful than it already was.

Shortly after that so did I. My crude pack of stuff salvaged from the car got its fill of bouncing and bellyaching, split open and scattered feeble expressions of American "culture" across the gravel. How appropriate. The phrase "World Without Slack" kept taking on new and more exasperating significance.

While I was crouching there, telling various inanimate objects how stupid they were and patching the pack by tying my shirt around it, all my arm and neck hairs suddenly stood up.

I turned around, and there was the smoothest-looking sports car I've ever seen, standing with the passenger door open. Instant floods of relief struggled with major danger signals for control of my legs. There was no way I could have missed seeing that car miles ahead of its arrival. I'd been looking back a lot oftener than any logical expectations could justify. And even with all the smog that's crept into the desert basins, visibility was still at least twenty miles, on a road going straight over the horizon.

The desperate craving for shade won out. Dehydration makes me capable of superhuman rationalizations. The car was actually the same shimmery color as the road, and might have been mistaken for part of the constant mirage. The motor was too quiet to be heard over the mild desert winds—which, rather than cooling me off, tended to produce a slight blowtorch effect.

And anyway, how could something so beautiful be dangerous? Its curve was completely different yet thoroughly appropriate. The interior was a deep moss green, and a cool ocean breeze seemed to be flowing from inside it. This car was definitely not made in Detroit.

As I stepped up to the open door I could see that the kid at the wheel looked harmless enough—scrawny, and unarmed unless his swimming trunks had a secret compartment, or the car itself was one big weapon. I collapsed into the strange green upholstery and pulled the door shut. The sound reminded me slightly of a submarine hatch closing.

"Thanks," I rasped. "That was getting embarrassing."

The kid just smiled and floored it. We went from zero to about one-ten in seven seconds, with no gear changes that I could detect. The bucket seat yielded in all the right places, but I immediately discovered there were no seat belts. And all I could figure was that he must have some really ultimate soundproofing, because I could hardly hear any engine noise. There was just sort of a deep muffled pounding whoosh, like a distant waterfall.

"What kind of car is this?"

"You sound awful. Here, soak those vocal cords before you break something. Unless you're trying for a New Sound, maybe."

I seized the water jug, closed my eyes and swallowed until I had to stop for air. Then I sat there gasping and trying to identify some of the extra stuff in the car's instrument cluster. What little I thought I could recognize made no sense at all, so I looked at the driver instead.

He didn't seem to make sense either. For one thing, he was soaked, not from sweat but as if he'd just been swimming five minutes ago. He looked quite cool and comfortable, and smelled like seawater—of which the nearest had to be a couple hundred miles away.

Also, he didn't entirely look like a kid, up close. The face was maybe nineteen, but the eyes seemed much too confident and experienced. Though he looked thin, the muscle definition was unusually sharp. And his hands and feet looked like they'd seen at least thirty years of heavy work, and were up for plenty more whenever.

I acted mildly unastounded by our speed and silence and took another shot at conversation. "You're probably wondering how I came to be stuck out here."

"Not really."

Normally I'd expect to be annoyed at such indifference to human suffering, especially mine, but he was so matter-of-fact about it.

He added, "One dead car, three hours cold, and one overheated hitch-hiker two hours' walk past it. Nothing else around for miles. Fairly short list of possible explanations, eh?"

In these irritating times that sort of statement might be considered as a mild put-down, especially from a strange and evidently well-financed teenager. But here it came across perfectly straightforward.

I credited my extra tolerance to the relief of getting out from under the sun, and to the water's invigorating aftertaste.

"What's in this stuff?"

"A few trace minerals, some North Pole magnetism and extra oxygen."

My stomach started feeling rather odd. "How do you get magnetism into water?"

"Put the north face of a large, flat magnet against it for a while. Makes it more able to hold things in solution. Don't use the south face unless the water's for plants."

"Uh, just how much stuff is in solution here?"

"Very little. It's mostly to help it dissolve and carry out unnecessary stuff from whoever's drinking it."

I had to admit that sounded like a good idea. Depending of course on who was defining "unnecessary," and for what.

He took a giant swallow off the jug so I let it slide, then remembered something else. "How could you tell my car was three hours cold?"

"Infrared. Comes in handy when you drive at night a lot."

I was trying hard not to goggle at the instrument panel, but it was rather spooky. There were pressure and temperature gauges: internal, external and somewhere else. There were high-voltage dials, gas-mixture indicators, gauges for magnetic and gravitational field intensities, a ship's floating compass, little radar and sonar screens, dials I couldn't identify at all, and some sort of range finder.

But there was no fuel gauge anywhere. Also, the speedometer had no numbers on it, just colors, and the needle was shockingly low on the dial. Unless it read backwards, it was meant to be able to register speeds many times higher than what we were doing. If that wasn't weird enough, there was an altimeter, next to a depth gauge.

Looking at all this stuff, I didn't know whether to laugh or try to escape. A lot of it appeared to have been salvaged from other vehicles. Most of the controls were touch-sensitive patches behind the same clear shield that covered all the gauges. What should have been a gearshift obviously wasn't, since he hadn't touched it yet. There were extra knobs branching off it, and what looked like backhoe levers beside it. There were also several small video screens, all empty.

Seen against all this, the faded "Bob" sticker on the glove compartment was rather reassuring. I'd met lots of SubGeniuses, and while most were pretty peculiar, none seemed to be actually dangerous to me so far.

Just over the windscreen was a full-length detailed chart of the electromagnetic spectrum, with tiny indicator lights along the whole thing, including an extra upper section I'd never seen. Strangest of all, sprouting from among the gauges were nine different clock faces with little dagger-shaped joysticks poking out of them.

My stomach suddenly felt very peculiar, and I involuntarily shook like a wet dog for an instant, then let out a tremendous belch. Just as suddenly I felt all right, better than I had all day.

"What the heck was that?"

"You just clobbered the anaerobic germs in your stomach, and also boosted your oxygen saturation a bit."

"Huh?"

"You have a severe oxygen deficiency, like most people in this time period. Due to pollution and deforestation, right now your atmospheric oxygen levels are at an all-time low, so the oxygen pressure in your blood is insufficient to guard you against oxygen-hating microbes. You become slightly stagnant, and serve as a growth medium for anaerobic parasites. But all pathogens are inherently much weaker than your own cells, which are a lot more highly evolved than viruses, bacteria, fungus and such. So you can always get rid of them by just raising your internal oxygen concentration above what they can stand."

I was still working on the first part. "I've heard of all kinds of nutrient deficiencies, but oxygen?"

"Your body's supposed to be at least eighty percent water, which is eight ninths oxygen."

"Wait a minute, water is two hydrogens for each oxygen, right?" I was not exactly a chemistry whiz.

"Yeah, but the oxygen atom is sixteen times bigger, remember?" I hadn't. "You're supposed to be composed of over two thirds oxygen, twice as much as everything else in you combined. The bigger a proportion of something in a formula, the more margin there is in the high to low range of how much you can put in and still make that formula work. That also applies to the formula for an organism.

"So you can see how a person could exist anywhere along a wide range of oxygen saturation that can support his cells, though the lower levels are not much fun. But people can still function, more or less, even at oxygen percentages so low that anaerobic microbes can inhabit them quite comfortably."

"Well, how can you tell if your oxygen level is high enough?"

"If you get sick, it isn't."

"But everyone gets sick sometimes."

"Everyone you know about. You're all oxygen-starved, that's all."

I considered this while watching the desert race by. I was strangely reluctant to ask how we managed to hurtle over this beat-up old highway without feeling any real bumps or vibrations. Instead I asked, "Well, doesn't the encyclopedia still say oxygen makes up twenty-one percent of our atmosphere?"

"Have you measured it yourself lately? They haven't. They just keep printing the same figures from earlier editions."

"So what level is it at?"

"Depends where you measure it. In a healthy rain forest it can still get up over twenty percent. But most large cities have very few trees and lots of carbon monoxide, which, being electrically unstable, gobbles up free oxygen like crazy, to become carbon dioxide, which is more stable. In those cities it gets down to twelve percent or less at times. In Eastern Europe, with the whole Western world's pollution blowing at them, even wooded areas can drop below fifteen percent. Entire forests are dying there. For humans, suffocation occurs at around seven percent."

"You mean the cities are already more than halfway to suffocating?"

"Right. What do you think causes early heart attacks, crib deaths and crashed immune systems? Very little of that happening in mountain villages. A mammal's immune system uses lots of single-atom oxygen in knocking off germs, and carries it around in H_2O_2. That's because singlet oxygen itself is so reactive it only stays loose for maybe a millionth of a second before oxidizing the nearest appropriate molecule. You should be internally producing and using several quarts of H_2O_2 every day, but you can't if there's not enough oxygen available from your air."

A little of this was coming back now. "H_2O_2? You mean hydrogen peroxide?"

"Yeah, oxygen water. The tiny amount in what you drank oxidized the pathogens in your stomach."

"That stuff they sell in brown bottles?" Yucko.

"No, the pure food-grade kind, thirty-five percent, which can hurt you if you don't dilute it enough. Lots of health-food stores carry it now. The drugstore variety has chemical stabilizers in it. Okay to put a little on a wound, but not much else."

"Stabilizers?"

"Supposedly to keep the oxygen from escaping, but it's really more stable than they let on. Mainly it's so no one will use enough of it all at once to get rid of a major disease that should've netted some hospital at least twenty grand."

"What? Which diseases can you get rid of with it?"

"All of them. But oxygen water is too simple and cheap to draw any commercial interest. Unpatentable."

"What do you mean, all of them?"

"Like I said, all disease organisms prefer much lower oxygen saturations than what your cells function best at. Their primitive, fragile membranes break down at concentrations a healthy human cell merely finds invigorating. You need it constantly; oxygen's the only thing you can die in minutes without. Get enough and it protects you from disease."

"What about cancer?"

"Especially cancer. It's anaerobic; high oxygen levels kill it pretty fast. Otto Warburg won a Nobel Prize back in the 1930s for pointing that out, but your medical establishment has ignored the principle since then. Too unprofitable. Cancer cells get energy from glucose by fermentation instead of by oxidizing it like normal cells. This wastes so much energy that the healthy cells can't get enough to function and the cancer squeezes them out, unless you intervene by raising the oxygen level one way or another."

I thought of a couple of friends who should be hearing this. My growing exhilaration wasn't just from watching the now-painless desert zooming past. "Why isn't this all written up somewhere?"

"It is, it's just unpublicized. Hundreds of physicians have independently reported curing all kinds of supposedly incurable diseases by raising the patient's oxygen saturation, whether with intravenous H_2O_2, ozone blood infusions, taheebo or hyperbaric oxygen tanks, all of which simply raise the level of H_2O_2 in the blood. But the way of modern science is to disregard any facts that don't fit the accepted lucrative theory. And disease is a multibillion-dollar industry, in case you hadn't noticed."

"For someone so young, you are well informed but awfully cynical."

He chuckled lightly. "Just how old do you think I am?"

I was spared the embarrassment of guessing completely wrong by a small interruption. A kamikaze jackrabbit apparently decided we were its ticket out of this desert and maybe out of rabbithood, and scooted right in front of us. The kid's hand twisted part of the steering wheel like a motorcycle throttle, and the whole car smoothly lifted a couple of feet then dropped back to the road. I turned and glimpsed a surprisingly complicated expression on the receding rabbit.

"Would you mind telling me where this car was made?"

"Detroit, mostly."

"Uh, Detroit in Michigan?"

"Where else?"

I really wasn't holding up my end of the discussion very well. But I was still determined to at least be too cool to ask why he was dripping wet in an air-conditioned car ninety miles from any water.

That was another thing I realized just then: The air conditioning was supreme. Instead of the usual dry, synthetic-tasting car air, this air was cool, moist, and invigorating, like the air near a waterfall. The roasted landscape whizzing by, and the relentless sun beating down all around, might as well have been on a movie screen for all the effect they had on us.

I tried a different approach. "Is your air conditioner a custom job as well?"

"Actually it's fairly standard at this car's point of origin. Nice, eh? The extra moisture, oxygen and negative ions make it pretty close to the optimum breathing mix for humans."

I spotted the inside air-mix gauge. "Thirty percent oxygen? Isn't that supposed to be twenty-one?"

"Just because it was twenty-one when the encyclopedias first came out doesn't mean that's optimum. Desertification of Earth has been going on a long time, though the current rate is unprecedented. Remember hearing about those scientists who measured the air mix in bubbles trapped in fossilized amber? It tested out around this high. Those samples were trapped about the time the mammals took over. Not much tree-cutting or gas-burning going on back then, and the plant-animal ratio was ideal. Under those conditions eventually humans appeared, designed to operate at that oxygen percentage."

"So it's dropped by a third since then?"

"It's had lots of help. Currently the manufacture and operation of your machinery consumes eighteen times the oxygen you use up through breathing. That's the equivalent of another ninety billion people standing around sharing your air, all so someone can keep selling oil and cars and such. Talk about wasteful, it works out that driving twenty thousand miles uses up as much oxygen as breathing for two years."

"Folks do have a right to travel, though."

"Absolutely, but there are much cleaner, cheaper and safer methods, ready and waiting, still as effective as back when they were invented and neglected. Same with oxygen as a healing principle. It's an ancient concept, appearing in various forms throughout history, but you all need it now more than ever. It stands to reason that if your body contains over three times the percentage of oxygen that's in the air, it has to work a lot harder at concentrating whatever it extracts through breathing when the atmospheric oxygen level drops. So supplementing it with oxywater or other high-oxygen substances becomes the most logical short-term solution."

"How about long-term?"

"Re-establish a healthy global oxygen production-consumption balance, if you're up to the task. It can be done, though the situation may need to get even worse before enough folks get their priorities straight. Like a lot of things, oxygen is taken for granted, but since it is so reactive, free oxygen has to constantly be replenished or it all gets bound up in other compounds. Keep trashing your forests and your oceans' phytoplankton, and you'll all be gasping long before X-Day."

"Oh yeah, when's that again?"

"Soon enough that you'd better get cracking. It'll be hard enough as it is, trying to mobilize a bunch of oxygen-starved Normals, and the longer you wait the more sick and tired and useless they'll become."

I had a sudden flash. "Is this why people were supposedly stronger and lived longer in early Biblical times?"

"Precisely. Though by then there was already some atmospheric damage from earlier civilizations."

"What, like Atlantis?"

"Among others. Many civilizations go through a brief deforestation and fossil-fuel-burning stage, but this one has been artificially retarded and kept there for over a century."

"By whom?"

"When you find the answer to that question, you will then know what to do about it."

"Some reason you can't just tell me?"

"At this point you'd never believe it, and that would interfere with your grasping certain other necessary facts first."

I made a disrespectful noise. "You sound just like my old college professor, Mr. McSploont."

"How clever of him. What'd he teach?"

"Disregard for college professors, mostly. I expect he eventually melted down in the white heat of his own brilliance."

He smiled a knowing smile that wasn't smug or irritating, but rather a bit frightening, hinting at vast hard-won experience.

"So besides being physically less healthy overall, noticed anything else wrong with city folks?" he asked quietly.

"You name it, they've screwed it up. Basically most of them just act unbelievably lame, and tolerate the most absurd stuff you can imagine.

There's some exceptions, but I mean, like, have you switched on a TV set lately?"

He casually touched part of the spectrum chart overhead. One screen lit up with a retina-wrenching ten-second montage of about ninety different TV channels, then he switched it off. "Yup, pretty pitiful."

I was staring at the blank screen. "Uh, well, yeah, there you are."

"So what do you reckon makes them act like that?"

"Beats me." It was reassuring to refer to "them" as if I had rarely lived in a city. "It's like they're all brain-damaged. Which is a real drag, considering that's where all the governments are located . . . hey, wait a minute."

He grinned. "Exactly. What happens to a brain that gets oxygen-starved?"

Mine seemed to be slipping gears a bit. "It goes to that big scrap bucket in the sky, eventually. But continuous gradual oxygen starvation, over a period of years . . ." I had to admit this could explain an awful lot of modern human behavior. "Earlier you implied all this was somehow deliberate. Does someone actually want people brain-damaged and stupid?"

"Did you attend a public school? Do you follow the so-called news? Have you browsed through a pharmacy recently?"

"Well, okay, but aren't most of the guys behind all that living right there in the cities too?"

"The most powerful ones all have their own remote strongholds, and can afford to have many others fronting for them. A good rule of thumb is, if someone's in the news, that person's not actually running things. And hired help are seldom in on the big picture, or the true purpose of their assigned tasks."

We reached the crest of a long, low rise and started down the other side. There was a slight bend ahead, with another road feeding in from the south, all of which seemed a lot more interesting than it really was, due to following so many miles of straightness. At the very edge of visibility it looked like there was a little town. It struck me that I had one hell of a lot of unasked questions still, and for all I knew this could be his destination coming up.

I took a wild guess. "Since you're not a big fan of air pollution, I assume this car is electrical, somehow."

"You could say that. It has more than one system, but the motor we're using at the moment is a variation on the Noble Gas Plasma Engine invented by Joseph Papp in the early seventies. Of course, since it's cheap and fuelless it was never allowed to be commercially developed."

"Of course. How does it manage to be fuelless with gas plasma?"

"Noble gases. They're inert; with their outer electron shells already full, they've got no incentive to hook up with other atoms. So they aren't being burned or broken down, just induced to expand repeatedly. Put a certain mix of noble gases in a sealed cylinder with a piston, spark it and pulse a magnetic field around it, and the gases repel each other quite fiercely for an instant, then collapse back to their previous state, to be sparked again. The energy delivered by the piston's displacement greatly exceeds that required to spark the gases, providing a net excess from a self-powering system."

"Are you saying this thing is a perpetual motion machine?"

"We're living on the surface of a great big perpetual motion machine and composed of godzillions of little tiny ones, so shouldn't they be able to exist on our scale as well?"

"Well, those things'll all wind down eventually, right?"

"They'll run long enough for whatever you plan on doing with them. Anyhow, this design is somewhat less than perpetual; every hundred thousand miles or so the gases lose their elasticity and need to be replaced."

"Sounds pretty tough."

"Sure beats making your whole lower atmosphere taste like a monoxide suicide's garage."

"Couldn't we retrofit existing car engines to run off this?"

"Simpler to start from scratch, but maybe. Seal off the valves, throw away the carburetor, fuel lines, exhaust manifold and so forth, evacuate the cylinders and let in the inert gas mix. It'd become two-stroke, since there's nothing for it to suck in or exhaust."

"So this gas is some combination of helium, neon, argon, krypton and xenon?" I was amazed I could still remember their names. "I suppose the exact mixture is privileged information."

"Technically, but it's locatable. The inventor's still alive, last we heard, but understandably rather frustrated. It's always disillusioning to work out a practical solution for some major problem, only to find out there's someone profiting hugely by keeping the problem just the way it is."

For some reason I didn't resist this notion as much as I usually would, even though it implied my having to eventually help do something about it. But at the moment what I really wanted was details. "Where could I find diagrams and such? I'm no engineer but I know a couple. While we're at it, how's that gearless transmission work? And what was that hopping trick? I'm assuming you'd like others to pick up on these inventions."

"Naturally. The drive gear consists of long cones pointing in opposite directions, with a heavy triangular belt that slides along them, giving a smoothly variable ratio between their cross sections. Again, it's not a new idea, but it had anti-commercial potential, being much too efficient and durable, so no way was any major automaker going to retool for that."

"I'd think the first to do it would make a fortune. Who wouldn't want one?"

"You're kidding, right? At first, sure they would, but then that'd be the end of selling replacement transmissions, and cost billions in lost engine sales and repairs, from the greatly reduced wear. Plus billions more in lowered gasoline consumption, due to improved efficiency. As for the rest of it, remind me to give you a few patent numbers and such before you get off."

It occurred to me that during all this I still hadn't asked how far he was going. Wherever it was, we'd be arriving a lot sooner than expected.

There was a billboard, of all things, about four miles ahead of us. Mr. Science touched something under one of the video screens and it gave us a zoom picture of the road ahead. He reached up and pushed a spot just below the visible-light band on the spectrum chart, and a little car-shaped pink spot with a bright center appeared on the screen at the bottom of the billboard.

"Nice of 'em to build that feller some shade. Though I doubt he's been there long."

"Well, don't you think you should slow down a bit?"

He shook his head. "My, aren't you well-conditioned. Don't sweat it; this car's not under any local jurisdictions."

While I considered my response, trying to choose between sounding real law-abiding and getting some clarification, we zipped past the billboard. He touched a spot on the radio portion of the spectrum, just as a very dusty police car lurched out after us in a cloud of gravel.

"Got a live one, Charlie," buzzed a small speaker in the dash. "No plates, too fast to get the make. At least one-twenty."

"Want me to come on out?" A fainter voice, younger.

"May need you for a roadblock, so stand by. Let's see if this new engine is as good as Clyde says."

We were already nearly a mile past him but now we could hear a faint siren, slowly getting louder. We slowed down slightly, a move which sort of seemed at cross-purposes with rocketing past a sheriff in the first place. My ever-unpredictable benefactor hit a button under the speaker and said, "Are you attempting to get my attention, officer?"

There was a brief spluttering noise, then a few clenched words. "Smart boy, huh? Pull your fancy self over, before I get irritated."

"That shouldn't be necessary. I can easily answer your questions in this manner, without being late for my destination."

"You think this is open for discussion? Identify yourself."

"Changesmith. Or CS, whichever. Who's this?"

"Officer Harry Scrotum. You have about five seconds to pull off of my highway."

"I see," said CS sympathetically. "What seems to be the trouble?"

"Are you nuts? Reckless endangerment, doing twice the limit, unauthorized use of police bands, no plates; hell, I expect your fine'll buy us a whole new station. You're even hauling drugs for all I know."

CS smiled questioningly at me and I shook my head. "Nope," he said. "And no one uses them where I'm from."

"Drugs?"

"License plates."

There was a strained silence. He evidently was not up for pursuing the implications of that. We were now less than a quarter mile ahead of the sheriff's car, which was still creeping closer, apparently at its top speed.

Changesmith added helpfully, "If our velocity is causing concern, be reassured that this vehicle is crash-proof and does not threaten the safety of local traffic, should there happen to be any."

There was a heavy sigh. "Charlie, get that block up, now. Don't use any working vehicles; drag over some clunkers from Philo's lot.

"And as for you, snakebrain, consider yourself warned. This is your last chance to pull over in one piece."

"Sorry to disturb your programming, but it's a mistake to assume that everything that moves through your area is subject to your rules and limitations."

"That's it, pal, your death wish is granted."

A sudden shimmy from the left hind wheel was followed by the faint sound of two gunshots. Changesmith touched a panel on the dash and a small sign lit up that said GUNJAMMER, then he accelerated us a bit. The shimmy grew more pronounced, then there was a loud clank and it stopped entirely.

No flat tire, and no more gunfire that I could hear. I looked back to see a pistol being violently shaken out the cop's window, accompanied by some general-purpose curses coming over the speaker.

CS said, "Sorry, but we couldn't chance a ricochet hitting someone in your town up ahead," and switched off the speaker.

"What'd you do?" I asked.

"Ever hear of a subject known as sonochemistry? Production of chemical changes with sound waves? This is related; we're broadcasting a simulation of the wave pattern that occurs when water blocks the oxidizing spaces in gunpowder. Since matter is junior to energy, many effects can be induced on the physical level simply by emitting the kinds of vibrations which accompany and direct them."

"Now that I like. How wide an area is affected?"

"The range varies with the power and circuit design. At the moment, no one can shoot anybody within about twelve miles of us."

"Well, all right! Does it interfere at all with organic oxidation?"

"Good question, but no; cellular processes are all much less explosive. Different frequencies altogether."

"Couldn't someone just mass-produce these things, hide them all over the world, and stop wars and murders once and for all?"

"With enough time and materials, yes. Appealing idea, isn't it? Like taking matches away from children."

I thought about it. "On the other hand, I suppose the more extreme gun lovers would all come after you with crossbows, until it sunk in that now they'd be protected as well. You'd have to be pretty discreet."

He zoomed the picture on the screen a bit more, and the rusty town became quite visible, complete with roadblock. The crew that was pushing it together seemed to be engaged in a lively argument with some old desert rat over one of the cars they'd included.

CS chuckled and switched the speaker back on. "How's your engine holding up?"

"Oh, so you're back, eh? I see we can add Giving False Names to the list of charges."

"Not at all. That is indeed my usual designation."

"You mean you don't even have a license, on top of everything else?"

Apparently neither of them considered it tasteful to mention the brief shooting incident. "Did you punch it in under Change or Smith?"

The speaker was silent for a moment, then Harry came on again, his voice containing a curious blend of triumph, respect, bravado and near-panic. "Let me guess. That thing you're driving is some sort of a stolen Pentagon experiment, right?"

"If so it'd be the most intelligent expenditure they ever made. But no, it was assembled entirely by unarmed forces."

"Well, either way, it might interest you to know that this here computer advises capturing and/or killing you with extremely hasty prejudice, in the urgent interests of national security."

"How thoughtful of it. You'd be awfully disappointed to learn exactly whose interests are now considered to be a matter of national security."

"Do I sound like the kind of character who goes around second-guessing the government? Look, it doesn't matter to me if you crash and burn at the roadblock, or among the boulders and ravines around the town, in case you were figuring on leaving the road. But since we'll miss out on your nice big fine, tell me something first: I know I saw the second shot hit your tire, so what's the deal? Tire armor or something?"

"Actually, why aren't we leaving the road?" I asked softly. "Is that trick only good for little hops?"

"He'd have to try and follow us, and I don't want to be responsible for him racking up his car and possibly himself." He added in a louder voice, "The tire's full of a type of semisolid high-pressure sorbothane foam, which hardens to a tough elastic crust on contact with air. Anything causing a puncture gets forced out through the surface by the internal pressure and centrifugal force, then the opening seals itself. Makes a flat tire impossible." He sounded awfully calm, for someone who was closing in at high speed on a barrier of old cars, and wanted by federal agents besides.

There was another brief silence. The screen was reducing its zoom as we neared the town, holding the image at a constant size. It showed the roadblock crew and a few dozen spectators scrambling back from the impending impact zone, everyone but the old-timer who appeared to be trying to start one of the cars.

Harry spoke up again. "If that's true, how come I never heard of that stuff before?"

"Ask the chief executives of your tire companies. It's in their files."

Right when I was sure this couldn't get any more complicated, another small speaker spoke up, with a completely different voice. "CS, there's some action about sixty leagues north of you."

"How bad?"

"Just heating up, max it but stay low."

"No kidding."

"And watch for monitors."

"Whose?"

"Anyone's."

"Okay, Xandy."

By now I was just about ready for what happened next. He pulled back hard on the wheel and the steering column stretched toward him. The road, roadblock, desert and town suddenly dropped away under us and shrank with its collective jaw hanging open. I looked down and back at all the little upturned astounded faces and laughed like an idiot, despite the fact that my gonads were trying to crawl behind each other.

The engine's faint whooshing sound didn't get much louder, but now it had a kind of underwater ringing quality.

"Real professional," remarked the speaker. "Maybe you could hold a seminar on how to keep a low profile, when you get back."

"Oh, hush. They'll probably be too embarrassed to even report it."

"You think anyone can run a check on your name without triggering a follow-up inquiry as to why?"

"Fret not; he can't tell them anything they don't already know, and by the time they respond we'll be extremely elsewhere."

As we tilted north and leveled out at less than a thousand feet, I wondered why I wasn't more disturbed at being, for all practical purposes, kidnapped by a UFO. Getting nowhere with that, I started wondering why I wasn't being flattened into the seat by our steep ascent, unable to turn my head like this without extreme and possibly terminal discomfort. Some sort of high-tech shenanigans were keeping my weight from being affected by these abrupt speed and direction changes.

"So, you can even get away with breaking the laws of inertia?"

"Not exactly, but there are conditions under which they don't apply. Those equations only described mechanical interactions at the low electrical intensities familiar at that time. At high enough voltages a local electrogravitational field can override the surrounding gravity well, and suspend inertia within the field."

I recalled my arm-hair reaction when the car first got near me. "How high a voltage?"

"Millions, but the current is so low it's practically a static charge. You also need to know what frequency to pulsate it, among other things."

The speaker switched itself on again, a different voice with more background hiss. "Try and stick to the information already available there and then."

CS ignored my startled look. "All this can easily be dug up through the scientific underground here. Like, the Biefield-Brown effect is already sixty years old, and it's been written up all over the place."

"I've never heard of it," I said, in a tone intended to encourage generosity with details.

He looked straight into my right eye. "Do you ever seek out information through any sources which are not approved and controlled by some tentacle of the Conspiracy?"

I squirmed a little. "Probably not. It's all just so . . . available."

"So even though you know they're a pack of liars, you still get all your news from their broadcasts and publications?"

"All right, so where do I find out who's got the real scoop?"

"Depends on what you want to know and if you really want to know it. But one way is, the most honest sources seldom seem to have much money, or charge much for their reports. Nor do they tend to get much coverage in any media owned by anyone with economic interests that could be harmed by such information getting out."

"Could you please just tell me how we manage to fly with no wings, propellers or jets?"

"Have you ever noticed what happens when you hang a charged condenser on a thread or a balance beam?"

"Can't say as I have. You mean a capacitor, right? An insulator between two conductive surfaces for storing charge?"

"Same difference. It can be any shape as long as its poles are at opposite ends, and it holds a substantial charge. Try it and you'll see it try to move in the direction of its positive pole. Hang it on a scale with the positive pole up and it'll get lighter. Shape the charged surfaces properly, put a huge positive charge on the leading edge, pulsed at a high enough frequency, and you can make that sucker fly."

"Let me get this straight. Right now the hull of this thing is carrying umpteen million volts, and we are sitting inside of a humongous capacitor? Why aren't we electrocuted, or did I just miss it in all the excitement?"

"The frequency's too high to bother our cells, and we're insulated from it anyhow. See, the condenser is the linking device between electricity and gravity, like the coil is between electricity and magnetism.

"We're riding on a temporary artificial gravity hump, sliding down it continuously like a surfboard on a wave, and carrying it along with us. In different terms, we're putting electrical stress on the local fabric of space, which tries to correct or balance it out by drawing us forward into the slight relative vacuum we're creating in the space-juice ahead of us. This here's the simplest version of the most widely used transportation method in this arm of the galaxy."

"Watch it," from the speaker again.

"What is this?" I yelped. "You got someone monitoring us?"

"Yeah, we always leave the line open. If anything happens they can learn a lot from the final transmission."

"WHAT??"

"Oh, relax, would you? Here, put some of this on your arms and legs, while you're sitting there gawking." He offered me a clear plastic squeeze bottle of what looked like water.

"What is it?" I had a lot to gawk at, with the desert tearing by right under us. This guy was crossing jet speeds with hang-glider altitudes, and it tended to keep the adrenaline pumping quite briskly. "And what's the anything that might happen?"

"A lot less than you were subject to back where I found you, so settle down and enjoy the heightened sensory input. This is three percent oxywater; you can absorb it through your skin." He splashed some on his chest and rubbed it in, then handed me the bottle.

"What will it do?"

"Weren't you listening earlier? Try it and see."

I smeared a bit on my arm and it felt just like water, so I went ahead and did both my arms, my legs and my chest. It was actually rather soothing somehow.

While I was rubbing it in I suddenly remembered why we were up here. "What'd that mean earlier, some action up north?"

"We have to go put out a forest fire."

Now I was really amazed. "When did the forest service get this sort of funding?"

"Dream on. This is an independent action; all the regular fire fighters are already tied up at other zones closer to populated areas."

That much I could believe; I'd recently heard the fire season was in full swing out here. I started to hand back the bottle.

"Put a little on your neck and behind your ears; it'll get into your cranial blood more quickly."

I did so and smelled something rather pungent, then realized it was my own arm. I smelled the bottle and it was completely odorless, so I put my forearm up to my nose and sniffed, and it smelled like a locker room with smoke damage. "What gives?"

"H_2O_2 enhances membrane transport, among other things. Your pores just expelled most of their accumulated toxins to the surface of your skin. They were there in you all along, but now you can smell them. The oxygen goes in and the garbage comes out. Here, use this." He pulled a wet towel out from under his seat and gave it to me.

Parts of my skin were starting to itch slightly, so I vigorously rubbed everything off with the towel, while noticing that I felt more alert and clearheaded than a minute ago. It was subtle and totally undruglike, as if it were a notch closer to the way I was actually supposed to feel normally.

"Does that improve things?" he asked.

"Yes, actually, though I can't explain just how." I figured I'd better try to get a clearer picture of my exact situation here, without seeming too obvious. "So now I'm germ-free, simple as that?"

"Hardly. You are absolutely riddled with anaerobic opportunists. But they've gotten the message, the party's over."

Apparently even fewer things were under my control than I thought. "Are they likely to be upset?"

"You better believe it. And their death struggles can be most uncomfortable to be around. You just don't back down once the battle's joined, that's all."

"I suppose it's too late to re-establish a truce?"

He looked at me and was no longer smiling. "It's way past too late. Any truce with them is on their terms, and they know a lot more about you than you do about them. For them you are a walking food supply, among other things, but you have no idea what they really represent."

My spine literally tingled at that, but I said, "How can you attribute intelligent behavior to a bunch of bacteria and viruses?"

"Individually they aren't very bright, but neither are your cells. When vast numbers of them get together, that's another story. You've heard of colonial organisms like beehives and army ants?"

"But germs are so tiny."

"Lots of your cells aren't much bigger. But enough microorganisms all working together can collectively act as a much larger intelligent life-form, such as you presumably exemplify."

"Look, those disease microbes aren't even physically connected."

"Neither are army ants, but they still manage to stomp the daylights out of anything that gets in their way. Since they're genetically identical, their DNA coils all oscillate at exactly the same set of frequencies; being on the same wavelength gives them telepathic linkage."

"Well, maybe, but ants at least have some sort of rudimentary brains to be telepathic with; germs do not."

"Your individual cells have no brains as such, and they sure wouldn't last long on their own, but when enough of them team up, they're a critter to be reckoned with."

I started getting a weird flashback from something I occasionally experienced during my mushroom days. It involved becoming somehow slightly aware on the cellular level, and it contained a sense of high drama that always made me feel vaguely guilty. Here were all these fearless hordes of cells, putting everything they had into keeping this body going, working nonstop, every moment of their brief lives, all so I could . . . do what? I was never able to think of an activity I could engage in that would be truly worthy of all that selfless cellular effort, so I sheepishly buried the vision under more normal memories.

Now it was back, and I remembered something else about it, some additional vague presence I had never felt like examining closely, and always forgot about as quickly as possible. There was something else in there that wasn't part of me or my cells. It felt cold, silent, disinterested, and very, very old. Now for the first time I actually tried to wrap my wits around it, and I got the distinct impression it was not pleased with me.

But there was nothing in the way of a personality to relate to. It felt like a minor part of something much bigger, patiently engaged in some vast operation that spanned millions of years. Most disturbing of all was the definite feeling that this huge project was nearing completion.

"Did you find your answer?" Changesmith's quiet voice brought the "real world" back to center stage, while the microdrama faded. The landscape streaming past was a lot more jagged now, and had picked up a few Joshua trees.

"Answer?"

"Earlier you asked, in effect, who is really behind the Conspiracy. The question to consider is: Who ultimately benefits the most from the overall effects of the things the Conspiracy does, or forces others to do?"

"That's what's always been so maddening. I just can't figure someone being both brilliant enough to pull off all these amazing scams, and stupid enough not to be able to foresee the disastrous consequences. It makes no sense that they'd try so hard to gain control of the whole planet, just to destroy it in the process. Especially if, as you say, they know about and choose to suppress alternative technologies that could head off eco-disasters altogether."

"What does that leave?"

I looked at the increasingly rocky scenery and thought about it. My sense of urgency was heightened considerably by the way CS seemed to just barely avoid the taller granite formations rushing past us.

"I guess whoever they are, either they're as suicidally psychotic as they are diabolically clever, or they've arranged someplace else to go after they've trashed the Earth." I let out a deep sigh. "Or they aren't even human at all and they have some totally different set of priorities."

He smiled grimly. "Or some combination of all three. So, since we're assuming the Conspiracy is smart enough to be actually accomplishing its goals, and since the overall effect of all the Conspiracy's actions is to eventually ruin this planet's oxygen cover and render it uninhabitable for humans and other higher life-forms, apparently that must be one of their actual goals. Who might possibly desire such a thing?"

"Lower life-forms, right?" Something in me felt it might be true, and something else was fiercely denying it. "Are you saying that all the activities of modern civilization are ultimately aimed at serving the interests of a bunch of germs? The heads of the Conspiracy are actually microbes? Who's going to believe that?"

"All the most successful conspiracies have been so outlandish they were impossible for anyone to believe, until it was too late. And no, none of our truly civilized activities serve them, only our ecology-wrecking ones. The germs may be merely a physical extension of something bigger and uglier that exists mostly on a different plane, feeding on death-energy. And humans themselves are actually making most of the decisions, but they are unaware of the neurological influences of the anaerobic entities hiding among their cells."

"A gang of viruses has stolen our brains? Give me a break."

"That's what all this is for. Actually, there is ample precedent for a lower life-form temporarily seizing control of a higher one's nervous system for its own purposes."

"Can you give me a for instance?"

"Certainly. Viruses routinely take over their target cells' manufacturing processes, to create more viruses. On a slightly larger scale, the ant brainworm needs to complete its life cycle in a sheep's gut, which is hardly an ant's favorite hangout. Nonetheless, when the time comes, the worm induces its host to climb up to the tip of a blade of grass and wait to be grazed. Then there's the parasitic bee worm that eventually persuades its bee to go drown itself, just so the worm can reproduce in the water."

"Gack. Okay, but what about bigger creatures?"

"Well, the problem is, if an animal's actions are not in fact serving its own needs but those of some parasite, how does it tell the difference until after it's too late, if even then?"

"Good Lord." I had several really sickening thoughts, each worse than the one before it, so I mentioned one to sort of hold off any others. "Do all those beached whales somehow tie in with this?"

"Interesting possibility. You mean like something uses whales to get up on land with a giant food supply? That'd be a tough one to verify."

"Why's that?"

"If someone hung around a decaying whale long enough to detect any monster parasites slithering away from it, would you let him stand close enough to tell you about it?"

"Heh, not without a strong crossbreeze."

"Anyhow, who knows, with whales? Some of the beachings could be their equivalent of those monks who set themselves on fire in protest."

"Of what?"

"I'm sure you can think of a few things people are doing that the whales might not be particularly enjoying."

"Wouldn't they get their point across quicker by sinking a few factory ships?"

"Perhaps that would compromise their sense of ethics. Likewise, the monks could go around blowing up this and that, but choose to make a more lasting impression."

There was another disturbing notion demanding closer examination. "What really gets to me is the idea that a bunch of germs could be influencing us all to use ineffective methods of dealing with them. What if the entire modern medical industry was really designed to prolong and spread disease rather than conquer it?"

"You would probably see a proliferation of treatments intended to mask the symptoms of disease, while the basic causes continued unchecked. Like turning your car radio up so you don't have to hear your ailing engine's warning noises. Increasing numbers of people would keep on getting sicker, from an ever-growing list of diseases, as more and more money gets poured into drugs, surgery and other accepted medical practices."

"Basically just like it is now. What a mess."

"It's not as if all the doctors have sold out the human race or anything. They're under the same subtle microbial influences as everyone else, plus their very unsubtle medical indoctrinations under others similarly afflicted. And a lot of what they've managed to develop within the limitations of their accepted theories is quite clever. Especially for patching up accident victims; some of those procedures are absolutely brilliant. Unfortunately, that doesn't quite make up for the technological stupidities that cause the accidents which make such repairs necessary in the first place."

"Oh yeah, what were you saying about this thing being crash-proof?" This was not just idle curiosity; we were into the foothills now, wiggling along canyons at the same fiendish speed that had felt excessive even over an open desert.

"When it's switched on, the cushion field that wraps around this craft repels any solid objects away from it, like the repulsion between two identical magnetic poles but much stronger. The force increases with the object's proximity and speed of approach. Ground vehicles with such fields were tested in Detroit back in the 1950s, then buried so as to postpone having to cope with all the inevitable industrial upheavals. But it's utterly foolish to build high-speed vehicles without designing in some such feature to protect the occupants and whatever might get in their way, except where the chance of getting creamed is truly meant to be part of their game."

I could only take his word for it, but we seemed to be cutting awfully close to the digger pines now whizzing by under us. As we slipped over a ridgeback and dropped into the next canyon, I recognized a few Coulter pines with their giant cones.

"Pretty, aren't they?" CS pointed out two eagles, off to our left and downslope, leaving the area with dignity but wasting no time at it. Then they vanished behind us as we climbed again, up and over into the next valley, continuing our convoluted northern course.

"I have to admit my appreciation of the scenery is tainted somewhat with the constant feeling we are about to become part of it. I assume all this ground-hugging is to keep us from showing up on somebody's radar."

"That and for better appreciation of the land's organic detail." He lit up one screen with a transparent-looking relief map, oriented with our flight path. A tiny blue dot was creeping along one of the crinkly furrows, and I realized the map must be showing the whole southern range we were entering, a thousand square miles at least.

He reached up and poked the upper infrared part of the spectrum, and a small red patch appeared at the top of the map. "There it is."

"How will you put it out?"

"You'll see. It'll be quite picturesque." He was fiddling with parts of the radio-TV-radar section of the chart and frowning slightly at some of the indicator lights.

He tapped the mike under the smaller speaker. "Hey, is Arg back yet?"

"A few minutes ago," said a high-pitched voice. "He could use some rest, though."

"Sorry, he'll have to rest on the run. Better send him on through; it's the price of being the best. This should be a perfect chance to apply the Third Unclenched Fist."

"All right, but don't wear the little guy out. He needs his edge."

"He'll be fine." Then he added semi-apologetically, apparently to me, "Elapsed time is practically the same at both ends."

"You must have me confused with someone who knows what you're talking about."

He blinked at me and said, "Oh yeah, reference list," then reached over and twisted the knob on the glove compartment. It opened stiffly, to the sound of gaskets separating, and he pawed through a heap of computer printouts floating around in there. He squinted at one, then handed it to me, shaking his head. "I think that's the right one for this branch," he muttered.

The print was very small. I stared at it and got as far as "Unauthorized Information Sources Available as of Late 1980s (Dobbs-Approved)" before my eyes glazed over, so I folded it up and put it somewhere for later.

We were now hurtling over mountainsides covered with orange-barked ponderosa pines, including some really big ones, with a few Jeffrey pines along the crests. An ominous smoky haze was now visible far ahead, whenever we topped a ridge—which wasn't often; he was keeping us down in the valleys and lower passes as much as possible. I was finally starting to get used to it, but my fingers must have left permanent dents in his weird upholstery.

"What is this stuff, anyway? It feels just like moss."

"That's because it is, mostly. Not all products of gene-splicing are dangerous, thank goodness."

"Uh, which ones are, in case I run into any?"

"The vast majority are still pretty nasty. Virtually all present funding of genetic engineering research is tied to biological-warfare projects. Again, the people involved think they're carrying out their own strategies, but in fact they are providing their parasitic masters with customized new vehicles, so they can more efficiently infect and take over large populations. Surely you've heard the rumors about AIDS being cooked up at Fort Detrick, Maryland?"

"Who hasn't? But why would they turn something like that loose on their own people?"

"Their own people do not include blacks, Latinos or Native Americans, the ones with the highest infection and mortality rates. Deliberate population reduction didn't stop when the Nazis fled Germany; it went international and got very covert. Here, check this out."

He activated the screen with the miniature computer keypad under it, and entered some brief request. It lit up with a map of Africa, which had a lot of small gray patches here and there. "Those are the zones where high numbers of AIDS infections have been reported."

He punched in something else, and a series of brown patches appeared, overlapping the gray ones almost exactly. "Those areas are where the World Health Organization conducted its massive smallpox vaccination program in the mid-1970s."

"They did that deliberately?"

"Not the individuals delivering the vaccinations; how could they know exactly what they'd been given to inject? But somewhere along the line, someone apparently contaminated the whole batch. It certainly wasn't the first time health personnel got duped into poisoning the people they were trying to help. Anyway, that's the bad news."

I stared at the screen, shaking my head. "What's the good news?"

He switched it off. "Mainly that nobody really has to die from it, if someone gets the word to them soon enough about oxygen therapies. Ozone blood infusions, and/or slow intravenous H_2O_2 at 0.035 percent, two hundred fifty cc's at a time, seem to work the most swiftly.

"But as far as beneficial applications of gene-splicing, Dr. Ananda Chakrabarty's work is one early example. He came up with modified bacteria that can break down dioxin and 2,4-D and other deadly long-lived poisons. Unfortunately, no one so far is producing them at anywhere near the volume the bio-warfare germ labs are up to."

Sitting and breathing heavily was about all the reply I was up for. Years of missing pieces were getting plugged in all at once, but I was undergoing extreme brain strain trying to keep up with it. At least it can't get much more intense than this, I told myself unconvincingly.

There was a loud gurgling slooshing sound right under me, so I looked down and there was an otter between my knees. I squeezed my eyes shut, then looked again and it was still there, paused in mid-crawl from under the seat, looking up with a this-better-be-worth-it expression.

"Hi, Argle."

The otter squinted at him, blinked at me, shook his head and sent an amazing quantity of cold water onto my legs. He slithered to the deep end of the footwell, yanked a short tube loose from under the dash and took a drink from it. Then he looked at me and shook his head again.

He was a fairly small specimen, some sort of northern river otter, and he was wearing a miniature backpack. "His name is Argle?" was the least stupid question I could come up with.

He sloshed over and surged right up into my lap, still carrying at least a gallon of ice water in his fur. As it sunk in, it struck me that this might just be the coldest water my lap had ever experienced, if you catch my drift. Then he stuck his face right up to mine, whiskers nearly poking my eye, and let out a revolting gargling belching noise.

CS cracked up. I sort of laughed, whimpered and gagged all at once; Argle seemed to be on an all-fish diet. Then I encouraged him to get off my lap, with what I hoped would be read by an otter as non-hostile body language, since I'd just had a close look at a very respectable set of fangs.

"Okay, I'm ready. Why an otter?"

"He's a bugging expert. Doesn't know a blessed thing about electronics but he's an ace at planting them."

Argle slooshed over to him, stood on the seat divider and yawned in his face. CS continued, "Ferrets are smaller, but otters are better at getting things open and finding hiding places. A bit undisciplined maybe, but slack is Slack."

By way of agreement, Argle chittered like a deranged raccoon and leaped into the backseat, splashing against CS along the way.

"Security at even the most top-secret complexes is still basically geared to human intrusions only. Argle is so fast, compact, nonmetallic and preposterous that he can go almost anywhere undetected. That is, when he remembers to dry off first," he added in a louder voice. A high-pitched snoring noise answered him from the backseat.

"How can he break into some high-security installation?"

"Usually he gets through the gate by running along under a car that's coming in."

"Isn't that kind of risky for him?"

"You bet. It's his career; lots of otters to avenge. And without actually hurting anyone, he can help bring an end once and for all to the murder of rivers and streams. He's a pretty brave little bugger." The snoring sound got louder, with a sarcastic edge to it.

CS grinned and studied the "experimental" portion of the spectrum chart for a moment, between radar and infrared. "Today he may get a chance to penetrate another central sourpuss sanctorum, and get us some feeds on just how organized or messed up their minds are, how many are having doubts about their agenda, or anything else that might help us salvage them or at least soften their impact." He nodded at the smoke column now taking up the middle half of the view ahead. "Then this might be less necessary."

We popped up over the final ridge between us and the fire, and raced toward it. I barely noticed the otter standing beside me again, as I stared slack-jawed at the onrushing blaze.

I'd never seen a forest fire this close. There were trees nearly two hundred feet tall, burning from the ground clear up past their crowns. The leaping flames were reflected in a river flowing through a narrow gorge off to the east. My fingers started a new set of dents in the seat moss as I realized we still hadn't changed course, and the blaze now filled the entire forward view.

I couldn't quite believe he was aiming us right into the fire. He sure didn't look suicidal, but whatever he had in mind was beyond me.

At last he grabbed the mutated gearshift. I managed to keep one eye on his hands as the wildfire bore down on us. Now we'd see something.

The conical hood ornament suddenly pronged forward, stretching out through a widening hole until it looked like a robot anteater snout. Then it shot out a brilliant sky-blue stream of some glowing, crackling liquid unlike anything I'd ever seen, all over the onrushing flames.

"Great Zot! What is that stuff?"

"Condensed space-juice. Supercooled fresh-squeezed electron fluid. Trees can't burn under a high negative charge."

There was a lot more of it firing out from under us through that nozzle than we could possibly have room for in any concealed tanks. "Where's it all coming from?"

"We draw it in as needed, and crush-cool it on the spot. No one misses it; there's at least ten to the ninety-fourth watt-seconds per cubic centimeter, everywhere in space, including space full of matter. The primary carrier wave of the physical universe is around sixty octaves higher than an electron's diameter." He switched hands, kept blasting away and pointed at a spot on the spectrum chart in the upper zone unknown to me. "The higher the frequency, the greater the energy density. Establish resonance with space-juice itself and you can obtain virtually unlimited power."

The sizzling, metallic turquoise liquid was spreading out incredibly fast wherever it hit, engulfing the flames in big round patches. It sounded like a cross between distant artillery and huge sails flapping in a gale as it rolled out over the blaze. The stuff went from shiny to blurry, and expanded into thick mats of blue-white fog, as if to cool and soothe whatever might survive of the forest.

We tilted around the western rim of the burned area, mopping up several hot spots missed by the main volley. The pulses of juice didn't follow exactly smooth trajectories but seemed to crackle slightly as if along lightning discharge paths.

The otter didn't appear to be even remotely scared by all this. He just stood resting a paw against my seat, watching and making chortling noises.

I found my voice again, "Is this another one of those suppressed inventions?"

"Not exactly; this one really was a bit ahead of its time. Liquid electricity doesn't have many useful applications until you make available a virtually unlimited electron supply. The basic idea was developed by a guy named Richard Diggs back in the late seventies, though he didn't foresee this embodiment at the time."

"How do you liquefy it?"

"Tell you what, since I sort of have my hands full, how about if you ask the computer instead?" He pushed something that woke up that screen again, with a blinking "info" message at the top. I stared at it for a moment and he said patiently, "Type 'liquid electricity,' then push Enter."

I did so and read:

```
The mutual repulsion of electrons can be overcome at
sufficiently high pressures and low temperatures.
Pump electricity into a nonconductive, supercooled
extreme high-pressure vessel, through a large sheaf
of fine emitting points, and the electrons can be in-
duced to flow together and behave as a dense fluid, as
long as conditions of great pressure and cold are main-
tained. Naturally the energy density of a drop of pure
electron fluid far exceeds that of any previous elec-
trical storage medium.
     To snuff forest fires, put a high-frequency oscilla-
tion into the fluid electricity as it leaves the
nozzle. At the proper frequency it will flow as a heat-
seeking surface charge over everything that's burn-
ing, simultaneously cooling the outside of all trees
and animals, and briefly removing the electrochemical
conditions allowing combustion. Released from the
pressure and cold of the container, the liquid will
flow very quickly over the entire blaze as it breaks up
into free electrons, then cling to all hot spots as they
drop below the flash point, to prevent them from
reigniting while the charge disperses.
     It is a surface charge only, so it shouldn't pene-
trate or harm any living organisms. While we're at it
we can add the blend of vibrations that stimulate rapid
cell growth, so as to accelerate the healing and re-
growth of the trees and other creatures in the damaged
area.
```

"Far out," was about all I could say.

We slipped around and under the main northern smoke column, blowing out lingering sub-infernos and plowing through a few blind gray
patches. Then we came out of one right under a Vietnam-era attack
copter that was not rigged for fire fighting. CS cut the main field for a
moment but didn't change course, and we cleared its landing gear by
maybe four feet.

At about thirty yards past it the field came back on and our seats
came back up under us. As we kept going straight the helicopter swung
around and pointed something black and ugly in our direction. A heat-
seeking missile, I assume it was, suddenly came after us with what
would have been an impressive smoke trail anywhere else.

Apparently it felt we weren't nearly as hot as the smoldering logs down off to its right, so it zoomed over there and enthusiastically re-ignited a section of what we'd just put out. They fired a second one immediately, which of course agreed with the first one, went straight over and made that spot even hotter.

A small screen began flashing a rotating exploded diagram of a Cobra pretty much like the one tilting after us now, but no one had asked and everyone ignored it while we cut a tight arc down and back toward the brightening flames. Holding us into the turn, CS let off a quick blue blast, snuffing the fire again with a heavy, resounding thump. He straightened out once we were heading directly away from the burned area, barely clearing the treetops, and put us into a steep climb.

I looked back and, sure enough, they were climbing higher and coming around, wobbling slightly. We continued to pull away, passing their altitude just as they fired another rocket after us. Its smoke trail bent sharply over and under like a giant white fishing rod, as it streaked down and back toward the still-warm debris from its two buddies, and poofed it into yet another hearty blaze.

"Goddamn it!" CS swung us around again, aimed the juice nozzle and fired a stream from long range. By now whatever life remained in the roots of those former trees must have felt like this was all some fiendish torture brought here just for their unrequested opportunity to work off a lot more bad karma all at once than any tree should have been able to accumulate.

At this distance the Cobra was nearly in line with the fire. Apparently its engines were hot enough to draw the attention of one strand of liquid electricity, because the stream forked and licked it briefly. Its rotors slowed as it glowed blue-white for a moment, then it dropped like a heap of scrap metal, in fact very like the one it would shortly become.

"Oops. That's going to be expensive."

"I thought you shalt not kill."

"They are unhurt but no doubt very excited. At this frequency it's only a surface charge, no matter how strong. Their ignition system, however, is history."

He was accelerating us toward the Cobra, which started to nose downward as it fell.

"Why couldn't you just use your gunjammer on it earlier?"

"That device is tuned to the frequency that makes gunpowder think it's wet. A different and rather elaborate sonochemistry is required to neutralize those more sophisticated explosives and propellants."

"Beyond even your capabilities?"

"Very funny. Beyond my finances, to be exact."

He hit a white patch on the dash and yanked back on one of the backhoe levers. Something like a big fat artillery shell with grooved sides lurched away from under us and headed for the falling Cobra, at a rather leisurely pace, all things considered. He reached over and switched off the blinking diagram.

The shell finally reached the Cobra's tail at maybe three hundred feet, for what point I could not see at all, then it blossomed on impact. The grooved sides split into straps that lashed around the tail frame, turning the shell inside out just as a huge green balloon burst out of it, swelling to its full size in barely over a second.

Suddenly converted to a wildly swinging pendulum under the balloon, the Cobra's cabin plowed drunkenly sideways through treetops that had been about to impale it a second ago. The balloon snagged and the Cobra jerked to a bouncing halt maybe twenty feet above the forest floor. Little uniformed figures crawled out and clung to the landing gear; they appeared to be undamaged but extremely annoyed.

CS was examining some sort of X-ray of the Cobra through various colored filters. Argle made a rather shrill enquiring noise.

"I'm not picking up anything of a high enough rank. Better wait."

The speaker came on. "If you're through, punch it for the next fire zone. They're getting creamed up there."

"I can imagine."

We vaulted up until the whole burned area was visible, most of it now fog-shrouded, but we didn't turn north yet. He touched something on the spectrum and another screen lit up with a ghost image of the geography in front of us. Some small yellow lights were clustered at the far corner of the fire zone, by the river. That was apparently what he was looking for, and we swooped over there.

He dropped us close to the river where we saw a thrashing clump of deer and other animals trapped between steep banks, a burning logjam, and rafts of flaming debris flowing toward them from upstream. With the same control stick but a different trigger, he fired a thin red beam from somewhere under us, into the logjam at the waterline. The jam came apart and the water rushed through it, raising more clouds of steam but opening an escape route for the animals, who surged through as it cleared.

As we whipped around and climbed toward the mountains farther north, I asked, "How could your infrared tell the mammals from the flames?"

"It didn't; that was the emotion scanner. Fear and pain signals tend to be among the strongest in the emotion bands, especially at a scene like this. No fear emissions would've meant they either weren't in danger or were already dead."

"You can actually read different emotions with that thing?"

"Just like notes on a scale. Humans and other mammals stand out quite distinctly in any case; trees have a very different set of emotions."

"Lucky them."

He looked mildly amused. "Their emotions are appropriate for beings who, among other things, can't get into trouble without someone else's help." Argle made a noise like a miniature walrus and hopped into the backseat again.

I watched the forest race by under us and something occurred to me. "Is that what you were looking for when you picked me up? Fear and pain?"

He snorted unsympathetically.

"All right then, just what emotion were you scanning for?"

"Sarcasm."

"Oh, really?"

"It's not that we particularly care to hear any of your sarcasm; we have quite enough ourselves as it is. But we do find it's an easy indicator to use, a sign of possible intelligence, should we ever happen to be looking for any."

Unable to think of an appropriately intelligent reply, I just sat there trying to think of any reply at all.

"Were you about to point out that sarcasm is not exactly an emotion?" he suggested. I nodded, wearing what would hopefully pass for an intelligent expression, if one allowed for all this unfamiliar information getting crammed into the close vicinity of my puzzled protoplasm.

"An important distinction. Sarcasm isn't what you feel, just what you do, when you feel this one certain emotion that has not itself been given a name yet. That emotion always occurs coupled with a certain mental state, which involves recognizing stupidity in some situation, so it's not like just a regular feeling. It has strong harmonics in the thought bands."

"What, you even have thought detectors?"

"Oh, such things exist, but they're very expensive. The frequencies involved are so fine, it requires sensors not much larger than molecules to distinguish different thoughts from each other. Might as well just use your head."

I closed my eyes, trying to coax my brain cells to hang in there a little while longer. One of the things dispersing my attention was the vigorous splashing from the backseat, where Argle was amusing himself by hydroplaning back and forth along the soggy mutated moss.

Looking out above the shifting horizon, I realized there was still a long strip of diffused smoke far ahead. CS had the map screen going again and appeared displeased with the red patch centered on it. He quickly glanced at the spectrum, then raised our altitude and speed a bit.

I cleared my throat. "What sort of metal was that shell? It acted like it was alive."

"Unfortunately it's a one-shot deal. Strips of Nitinol, a type of shape-memory-effect alloy, backed with an impact-activated heat-generating compound to trigger the alternate shape. The helium was compressed nearly to liquid, in a titanium sphere with a quick-release valve."

"I remember hearing about Nitinol, but I didn't know it was that strong. Nickel-titanium, right? Whatever happened with that stuff?"

"It never really became available to the general public in any useful quantity, once it was realized you could take advantage of naturally occurring temperature differences and build free energy motors with it."

"Just how many kinds of free energy devices are there?"

"We've lost count. The fact is, all energy is free, just like the land and water once were. However, if someone's methods of obtaining it are inefficient enough, they can justify selling it to others as if it were inherently scarce and expensive. Of course, for that to work they have to continuously ignore the vast energy underlying physical reality."

"So your noble gas motor isn't still providing all this power, is it?"

"That one's only for the wheels. The main power supply works something like a living organism, resonating in harmony with the oscillating space-juice, and inducing extra energy to well up within its circuits. There's theoretically no upper limit to what can be drawn off with a properly tuned transducer."

He switched on the FM radio band for a moment and quickly found a news station that was covering the fires. The newscaster was commenting on the unusual number of dry lightning strikes again this year.

CS turned it off. "Awful lot of lightning to be coming out of a cloudless sky. You'd think they'd at least wonder about it."

From this height the trees streaking by were almost soothing, and my pulse rate had finally started slowing down a little, when CS said, "Did I mention watch out for lasers?"

"No," I sighed, "not that I recall. Would these be coming from any particular direction?"

"From overhead." His tone implied I should have figured this out; actually I'd been avoiding doing so. But now I happened to remember a guy I knew a few years back, who was an investigator for the fire marshal's office.

In the summer of '85, something had turned him really paranoid, while working on that huge bunch of forest and brush fires in California. Officially the cause of most of the fires was arson, but they never said how or by whom, as the investigation was supposedly still under way.

One evening I got him to let me buy him a few drinks, to relax him a bit since he was always so keyed up lately, and since that was his preferred relaxant. He started talking about the fires and it came out that quite a few of them seemed to have started high in the treetops, as if by an intense heat source directed from above. But there was none of the shattered look typical of lightning strikes.

I didn't know what to make of that, and he didn't seem inclined to speculate. Not long after that he quit the fire marshal's office and disappeared. Now when I tried to picture him, all I could see was the way his eyes looked that night. As I recall it took me some time to persuade myself that it all had nothing to do with me.

The smoky haze up ahead was getting thicker and darker. I wanted to ask CS to clarify his warning, but the only possible answers I could anticipate I was very reluctant to hear right then.

CS seemed to sense another round of questions approaching. "I'm a little burnt out on all this jabbering at the moment. Why don't you pick us out some tunes instead?" He slid open the cover on the seat divider to reveal a row of ordinary tape cassettes. "This is the best stuff from the all-time greatest musicians and anti-musicians."

Some of the names were quite familiar: Beethoven, Miles Davis, Jimi Hendrix, Frank Zappa, Doktors for "Bob." Others I'd never heard of. "What do the Mutated Mudpuppies sound like? Or the Presidential Polyps?"

"You have to be in the right mood. Let's hear something more cheerful."

Argle reached over and patted one of the tapes. "Skraa-ook Chirrup?" I pronounced carefully. "What the heck is that?"

"One of the best human-dolphin combos. Yeah, put that on."

I opened it and popped it in the slot, while trying to make out the picture on the case. It appeared to be six dolphins and three people, playing several extremely weird instruments, and surrounded by coral reefs and curious fish. Two more dolphins were operating a presumably waterproof mixing board. Apparently I was not keeping up with the latest musical trends as well as I'd thought.

I looked up and there were now giant smoke plumes clearly visible, rising from beyond the farthest ridges. Shivering slightly, I put the case back in with the others and riffled them with my fingers. "Somehow I was expecting micro-CDs or laser cubes or something."

"Too much hassle to make copies. Cassettes are cheap and universal."

A startling burst of percussion filled the air. Whatever I'd been expecting, this wasn't it. Clicking, ratcheting, creaking, and tearing sounds wove in and out in fast, intricate multiple rhythms. There were only occasional pure notes and chords here and there like accents, sparingly describing a song that was somehow both thrilling and haunting. Despite the high density and underwater sound quality, it was all very crisp and undistorted.

The music contrasted sharply with the grim scene ahead. The mountains were taller here. Although our approach was from generally upwind, we were already well into the fringes of a huge smoke blanket. The valleys we were crossing were densely forested, but the last few ridgebacks between us and the central smoke columns were boulder-strewn and nearly treeless.

CS looked rather grim himself. He appeared to be silently wrestling with some sort of difficult decision. Argle was standing between us, perfectly still for a change, watching the smoke.

We shot through the last slate-gray pass and saw miles of scorched ex-forest ahead, with a blazing edge way off to the northeast.

"Bloody hell, we're too late. Well . . ." he glanced at the otter, who nodded briskly. "Close your eyes."

The speaker came on: "CS!"—a different voice with lots of static.

"Hey, all's fair and this is both. Fuzzy noncombatants."

"Fine. You get to do all the maps and paperwork for the new fork."

I grabbed the sides of the seat. "What are you about to do? And will throwing up electrocute me?"

The otter vanished into the back.

"Relax, close your eyes. You can always trust a SubGenius, right?"

He touched something out of sight behind the steering column and a loud bell sounded that was just like the one before they start up the boardwalk bumper cars. "I'm not kidding," he added and grabbed two of the bigger clock-face joysticks.

I squeezed my eyes shut just as a searing white light hit us for a second or two, along with a weightless feeling and a sound like a giant champagne cork.

When I looked again it seemed like the windows themselves were all swiftly fading from blue-black to transparent, but it might have been my own afterimages. I realized I was looking at the same landscape as a moment ago, but it was only late morning and most of the trees were still here. Right in front of us though, on a very inaccessible-looking hillside a few miles ahead, was a fire nearly as big as the one we'd snuffed back by the river.

"There, that's a bit more fair." A sudden puff of smoke went up a few miles south of the main fire. "There's a new one. They're still firing here."

"Who? What's going on?"

"Grab this stick, will you? I need to get a fix on the satellite. We have to get under the next one to reflect it back up and fry the laser. Use this button here as we pass the blaze."

"I'm not shooting anything until you tell me what we're up against."

He turned the wheel hard over and we plunged toward the rocks. "Oh, sorry, I didn't realize you wanted off here."

"Hey!" I clutched at the stick. "All right already, you can tell me on the way."

We leveled out and streaked toward the leaping flames. "Aim for the northeast edge first, then dump full power into the center."

He had a screen going that was full of stars, thinning out rapidly as he touched a series of colored patches under it. Finally one remained, and he hit a button that dropped a grid and target pattern over it. "Got it. Okay, we're in range; cool her down."

I aimed the hood nozzle as he'd done and touched the juice trigger. A thin stream of turquoise plasma licked out and curved away in the wind, lighting up a jumble of boulders way northeast. I hastily aimed further to the left and held the trigger all the way down, as the fire raced toward us. The stream connected and there were several deep thumps as the bright liquid blew out hot spots and dispersed into a powder-blue fog that immediately spread over the whole blaze. Just as we were about to tear right into it, we banked all the way over, hard left, and shot toward the vertical southern horizon.

As we leveled out and accelerated even faster, I looked back and couldn't see any flames, just thick, rising white mist. "Fantastic."

"Heads up. Snuff that little one there."

I looked where he pointed, tried to compensate for the wind, and arced a short stream toward the latest fire. Nailed it on the first shot, with a satisfying thump. Actually it looked like I'd overshot at first, but the tip of the blue stream bent toward the flames as the heat attracted it.

The star screen showed a small green blip rapidly closing on the targeted star. CS twisted something beside the seat and the whole center of the roof bulged downward until the top must have been perfectly flat. He touched a spot above the spectrum chart and small signs lit up with the words MIRROR ON and SHIELDFIELD REINFORCED.

As we fired through another jagged pass, the two blips joined and a big X appeared, locking them together. We angled slightly west, got perfectly level and held a constant speed. "Any time now. Probably at that next big valley ahead." He gently took back the control stick.

I found room in my midsection for another small knot of fear; there was a little town in that valley. I could see kids playing beside an ancient red one-room schoolhouse. "So the Strategic Defense Initiative never really was for defense, I take it."

"Afraid not. The Nazis first conceived it as an explicitly offensive weapon in the mid-forties. Look up Project Paperclip, the U.S. importation of Nazi scientists. In all fairness, though, very few of the folks working on it have any notion what their effort's actually going into."

"And that is?"

"Continuing destruction of Earth's oxygen-producing surfaces, removing native animals and peoples, and driving survivors out of the mountains into the cities, where they can be more easily weakened and controlled. Eliminating the wide variety of natural, harmonious cultures that might compete with the homogenized anaerobotoids."

There was a sudden shimmering flash around us, and the big X on the screen went out. He scanned the spectrum chart and smiled. Then he pulled us into a tight downward spiral, firing short blue bursts at the broken ring of new flames rising from the trees just below us. They were snuffed almost instantly, and he straightened us out, climbing into the western sky.

"That was it? Are there more of those?"

"A few, but not within reach at the moment."

"Was anyone alive on board, do you think?"

"Those platforms are awfully toxic, and supposed to be unmanned. If anyone was there they'd have to have been severely modified to tolerate the radiation while they lasted."

"So we possibly just fried some poor slave?"

He sighed. "All I can go on here is the Golden Rule, and if I'd been kidnapped, neutered, mind-controlled, and turned into someone's expendable cyborg, I think I'd want to be freed from that nightmare existence as quickly as possible, and take a shot at something more natural. If anyone was up there and they were actually enjoying it, they have my apologies."

He was eyeing a pink spot on the main video screen, superimposed on the wooded edge of the next pass up ahead. He checked the lights blinking in the radio-TV bands, then dropped us right toward the blip.

An unmarked helicopter bristling with cameras and listening gear peeled out from behind the treeline where the pink spot had been. It dropped away from us down the far side of the ridge, gaining speed. As we closed on it I saw a gun barrel swing out and point toward us, and I nearly beat CS to the jammer switch. The gun protruded ineffectually in our direction for a moment, was shaken violently, then pointed at us again. Finally it was withdrawn and replaced with another, which must have annoyed its owner even more than the first one, since he hurled it out the door at us.

We swiftly overtook them and climbed slightly higher. CS thumbed the ungearshift's laser trigger. "I really don't want to waste another rescue shell, so let's just trim the blades a bit."

The thin red line angled down for an instant and snicked the edge of the rotor's whirring blur. Two dark rectangles spun off violently on parallel tracks, and the chopper immediately started losing altitude.

"Now they'll drop at around three feet per second all the way down, even at full throttle." As in the previous encounter, he made no attempt to talk with these guys. We soared away on roughly the same track as our approach, as if how they landed was of no concern. Along the way we happened to pass directly over the only chopper-sized clearing within their range.

Looking back we saw them pull out of a near-tumble and follow us toward it at the shallowest descent angle they could hold. We kept going, on around the valley's next bend, until we were just out of sight of the clearing, then dropped right down between the trees. CS cut the field and we crunched into a thick carpet of pine needles.

He opened a compartment in his armrest and pulled out a small bag. "Better take some extra fangs. This one could be a long way in and a short way out." Argle held still while CS stuffed a handful of little hollow white cones into an elastic pouch on his pack. They looked exactly like caps for an otter's upper canines.

"What're those, poison or something?"

They both looked at me a moment and slowly shook their heads, wearing remarkably similar expressions. "The bugs, naturally," said CS.

"That would've been my second guess. Does he bite them into a door frame or what?"

"A desk or chair leg works better, or sometimes an air vent, the underside of a briefcase or the heel of someone's shoe. If he gets in far enough and plants enough of them, a few are bound to pick up something useful."

"I gather he'll be hooking a ride with whoever comes to rescue these guys. How do you know they'll be taken straight to some inner sanctum?"

"He'll stick with whoever's the highest rank, and that one'll almost certainly go in for debriefing immediately. Otters don't have much personal use for social pecking orders, but they have no trouble spotting them in other species."

Argle came over and patted my back with a splatting sound. His fur still held quite a bit of water, but I didn't say anything. Then he shook his whole coat, thoroughly soaking both of us.

He stood and hitched up his pack, adjusting the quick-release clasp on the front of his harness. He leaned against CS and stretched his neck up until they were nose to nose for a moment. For a second there it was kind of touching, almost, then Argle blew his hair back with a racket like a blue jay getting stuffed into a mud hole.

"Need to get any more of that out of your system, or can we open the door now?" Argle nodded at the door and CS cracked it open. The scent of startled pine trees rushed in while the otter slithered out, managing to give CS one more hearty splat across the face with his thick tail, the only place where his fur was still full of water.

We watched him flow erratically back toward the clearing where his quarry had presumably come down in one piece. He paused and shook all over for several seconds, until only a fine mist was flying off. CS pulled a couple more hand towels out of the back footwell and handed me one, and we silently dried ourselves off while we watched Argle disappear into the underbrush.

CS stared thoughtfully at one of the stabbed clocks, which I noticed had thirteen hours marked on it. Then he switched on the main field. We popped up off the ground and rose between the trees until we were barely above them. Then we slid away as if the field were rolling lightly over the treetops.

"What are his chances?" I asked.

"Pretty good, actually. He has a one-shot escape route he can activate almost instantly, as long as he jumps the moment he's spotted."

"What if he doesn't see them first?"

"Back home his wife'll be having pups any day now. He knows where to go if he winds up needing another body."

I thought about it. "That's really something, putting his life on the line like that to help you guys."

"He knows we're all in this together. If our habitat goes down the tubes, so does his."

Somewhere along the way the background music had faded into serene counterprogressions of bubble and bell sounds, with barely a trace of percussion left. I was still hunting for a discreet and trustworthy-sounding way of mentioning I'd noticed that along with everything else we were flying a time machine.

We rounded another bend in the valley, then accelerated and started climbing. Finally I said, "I couldn't help noticing that this car is a time machine."

CS grinned but made no reply. I added delicately, "Could you tell me how it works?"

"Afraid not. It hasn't been invented yet. You can already find some good clues, though, in current popular neophysics texts, the multiple-worlds hypothesis, Professor N. A. Kozyrev's time experiments, and certain past-life regression techniques."

"How long before, uh, this gets invented?"

"Only a few more years. As with most breakthroughs, necessity is the mother. If you want something bad enough you can usually make it happen. In this case, some young electronics prodigies will get together and decide a time machine would be their only chance to personally witness some of those Jimi Hendrix concerts they weren't old enough to go to when they happened."

"You're not kidding, are you? Talk about devoted fans." I thought for a moment. "So how did you come to be this thing's owner?"

"After experiencing all that soul-washing music they couldn't resist interfering with his assassination. One of them caught him backstage and warned him about the FBI's Cointelpro hit list, and about Monica Danneman. For some reason it hadn't occurred to him that a Düsseldorf banker's daughter would not normally be a strong supporter of black antiwar activists, considering interest payments on war debts are the biggest source of income for the major bank owners."

"But he really did die. Whoa, is that what you meant by a new fork?"

"Exactly. They chose, quite naturally, to remain in the branch where Hendrix was allowed to mature and continue his astonishing career. He got together with Miles Davis as originally planned, and they changed history in precisely the way that those who ordered his removal had feared.

"Quite apart from the surge in musical breakthroughs, and completing Jimi's graduation from Conspiracy-created drugs, the collaboration drew Miles into an active role in the antiwar movement in the early seventies. Dozens of jazz artists followed his lead, as they had in music, and that entire somewhat hipper subgroup of the establishment that appreciates jazz followed after them. They injected new energy and major funding into the peace movement, and made it impossible for the warmongers to maintain the fiction that only Commies and hippie radicals wanted to end the wars.

"The program of eliminating politically active musicians and minority leaders ground to a halt, hate music and other false rock never really took hold like it has here and the Age of Slack arrived there earlier."

The tape had ended and we were high enough now to make out a spectacular multilayered cloud bank off to the west. We weren't really climbing so much as allowing the mountains to drop away under us, but it gave us a higher altitude than any so far.

"Weren't you tempted to join them?"

"Sure, and I may splice into their stream again later, but meanwhile someone has to tend the home branch. Anyhow, great danger can still make for some of the most thrilling challenges. Which brings us back around to your reason for being here. You're looking for work, right?"

"Sort of. However, my choice of positions tends to be influenced by the probabilities of getting killed on the job."

"Fair enough. I imagine you'd also prefer something that calls for a minimum of heavy perspiration."

"Now that you mention it, that could be a factor. What sort of work are you offering?" Until I learned otherwise, I was going to keep acting as if I was up here entirely by my own free choice.

"There are five billion humans down there, who in most cases through no fault of their own are locked into some suicidally shortsighted technologies. Many are already well aware that they need to clean up their methods, but they need a lot of help getting informed about the more harmonious alternatives, and the economic transitions required."

"I do appreciate the urgency, but what exactly can I do about all this?"

"By now you should have a fairly clear picture of the fundamental struggle over Earth's future, and basically who's fighting who over what."

"Actually, I still have only the vaguest sense of what these oxygen wars are all about. And if I tried to explain it to someone else, they'd probably have me put away."

"Okay. There are basically two kinds of life here, the kind that thrives at high oxygen levels, which are the vast majority, and the little ugly slimy things that would prefer an atmosphere with a lot less oxygen and a lot more methane, ammonia and that sort of stuff. They had their run of the place way back when, but until humans came along the expansion of forests and all the accompanying high-oxygen-based creatures was continuously pushing the other kind into smaller and less significant roles in the ecology.

"Now humans are more capable than any other life here of things like expanding forested areas and pushing back deserts. But if they had any grasp of the existing natural order of things, very few of them acted like it. They threw in with the anti-oxygen gang, against their own entire kind of life-forms, unaware in most cases of the long-term effects of the things they were trained to do. As humans became more heavily affected by parasites, they acted more and more like parasites themselves.

"The possibility that some sort of organized nonphysical predators are using the upstart micro-lowlifes for reasons of their own, and/or the other way around, have not been ruled out.

"Earth's time track has some enormous forks coming up. Who goes which way is up to everyone involved. On one of the least enjoyable branches the entire planet's water-oxygen cycles all collapse and an Age of Decay really sets in."

"You went there and saw it?"

"Only the most miserable of higher life-forms bother with the place. The point is, here and now, the future is still entirely up to those who are going to experience it. The first thing they need fixed up is their health; can't do much else while they're getting sick all over the place."

"Isn't there a lot more to it than just getting them to raise their oxygen levels?"

"There are other factors, of course. Attitude, behavior, whether their blood is clean or loaded down with useless extra matter, whether they have enough trace minerals or are trying to live off just a few elements, all that sort of thing. But oxygen is the key.

"Your personal fluidity varies with your oxygen-hydrogen ratio. Oxygen loosens your cells, speeds up your internal flows, atomic turnover and energy level. Oxygen is biomolecular Slack. Hydrogen sticks things together and slows the flows, ideally just enough to hold your form solid, but too much makes you sort of gluey, not as fluid or adaptable.

"Oxygen is the physical counterpart of *prana,* vital energy. All your metabolic functions require it, and run better as you increase it. Also, it's no accident that humans can potentially run at higher oxygen percentages than any other land creatures, though few manage it or even try in these sluggish times. Thus, the vast majority never discover the additional marvelous capabilities designed into their bodies, which very rarely switch on at the usual low energy levels.

"At any rate, your job would be to first inform yourself more completely as to the details on all this, then help get the word out and turn the tide. Anyone with a little imagination and sense of humor should be able to take all this information and make a decent living and a lot of good karma out of it."

"It certainly would be different. What sort of pay is involved?"

"Up to you, since you'd be your own boss. The benefits include avoiding what'll happen if you don't do it." He noticed my expression and grinned, then added, "That's general prophecy, not personal threat."

"I knew that. Does the deal include time travel?"

"In a way. You can help the future to hurry up and get here."

"Say, couldn't you take me ahead a few years to just after this was built, then tell me how it works?"

"Nice try. You'll have your hands full with what you've already got, and the rest'll be along before you know it. Meanwhile, it'll help if you bear in mind that the sensation of time itself is generated by certain constant universal rhythms, at nearly unmeasurable frequencies, high enough to continuously grab the part of your attention that makes memory recordings."

"That's supposed to help?"

"It might, later on."

I wondered how much of this I'd even be able to remember later on. My attention couldn't help dividing itself between the words and the stirring scenery flowing by, at a lot less threatening proximity than earlier. Not far ahead the dark green forest faded into brown and yellow foothills, then nearly white desert at the horizon.

"I have this tendency to hesitate on tough decisions," I said carefully. "With this one it's not so much a matter of whether, but how. And there are some things I'm still not sure about. Like, what if it turns out that this great master-germ takeover theory is wrong after all?"

"It wouldn't change any of the rest of it, apart from giving the humans a lot less of an excuse for their behavior. No matter who's really behind the constant all-out assault against higher life-forms, the basic means of reversing it are the same. Shift over to fuelless energy sources, massive reforestation, and oxygen therapy, and don't wait for official permission.

"That applies to any of this information, by the way, from gravity control to the multi-worlds hypothesis. You don't have to swallow all of it, to use the parts you like."

"Imagine my relief." There was something else I just had to ask. "So, does the Church of the SubGenius really wind up being the number-one religion worldwide?"

"Work out the numbers and see what you come up with. Since any new member's first duty is to splinter off and form a new denomination, how long can it take before the sheer number of SubGenius splinter groups exceeds all other denominations combined? Since they borrow the least foolish points from all the other religions and mock the rest, how can they help but attract away the brightest followers of those plundered faiths? As the Conspiracy's actions become more and more obvious, who can resist the only church that even acknowledges the Conspiracy exists? And what other church provides such laughter? For its own members, I mean."

"Sounds like everything turns out all right, then."

"Don't take anything for granted. The AntiSlack Masters still think they can win."

The speaker came on with a burst of static. "CS, can you hear me?"

"Why, has it started already?"

"Yeah, it's getting pretty intense here. Can you spare yourself?"

"Of course. Want the car?"

"No. It has no dependable dream body, and you'll be needing yours, at full power."

"Good, I should leave it for Argle anyhow." He stretched for a moment, then put his hand behind the steering column. A small sign lit up with the words IDIOT MODE.

He started climbing out of his seat into the back. "Take the wheel."

"Wait! How do I, uh? . . . "

"Look, it's very simple. Turn the wheel right or left, pull it up and down to rise and descend. The accelerator and brake pedal work pretty much like you'd expect. The car won't let you crash it."

"But what if it, uh? . . . "

"Hey, either you achieve a state of hole-in-oneness or you don't."

I got into the driver's seat and gripped the wheel, feeling a strangely enjoyable mixture of power and incompetence.

"There you go. You are now headed toward your original destination. Hold at this altitude almost to the coast, then turn south and descend. I suggest you park somewhere discreet, outside city limits, and walk from there. I'll find it later with the beacon."

I glanced back and got a bit panicky; he was strapping on a small pack. "What the hell? Are you bailing out here or something?" I didn't remember seeing any back doors.

He pointed over my shoulder at the map screen. It still showed no new red lights. "There are no more fires from here to the coast," he said, as if that made everything okay.

"But what are you doing?"

"I have to go take care of something that'll get a lot more complicated if I put it off."

I made various ineffective protesting noises, then glimpsed something truly awesome out the right window. A huge bright silver disk was pacing us, far off to the northwest.

I looked at CS and his eyes were gleaming like a child's, so I figured this wasn't an enemy craft. He put a hand on the wheel for a moment and rocked us slightly from side to side. The silver disk made a similar small rolling motion, then shot straight up at an impossible speed and vanished in about three seconds.

I gave him a stunned look and he said happily, "Some modes of transport are a lot more advanced than others."

I stared again at the outrageous dashboard and my eye fell on the "Bob" sticker, so I asked, "Have you ever actually met "Bob" personally?"

"Has anyone ever truly met "Bob"? Even "Bob" himself?"

With that he slipped further into the back seat and added, "Check your map. You'll reach the coast in a few minutes."

I looked at the map with a fizzing sensation in my ears. Then I heard a roaring, whooshing sound behind me and spun around. CS was crouched on the seat with his back to me. He had a strip of blue-white fabric stretched between his hands, and it appeared to be trying to get away. He hooked an elbow into it and spread it sideways, as the roaring grew louder and my ears popped. The fabric was writhing and whipping around and its actual pattern seemed to be spinning. I couldn't pull my eyes away from it.

He wedged his other elbow and a foot into this escaped hallucination and stretched it like a sheet of rubber, and the roar grew deafening. I got a blast of ocean mist in the face, and suddenly I was looking into the thundering tube of a fifteen-foot wave, with sunlight gleaming through and a flash of blue sky beyond the churning mist at the far end. For an instant there was this flapping window right through the throat of a great tumbling tunnel of water, then he leaped into the pounding chaos and it snapped shut behind him.

I sat turned around like that, staring at the empty backseat long after the last tiny blue spot had faded away and the foam had all soaked into the moss. Then I recalled I was at the wheel of a car going several times faster than I'd ever driven, and up in the air besides, so facing forward might be a good idea.

I did that and my adrenal glands really outdid themselves. There was nothing but ocean far below. My head thumped as if my brain intensely desired to be somewhere else, then I realized the coast was behind me and sheepishly turned the wheel in a slow curve to the south.

About the only coherent thought I remember from the remainder of the flight was how much I needed to take a leak. The car covered the remaining miles to the mountains above L.A. a lot faster than I asked it to. It also didn't seem to care if I steered it or not, since it always corrected gently back to the same heading afterwards, resetting the wheel's relative orientation each time. It ignored the altitude control, brake and accelerator altogether. I felt around behind the steering column but didn't find any hidden switches, and the IDIOT MODE light stayed on.

Without any help from me the car zeroed in on a small canyon facing the coast and hurtled toward it at a truly sphincter-testing velocity. I was standing on the brake with both feet when finally we slowed to a crawl all at once. Now even the steering wheel ignored me as we floated down and landed among boulders and sagebrush. We were in a state park, judging from the maze of trails that had flashed by.

I started breathing semi-normally and blinked quite a few times. My eyes seemed rather dry, probably from bulging so much. As my hand went for the door handle, I noticed the INFO light blinking on that screen above the keypad, and hesitated. There was an appropriate bush only about thirty feet away, but I had to try something first.

I typed "time travel" and pushed Enter. A short menu of subtopics appeared: General Theory, Useful Discrepancies, Circuit Diagrams, Backup Systems, Special Features, Fork-Mapping Suggestions, Unmapped Warpjumping Cautions, and Now That You're Stranded. Unfortunately, nearly all the choices were followed by the words "Unavailable in This Mode and/or Time Period," flashing at the same dull rate as the IDIOT MODE light.

The only option that wasn't marked unavailable was number nine, Brief Demonstration. Curiosity continued to override bladder pressure. I pushed 9, and read: →Select date and location.

This couldn't be for real.

I grabbed one of the joysticks and twisted it around. It offered more resistance than I expected, but it also could be rotated on its axis, and pulled in and out several inches. Apparently it let you control four directions with one hand, and it really was almost like reaming a clock with a big knife, but nothing seemed to be happening. Some of the clocks had thin flat rings around them, calibrated with numbers and other less familiar symbols. I started to rotate one of them, then noticed some more words had appeared on the screen: →Preset destinations available only. List? (Y/N). I punched Y, ignoring my hydraulic discomfort.

→Dating system? 1) Euro-American 2) Chinese 3) Mayan 4) Other. I pushed number 1.

A chillingly plausible string of dates and places appeared, with an inquiry as to whether I was interested in seeing more. (Y/N). I pushed Y. Would this turn out to be some sort of intelligence test, or a practical joke? But I'd already seen some of what this machine could do.

The selections formed odd clusters. Most of the first screenful was 1969 and 1970. These guys had some peculiar criteria for choosing important moments. I recognized things like November 22, 1963, but only a few of what would usually be thought of as key historical events were included. Hardly any wars were represented, though there was a cluster right around the "end" of World War II. Except for a few in 1899 at Colorado Springs, the dates grew farther apart as they got into earlier centuries. They'd skipped the Middle Ages entirely.

There were a few selections around A.D. 33 in the Middle East, and several more around the mid-fifth century B.C. in India and China. Then the Nile Delta at 1500 and 3100 B.C., something in Northern Europe at around 11,000 B.C., a string of five- and six-digit dates and places that meant nothing to me, and then Greenland at 5,000,000 B.C.

There was another big gap, and the next choice was 63,000,000 B.C., Cliffside, Lizard Vista, North Pre-America.

I read no further. Dinosaurs! This couldn't wait. With trembling fingers I tapped in "179," the number for that selection, and then pressed Enter.

The screen said: →What, you want to go there? (Y/N). I pushed the Y.

→Are you sure? (Y/N). I pressed Y again.

A long list of instructions and cautions appeared, that sort of got on my nerves: →Ensure eyes are closed before engaging temporal displacement, but not before reading remaining instructions. Do not attempt to open door after displacement, or while it is occurring. Do not attempt to move vehicle from preset destination during or after displacement. Duration of excursion is subject to conditions at selected viewpoint. Rebound may occur with little advance notice, depending on conditions, etc. Very few controls will respond until vehicle withdraws to origin point, so quit screwing around and enjoy the show. This vehicle is not to be considered specifically liable for anything whatsoever.

→Do you still wish to move to viewpoint 179? (Y/N). I hit the Y.

→You're quite sure about this? (Y/N). I hit the Y again, with unnecessary force.

→Close your eyes and press any key.

I pushed the exclamation point, but hesitated on closing my eyes; I had to see if the time daggers moved around by themselves. Instead the screen said: →Are your eyes closed? (Y/N). There was a five-second pause, then the warning bell sounded and I covered my whole face with my arms.

The white flash and deep thump seemed no more intense than when we made the several-hour hop. But when I opened my eyes I instantly wished I'd held off on this little jaunt until after soaking some unsuspecting bush.

I was looking straight down into a river canyon from the side of a cliff, maybe two hundred feet up, from a shallow cave barely larger than the car. The cliff sloped sharply back away from under us, and the opposite cliff was also heavily undercut, making the canyon much wider at the bottom than up here. But this was just a small side canyon feeding into an enormous river valley off to our left, where the view opened out.

At the far end of the valley, the biggest waterfall I'd ever seen was thundering in over a much taller cliff, from what looked like an inland sea on the horizon. Its mist filled the entire valley. The sky overhead was the deepest and most intense blue I'd ever seen outside of dreams.

Through the mist I could make out these strange enormous shapes lying around down there on the rocks and mud, like gigantic seals. Presumably these were the dinosaurs, but they weren't actually doing anything.

The visual scale kept trying to shift around on me. I finally realized it was because all those trees along the river were giant-size versions of plants I was used to seeing only a few feet tall, if ever, so it threw everything else's apparent size off.

The cliff across from me was only about fifty feet away, and it had several cave openings. A small, scaly face with big eyes suddenly appeared in the one just opposite, peeking over some rocks on the ledge. It made a chittering noise a lot like Argle and disappeared back into the cave.

I heard a chorus of honking and bleating sounds, and three of the cave openings filled with long-legged monkey-sized lizards. They all had light-brown scales and, as it turned out, opposable thumbs, which they put to immediate use by hurling rocks in my direction. I ducked instinctively, then realized the cushion field was still on; the rocks were all bouncing off like they'd hit a wall of springs.

There was something wrong with this picture. These ape-lizards were all bouncing around throwing rocks and dodging each others' ricochets, screeching and cackling as if this were some sort of a game. Their voices had that shrill, annoying quality that seagulls have, probably from trying to be heard over the constant noise of pounding water.

I watched some of the bigger ones in the left-hand cave until it was quite clear they were trying to bank their rocks off the car's springy field and hit their friends in the adjacent caves. Most appeared to have done this before. Several were already bleeding from direct hits but they all seemed to be enjoying it immensely.

Just as I figured it out, they all stopped and stared at something on my side of the gorge, off to the left. I looked and saw two iguanodons, I think they're called, approaching the top of the cliff from above.

Each was carrying a very angry pterodactyl folded up under its arm, and holding the long beak shut with the other hand. Both were rather scratched up and missing a few scales, but they seemed in good spirits, honking boisterously at each other as they walked right up to the edge of the cliff.

It was hard to imagine the iguanodons thought their rate of descent would be slowed much by the pterodactyls, which they must have outweighed by ten to one, but they seemed pretty confident. With no particular ceremony they stopped at the very edge, grabbed their pterodactyls' hind feet and jumped off.

The winged lizards went into screaming overdrive, flapping frantically all the way. Everyone watched as they fluttered erratically down and splashed heavily into the swamp. I guess I'd just witnessed the invention of hang gliding, or something.

That done, rock throwing resumed immediately.

A lot of the rocks weren't bouncing all the way back to the opposite cliff. Far below I noticed a mass of ferns disappear into one end of a big long mud bank, and began doubting it was a mud bank. It confirmed this suspicion by raising that end and looking around to see what had just bonked it on the head.

I forgot about the rocks as the head continued to rise. This thing was even bigger than that supersaurus or whatever it was they wrote up awhile back, or ahead, depending. As I watched it lift its neck higher and higher, it occurred to me I hadn't noticed any instructions for activating the departure mechanism.

A deeper and more authoritative honking across the way made me look back up at the caves. A larger and less fun-loving version of the rock-throwing reptiles had appeared in the opening and was shooing everyone back inside. The other cave entrances emptied almost as quickly. I looked down and now the humongosaurus was definitely looking at me, and the head was still rising.

I rapidly typed, "How do we get out of here?" and pushed Enter.

→What, you want to go already? (Y/N). Y.

→Didn't we just get here? (Y/N). Y.

→So what seems to be the trouble?

Not having prepared for an essay question, I typed, "A very large dinosaur is about to try and swallow us or maybe hatch us," Enter.

→Now let's go over that again: You say you saw some sort of monster? (Y/N).

No wonder most of the paint was worn off the Y. I tapped it again, trying not to punch it right through the keypad. The neck was nearly vertical, and that little head was looking a lot bigger.

→And so you want to leave now, just like that? (Y/N). Y.

→Were you expecting maybe cows and bunny rabbits? (Y/N). Tricky; N.

→Well what, do you need to take a leak or something? (Y/N). Y!

The stupendosaurus ran out of neck about thirty feet below us, then rocked back onto its hind legs and tail, raising its shoulders and front legs until its lumpy face was less than ten feet away. Now the creature looked like a mountain of mud with a giant tentacle on top, with eyes and a big mouth instead of suckers.

The screen wasn't through with me yet: →But are you sure you want to leave right this minute? (Y/N). I got some sweat on the Y this time.

→Are you positive? The view is quite spectacular from here, (Y/N).

I was close to losing it. I pushed the Y some more, with considerable restraint, considering. The giant head was tilting to one side in a way that might have struck me as sort of grotesquely cute, if I'd been feeling more detached about things. It wasn't easy to be terrified by something with a big heap of swamp mud dribbling down its face, but I was managing.

A tongue bigger than a surfboard flopped out and slurped toward us, compressing the field to less than three feet from the windshield, and rocking us back slightly. The head reared back a couple of yards and seemed to ponder the cushion field's electric taste, then it let out a noise like a giant rusty hinge, amazingly similar to the sound in the old Godzilla movies.

Still we sat there in our hole in the cliff. I wondered just what it took for this machine to register something as dangerous.

→Sure you don't want to take a few pictures before we go? The lighting is perfect right now, (Y/N).

What was this, hitchhiker torture time? I hit the Y and most of the keys next to it, hoping I'd read the question correctly.

The giant mouth was swaying toward us again, and opening wide.

The teeth all appeared to be plant-grinding molars, with big chunks of fern gumbo wedged into all the crevices, but somehow I was not reassured.

→All right then, you're absolutely certain? (Y/N). I typed, "CAN WE PLEASE GO NOW!" and hit Enter, just as the whole mouth started rocking us.

→Oh, relax. Close your eyes and press any key.

Certain parts of my endocrine system were sure getting a workout today. I pressed about ten keys at once, and this time, instead of the bell, the thump and blast of light were preceded by something like a flashbulb going off that made me blink just in time.

I thought I saw, fading from the screen: →Wimp. But I was in too much of a hurry to pay attention. Now I truly was in dire need of a leak. For all I knew, the way this vehicle could move around, its moss seats might very well be designed to safely absorb large amounts of urine spontaneously released by startled passengers. But I didn't want to test that possibility right now; I'd managed to hang on this long.

I nearly lost it, struggling with the door handle; it turned out I needed to twist and pull at the same time to unseal it, then the pressure difference popped it open. Apart from the smell of sage, I noticed a slightly unpleasant scent, then realized it was just typical L.A. County air. I slid out and staggered to the nearest bush, and the next few moments were the least stressful I'd had all day.

As the pressure started to ease, my mind was filling with possibilities. All I needed was to scrounge up a movie camera somewhere, and the film world would soon be in an uproar. Incredibly realistic historical epics for just the cost of the celluloid. Dinosaur scenes that'd make Ray Harryhausen himself wonder how they were done. The ultimate in quality bootleg concert videos. And imagine what a determined investigative reporter could accomplish with a camera, a tape recorder and a time machine.

While I was at it I was sorely tempted to go buzz downtown L.A. in this thing, just for old times' sake.

There was a half-familiar gurgling whooshing sound behind me. I turned and saw Argle climbing out from under the passenger seat. As I walked toward the car he got into the driver's seat, shoved my pack out onto the ground and put his paw behind the steering column. The door closed itself and the IDIOT MODE light turned off.

Great, I thought to myself; even an otter from the future is smarter than me from now. I walked up and tapped on the glass. He made a shooing motion with one paw and placed the other paw meaningfully on the main field switch. I backed away hastily; he had a black singed-looking streak across the top of his head and a no-nonsense expression.

I watched helplessly as he yanked down on one of the time daggers with both paws. There was a sound like a giant champagne cork played backwards and the weeds and bushes all jerked toward the place where the car suddenly wasn't. Then the birds and insects all started up again and the world sort of went normal on me.

There was no physical trace of anything I'd just experienced, except for my dead car somewhere back in the desert. Apparently I was up a wild story without any proof.

Then I remembered the reference list and started going through my pockets.

As a child, at the end of a dream I would often try to grab something in the dream and take it back with me to the waking world. But whether I grabbed sticks, dirt, rocks, toys, money or whatever, it always turned out what I was clutching was part of the sheet, or my own arm or hair. Though even now I still felt it should somehow be possible, I'd never managed to drag any physical souvenirs awake with me from dream-time.

So it was with a once-familiar sinking feeling that I came up empty in every pocket. Then I pulled open my pack and there it was, a bit crumpled but quite readable: a long list of what appear to be legitimate publications, book titles, patents and contacts. These are some of the main ones. What do you make of this?

- Rex Research, P.O. Box 1258, Berkeley, California 94701. Some 250 different photocopied folios of the original reference material on various ignored, suppressed or otherwise little used but highly promising breakthroughs in energy, transportation, healing, agriculture, unconventional water sources, gravity and weather control, and other areas. Catalog $2.00.
- *Now What,* P.O. Box 768, Monterey, California 93940. Unauthorized information: oxygen therapy, free energy and other exotic sciences, clean resources, transition logistics. $15.00/four issues, $4.00 each.

More Info on Oxygen Therapy

- *ECHO,* a newsletter on oxygen therapy, is available from Walter Grotz, P.O. Box 126, Delano, Minnesota 55328. 8 pages, $2.00. Extensive references and case histories of successful treatments.
- *The Peroxide Story: Update on Oxidative Treatments and Remedies* by George L. Borell, P.O. Box 487, Stanton, California 90680. 83 pages, $7.00.
- *The International Bio-Oxidative Medicine Foundation* (IBOM) *Newsletter* contains technical updates for physicians offering H_2O_2 therapies. P.O. Box 61767, Dallas/Fort Worth, Texas 75261, 817-481-9772. Physician referrals $10.00.

☠ The International Ozone Association, 83 Oakwood Ave., Norwalk, Connecticut 06850 (203-847-8169) has available *Medical Applications of Ozone,* the largest single volume on the subject. $50.00. (Ozone in water or blood forms H_2O_2.)

☠ *The Use of Ozone in Medicine: A Practical Handbook* by Drs. Siegfried Rilling and Renate Viebahn, Karl Haug Publishers, Heidelberg, 200 pages. English version: Medicina Biologica, 4830 N.E. 32nd Ave., Portland, Oregon 97211. $29.00. (Two of the physicians reporting complete cures of AIDS patients.)

See also the "Medica Media" subcatalog from Rex Research.

Free Energy

☠ "Noble Gas Plasma Engine," Joseph Papp, U.S. Patent #3,670,494.

☠ "Permanent Magnet Motor," H R Johnson, U.S. Patent #4,151,431 (one of many).

☠ *Suppressed and Incredible Inventions,* by Al Fry, 9237 Craver, Morongo Valley, California 92256. $9.00.

☠ *The Manual of Free Energy Devices and Systems,* Electrodyne Corporation, P.O. Box 11422, Clearwater, Florida 33516. $10.00.

☠ *Living Water: Viktor Schauberger and the Secrets of Natural Energy* by Olof Alexandersson, Turnstone Press Ltd, Wellingborough, Northamptonshire, England.

☠ *The Sea of Energy* by John E. Moray, Cosray Research Institute, 2505 South 4th East, Salt Lake City, Utah 84115. $22.50 (cloth), $9.35 (paper).

☠ *The Energy Machine of Joseph Newman: An Invention Whose Time Has Come* by Joseph W. Newman, Route 1, P.O. Box 52, Lucedale, Mississippi 39452, 601-947-7147. $39.00.

☠ *The Principles of Ultra-Relativity* by Professor Shinichi Seike, Gravity Research Lab, P.O. Box 33, Uwajima City, Ehime (798), Japan. $40.00.

☠ *Tesla Said* and *The Nikola Tesla Patent Wrappers,* edited by John T. Ratzlaff, Tesla Book Company, P.O. Box 1649, Greenville, Texas 75401, 214-454-6819.

Rex Research has approximately twenty different folios on fuelless power sources.

Gravity Control

☠ "Electrokinetic Apparatus," Townsend Brown, U.S. Patents #2,949,550, 3,018,394.

- "Secondary Gravitational Field Generator," H. W. Wallace, U.S. Patents #3,626,605.
- *Ether-Technology: A Rational Approach to Gravity Control* by Rho Sigma, Tarnhelm Press, Lakemont, Georgia 30552. $7.00.
- *The Gravitics Situation* (Gravity Rand Report), Rex Research. $5.00.
- *Moongate: Suppressed Findings of the U.S. Space Program* by William L. Brian II, Future Science Research Publishing Company, P.O. Box 06392, Portland, Oregon 97206. $14.95.
- *UFO's and the Complete Evidence from Space: The Truth about Venus, Mars, and the Moon* by Daniel Ross, Pintado Publishing, P.O. Box 3033, Walnut Creek, California 94598. $9.95.
- "The Hans Nieper Gravity Papers," Keith Brewer Library, Richland, Wisconsin 53581.
- *The Secrets of Flying Saucer Propulsion* by Noel Huntley, Prescience Publications, 1330½ Sutherland Street, Los Angeles, California 90026. $9.00.
- *The Cosmic Pulse of Life* by Trevor James Constable, Merlin Press, P.O. Box 12159, Santa Ana, California 92712. $6.95.
- *Clear Intent: The Government Cover-up of the UFO Experience* by Lawrence Fawcett and Barry J. Greenwood, Prentice-Hall, Englewood Cliffs, New Jersey 07632. $8.95 (out of print).
- *Genesis* by W. A. Harbinson, Dell. $4.50. (Fiction, but lists useful sources.)

Liquid Electricity

- Richard Diggs, Custom Invention Agency, P.O. Box 11, Carthage, Missouri 64836; patent process on hold, though he has over two hundred others.

The Conspiracy

- Mae Brussell Research Center, P.O. Box 8431, Santa Cruz, California 95061.
- *Endless Enemies: The Making of an Unfriendly World* by Jonathan Kwitny, Penguin, New York. $8.95.
- *Out of Control* by Leslie Cockburn, Atlantic Monthly Press, New York, 1987. $18.95.
- *Inside the League: The True Story of How Nazis, the Unification Church, South American Death Squads, and the American New Right Have Joined Forces to Fight Communism* by Scott and John Lee Anderson, Dodd, Mead, 1986. $19.95.
- *Blowback: America's Systematic Recruitment of Nazis and Its Disastrous Effect on Our Domestic and Foreign Policy* by Christopher Simpson, Weidenfeld and Nicolson, New York, 1987. $19.95.

℣ *The Creation of World Poverty: An Alternative View to the Brandt Report* by Teresa Hayter, Pluto Press, 1981, published by Longwood Publishing Group, 27 South Main Street, Wolfeboro, New Hampshire 03894-2069, 603-569-4576. $5.50.

℣ *In Banks We Trust* by Penny Lernoux, Anchor Press/Doubleday, Garden City, New York, 1984.

℣ *Cointelpro: The FBI's Secret War on Political Freedom* by Nelson Blackstock et al., Anchor Foundation, Inc./Pathfinder Press, New York; Vintage, New York.

℣ *Deadly Deceits: My 25 Years in the CIA* by Ralph McGehee, Sheridan Square Publications, P.O. Box 677, New York, New York 10013, 212-254-1061. $7.95.

℣ *The Warmongers* and *The Paper Aristocracy* by Howard S. Katz, Books in Focus.

℣ *The Secret Team: The CIA and Its Allies* by L. Fletcher Prouty, Ballantine, New York; Prentice-Hall, Englewood Cliffs, New Jersey (out of print). (CIA "controls" world.)

℣ *Spooks: The Haunting of America—The Private Use of Secret Agents* (Wm. Morrow & Co., New York) and *Secret Agenda: Watergate, Deep Throat and the CIA* (Random House, New York; Ballantine, New York) by Jim Hougan (out of print).

℣ *A Higher Form of Killing: The Secret Story of Gas and Germ Warfare* by Jeremy Paxman and Robert Harris, Hill and Wang, New York. $7.95. (Is AIDS a weapon?)

℣ *Nomenclature of an Assassination Cabal* by William Torbitt (removal of JFK).

℣ *The Taking of America, 1, 2, 3* by Richard E. Sprague.

℣ *The Nazis Go Underground* by Curt Riess, Doubleday Doran, 1943.

℣ *Project Paperclip: German Scientists and the Cold War* by Clarence G. Lasby, Atheneum, New York (out of print). (Imported Nazis.)

℣ *The Great Conspiracy* (Little, Brown, Boston) and *Sabotage! The Secret War against America* by Michael Sayers and Albert Kahn, Harper and Row, New York (out of print).

℣ *International Terrorism and the CIA* by V. Syrokomsky, Progress Publishers, U.S.S.R./Imported Publications, Chicago (out of print).

℣ *The Real Terror Network* by Edward S. Herman, South End Press, Boston. $9.00.

℣ *The Great Heroin Coup* by Henrik Kruger, South End Press, Boston. $8.00. (CIA and narcotics.)

℣ *The Crime and Punishment of I. G. Farben* by Joseph Borkin, Pocket Books, $2.75.

℣ *The Glass House Tapes* by the Citizens Research and Investigation Committee and Louis Tackwood, Avon Books, $1.75. (L.A.P.D. and Cointelpro.)

Many titles no longer available from publishers can be obtained from Tom Davis Books, P.O. Box 1107, Aptos, California 95001.

 *Covert Action Information Bulletin,* P.O. Box 50272, Washington, D.C. 20004, 202-737-5317. $20.00/four issues.

 *Citizen Alert,* P.O. Box 51332, Pacific Grove, California 93950; $10.00 info package documents the "October Surprise," the 1980 Bush-Reagan deal with Iran to delay the release of the American hostages until after the election.

Reality Engineering

 Everything by Carlos Castaneda. Widely available. (Start with *Tales of Power* or *The Power of Silence,* unless you expect to have lots of time.)

General Interest

 *Three-Testicled Tales of "Bob"* by Rev. Yvonne Stang, Simon, Schuster & Shonuff.

ABOUT THE CONTRIBUTORS

St. Paul Mavrides
(aka "LIES")

"Spam" is internationally known for his acidly etched, vividly bleak view of life, as deluminated through uncounted sardonic paintings, writings, album covers, Church revival productions and so-called "underground" comics. Possibly the most prolific word/art designer of the hundreds of SubGenius contributors, he also polices the Church against all hints of cuteness or positive thinking. The veritable "Eeyore" of the early Dobbs Apostles, Mavrides is simultaneously both the religion's main heretic and its primary artistic buttress against Pinkness and normality. Though he enjoys his own quasi-independent life outside the Church, his emotional existence is still tied inextricably, if reluctantly, to Churchly matters. And vice versa; as Dobbs said, *"There can be no Truth without LIES."* His otherwise handsome appearance is inappropriately punctuated by his trademark weird Egyptian-wedge haircut, tribal scars and Beefheartian chin beard.

Dr. Philo Drummond

This once-humble *Yellow Pages* salesman is now enthroned at the right hand of Dobbs, being not only His Primary Apostle but also the first "human being," so to speak, to be surgically altered, under Dobbs and his Tibetan lama buddies, into full OverManhood—the "Adam" of our new race. Of the Twelve Original Fishers of Wallets, Philo is Dobbs' Right Brain Man and also most resembles "Bob" psychically and physically. A multitalented True Individual and Great Man, Philo is at once a consummate salesman, Slackhead, 'Fropmeister and dad, yet still finds time to lead St. Louis' fave mystery-jazz acid-surfer-rock band, the Swinging Love Corpses. He looks like a plainclothes policeman: Wherever he is, it seems to everyone else that he shouldn't be there. His renowned and inhumanly loud cough has, however, endeared him to all who dare take the time to buy from him.

Rev. Ivan Stang

"Bob's" Second Apostle, and unquestionably the hardest-working of Dobbs' permanent wage slaves. Film producer, stop-motion porno animator, and professor of crackpotology, Stang also hosts the weekly "Hour of Slack" radio show (heard in many cities), and preaches the *Wor* of Dobbs at Church Devivals everywhere. Though he is a bad actor, his performances are immeasurably aided by authentic schizophrenia and his total, unquestioning faith and religious mania. Resembling a bespectacled Clint Eastwood, he has been described as "sounding like Rev. Jimmy Swaggart on acid." He previously penned the Simon & Schuster nonfiction books *High Weirdness by Mail* and (with the help of almost all the other people listed herein) *The Book of the SubGenius.*

William S. Burroughs

The youngest of our contributors, this newcomer shows great promise despite his lack of experience. (This is his first SubGenius publication.) In fact, his introductory piece was written *before* he heard the Good News of Dobbs—yet despite his literary handicaps, it bears as uncanny a pertinence to the subject as it does sales-bolstering name recognition among Humans. Burroughs has previously authored many obscure humor books such as *Naked Lunch* and *Exterminator!*, and is widely regarded by beatniks, hipsters and avant-garde policemen as the original 'Fropmeister and America's Greatest Living Writer. To us, though, he's still just "Young Bill," another fellow Midwestern good ol' boy with a sick sense of humor and a croaky, fucked-up voice.

Ipsissimus John Shirley

Coming to us from the world of science fiction (where he has been unfairly dubbed and drubbed as a founder of the rowdy and disreputable subgenre "cyberpunk"), John is also an undiscovered rock and roll star as well as a screenwriter of children's Saturday morning cartoons. His spectacularly disturbing novels have run the gamut from horror to romance to horror/romance, including such bedtime stories as the *Eclipse* trilogy, *Cellars, In Darkness Waiting, A Splendid Chaos, The More Man,* and the short-story collection *Heatseeker.* (His *Black Hole of Carcosa* also features "Bob" Dobbs as a main protagonist.) Feared by all cyberpunk rivals, scourge of the SF fan "scene," this handsome satyriasis victim doesn't just *write* about the SubGenius universe—he *lives* it. And, unlike most of us, he gets paid for it as well.

Dr. Harry S. Robins
(aka "Dr. Howl")

Wielding the largest vocabulary and, consequently, most driven improvisational tongue in SubGenius radio, Dr. "Hal" Robins can be heard weekly on the KPFA-Berkeley program, "Less Than an Hour, More Than a Show." Expert in such diverse fields as paleontology, magazine illustration, Shakespearean acting and dowsing, Robins is now in great demand and finds it increasingly difficult to maintain his anonymity as he furtively prowls the streets of his beloved San Francisco Tenderloin district by night, searching for new story or rant material. He was born far too late and to too distinguished a family for this plebian modern world—his scholarly erudition, painstaking artistic skills and even his physical presence bring to mind the young H. G. Wells or Charles Fort, both of whom he also resembles sartorially. Robins can recite Dante in Latin and *Famous Monsters of Filmland* magazine with equal ease, proving him a model SubGenius. In his spare time he collaborates with St. Paul Mavrides on the comic-book saga of *Dinoboy,* and narrates all SubGenius recruitment videos.

St. Larry Sulkis

This much-sought-after (and all too often found) film/video director is an Ascended Master of gray-matter manipulation in the bowels of Hollywood. You see his work, barely credited, on TV every month, no matter how infrequently you watch. He is, in point of fact, the real-life Golden Boy self-described in his Tale—a Tale which is not only true, but MORE than true: indeed, MOREAL. Sulkis is possessed of an almost supernatural ability to extract the most touching testimonials from whomever he is filming for whatever project, possibly because his easygoing but chameleonlike nature inspires (occasionally undeserved) trust from his subjects. But, like so many of the "worldly"-type SubGenii, the abilities for which he is most often hired ironically also provoke the greatest fear and jealousy in his employers, making his life an unending Hell of Contradiction assuaged only by his gentle and almost-all-forgiving nature. Having asked what the Conspiracy can do for *him* rather than vice versa, he's gotten the lucrative but often heartbreaking answer.

Rev. Lewis Shiner

Lewis Shiner was one class ahead of Ivan Stang at the same Texas private school from which they are now both banned, and twice purchased liquor for the underage Stang before they both swore off the hard stuff. However, that isn't why he's included in this anthology. Shiner, an accomplished mystery and science fiction writer, has been nominated for the Nebula and Philip K. Dick Awards for such novels as *Frontera, Deserted Cities of the Heart,* and *Slam,* and the upcoming collection of his short stories, *When the Music's Over* (a benefit work for the Greenpeace organization). He is also writing and designing a new character series for DC Comics. Witty and gracious, handsome and skinny, Lew's friendly exterior suggests no hint of the deeper sickness that lurks within. He seems like such a nice fellow that few would suspect his SubGeniusdom nor the broiling subpsychic forces which drive his writings.

Pope Michael Peppe
(aka "Pope Bubba Free Im-Ho-Pep Innocent I")

Peppe's Tale is included herein only because of his bribes and whee-dling, for it is against our religion to admit geniuses. Believe it or not, this "Aesop" of SubGenius fables TALKS even better than he writes, and he obviously writes *loudly*. He is best known for his "performance art" pieces, in which he transcends both performance and art com-pletely through an incredible barrage of ranting, self-invented arche-typal characters, made all the less credible by the fact that he has memorized each of those carefully prepared ten thousand spoken lines. To make things worse, Peppe also invented an entirely new form of written verbal music, "behaviormusik," which incorporates all human grunts, gestures and body language into "concertos" of mind-blasting power. All other highfalutin conceptual artists are put to shame by Peppe's seemingly effortless, intensely meaningful, yet hopefully commercial spewings. He is a slender, good-looking biped of Italian extraction, and, like most SubGenius Hierarchy males, has more than three fairly large penises. A professional at LIFE, no doubt Michael Peppe will someday become equally proficient at DEATH as well.

Dr. Onan Canobite
(aka ___ ___)

The oldest SubGenius writer, Onan resides in a rest home in East Tennessee and, while seeing the past and future in his bedpan, is some-how able to psychically command people to think he's only in his early twenties. A mainstay of underground publishing and STILL a very polite, mannered old gent who has DESTROYED THE ENTIRE CON-SPIRACY (in blueprint form) more than once, he is a hideously sensi-tive *survivor*—a rare but typically SubGenius (if there were such a thing) combination! Our favorite kind. Onan is also known for his mu-sic, which might be likened to earliest DEVO reworked through a late-1990s sensibility. At 6'9" he is also the second-tallest SubGenius, his giantism-afflicted height coveted by royalty of the European courts. He has unfashionably short hair and a sort of "all-purpose" face, which has helped make him the secretly famous media mogul he is today. Watch for Onan to become a superstar and idol of YOUR KIDS in the future simply by virtue of his highly reticent, unbragged coolness.

Rev. Brooks Caruthers

This gentle, conscientious resident of Little Rock, Arkansas, is being first published "big-time" here. That is to our honor. Too bad he couldn't have been paid more. Brooks' is the only play in recorded history that

can be "seen" like a movie—without the reader even *reading* it! We at
SubGenius Foundation Headquarters have sworn to produce the play
onstage, no matter our own lack of any experience, budget or schedule.
It is rare, mayhaps even previously impossible, for any manuscript to
provoke out-loud laughter from SubGenius Hierarchites, but this one
did. Moreover, unlike all other stories herein, there were NO MISPEL-
LINMGS in the original manuscript. Brooks could claim to be the
youngest and best-looking of all the Drs.-for-"Bob"-associated Arkan-
sanian SubGenii, most of whom are getting pretty seedy looking these
days, but his sweetie Sandy "Bubbles" LaFlame wouldn't want him to,
nor would we.

Dr. Christopher Gross

The shy, visionary Philip K. Dick of the Church of the SubGenius,
Chris relies on trances for his story fodder. (We do not recommend this
method to beginners or anyone else unschooled in Invisible College
tactics!) A Fortean researcher who has unearthed one secret too many,
he is now troubled by nearly nonstop poltergeist and spontaneous-
combustion phenomena which, luckily, seem to afflict only his bosses—
but holding down a job has therefore become somewhat problematical.
Besides writing, he also works as a cartoonist, video artist and com-
poser with the band, Men in Black. He claims that his best tapes,
however, have been erased by uncontrollable outbursts of his unwanted
telekinetic gifts. Gross is primarily a dark humorist, yet herein he
offers us two deadly serious Tales. Only he knows to what degree they
are autobiographical.

Pope Robert Anton Wilson

"Pope Bob" might have been disqualified from inclusion in this volume as just another hopeful newcomer, but for one extenuating circum-
stance: Despite his abysmal ignorance of things Dobbsian (relative to
the old-time Church Hierarchy, anyway), he alone among us has *gotten
drunk with Dobbs!* This "close encounter of the fifth kind" has allowed
him to intuitively comprehend the Dobbs Nature, as is obvious from a
close look at his Tale—which is a big one. Some readers may also
recognize his name as a primal co-sub-founder-in-law of the Discordian
faith, a sort of good-natured little precursor to our present-day mighty
empire of bad-natured prophecy. The author of some thirty or forty
books, including the *Illuminatus* trilogy (to which many SubGenii owe
their illumination), Pope Bob is probably the best-educated SubGenius,
yet also the worst-accented. He's from Brooklyn. Despite this profound
handicap, ANY BOOK with his name on it is mandatory reading for all
Initiates.

Dr. Ahmed Fishmonger
(aka "Seth Deitch")

Dr. Fishmonger is the black sheep in a family composed entirely of black sheep (the Deitch cartoonists and artists). He has successfully transcended the strangeness even of his clan by inventing whole new art forms of highly alien natures, and by his development of the pataphysical theory of *Retrocausality*. Still, "Seth" likes to think of himself as, at the very least, the *ugliest* of his peculiar dynasty. His metal-reinforced bald pate and fantastically tweaked handlebar moustache make him an instantly recognizable figure on the streets of his native Boston, where he peddles his world-shattering scientific discoveries to the unheeding Pink-punk masses. He publishes artistic and scientific folios including *Get Stupid,* the smartest magazine in the world. His excellent taste in bad taste has garnered accolades from all quarters of the worlds of kitschmania and bulldada, as has his discovery of a new subatomic particle, the mutron.

Rev. Ken DeVries

Despite his tender age (7½ at this writing), this savant is a truly "hep," "with-it," sensitive but extremely secretive painter, anti-Communist, cartoonist, stud, poet and general all-around bohemian. Forceful, painstaken and poignant, his comics and essays can be seen in *The Stark Fist* and *Get Stupid* magazines, among many others. Rather more "serious" than most of his Churchly brethren and sistern, this cultural garbageman is a master of sheer and unadulterated hate (a prerequisite for SubGenius Doktorhood)—although little "KDV" does tend to restrict this prodigious hatred to tool-using bipeds in the Conspiracy. He is a small, gnarled child benefiting from an accusatory gaze so intense and unblinking that most adult people avert their eyes in shame and fear. His main companions are the wraiths and spirits that share his haunted Boston garret; neighbors report that he may be heard conversing with these invisible "friends" at all hours of the night.

St. G. Gordon Gordon

"The Most Dangerous SubGenius." Gordon's head would fetch a high price in several Marxist countries where he is wanted for his violent "acts against the state" in defense of Slack and PatrioPsychotic AnarchoMaterialism. Never caught, always sought, Gordon is in real life a professional assassin and mercenary, ready at a moment's notice to perform whatever acts are necessary to the Church's Nameless Mission—for the right payment, of course! One of Dobbs' few confidants, Gordon is also the SlackMaster's primary (if not always effective) bodyguard, and a dreaded "Deliverer of Eternal Slack" to all the Church's political and corporate enemies. He is the sole Hierarchite besides Philo Drummond to have undergone alien Xist surgery; the skills resulting from this enhancement are only slightly exaggerated in his Tale— which is actually a memoir, rewritten by him in a futuristic setting to protect the innocent. Gordon physically and vocally resembles a moustachioed Arnold Schwarzenegger, only louder, as do his lady concubines.

Prof. Mark Mothersbaugh

Mark "The Perfessor" Mothersbaugh is best known as the lead singer and songwriter for the freakish rock 'n' roll phenomenon, DEVO . . . but only a small audience has had the fortune to experience his turgid, disturbed writings and doodles, such as *My Struggle* (a collaboration with his friend, Booji Boy) and *What I Know,* the book from which these pieces are excerpted and editorially mangled. The first big-media Adept adept at popularizing mutation in general, "Von Marko" must shoulder some responsibility for the continued existence of our persecuted Church. Though he is, technically, a rock star, he has the decency not to behave like one, and has consequently seen continued financial success in the scoring (and scouring!) of films, commercials and groupies. And this in spite of the fact that he is a short, nerdy-looking, nearly blind mutant spud! He lives in seclusion in the Hollywood Hills with his computers, startlingly beautiful wives and the best-stocked refrigerator in SubGeniusdom.

To dispel certain rumors: While DEVO and the Church did evolve simultaneously and certainly parallel each other, both are equally loved by their mutual owner, "Bob."

St.^{2} Guy C. Deuel

A close personal friend of G. Gordon Gordon, Deuel was born English, raised in South Africa and Texas, and has since lived on every continent. The most visible rich jet-setter of the Church, he and his "guileless" wife Autumn supervise the Dobbstown II and III encampments in Brazil and Bolivia, where new SubGenii are sent for regrooving and indoctrination. A professional writer, radio personality, gun collector and genital geneticist, Deuel has become something of a historian of the long SubGenius crawl from the slime of obscurity to such towering recent heights as our 1989 reception at the Great Vault in Rockefeller Center. A true "insider," Deuel writes gossipy reports on inner Church workings that have netted him as many paychecks as enemies. This tall, multicultured and multihued gentleman has served also as biographer to G. Gordon Gordon, and is the author of many upcoming spy thriller novels.

Admiral Doug Wellman

(aka PUZZLING EVIDENCE, D. Woodwell Atman, Überbrow, Unibrow)

Wellman: the *Judas* of the Original Twelve SubGenius Apostles. HE SHOT "BOB" AND KILLED "HIM" on the stage of the Victoria Theater in San Francisco, on January 21, 1984 ... proving rather succinctly that our High Epopt is at least *intermittently* mortal. Not that a brainpan full of bullets slowed "Bob" down! But—who other than "Puzzling Evidence" would have had the brazen GONADS to even *consider* such extreme unction?? Wellman's military background surely had much to do with it; he served in naval intelligence during the Vietnam years and has, since 1963, nursed an ill fascination with the Kennedy assassination(s). Strangely, *after his own death,* Dobbs apparently forgave Wellman for his act; "Puz-Ev" is still allowed to broadcast (with Hal Robins and Gary G'BroagFran) his weekly radio show on Berkeley station KPFA. And, despite his sins against Dobbs' cranium, this professional photographer, filmmaker and radio producer remains the official photographer and sound recordist at all major Church rituals. Whatever *other* organizations he may be involved with remains a matter of paranoid conjecture by Bobbies and other Church "conspiracy" fanatics.

Pope of All New York, Idaho and the Great Pacific Northwest David N. Meyer II

Undeniably the greatest, most charismatic of SubGenius preachers, Pope Meyer is also an established critic, satirist and writer of, among other things best not discussed, historical fantasy—as vividly exemplified by his amazingly accurate "pirate Tale" herein. His books in the *Dreamquest* series (written under the pseudonym Lloyd St. Alcorn) include *Halberd: Dream Warrior, On the Shoulders of Giants,* and *The Serpent Mound.* The Pope preaches at only, but at all of, the biggest Church Devivals, and his gut-blowout harangues and layings-on-of-hand are the stuff of legend. Tall and athletic, this sweat-besmeared "mad prophet" has rendered all his audiences either limp or joyously knuckle-walking to Jerusalem. He steals the show in the SubGenius video feature, *Arise.*🕱 The Pope is his own man, however, and in his sermons he has somehow managed to juggle orthodox Dallas-based SubGenius belief alongside foul and venal heresies entirely of his own

---

🕱 The SubGenius Video, *Arise,* as well as free information on all available Church of the SubGenius books, audiotapes, radio shows, comics, T-shirts, jewelry, pamphlets, amulets, magic tokens and magazines, is available from The SubGenius Foundation, P.O. Box 140306, Dallas, Texas 75214. (The 2-hour *Arise* video is $39.95 postpaid in VHS format.) Any of the authors of this anthology may also be contacted in care of that address.

making. Dobbs needs more like him. He also plays eardrum-busting drums with the Seattle band, the Hanks.

Pope Sternodox "Michael" Keckhaver

Sterno's importance to the Dobbs Outreach is as hard to define as it is unquestioned. Firstly, this Little Rock native formed (with Janor Hypercleats, Snavely Eklund, the late Drelloid Mutant and others) the mythos/concept/style of Doktors for "Bob": a "band" (for that is what "it" would be "called" by ordinary "third-dimensional" "persons") which has influenced all SubGenius output since the Church's decanting in 1953. He has overseen all known Launchings of the Bleeding Head of Arnold Palmer in this century; he has thrown every nearby Conspiracy agent into confusion through daring anti-Con real-world Bold Surrealist activism; and, as a family man yet unfettered by vile Normalcy, he has served as a model for SubGenius NonBehavior both to Bobbies and to his Hierarchy peers in the quest for True Slack. Although Sterno is more often the author of penultimately rude lifestyle statements, he nevertheless puts words on paper for the Little Rock weekly, *Spectrum,* designs logos for Pinks, sells diamonds to Pinks, sells Crystal Cages™ to Pinks, does computer consultation for Pinks and otherwise takes vast, inordinate amounts of money from Pinks. Always ready, like the Good Samaritan, to pee another's fuck, or even to hang a damn *pack* up their ass, Sterno represents a kind of loveshit of dickpussy and Slackfuck to all of Dobbs' children. He has soft, doelike eyes, eighteen working dicks, and plays killer bass for the Glands, Homicidal Briefcase, Drs. for "Bob," and (the original versions of) the Gun Klowns, the Butt Pluggz, Drs. for Wotan and the Shitty Beatles.

St. Janor Hypercleats

Janor, Janor . . . oh, Janor. Who can CHANGE JANOR??

Many, many SubGenius groupies have asked this question, for Mr. Hypercleats is truly the Rasputin of the Church—that one scrawny little nerd who FOR SOME UNKNOWN REASON seems to "sum up" all SubGenius sexuality, at least to the gals who only see him up on stage ranting, singing and dancing like an electrocuted puppet . . . until he gets them alone, that is. This poor dumb skinny hick, this rubber-jointed, gangly, unexplainably dynamic "idiot savant" of ranting and conceptual art-'n'-roll, this veritable Panzer attack of the funniest lines anyone ever heard anywhere, is . . . well, you might say he "begs description." For Janor is the veritable TONGUE of our Church, ultimately the most *dependable* trance medium for the Word of Dobbs, no matter that it makes no sense in this "linear" world. Anything he says, during whatever mundane manual job like lawn mowing or pizza delivery, is automatically rendered Orthodox Church doctrine. WHY

NOT!!!!?! MY LEGS ARE ON FIRE. Though unable to function as a normal human being, Janor has nonetheless channeled his abnormality perhaps more *purely* than anyone else. EVER. He does stand-up "comedy" throughout the Southwest and has big if unfathomable followings on both coasts.

That Janor Hypercleats has lived this long is ULTIMATE PROOF that DOBBS EXISTS.

Connector Waves Forest

The Most Sincere SubGenius. Waves has been called by the Highest Powers to locate, preserve and circulate at some risk all scientific and medical information that the Conspiracy otherwise would suppress. He publishes news of these various boons to Earthkind in his newsletter *Now What,* each issue of which is sure to knock loose some cobwebby paradigms in ANY skull. When he turns to fiction, this wily Californian somehow manages to combine both crucial educational information with slyly seductive entertainment to create such stories as the undeniably controversial one included here. Watch for his upcoming novel, *Corralberg.* The most hardened skeptics would have to agree that *if* Waves is a crackpot, he's a *damned good one;* and if he *isn't* nuts, his work contains clues to solving practically every serious environmental (and just plain mental) problem currently afflicting humanity. You may discover the truth by sending four dollars to: Waves Forest, *Now What,* P.O. Box 768, Monterey, California 93940.

St. Byron Werner

Height: 6'1"
Weight: 150 lbs.
Color hair: brown
Color eyes: blue
Number of dicks: 36
    # of functional dicks: 14
    # of dicks over 2 feet: 3
    # of prehensile dicks: 2

Byron is a "cummer" on the Los Angeles art scene, with his stupefyingly psychedelic paintings and sculptures seeing ever-increasing exposure and prices. His extraordinarily complex mandalas are said to possess magickal powers, as are his intricate collages and sick underground comics. Moreover, Byron has the largest collection of weird old records in the whole Church, and his warped audiotape montages have become crucial components of any Church radio program or Media Barrage tape. However, he is best known to his close SubGenius friends as one of the most merciless pranksters in this business of monstrous pranks. We could return the favor here by mentioning a certain "curtain," but we won't. He is married to a former Miss Bull Shoals, Arkansas, beauty pageant winner, and works in Hollywood as a highly paid special-effects craftsman.

Rev. Kenneth Huey

A heck of a nice guy, which is surprising when one sees his work. Originally a Yankee hatched from the Pennsylvania swamps, "Ken" has become one of Dallas' more successful commercial artists, even though he is also a main contributor to the comic book *Commies from Mars* as well as *The Book of the SubGenius* (for which he did the second edition's cover, a color portrait of Dobbs). His eyeball-devastating paintings grace many a gallery and product in the science fiction world, inspiring awe and amnesia in all who survey them. He lives with his lovely wife "Barbie" in a Dallas mansion surrounded by barbed wire, guard dogs and gun emplacements, venturing out only when necessary to fill his cupboard or to frighten Pinks for fun. At 7'6", that isn't difficult!

Sacred Agent Jane Jordan Browne
(aka "Multimedia Product Development, Inc.")

Jane Browne, as literary agent for the Church, has held our hands and upped our prices through seven years of SubGenius "mainstream" publishing. From her offices in Chicago, she deftly negotiates all book and screen deals before Dobbs steps in, absentmindedly, to close them. Her savvy and wisdom are well illustrated by the fact that she has arranged things whereby she must only talk with the staid, conservative Ivan Stang, and not the dozens of eccentric Doktors and contributors. With years of distinguished work on both coasts behind her, she lends a false air of legitimacy to our projects, and translates the arcane jargon of literary/film contracts into the SubGenius language so that we might know on just what shaky ground we actually stand.

The SubGenii Whose Stories Are Not Published in This Book

At the inception of this project, Ivan Stang, as is his wont, went overboard and invited thrice as many writers to contribute to this anthology as could feasibly have been published, wrongly thinking that only one third would respond—given the pay. He was mistaken, and we are now left with two more *Tales* collections' worth of stories, all just as incisive as those chosen. The selection process involved much flipping of coins, and the ones included in this first *Tales* anthology were the *lucky* ones. There now exists a huge backlog of Dobbs yarns just as worthy, and they await inclusion in future *Tales* collections (*Four-Fisted, Five-*

Fisted, and so on)—but only on the condition that *you,* the reader, purchase *multiple copies* of this book as both Christmas AND birthday presents for all your friends, relatives and in-laws. SubGenius is not exactly best-seller material, but our previous books have all enjoyed perpetual shelf lives and have sired sequels in every case. This series can too, and with a lot less work (so many stories already having been penned), but that will happen only if our audience continues its loyal, profligate buying of Churchly publications. Wonderful stories by your favorite big-name authors await you if only you will squander every spare penny on "gift" copies of this particular magnificent tome. Not only we, the mortal authors, but J. R. Dobbs himself DEMANDS that you do so. Look at it this way: we have never demanded that you *like* this stuff; we, unlike the Conspiracy, WANT you to make up your own mind. However, we do request, not all that humbly, really, that you spend your pathetic, useless dollars on us, if for no greater reason than the Hope of Future Generations. Amen.

Rev. Ivan Stang